Language Corpora Annotation and Processing

Niladri Sekhar Dash

Language Corpora Annotation and Processing

Springer

Niladri Sekhar Dash
Linguistic Research Unit
Indian Statistical Institute
Kolkata, West Bengal, India

ISBN 978-981-16-2962-4 ISBN 978-981-16-2960-0 (eBook)
https://doi.org/10.1007/978-981-16-2960-0

This Springer imprint is published by the registered company Springer Nature Singapore Pte Ltd.
The registered company address is: 152 Beach Road, #21-01/04 Gateway East, Singapore 189721, Singapore

Dedicated to

Amma

Annamalai Murugan Temple

Kundah, Nilgiri Mountains, India

Preface

During the last few years, innovative techniques, strategies, and methods are introduced to annotate and process natural language texts. This has been possible due to the widespread application of texts for various academic and commercial purposes. The value of texts is multiplied if texts are normalized, annotated, and processed properly. Such texts are utilized for the development of various language-related systems and applications. These are indirect incentives for scholars engaged in designing new and innovative techniques for text annotation and processing. Some of the text annotation and processing techniques are discussed in this book. It gives more attention to text annotation as text processing issues are addressed more widely in earlier literature.

People working in various domains of machine learning, artificial intelligence, information technology, language technology, and linguistics realize that they need to devise new methods and techniques to make texts more user- and system-friendly. Texts should be easily accessible so that one can utilize data and information from texts in research and development activities. This has been another factor behind the development of innovative ways of text annotation and processing. The application of innovative techniques on texts generates new kinds of results which have an impact on looking at a language from a new perspective as well as addressing various language-related needs.

New text annotation techniques open new ways of looking at language. New annotation processes are applied to texts to make text data suitable for new applications. It generates new perspectives toward a natural language and its properties. In essence, annotation contributes to looking at a language beyond the traditional frame of analysis and description. The introduction of new text processing techniques, on the other hand, makes us more powerful in gathering offbeat information from texts, furnishing rare and irregular evidence, and modifying existing theories and models based on newly found examples and information. Moreover, analysis of annotated texts produces results to mark limitations and deficiencies of existing theories and intuitions about a natural language and its properties.

A language-based application requires special tools, systems, and techniques to interact with raw and processed texts. The application strength of a tool increases when it works on annotated and processed texts. Proficiency and precision of a system also increase when it is able to access data and information of an annotated text. Keeping these advantages in mind, we discuss some of the conventional and some non-conventional text annotation techniques in this book. We propose to apply these annotation techniques for language-specific research and applications. We have noted that text annotation techniques play a crucial role in devising new methods for language study, developing new skills for language analysis, and identifying new domains for language use. New text annotation techniques also help to collect new evidence from texts, process texts for new usages, and apply language data for new purposes. We collect information from annotated texts to explain non-canonical linguistic phenomenon convincingly, rather than reshaping language data to support the existing theories.

The majority of text annotation tools and systems that are available at present are useful for advanced and resource-rich languages. Scopes of application of these tools and systems in less-advanced and resource-poor languages are quite low. The majority of world languages fall under "resource-poor languages." In this context, the present book could have tried to demonstrate how tools and techniques developed for advanced languages could also work elegantly for less-advanced and resource-poor languages. Perhaps, this would have been widely appreciated by the scholars of resource-rich languages. The goal of this book is, however, not fixed on it. It does not desire to show how annotation and processing techniques used in advanced languages are working fine for the less-advanced languages. Rather, it shows that less-advanced languages require similar tools and systems which are characteristically different and which can address language-specific requirements of the less-resourced languages. Since this book focuses on a specific group of languages, the prospective readers are likely to be specialized. This book, however, can find a home in university and research libraries as well as become a text-cum-reference book for corpus linguists in universities and colleges. The importance of this book may be realized when we understand that it discusses some of the crucial issues and aspects of text annotation keeping in view the requirements of less-advanced and resource-poor languages of the world.

Kolkata, India
March 2021

Niladri Sekhar Dash

Acknowledgments

I humbly thank my seniors, peers, and juniors who have helped me in different capacities to represent my ideas, concepts, and information in this book. I also thank those scholars who have given me insights and information to shape up new ideas and concepts presented here. I thank those unknown reviewers who have suggested changes and modifications in the manuscript for improvement of content and quality of the volume. I sincerely appreciate their constructive comments. Their suggestions have helped me to revise and upgrade the present book to a large extent.

I humbly acknowledge the support I have received from parents, teachers, colleagues, friends, and students. I express my sincere thanks to my wife Soma, daughter Shrotriya, and son Somaditya for their emotional support and encouragement during the course of writing and revising the manuscript. I also thank Satvinder Kaur of Springer Nature who played a crucial role in shaping up my proposal in the form of the present book. This book would not have been possible without her continuous encouragement and support. Finally, I express my gratitude to Shri Sunil Kumar Bhar—my friend, philosopher, and guide—who is always there to boost up my morale and steer me through thick and thins.

I shall consider my efforts are amply rewarded if readers find this book useful for their academic and extra-academic works. All limitations and errors found in this book are my faults; and for that, I take full responsibility.

Kolkata, India
March 2021

Niladri Sekhar Dash

Introduction

Why This Book

This book describes some of the methods of text annotation and processing that are developed and applied to digital texts. Although enough advancement is made in corpus development, limited progress is made in text annotation and processing. We have tried to put these annotation and processing issues within a single volume so that people of information and language technology, corpus linguistics, and other disciplines can refer to this book to explore these crucial aspects, issues, and challenges of text annotation and text processing. There is a need for a book of this kind in the global market, and this book fulfills this need. It can be used as a course-cum-reference book for teaching text annotation and processing at undergraduate and postgraduate levels. This book, in essence, fulfills the requirements of both academic and commercial domains.

The topics addressed in this book have high academic and industrial relevance. Over the last few decades, we observe a strong wave of corpus-based language study and application. It provides answers to many questions relating to the importance and application of texts in the advancement of our understanding of a language in life and living. Through reference to new ways of interpretation and analysis of empirical data, we search for answers to the basic questions of human understanding of language beyond the realms of our age-old methods of language description. The present book thus reiterates the utility of language corpus in academic and commercial applications.

Within a wider spectrum of speech and language research, the functional value of an annotated text is beyond question. However, the generation of an annotated text is a daunting task. We require a large amount of text for hands-on experiments, implementation, and verification of systems and techniques. We also require a long-time engagement of scholars on specific text annotation mechanisms. This implies that success in text annotation and processing is a hard-earned result. This book highlights some of these issues and aspects.

Text Annotation Versus Text Processing

It has been noted that *text annotation* is often mixed up with *text processing* in academic discourse, technical talks, informal lectures, classroom teachings, academic meetings, and commercial deliberations. This is inevitable since the concepts are interrelated and share some common functions. It is, therefore, expected that during discussions on text annotation and processing, one may mix up the concepts. Let us look at the concepts theoretically and practically to know that they, in reality, are two different concepts with different operations, purposes, and outputs.

Text annotation, in principle, is a process of adding external information to a text included in a digital corpus. Without the annotation, a text does not lose anything. But with annotation, it becomes more informative, better organized, and more application-friendly. Text processing, on the other hand, is primarily a technical process of analyzing a digital text for extracting customized data and processed information for different application purposes. After processing, a text remains as before; it neither loses nor gains anything. But a machine or an individual, who is interested to utilize data and information from a text, is able to gather appropriate data and information from a text that he considers useful for a particular study or application.

Text annotation can be done by an individual on a small amount of text. In the case of a large and varied amount of texts, it is normally done by a computer trained with appropriate algorithms and programs. The resultant output is a new version of a raw text which is marked with annotation. An annotated text is understood by both a human and a machine, but in a different manner. The nature of understanding is also different. Text processing, on the other hand, is done entirely by a machine. The outputs are, however, understood and utilized by a man and a machine. For instance, an individual may not be able to manually count the number of characters used in a text which is made up of a million sentences. But a computer can do it quickly and accurately. Moreover, if an individual does it, there is a possibility that he may make mistakes in counting or may come out with different results after each counting. If more people are engaged in the work, it is more likely that each person comes up with different results. In case of a computer, it is always a fixed answer. Even if the number of computers is increased or the same computer is used several times, there is a little chance that the count will vary.

After annotation, we get a new kind of text. It is called an "annotated text." When placed against a raw text, it shows additional information marked in the body of the text. For instance, when a raw text is annotated at the part-of-speech level, it is known as a "POS annotated text" (or *grammatically annotated text*). Similarly, when a raw text is annotated at the sentence level, it is called a "parsed text" (or *syntactically annotated text*). It is a new version of text where each phrase of a sentence is marked with phrasal identity and dependency relation. Text processing, on the other hand, does not generate a new version of a text. What we find after text processing is an output that is generated from a text—either unannotated or annotated. The output is invariably of different compositions and characteristics. It is characterized by some

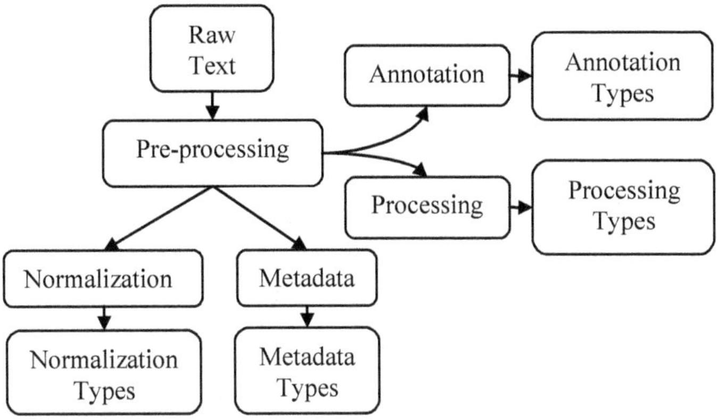

Fig. 1 Three-point scheme of corpus text management

internal features or criteria that work as controlling factors. For instance, after we run a concordance program on a text, we gather a large number of individual sentences where a particular word of our choice is found to be used in each sentence. The total set of sentences is known as a "concorded text," which is generated from a raw text through the application of a text processing technique called "concordance." Unlike a raw text, a "concorded text" has specific formation, representation, purpose, and application.

A text annotation technique does not need a processed text. It works better on a raw text which, if required, is normalized to a certain level to make a process of text annotation useful and robust (Wolfe 2002). Text processing, on the other hand, usually likes to work on annotated texts. Although it can work on the raw text, it works better on an annotated text. For example, for counting the number of words of different part-of-speech in a text, a part-of-speech (POS) classification tool, which classifies and counts part-of-speech of words, takes a POS annotated text as an input. Only when a POS annotated text is given as an input, a POS classification tool classifies and counts the numbers of words of different POS in the text.

The term *text processing* is a complex term. It puts us in doubt to think if it is an additional work that is mandatory before we use a text. It is used in one sense in corpus linguistics and language technology but used in some other sense in information processing, knowledge processing, food processing, and data processing. In each sense, it denotes a set of specific tasks that are to be executed before the materials or resources are made more useful and worthy for end users. In corpus linguistics and language technology, we apply text processing methods on texts to streamline text data so that it is organized, classified, and processed to be useful in linguistics, artificial intelligence, and language technology. We may refer to the diagram (Fig. 1) to show the "three-point scheme" of text management and to understand how text annotation and text processing are to be interpreted and interlinked.

As the diagram shows (Fig. 1), after we get a raw text (spoken or written), we carry out a series of activities on the text before it is made ready for use. While the tasks of preprocessing go on, we can also start text annotation, although it is better to start annotation after a text passes through stages of preprocessing (and normalization) and is declared fit for text annotation. This reduces many problems relating to a text itself. Moreover, it makes the outputs of annotation accurate, error-free, and reliable. In the same manner, it is better to apply text processing techniques on a text after the text passes through text normalization processes and is certified as an error-free version representing a particular genre or variety of a text. That means text annotation and text processing can be done sequentially or parallelly based on the priority of a project. However, it is to be noted that these are characteristically different and therefore should be done separately after a text is preprocessed and normalized.

Both annotation and processing are, however, fixable issues. These are not mandatory to be used on a text. Moreover, they represent different types and levels of information and knowledge for text users. Within the generic scheme of text understanding, the "3A Cycle Model" (Wallis and Nelson 2001, Wallis 2007) is quite useful as it distinguishes different levels of knowledge in texts and the cyclical processes that are used in text management. Text annotation is one of those processes. Once we are able to distinguish levels of knowledge, it becomes easier for us to understand (a) what particular annotation processes, tools, algorithms, etc., we actually apply and (b) what new necessary tools and processes we require to bridge certain gaps. For instance, in bootstrapping POS annotation, most of the processes are likely to involve a certain amount of manual intervention to build a micro-database as well as a certain amount of computation. However, both manual annotation and automated annotation have the same ultimate goals.

Summary of the Chapters

In Chap. 1, we define the basic concept of text annotation. We also present some preliminary ideas about the central theme and content of the book. We discuss characteristics, kinds, criteria, and maxims of text annotation. We discuss these issues in different sections of this chapter keeping in view their theoretical, functional, and referential value in analyzing and understanding a piece of text by man and machine. We also justify text annotation, highlight different annotation schemas and models to record conceptual differences, and present a short discussion on intralinguistic and extralinguistic annotation. In the last part of this chapter, we look at the present state of text annotation in less-resourced languages (including Indian languages) and explore possibilities of building annotated texts for developing language technology resources, tools, and systems. Finally, we highlight referential value and application relevance of texts that are annotated at various levels with different types of linguistic and extralinguistic information.

In Chap. 2, we define principles and rules for text annotation. We apply the principles and rules when we design methods for POS annotation of words in a text. Moreover, we define strategies for formulating algorithms for automatic assignment of part-of-speech to words. Although we address some theoretical and practical issues relating to these tasks, we do not dwell on those complex technical issues and computational aspects that are needed when a computer system is trained to do POS annotation automatically. We keep these issues relatively simple here as an area of general inquiry so that non-linguists and common people have some ideas about how words in a text are annotated at the POS level and how principles and rules are used during POS annotation. This chapter has two broad parts: (a) the first part describes some principles to be followed during POS annotation and (b) the second part refers to some rules that are indispensable in POS annotation. This chapter supplies necessary guidance about the nature and characteristics of POS annotation, and insights for the application of POS annotation principles and rules to make works of text processing and analysis easy and user-friendly.

In Chap. 3, we discuss the process of manual and automatic annotation of words at the part-of-speech level. We can do it effectively when man and machine are adequately trained in identifying morphological identity and grammatical role of words in a text. Here we discuss the basic theoretical issues and aspects of POS annotation. To do this, we avoid all issues involved in the development of an automatic POS annotation tool that requires computation. To keep things simple and within the capacity of non-experts, we address some of the primary concerns of POS annotation. Starting with basic concepts of POS annotation, we show differences between POS annotation and morphological processing, define levels and stages of POS annotation, refer to some early works on POS annotation, present a generic scheme for POS annotation, and finally show how a POS annotated text is utilized in various domains and sub-domains of theoretical, descriptive, applied, computational, and cognitive linguistics. The ideas and information presented here are useful for designing linguistic and computational models for POS annotation in a language.

In Chap. 4, we portray a perceivable sketch for extratextual annotation, which in the present state of text annotation is indispensable. Through the application of this process, we add representational information to a text that is included in a corpus. Extratextual annotation is important when a corpus is built with different types of texts obtained from different genres and text types. To develop a workable frame for extratextual annotation, at each stage, we propose to classify the existing processes of corpus annotation into two broad types. Moreover, we explain different layers that are embedded in extratextual annotation of texts and identity applications which enhance extractability and accessibility of language data from a text for works like text file management, information retrieval, lexical items extraction, and language processing. The techniques that we propose and describe in this chapter are unique in the sense that these are useful for expanding the utility of a text beyond the immediate horizons of language processing. In this chapter, we also argue that we should annotate all written texts at an extratextual level in a uniform manner so that text samples stored in a corpus are uniformly accessed for various works of descriptive, theoretical, and applied linguistics. This annotation scheme is applied on a Bengali corpus, and it is found that accessibility of data and information from the corpus is more flexible and user-friendly than a non-annotated corpus.

In Chap. 5, we discuss the process of etymological annotation of a text. It is a new kind of annotation where our primary goal is to tag etymological information to words used in a text. It is a crucial scheme of text annotation as lexical borrowing is a common linguistic phenomenon of all the natural languages. Through lexical borrowing, each language is enriched with a new stock of vocabulary. It helps a language to grow with time and adjust itself to new ideas and concepts. Since lexical borrowing is a prominent linguistic feature for all languages (more prominent for advanced languages), it is necessary to annotate the origin of words in a text to know how words are borrowed from different languages. Keeping the issue in mind, we propose in this chapter a new scheme of text annotation, namely the etymological Annotation. We apply a new method for annotating the source of words used in a text to identify and document the "mother language" from where words are borrowed, assimilated, and naturalized in a language. Etymological annotation is necessary when a large quantity of words of a language is accumulated from other languages, and these words are assimilated with indigenous lexical stock. The source of origin of words needs to be annotated for linguistic reference in dictionary compilation and source-based lexical classification. In this chapter, we classify Bengali words based on their etymology, define an elaborate tagset that we use in etymological annotation, discuss the methods that are used for annotating words at the etymological level, note challenges involved in portmanteau words (a word made with two words taken from two different languages), discuss application relevance of the etymologically annotated text in various domains of linguistics and language technology, and finally, establish the scheme within a wider frame of text annotation.

In Chap. 6, we discuss some non-conventional types of text annotation, which due to many factors are not frequently applied to the text. This discussion gives readers some preliminary ideas about the ways and means of annotating a text at various other levels for making a text useful beyond machine learning and language technology. The availability of texts annotated at different types and levels is useful for various academic and commercial applications. The primary goals of each type of text annotation are characteristically different based on the type of text as well as proposed applications of an annotated text in customized requirements. Based on different goals, annotations vary following the nature and composition of a text considered for annotation. In essence, non-conventional text annotation techniques are not always useful for all kinds of standard linguistic investigation of texts but are useful in those contexts where the non-standard interpretation of texts is applied for better interpretation of a text. The non-conventional annotation yields outputs which are not required in the standard process of language description and analysis but are necessary for language application and language data management. The non-conventional annotation processes require a different kind of capability in understanding a text, which, in return, generates a new kind of insights and expertise in text interpretation and textual information management. In this chapter, we focus on some of the non-typical text annotation techniques which are not often used in written text annotation. Our discussion refers to English and Bengali language data for necessary examples and explanations.

In Chap. 7, we describe the morphological processing of words. It is a process that is applied to retrieve various kinds of morphological information from inflected words used in a piece of text. We make the process of morphological processing clear keeping in view that this concept is often mixed up with part-of-speech annotation and syntactic annotation. To make things easy, we define the concept of morphological processing, discuss methods and approaches that are developed and used across languages, and describe how a morphological processing system is developed for processing inflected words in a text. Also, we show how processing of inflected words puts up challenges in generating acceptable outputs; how orthographic inconsistencies posit strong barriers in proper recognition of inflected words; and how detached words, isolated and sequential lexical ambiguities mar robustness of a morphological processing system in analysis and generation of appropriate outputs. The success of a morphological processing system largely depends on two basic components: (a) ability in dealing with inherent morphological complexities of inflected words and (b) algorithm in management of linguistic data, information, and grammatical mapping rules. These issues are addressed in this chapter with reference to examples taken from a Bengali corpus.

In Chap. 8, we describe a process of lemmatization of inflected nouns. Nouns are used in a high frequency in Bengali, a language, which is known as one of the most inflectional languages in the world. We execute the process of lemmatization on a large lexical database of inflected Bengali nouns that we collect from a modern Bengali multidisciplinary text corpus. After applying several intermediate stages, we decompose all the inflected Bengali nouns to separate inflections from nominal bases. All the stages are executed by a set of grammatical mapping rules (GMRs) that operate to concatenate inflections with nominal bases. The GMRs are initially designed manually after analyzing a large representative set of inflected nouns for procuring necessary data, information, and insights. At the subsequent stages, the GMRs are applied in machine learning so that a system can separate inflections from all inflected nouns with controlled human intervention. Our present strategy is successful as most of the inflected Bengali nouns, which are stored in a central lexical database, are rightly lemmatized. Moreover, as the outcomes of a multilayered process, we generate a set of nominal inflections and a large set of lemmatized nouns to be used in translation, dictionary compilation, lexical decomposition, and language teaching. The method that we present in this chapter is useful for lemmatizing inflected nouns and adjectives of other languages that follow the same pattern of inflection in word formation.

In Chap. 9, we describe an analytical method that we apply to decompose inflected verbs in Bengali. For this, we consider inflected verbs as isolated and autonomous lexical units, which are physically free from their contextualized frames of occurrence in sentences. The primary goal behind using this method is to retrieve various kinds of morphological information from surface forms of inflected verbs. Some other goals of this work are to use the information for developing a root database, compiling a verb suffix database, and designing a semi-supervised Bengali verb analyzer. To accomplish these goals, we apply a rule-based suffix stripping method based on knowledge and information that we obtain from manual analysis of a large number of inflected verbs used in modern Bengali texts. Our present system first accepts an inflected verb as a separate lexical input, treats it as an independent unbroken string of characters, applies stripping rules for root–suffix segmentation, matches segmented parts with respective roots and suffix lists, extracts relevant information from a machine-readable dictionary supplied to the system, and displays output with information of constituents that are used to generate inflected form. The outputs of this method are root lists, suffix lists, morph lists, grammatical rules, and a set of matching algorithms. These are useful for developing a verb analyzer and a verb form generator for Bengali. The lexical database, morph lists, and metadata that are generated through this process are also used for developing tools for stemming, lemmatization, lexical information retrieval, and lexical teaching. The methodology that we propose in this chapter is useful for decomposing inflected nouns, pronouns, and adjectives used in Bengali by replacing respective stem and suffix databases as well as their morphological concatenation rules.

In Chap. 10, we discuss the problems and challenges of syntactic annotation of sentences. We define the basic concept of syntactic annotation followed by its nature, method, and function in a language. We refer to purposes that operate behind developing a tool of this kind for a language. Since it is possible to get ideas and algorithms for developing a syntactic annotator for a language from literature and guidelines available online, we do not discuss these issues again in this chapter. Rather, we evaluate the theoretical importance of a syntactic annotator in extracting hidden information of a sentence, which otherwise is not possible for a machine to extract. When a natural language sentence is provided to a machine as an input, a machine is asked to mark out syntactic functions and grammatical roles of words and phrases used in the construction of a sentence. This implies that it is necessary to know the function of a syntactic annotator so that we understand how a natural language sentence should be analyzed from the perspective of syntactic function and semantic information of words and phrases. It also guides one to know how syntactic-semantic roles of various syntactic units are controlled based on their lexical association and morphological function in understanding the information embedded within a sentence. We address all these issues in this chapter while we present ideas and processes involved in syntactic annotation. In the course of formulating the idea, we refer to the rules of context-free grammar and show how outputs generated from syntactic annotation are utilized to cater to several needs of descriptive, cognitive, and applied linguistics, language technology, and language teaching.

Value of this Book

This book contributes to the concept of "corpus text annotation and processing" in a significant manner. The value of the book is summarized below:

- It makes us aware of many new methods and techniques of corpus text research and application.
- It shows how language data and information in a text are possible to annotate for different purposes and applications.

- It shows how findings from annotated and processed texts can affirm or refute earlier observations and findings.
- It directs our attention toward new avenues and areas of application of annotated language data for academic and commercial purposes.
- It makes relevant and important contributions toward the growth and maturity of corpus linguistics as a more useful area of study.

The present book is written to make issues of text annotation and processing useful to those people who can reap a good harvest from the areas related to text annotation and processing. It addresses all major issues of text annotation with reference to notable methods and works known to us. It lucidly discusses things for its use in a classroom situation to teach methods and techniques of text annotation and processing. It also contains adequate empirical data and information for understanding the nature, feature, function, and relevance of text annotation and processing techniques. Readers will get better insights into the linguistic challenges involved in text annotation and processing. Moreover, they will learn how linguistic and non-linguistic data and information are annotated and extracted from a text to develop innovative systems and devices of information and language technology. Knowledge of linguistics is enriched with new findings retrieved from different types of text annotation presented in the book.

The value of the book can be adequately measured when we understand the theoretical significance and applicational value of an annotated text in several language-related technology and applications development. The book draws attention to those areas, which are going to be the areas of attention in academic and commercial domains for the next few years. People working in different areas of linguistics, information technology, machine learning, data processing, grammar writing, content development, dictionary compilation, translation, corpus linguistics, and others will be directly benefitted from this book.

References

Wallis, S. A. & Nelson, G. (2001). Knowledge discovery in grammatically analyzed corpora. *Data Mining and Knowledge Discovery*, *5*(4), 305–336.

Wallis, S. A. (2007). Annotation, retrieval, and experimentation. In A. Meurman-Solin & A. A. Nurmi (Eds.), *Annotating variation and change*. Helsinki: Varieng, UoH (ePublished).

Wolfe, J. (2002). Annotation technologies: a software and research review. *Computers and Composition*, *19*(4), 471–497.

Contents

About the Author

Dr. Niladri Sekhar Dash is Professor and Head, Linguistic Research Unit, Indian Statistical Institute, Kolkata (The Institute of National Importance, Government of India). For the last 28 years, he is working in corpus linguistics, language technology, computational lexicography, computer-assisted language teaching, language documentation, translation, clinical linguistics, and digital ethnography. To his credit, he has published 18 research monographs and more than 285 research papers in indexed and peer-reviewed research journals, anthologies, and conference proceedings. As an invited speaker, he has delivered lectures at more than 50 universities and institutes in India and abroad. He acts as a Research Advisor for several multinational organizations that work on language technology, artificial intelligence, lexicography, digital humanities, and language resource development. He acts as Principal Investigator for several LangTech projects funded by the Government of India and corporate houses. He is the Chief Editor of the *Journal of Advanced Linguistic Studies*—a reviewed international journal of linguistics. He is an Editorial Board Member for several international journals. He is also a member of several linguistic associations across the world. He is a British Academy International Visiting Fellow (2018), Visiting Research Fellow of School of Psychology and Clinical Language Sciences, University of Reading, UK (2018–2021), and Visiting Scholar of Language and Brain Laboratory, University of Oxford, UK (2019). At present, he is heading five projects: (a) 'Upgradation of Bengali WordNet' funded by the Ministry of Statistics and Programme Implementation (MoSPI), Government of India; (b) 'Sound Imitative Words in Bengali' in collaboration with the Dept. of British and American Studies, Faculty of Arts, P. J. Šafárik University, Slovakia; (c) 'Bilingual Dementia of Patients with Broca's Aphasia' in collaboration with the School of Psychology and Clinical Language Sciences, University of Reading, UK; (d) 'Public Announcement System at Airports and Railway Stations in Indian Sign Language with Animation' in a consortium-mode project headed by the Department of Computer Science, Punjabi University, Patiala, India, and (e) 'Dictionary for Sabar Speech Community'—an endangered tribe of West Bengal, India. Details of Niladri: https://sites.google.com/site/nsdashisi/home/.

Abbreviations

AGBA	Acyclic graph-based approach
AI	Artificial intelligence
BIS	Bureau of Indian Standard
CALT	Computer-assisted language teaching
CLAWS	Constituent Likelihood Automatic Word-tagging System
DI	Division indicator
DLA	Deep lexical acquisition
DLD	Digital lexical database
DLP	Deep linguistic processing
DP	Delayed processing
DPM	Dynamic programming method
EAC	Extratextually annotated corpus
EAGLES	Expert Advisory Group on Language Engineering Standards
ELRA	European Languages Resource Association
FoS	Figure of speech
FSA	Full syntactic annotation
GA	Grammatical annotation
GD	General dictionary
GMR	Grammatical mapping rule
GRD	General reference dictionary
HMM	Hidden Markov model
ID	Inflection database
ILMT	Indian Language Machine Translation
ISLE	International Standards for Language Engineering
KWIC	Key Word In Context
LAF	Linguistic annotation framework
LB	Lexical block
LD	Lemma database
LOB	Lancaster-Oslo-Bergen
LT	Language technology
LWG	Local word grouping

MMPS	Multimodal morphological processing system
MRD	Machine-readable dictionary
MRED	Machine-readable etymological dictionary
MWU	Multiword units
NBD	Nominal base database
NID	Nominal inflection database
NLP	Natural language processing
NP	Noun phrase
POS	Part-of-speech
PP	Preposition phrase
PSA	Partial syntactic annotation
PSG	Phrase structure grammar
RL	Root lexicon
SC	Subject category
SGML	Standard Generalized Markup Language
SIC	Sentence identity code
SL	Suffix lexicon
TAB	Trie structure-based approach
TC	Text category
TDIL	Technology Development for the Indian Languages
TEI	Text Encoding Initiative
TT	Text title
USAS	UCREL Semantic Analysis System
VLD	Verb lexical database
VP	Verb phrase
WCD	Word category disambiguation
WCM	Word category marking
WFE	Word-formative element
WFR	Word formation rule

Chapter 1
Corpus Text Annotation

Abstract Some of the basic and preliminary ideas of text annotation and text processing techniques, which are normally carried out on a corpus of written and spoken texts are addressed in this chapter. Keeping non-trained linguistic scholars and common linguistic readers in view, we briefly discuss the basic nature and goal of text annotation, describe the purposes of text annotation, and refer to the common maxims of text annotation. A common reader may need these ideas to understand the tools, systems, and techniques of text annotation and processing that are discussed in this book. Next, we report on different types of text annotation, which we apply to written and spoken text corpora. We address these issues keeping in view the theoretical, functional, and referential importance of text annotation and text processing in the analysis and application of a natural language data by man and machine in various domains of linguistics and technology. We also draw theoretical differences between text annotation and text processing to dispel the confusions faced by both academicians and corporate scholars who use annotated and processed texts as an indispensable resource. We look into the present status of text annotation and processing in both resource-rich and resource-poor languages and propose to take the necessary initiative for building raw corpora, annotated corpora, and processed corpora for the resource-poor languages to address the requirements of language technology, linguistics, and other disciplines. Finally, we discuss how the applicational importance and referential relevance of corpora are increased after corpora are annotated with various kinds of linguistic (and extralinguistic) information and processed at various levels.

Keywords Annotation · Orthography · Prosody · Semantics · Discourse · Anaphora · Etymology · Rhetorics

1.1 Introduction: What Is Text Annotation?

By definition, annotation is a special kind of task where we add additional information to a piece of text for its better interpretation, analysis, comprehension, and application. In earlier days, when texts are primarily prepared manually and are sent to publishers, a critic or an editor used to add notes on a text during text revision or

N. S. Dash, *Language Corpora Annotation and Processing*,
https://doi.org/10.1007/978-981-16-2960-0_1

final text preparation. At this stage, editors or critics used to add some annotations in the form of notes which are addressed by text composers before the text is sent for printing. In dictionary-making (i.e., *lexicography*), on the other hand, annotation is applied as a process by which a dictionary-maker adds a short note, explanation, comment, and assistive information to a piece of text based on which a dictionary composer can understand a text and retrieve necessary information from a text to be included in the dictionary.

There are some genuine purposes of annotation of a piece of text—the text may be handwritten, printed, or digital. The addition of annotation provides aids to a new understanding of a text, engages readers in a conversation with the author of a text, provides useful guidance to a text composer for final preparation of a text, and records reading experiences when we return to a text. When we annotate a text, handwritten and composed, we write down quick notes, short summaries, relevant points, pertinent questions, and critical observations on the margins of a text as well as encircle, underline, highlight, and comment on the body of a text. In a traditional sense, these activities fall under text annotation. In office and administrative works, annotations are normally made by using sticky notes on texts. In the case of digitally developed texts, a typical technique of text annotation is "insert-comment feature" that we come across in word-processing software. The bibliographic annotation, which is typically applied in academic research, is a different kind of text annotation. Here a researcher lists up the research sources (called a *Works Cited*) with an annotation under each work cited in the research. The resultant output is an *annotated bibliography* which shows how a researcher accesses earlier works to frame and formulate a new research work.

There are several practical advantages of text annotation, some of which are summarized in the following manners.

(a) Through text annotation, we understand the additional linguistic information embedded within a piece of text.
(b) By referring to annotations we can retrieve orthographic, phonological, semantic, syntactic, discourse, and figurative information from a text.
(c) Through citation of an annotation, we know about the time, place, and purpose of the creation of a text as well as about the creator of a text.
(d) By referring to annotation, at a non-linguistic level, we can gather register and ethnographic information of a community from a text.

Corpus text annotation is a typical practice of adding interpretative information to an electronically developed corpus. The corpus contains text samples either from a written or a spoken discourse. Annotation is done by invoking a value-encoding mechanism which attaches interpretative information at the different levels of a text. The interpretative information can be of many types. It may be related to *prosody, pronunciation, orthography, grammar, meaning, sentence, anaphora, discourse, rhetorics, etymology,* or some other issues. Based on this, we classify interpretative information into two broad types, intralinguistic and extralinguistic.

(a) Intralinguistic issues are linked with linguistic features and properties of a text.

(b) Extralinguistic issues are related to some issues which are not directly connected with linguistic properties and features of a text.

Apart from pure intralinguistic information and data, a corpus is also capable of carrying extralinguistic information. Intralinguistic information helps us to understand the internal issues and aspects of a text. Extralinguistic information, on the other hand, helps us to know that information based on which we can have a better interpretation of a text. Analysis of extralinguistic information provides better insights into a text. Both types of information are annotated to a text—either attaching them to a text or interspersing them within a text. The purpose of the annotation is to add additional information to a text so that future analysis and interpretation of a text becomes easy, accurate, and useful. Compared to a raw text, an annotated text is complex in structure and difficult to access, but easier in analysis and more user-friendly in an application.

In Sect. 1.2, we mark out some characteristics of annotation; in Sect. 1.3, we discuss different kinds of text annotation; in Sect. 1.4, we reflect on the primary criteria of text annotation; in Sect. 1.5, we refer to the maxims of text annotation; in Sect. 1.6, we justify the purposes of text annotation; in Sect. 1.7, we refer to some annotation methods and models; in Sect. 1.8, we describe the major types of text annotation; in Sect. 1.9, we look at the state of text annotation in resource-rich and resource-poor languages; and in Sect. 1.10, we discuss how the applicational value of an annotated text increases in information technology, linguistics, and other domains.

1.2 Characteristics of Annotation

Annotation, should in principle, be supported by a "**theory**". Moving from naive assumption to a systematic scheme requires a commitment to an apriori framework that is likely to develop cyclically as it is applied to texts (Wallis, 2007). If data in texts is not systematically annotated, we cannot evaluate it empirically. Only when a text is systematically annotated, we can abstract datasets, analyze models, and test hypotheses to measure the power or weakness of an annotation framework. By annotating texts, we are engaged in the process of building theories cyclically and validating the process. At different cyclical stages, we discover many new instances which are unanticipated by the framework that we set out at the beginning (Wallis & Nelson, 2001). We are engaged with, as part of the theory-making system, in deciding how to annotate the new instances.

Annotation is fundamentally "**dual**" in nature. We apply a label to an instance, a token to a type, but we also simultaneously *instantiate* that label to assert that this *type* does correctly distinguish this *token* according to the rules of an annotation framework (Wallis, 2007). The philosophical issue of "theoretical plasticity" is involved here. How far can we stretch a definition before we break the theory? The postmodernist theories would argue that by varying the way a term is applied to new instances we change the theory entirely, implying that every new instance requires a thorough reanalysis. On the other hand, conventional scientific rationalism allows for greater ambiguity and plasticity, emphasizing ultimately on empirical verification and critique of experimenter bias: In other words, putting our faith in the empirical process. Either way, this is a non-trivial question in the face of multiple schemes or allowing for a cyclical development.

Annotation is fretted with "**decidability**." It is understood that instances are decidable. But at what level of granularity is the question. Although "non-ambiguity" is a necessary condition in annotation, there are cases where "decidability" is controlled by the granularity of information assigned to an instance. If an expression is grammatically ambiguous, e.g., *time* (noun versus verb) in *time flies like an arrow*, then POS tags need to record one or multiple interpretations (depending on the ambiguity-encoding principles). Faithfully deciding on only one interpretation indicates that interpretation is based on usage of the instance in a text. Conventionally we do this, but we should not claim that what we are doing is objective and final.

There is a related issue of "**centricity**" (i.e., orientation) in an annotation. Should we annotate a text from the perspective of a language producer or from the perspective of a language user? So far, it is a *producer-centric* annotation (i.e., *writer-annotation*) where we try to infer the intended meaning of the writer of a text. Annotation, in corpus linguistics, is a part of a descriptive linguistic tradition. We do not insert words that are implicit; we describe what is explicit in a text. We assume that it might be insightful if we try to annotate a text from the perspective of a reader (i.e., *reader-annotation*), especially when we have evidence of reader's misinterpretation or new interpretation of what is intended in a text. Such a practice will, however, open up many controversies as interpretation of a text varies based on the understanding of readers. This, however, can be an interesting exercise to explore how misinterpretation or new interpretation by readers leads to "**erroneous encoding**" of a text, thereby reflecting on the nature of cognitive processing of a text by readers.

In annotation, we are eventually driven by goals of "**applicationality**". It is natural to have a broad goal of *future anticipated reuse,* as distinct from merely annotating the useful distinctions for a narrow set of application ends. But whatever we decide, the ultimate test of an annotation scheme is one of research *power*—whether it advances our linguistic knowledge by revealing linguistic processes that are otherwise undetectable (Wallis, 2014). For example, empirical scientists like to distinguish between primary information derived from raw data and secondary interpretation of that data. From this perspective, a spoken audio text is primary data, and its transcription is secondary data. An annotation of an audio text may be time-aligned to it. From this perspective, none of the transcriptions is *authentic, un-interpreted,* and *natural.* Similarly, there are confusions whether a "word" should be linguistically analyzed as a single item as noted with respect to multiword units, but not with respect to clitics or abbreviated forms. Therefore, whether expressions like *I'm, haven't, can't, I'll,* etc. should be considered as single words is still an open issue of debate.

A critical problem in text annotation is "**divisibility**" that refers to the problem of sentence sub-division that impacts syntactic annotation (i.e., parsing). We, from a simple descriptive perspective, assume that language consists of sentences, phrases, and words. However, it is noted that real recorded conversations include so many "incomplete" sentences, fragments, and phrases that even a concept like a "sentence" in an audio text cannot be assumed. It has been studied and recorded that in a spontaneous parsed corpus of English (*Diachronic Corpus of Present-Day Spoken English*), up to a third word string of utterance segments that are distinguished for parsing purposes, are "clause fragments" of one kind or other (Wallis & Aarts, 2006). These categories, from the perspective of linguistic analysis and interpretation, are much more problematic, and thus linguistically interesting than the age-old description implies.

1.3 Kinds of Text Annotation

According to Leech (1993), information that we add to a text can be divided into (a) representational information and (b) interpretative information. "For a written text corpus, the representational information is the actual form of text, consisting of spelling, punctuation, etc. The interpretative information is something added to the basic text, usually by human "linguistic experts" presumed to have insight into, or knowledge of, the linguistic features of the text" (Leech, 1993: 275). Keeping this argument as well as various other issues and constraints of a text in view, the process of text annotation may be divided into two broad kinds:

(a) Representative annotation
(b) Interpretative annotation.

In case of representative annotation, we attach information that represents the form and structure of a text. In a written text, for instance, representative annotation carries information relating to the orthographic representation of a text. In a broad sense, it includes information on orthographic symbols (i.e., *characters*), punctuations, diacritics, words, spellings, phrases, sentences, and similar visual elements that are used in the formation of a text. In case of a spoken text, on the other hand, representative annotation carries information relating to the actual process of production of a spoken text. It includes information related to the impromptu nature of an utterance, adjacency pairs, intonation, backchannels, pauses, repetition, discourse markers, false starts, non-beginnings, non-ends, hedges, suprasegmental properties, and other features that are normally found in a text generated through informal verbal interaction.

In case of interpretative annotation, we add that kind of information which is not directly available from a text but hidden in it. These annotations carry information that helps us to interpret the theme and content of a text. This annotation is added by experts who have good insight into, or knowledge of, linguistic features of a text. In most cases, interpretative annotation is linked with meaning, discourse, pragmatics, and sociocultural issues and features that are normally concealed in a text and are obtained through analysis of a text. The interpretative annotation of a spoken text, on the other hand, carries information relating to demographic details of speakers, situational issues in verbal interactions, and contextual information underlying a dialogic interaction. It is also linked up with the intended meaning, discourse, pragmatics, and sociocultural factors linked to the text of verbal interaction. These properties are usually embedded in a spoken text to be understood through analysis and interpretation (Greene & Rubin, 1971). In this case, also, interpretative annotation is added to a spoken text with a clear knowledge of linguistic features and properties found in normal and fabricated spoken interactions.

1.4 Criteria of Text Annotation

According to scholars (Leech & Smith, 1999), there are at least three criteria that may be indispensable in text annotation. They include the followings:

(1) **Consistency**: It asks for a kind of uniformity in the scheme of annotation throughout the text data stored in a corpus. That means the annotation scheme should be consistent from the beginning to the end of a text annotation process so that subsequent use of a text does not posit a serious challenge to text users.

(2) **Accuracy**: It asks for freedom from any kind of error in the tagset that is developed for a specific type of text annotation. It also asks for the removal of mistakes of any kind in an annotation. This implies that the annotation guideline should be clearly defined so that mistakes are avoided or minimized in an annotated text. It also asks for adherence to definitions and guidelines of a strategy designed for text annotation.

(3) **Speed**: It directs toward the automatic implementation of the process of text annotation on a large amount of text within a short span of time after an annotation process passes through exercises, trials, and learning. At the initial stage, when the annotation guidelines are at the early stages of development, humans are engaged to annotate a text. Once this manually annotated text is certified, it is used as a trial text for the finalization of an automated annotation process. At this experimental stage, speed may be slow. At a later stage, when annotation guideline is finalized and a computer system is sufficiently trained, speed has to be accelerated so that a large amount of text is annotated within a short span of time.

These three criteria are important in any kind of text annotation. Due to this reason, a high level of accuracy in text annotation is no more a distant dream. There are, however, still some hurdles in annotation which are not yet solved. This is due to the fact that each type of text is characteristically different and a potential candidate to throw up many unprecedented decision-making challenges. Therefore, it the duty of text annotators to maintain consistency in annotation even their decisions may show some traits of arbitrariness.

In reality, however, it is not much conducive to stick to the criteria that are already specified for text annotation. We have to keep in mind that due to the rapid advancement of computer technology, the amount of digital text is increasing very fast in all major languages. Therefore, it is a challenge to annotate different kinds of texts accurately within a short span of time. Because of this factor, the level of accuracy in text annotation is slightly affected. It is a challenge for both resource-high advanced languages which have a huge amount of digital texts and less-resourced languages where the amount of digital text is increasing day by day. Each new text shows up many new features which require new ways and strategies for interpretation and annotation. For instance, in Bengali, a word might be used as a pronoun in a text; in another text, the same word might be used as an adjective. Therefore, an annotator has to be quite vigilant during annotation because decisions have to be revised in accordance with the phenomenon observed in a new text.

1.5 Maxims of Text Annotation

The majority of schemes of text annotation are yet to be standardized for most of the less-advanced languages, including many Asian and African languages. Therefore, acceptance of annotation standards and annotated texts largely depends on the text evaluating skills of linguists engaged in developing tagsets and defining annotation guidelines. Keeping the application of tagsets and annotation schemes adopted for implementation on a text in mind, Leech (1993) proposes the following seven maxims of text annotation.

(1) "It should always be easy to dispense with annotation and revert to the raw corpus. The raw corpus should be recoverable.
(2) The annotations should, correspondingly, be extractable from the raw corpus to be stored independently or stored in an interlinear format.
(3) The scheme of analysis presupposed by the annotations—the annotation scheme—should be based on principles or guidelines accessible to the end-user. The annotation scheme should consist of the set of annotative symbols used, their definitions, and the rules and guidelines for their application.
(4) It should also be made clear beforehand about how and by whom all the annotations were applied.
(5) There can be no claim that the annotation scheme represents 'God's truth'. Rather, the annotated corpus is made available to a research community on a *caveat emptor* principle. It is offered as a matter of convenience only, on the assumption that many users will find it useful to use a corpus with annotations already built-in, rather than to devise and apply their own annotation schemes from scratch (a task which could take them years to accomplish).
(6) Therefore, to avoid misapplication, annotation schemes should preferably be based as far as possible on 'consensual', and 'theory-neutral analyses' of the corpus data.
(7) No annotation scheme should claim authority as the standard, although de facto interchange of 'standards' may arise through widening availability of annotated corpora. And this approach should be encouraged".

In simple terms, we can remove the annotation from an annotated text in order to revert to raw text. In many cases, it is an easy process. For instance, we can remove POS (part-of-speech) tags attached to words with an underscore in a text (e.g., "The_AT boy_NN is_AUX going_FV to_PP school_NN") to get back to the original raw text (i.e., *The boy is going to school*). This, however, will not be an easy task for a spoken text where pitch variation is interspersed within a single-word string. For instance, in the London-Lund corpus, the symbol '/' is used to indicate a rising pitch on the first syllable of a word (e.g., 'g/oing'), implying that the original word cannot so easily be reconstructed by removing annotation.

It is, however, necessary that we can, if we want, remove annotations from a text. That means an annotated text should allow flexibility for manipulation of annotations by a text user. An annotation scheme, therefore, should be based on the guidelines which are available to the annotators as well as the text users. Such guidelines are actually manuals which contain detailed instructions of an annotation scheme. It enables an annotator to understand what each instance of annotation represents in a text without any guesswork and understand, in cases of ambiguity, why a particular annotation decision is made at that point. It is also necessary to record the names of the annotators who have carried out the work as well as modalities adopted in an annotation. At the starting stage, a text is normally annotated manually—either by an individual or a group. At a later stage, when an annotation is carried out in a semi-supervised or unsupervised manner by a computer program, outputs are reviewed by experts to verify the level of accuracy as well as make necessary corrections.

The people who are going to use an annotated text should understand that text annotation can never be a completely error-free process. An annotation is, in essence, an act of text interpretation—either of structure or content. An annotation process achieves a high rate of accuracy through several stages of trials, errors, and validation (Berez & Gries, 2010). And an annotated text developed in this process is far better and more useful than a raw text. Our typical expectation is that a text annotation scheme should be designed on widely agreed-upon and theory-neutral principles applicable to a language. For example, during part-of-speech annotation, it is expected that the regular sets of part-of-speech of a language should be used in a POS tagset designed for the language. Also, it is expected that a tagset made for syntactic annotation of a particular language should adopt a universally accepted grammatical framework (e.g., *context-free phrase structure grammar*) rather than applying a highly language-specific narrower grammatical framework.

Finally, it has to be pragmatically accepted that no annotation scheme is complete, final and ultimate. No annotated text, in principle, can be considered as a benchmarked standard however high level of accuracy it may possess. The standard and accuracy of annotation scheme tend to vary based on the type of text, the nature of complexities involved in a text, the kind of tagsets designed and the details of annotation guidelines devised for the purposes. Standards emerge through continuous practices as well as from collective consensus adopted in the process.

1.6 Justification of Text Annotation

What is the justification of text annotation? This is a very important and pertinent question. The answer has come not only from corpus linguistics but also from other domains and disciplines where texts from natural languages are used as valuable resources for their sustenance and growth (e.g., *Artificial Intelligence, Information Technology, Language Technology, Computational Linguistics, History, Culture*

Studies, Sociology, Cognitive Science, Forensic Sciences). Many of these disciplines use language texts both in raw and annotated versions as well as work on the results derived from annotated texts. Many studies, for years, have shown that the use of annotated texts is far more useful and beneficial in language text analysis, text processing, and text applications in various domains of human knowledge.

According to Leech (1997: 4), a text in a corpus is annotated for the following three basic reasons: (a) extracting information from texts, (b) reusability of texts, and (c) multifunctionality of texts. The first point refers to the idea of extracting linguistic information, ideas, and examples from a text, once a text is annotated at various levels of annotation. The second point refers to the phenomenon that an annotated text can be used multiple times by multiple users, and therefore, once a text is annotated, it can be reused as many times as we want. The third point refers to the fact that the application of an annotated text is not fixed to a few domains of linguistics like lexicography or language teaching. Rather, it refers to the fact that an annotated text is meant to be used in many domains and disciplines which are not directly linked to linguistics. Keeping these factors in view, we visualize the application of annotated texts in the following domains:

(a) Computer-readable annotated text generation
(b) Digital linguistic resources generation
(c) Language technology tools and systems development
(d) Translation support tools and systems development
(e) Man–machine interactive interface development
(f) Customized resource generation for IT industries
(g) Speech technology tools and systems development
(h) Resource generation for academic and commercial purposes.

The texts which are annotated with linguistic and extralinguistic information are valuable resources for different kinds of works of linguistics, language technology, and other disciplines. An annotation task, on the other hand, asks for the involvement of many experts, a huge amount of money, and a large amount of time. Besides, it asks for efforts leading to the development of workable standards which may be adopted uniformly across languages and their varieties for the creation of customized texts. Anyone who annotates a text has to deal with the following two basic questions:

(a) What kind of information is to be annotated?
(b) How this information is to be annotated?

With regard to the first question, we must come up with a well-defined plan and purpose. We must decide beforehand the kind of information we plan to annotate in a text. Based on our decision, the required tagset is designed and the annotation scheme is defined. As noted in present practices, the linguistic information that we annotate to a text includes information of orthography, prosody, part-of-speech, morphology, grammar, syntax, anaphora, semantics, discourse, named entities, pragmatics, etymology, sociolinguistics, or similar other aspects. It may include other aspects based on the future application of a text. The process of annotation will vary based on the type of information we want to annotate to a text.

We regard to the second question, we have to decide if an annotation task is to be carried out in a supervised, semi-supervised, or unsupervised manner. At the initial stage, it is always better to go for a supervised method as it has several advantages in checking input data, controlling an annotation process, revisiting operation stages, and verifying the outputs. Semi-supervised and unsupervised methods may be considered once a computer system is trained enough with supervised operations. There is a crucial aspect related to the second question. We typically annotate only one type of information to a text. Should there be a provision to augment another type of information to a text which is already annotated with a particular type of annotation? Will it be rational to put another layer of information on a text which is already annotated with one layer of information? Is it useful to annotate the same text at the sentence level after it is annotated at the part-of-speech level? Some may agree with this kind of proposal while others may disagree. In machine learning, it is possible that one type of annotation is used as an input for another type of annotation on the same text. For instance, a grammatically annotated text is the desired input for upper layer annotations like chunking and parsing. The lower layer annotation helps in the generation of better results for upper layer annotation. For human users, however, a multilayered annotated text is a visually complex text with limited human comprehensibility. We have to, therefore, decide whether we are comfortable with just one layer of annotation or ask for multilayer annotation. Whatever is the decision, a common consensus is that there should be no compromise with the amount of linguistic information that is annotated to a text.

A written text, when developed in a machine-readable form, appears in a raw state in plain text format. On the other hand, an annotated text is produced by attaching various kinds of intralinguistic and extralinguistic information to the text (deHaan, 1984). After annotation, a text is changed in its form, character, content, and functionality (O'Donnell, 1999). The tag values that are attached to a text usually increase the applicational potentials of a text by providing specificity in feature identification and accuracy in information detection (Aldebazal et al., 2009). Thus, annotation makes a text accessible to a computer for the extraction of data and information. On the other hand, such a text is handy for scholars interested in different aspects and properties relating to a language (Archer et al., 2008). The explicit information that is externally added to a text does not belong to the body of a text. It is a repository of external information in the sense that it provides relevant cues for retrieving implicit information from a text (Leech, 2005).

1.7 Annotation Schemas and Models

In the last forty years or so, we have come across several text annotation techniques, text encoding initiatives, text coding schemes, mathematical–computational models for text annotation, indexing, and processing. Most of these have undergone several phases of revision and upgradation. Some notable and often referred to techniques and standards are as follows:

(a) CLAWS: Constituent Likelihood Automatic Word-tagging System (Garside, 1987; McEnery & Hardie, 2011)
(b) TEI: Text Encoding Initiative (Sperberg-McQueen & Burnard, 1994)
(c) HMM: Hidden Markov Model (Kupiec, 1992)
(d) COCOA Reference method (McEnery & Wilson, 1996)
(e) DPM: Dynamic Programming Method (DeRose, 1988)
(f) EAGLE annotation guideline (Ide & Suderman, 2014; Sinclair, 1996)
(g) LAF: Linguistic Annotation Framework (Ide & Romary, 2003, 2004, 2007).

Besides major text annotation guidelines and initiatives, we also come across several indigenous techniques for text annotation (Bird & Liberman, 2001; Johnston, 2013; Carletta et al., 2004; Wolfe, 2002; Xiao, 2008; Gilquin & Gries, 2009; Wolfe & Neuwirth, 2001; Oostdijk & Boves, 2008; Ide et al., 2017; Thieberger & Berez, 2012). Most of the techniques are different from so-called standard text encoding systems. In most cases, however, the major concerns for annotation have been the following issues:

(a) Interface for annotation: manual versus mechanical, supervised versus semi-supervised versus non-supervised
(b) Encoding of information: extratextual versus intratextual
(c) Hierarchy of annotation: monolayer versus multilayer
(d) Levels of annotation: single-level versus multilevel
(e) Lexical block: single-word units versus multiword units
(f) Dispensability of annotation: dispensable versus non-dispensable.

1.8 Types of Text Annotation

In the last four decades, we have come across many innovative types and workable strategies for text annotation (Leech & Wilson, 1999; Sperberg-McQueen & Burnard, 1994; Smith et al., 2007). Some of these are quite straightforward and easily operational, while others are complicated and advanced (Zinsmeister et al., 2008). Most of the time, annotations are applied to texts keeping in mind the nature of a text, the goals of annotation, and the future applications of an annotated text on academic and commercial fronts. Keeping these aspects in mind, we propose to classify text annotation processes into the following types and sub-types (Fig. 1.1).

1.8.1 Intralinguistic Annotation

A text can have two types of annotation: (a) intralinguistic annotation and (b) extralinguistic annotation (Dash, 2011). Intralinguistic annotation involves encoding words, terms, phrases, and similar items which are physically present in a text. For instance, in a spoken text, we find words, sentences, and prosodic features physically present

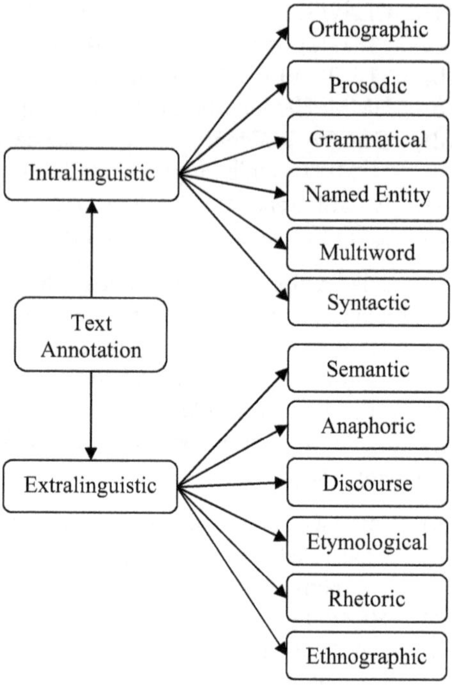

Fig. 1.1 Major types and sub-types of text annotation

in it. Similarly, in a written text, the physical presence of characters, words, and sentences is easily discernible. If we are careful and inquisitive enough, we can also trace the presence of part-of-speech with words and find the presence of phrases in sentences. We can annotate all these properties without going beyond the text itself. The annotation of such information in a text is called an intralinguistic annotation. Some common types of intralinguistic annotations are *orthographic annotation, prosodic annotation, grammatical annotation, named entity annotation, multiword annotation,* and *syntactic annotation*. Some ideas about intralinguistic annotation are presented below.

(a) **Orthographic Annotation**

In orthographic annotation, we identify various types of characters, symbols, and signs that are used in a written text and mark their exact function in the text. Through interpretation and analysis of the function of orthographic symbols, we know how a piece of text is developed, which script is used for the composition of a text, and in most cases, with reference to the script, we can identify the language of a text. In many cases, orthographic symbols are interpretative and representational. In a written Bengali text, for instance, orthographic annotation is needed to solve problems that arise due to ambiguous functions of orthographic symbols which are used to form compound words. A common type of ambiguity is caused due to the indiscriminate use of punctuation marks and spaces within and across words. Some of the major challenges of orthographic annotation include identification and encoding of punctuation marks, diacritics, graphic variants, mathematical symbols, non-textual elements, numerals, and digits.

(b) **Prosodic Annotation**

In prosodic annotation, we annotate crucial prosodic features on a spoken text. Our primary goals are to indicate and mark stress and accent in speech, patterns of intonation, spontaneous speech features, suprasegmental properties, and non-verbal cues like silence, pause, and similar properties present in a spoken text (Johansson, 1995). Moreover, differentiating between stressed and unstressed syllables as well as marking stressed syllables with pitch variations is a challenge which needs wide experience in the analysis of intonation patterns of speech. It is, therefore, a more difficult process than orthographic annotation. Prosody is primarily impressionistic in nature which requires careful listening and comprehension of a spoken text by trained ears before these are rightly annotated to a spoken text.

(c) **Grammatical Annotation**

In grammatical annotation, we assign specific part-of-speech to words after we understand their grammatical roles in a given text. That is why it is also known as part-of-speech (POS) annotation. To assign a POS value to a word, we have to first analyze the role of a word in a sentence and identify in which part-of-speech it is actually used. Once it is understood and confirmed, the word is annotated with that value and the resultant output is called a grammatically annotated text. In the majority of cases, numbers of POS values differ based on the number of part-of-speech types available in a language and the number of POS tag values included in a tagset used for annotation.

(d) **Named Entity Annotation**

In named entity annotation, our primary goal is to identify all proper names used in a text and mark them in different types of named entities based on their form and function in a text (Demir & Ozgur, 2014). The tagset used for this kind of annotation is sub-types under some common types of named entities, such as person names, location names, place names, organization names, event names, time expressions, quantity expressions, monetary terms, and others. The named entities are either single word names (e.g., *Kolkata*), double-word names (e.g., *New Market*), or multiword names (e.g., *Netaji Subhas Chandra Bose Public School*). There are many tasks involved in this annotation: identification of named entities in a text, assignment of specific IDs to them, identification of the type to which these IDs belong, and linking IDs to single-word named IDs or multiword named IDs (Roman et al., 2016). In essence, named entities are recognized and annotated based on their IDs, class, and function in a text.

(e) **Multiword Annotation**

A multiword unit crosses a single-word boundary (or spaces). An expression that is composed of two or more words and is not usually predictable by any of the words which are used to construct it is a multiword. In multiword annotation, we identify and mark multiword units with a set of tags so that, at a later stage, a machine can identify them to analyze their forms and functions to understand their role in a text (Damerau, 1993). Typically, multiword units are annotated with the following sets of information: (a) multiword ID, (b) POS value, and (c) lemma (Calzolari et al., 2002). Once these are identified and annotated, the functional roles of component words (*head* and *satellite*) are analyzed and information is generated for machine learning (Sag et al., 2002). Based on this information, a computer system recognizes multiword units from a text, assigns their POS values, and differentiates them from chunks and phrases (Baldwin et al., 2003).

(f) **Syntactic Annotation**

Syntactic annotation is also known as **parsing**. Here we try to identify and annotate all phrases and phrasal expressions that are used in the meaningful construction of a sentence (DeRose, 1988; Garside, 1987). There are different types of phrases (e.g., *noun phrase, verb phrase, preposition phrase, adjective phrase*) which are indispensable components for generating a grammatically valid sentence. Characteristically, each phrase type is different from the other with regard to its construction, component, and function. Since phrases are minimal constituents which allow a sentence to be meaningful, during syntactic annotation, each sentence is parsed (either at a shallow or a deep level) to define and mark out a hierarchy of dependency of phrases in a sentence (Kupiec, 1992). In syntactic annotation, we identify different types of phrases, annotate the nature of their dependencies, mark constituents and predicates and their arguments within sentences (Smith & McEnery, 2000).

1.8.2 Extralinguistic Annotation

In extralinguistic annotation, we annotate a text with that kind of information, which is not physically available inside a text. For instance, when we annotate a text at the anaphora level, there is no apparent information available in the text based on which we identify how words are linked with others in a relation of coreference. We have to go beyond the textual level to understand how words are co-indexed or bound with coreferential relations. Some common types of extralinguistic annotation include *semantic annotation, anaphoric annotation, discourse annotation, etymological annotation, rhetoric annotation,* and *ethnographic annotation*. Some preliminary ideas about some extralinguistic annotations are presented below.

(a) Semantic Annotation

Semantic annotation is also known as **word sense annotation**. Here we assign semantic values to both open and closed classes of words. The primary goal of semantic annotation is to identify the sense a word denotes when it is used in a text. This sense, which is normally known as **contextual sense**, may differ from the basic **lexicographic sense** of words available in a dictionary. The contextual sense is utilized in language applications such as word sense disambiguation (Löfberg et al., 2005), mapping sense span of words, assigning semantic fields to words (Piao et al., 2006), and representing semantic ontology in WordNet (Miller et al., 1990; Dash et al., 2017). In semantic annotation, we emphasize on the identification of semantic information of words and representation of semantic relationships underlying words, collocations, and co-occurrences.

(b) Anaphoric Annotation

In anaphoric annotation, we identify and co-index pronouns and nouns that are used in text in a coreference scheme following a broad framework of cohesion (Halliday & Hasan, 1976). Also, we identify different types of anaphora used in a text, list them, and sort these forms to dissolve anaphoric complexities in texts (Webber et al., 2003). Applied to a text, anaphora annotation indicates possible anaphoric and other equivalent internal relations underlying between neighboring parts of a text (Popescu-Belis, 1998). This annotation has strong application in studying and testing mechanisms like pronoun resolution, which are important for automatic text understanding and machine translation across languages (Mitkov et al., 2000).

(c) Discourse Annotation

In discourse annotation, we annotate a text at a level which is beyond the level of sentence and meaning. We do this to understand discourse and pragmatic strategies deployed in a text. It is noted that the identification of specific discourse markers and pragmatic functions of units in a text gives scopes to understand the purposes and goals of a text generation (Stenström, 1984). Also, it creates a background for the identification of many other forms of linguistic phenomena in a text (Edwards & Lampert, 1993). For instance, marking spatial and temporal expressions in a text gives scopes for identifying discourse relations among all spatial–temporal expressions. Also, it allows to identify and annotate discourse connectives and discourse particles, which help in the identification of contexts for the pragmatic interpretation of a text.

(d) Etymological Annotation

Etymological annotation is known as **lexical source annotation**. We apply this process to a text to annotate the source of origin of words and the milestones the words of a language have touched upon (Dash & Hussain, 2013). In a natural language, it is necessary to know how vocabulary is developed, how words evolved and came into use, how words of one language combined with words of other languages in generation of new lexical items in the language. These questions can be adequately addressed if a text is etymologically annotated. For dictionary compilation and language planning, it is necessary to know how a language borrows words from other languages over the centuries. For lexicological studies, it is necessary to know how a language increases its vocabulary, how it assimilates concepts by incorporating new ideas through lexical borrowing, and how it adapts words and terms through naturalization (Dash et al., 2009). An etymologically annotated text addresses all these questions and challenges related to the etymology of words.

(e) Rhetoric Annotation

Rhetoric annotation is also known as **figure-of-speech annotation**. Here we identify various rhetorical devices that are used in a text. We annotate these devices based on standard methods of classification and categorization of rhetorics. The use of rhetorics is a common practice in text generation. Each piece of text (either spoken or written) contains a few rhetorics—either explicitly visible or implicitly embedded. Analysis of rhetorics sheds new insights on the theme and structure of a text. For instance, a piece of text that is made with rhetorical devices is characteristically different from a text without rhetorics. A rhetorically developed text differs in choice of words, order of words, sentence structure, grammatical form, sense implication, and reference. Such properties put up challenges in scientific argumentation in a text (Fahnestock, 1999) and throw up hurdles in the proper representation of arguments within a text (Green, 2010). Moreover, such a text becomes a challenge in argument mining, machine learning, and text analysis, language computation, and artificial intelligence (Harris & DiMarco, 2017; Harris et al., 2018).

(f) Ethnographic Annotation

Ethnographic annotation is a carefully defined and expected deviation from discourse annotation. It involves marking of sociolinguistic cues, ethnographic elements, cultural traits, and extralinguistic elements that are normally concealed in a text (Archer & Culpeper, 2003). Such elements are hardly visible without a thorough analysis of a piece of text at the ethnographic level. Through ethnographic annotation, we mark the presence of various kinds of ethnographic properties in a text and apply these properties in the interpretation of a text from an ethnographic and socio-cultural perspective. For instance, following the scheme proposed by Hymes (1962, 1964) we annotate ethnographic properties (SPEAKING: *Setting and Scene, Participants, Ends, Act sequence, Key, Instrumentalities, Norms, and Genre*) in a spoken text to understand its form, purpose, and composition. Also, through ethnographic annotation, we annotate a text with different kinds of demographic and register variables that often remain hidden in a text.

Besides these major types of text annotation, we can also think of text annotation of other types. In most cases, these will produce new sets of challenges. We have to think of new strategies to solve these challenges. For instance, we have not yet decided how a poetic text should be annotated; what kinds of textual, linguistic, stylistic, prosodic, and figurative annotation techniques we should design for and apply to poetic texts. Problems and challenges are also there in the annotation of medical texts, texts of court proceedings, conversational texts, multimodal texts (where audiovisual elements are put together), mythological texts, and others. Further challenges are also involved in annotation of old heritage and classical texts which require separate tagsets and methods for annotation of mythological characters, events, anecdotes, ecology, and sociocultural traits.

1.9 Present State of Text Annotation

The number of grammatically and syntactically annotated texts is many and these are more or less easily available across several languages. These are developed mostly in advanced and semi-advanced languages. These are available either for on-site access or download. And most of these annotated texts are used heavily in linguistics, information technology, and many other domains. The other types of annotated texts cut a sorry figure even in advanced languages. There are many reasons for this—technical, linguistic, logistic, and others. Annotated texts of different types are available in *English, Spanish, French, German, Italian, Chinese, Japanese* and some other languages (Atwell et al., 2000). On the other hand, such texts are few and far between in less-advanced languages. For instance, grammatically annotated texts are found only in a few Indian languages. Moreover, these texts are neither large, nor diversified, nor widely representative, nor readily accessible. The other types of annotated texts are not yet developed in these languages for many reasons.

(a) The availability of a large number of written and spoken texts in digital form in advanced languages has made it possible for annotating these at various levels for works of linguistics and language technology. In case of less-advanced languages, the number of digital texts is very few and most of these are not designed properly.
(b) The availability of various text processing tools, systems, and techniques works as a catalyst in the development of annotated texts in many advanced languages. This kind of situation is not observed in less-advanced languages due to logistic, technical and motivational deficiencies.
(c) Grammatical annotation is comparatively easier than other types of text annotation. Even non-experts with limited grammatical knowledge can annotate words at the part-of-speech level in a text. Reports show that achieving a good rate of success in grammatical annotation is possible even with limited skill and sincere efforts (Leech, 2005). This strategy, however, does not work in other kinds of text annotation.
(d) Other types of text annotation require specialized knowledge and training for achieving success. For instance, without having adequate knowledge in phonetics, phonetic transcription, intonation, suprasegmental features, and other properties of speech we cannot annotate a spoken text rightly. Similarly, without having a strong understanding of semantics, discourse, and pragmatics we cannot claim success in semantic and discourse annotation.

Table 1.1 Text annotation situation in English and Indian languages

Annotation	English	Indian languages
Orthographic	Several	None
Prosodic	Few	One or two speech texts in Hindi
Grammatical	Many	Some texts (TDIL & ILCI project)
Named entity	Few	One or two
Multiword	Few	One or two
Syntactic	Several	Few (ILMT project)
Semantic	Several	None
Anaphora	Several	One or two
Discourse	Few	None
Etymological	None	One in Bengali
Rhetoric	Few	None
Ethnographic	Few	None

(e) The number of scholars working for advanced languages far exceeds the number of scholars working for less-advanced languages. Moreover, for advanced languages, scholars come from the background of computer science, linguistics, artificial intelligence, mathematics, statistics, and cognitive science. This is hardly noted in case of less-advanced languages. It is a crucial factor for making a less-advanced language advanced as well as making a language digitally accessible, computer-friendly, and useful for works of linguistics, language technology, and information technology. Direct and active participation of scholars coming from different academic backgrounds is hardly observed in less-advanced languages.

Due to these factors, the number of annotated texts in less-advanced languages is very few. The present scenario is, however, changing in a positive manner. The number of raw and annotated texts is increasing day by day in less-advanced languages also. The pressing needs of language technology play a crucial role here. Moreover, difficulties involved in text annotation works motivate many scholars to take up challenges. Keeping this in view, in the following table (Table 1.1), we present a rough estimate on text annotation in English with a reference to some Indian languages. The table reflects on the present state of development of annotated texts in the sphere of linguistic knowledge harvesting, knowledge generation, and knowledge management.

1.10 Utilization of Annotated Texts

The importance of an annotated text is enormous in language description, language processing, language technology, artificial intelligence, information technology, and many other disciplines. The utility of an annotated text within a wider canvas of

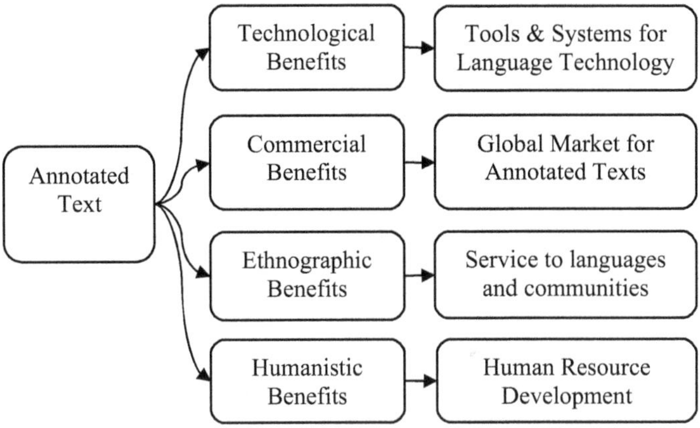

Fig. 1.2 Benefits of annotated texts in various domains

computational linguistics, cognitive linguistics, and applied linguistics may be visualized in the following manner (Fig. 1.2). It shows how an annotated text becomes a source of data and information for various academic and commercial purposes.

It is to be understood that all kinds of annotated texts are not useful for all kinds of linguistic or technology-related works. Each type of annotated text has a specific utility in a specific domain, although it may be used in other domains. For instance, a POS annotated text is useful in natural language processing applications like developing systems for grammar checking, putting words into chunks, recognizing named entities, and disambiguation of word senses. Similarly, a syntactically annotated text is useful in understanding the grammar of a language, addressing queries, retrieving information, translating a text, and language modeling. A semantically annotated text is indispensable in machine learning, computational lexicography, word sense disambiguation, cognitive linguistics, and language teaching. A prosodically annotated text is useful in speech recognition, speaker identification, speech processing, forensic studies, and clinical linguistics. Annotated texts of all types are used in various studies, investigations, and experiments in descriptive and applied linguistics. Such texts are also used in allied disciplines (e.g., *sociology, economics, semiotics, ethnology, ecology, culture studies*) to address many academic and commercial requirements.

One can visualize many applications of annotated texts in many domains of humanities, science, and technology. Even then, to date, we are not successful enough in the development of these highly useful linguistic resources. This implies that we have to take initiatives in this direction to develop annotated texts of various types with the following three goals: (a) develop digital texts of various types and subject content; (b) design a maximally accurate tagset to increase the level of accuracy of an annotated text, and (c) train computer systems to develop annotated texts in a large scale to address the present academic and commercial needs.

References

Aldebazal, I., Aranzabe, M. J., Arriola, J. M., & Dias de Ilarraza, A. (2009). Syntactic annotation in the reference Corpus for the processing of Basque (EPEC): Theoretical and practical issues. *Corpus Linguistics and Linguistic Theory, 5*(2), 241–269.

Archer, D., & Culpeper, J. (2003). Sociopragmatic annotation: New directions and possibilities in historical corpus linguistics. In A. Wilson, P. Rayson, & T. McEnery (Eds.), *Corpus linguistics by the Lune: Studies in honour of Geoffrey Leech* (pp. 37–58). Frankfurt: Peter Lang.

Archer, D., Culpeper, J., & Davies, M. (2008). Pragmatic annotation. In A. Lüdeling & M. Kytö (Eds.), *Corpus linguistics: An international handbook* (pp. 613–642). Berlin: Walter de Gruyter.

Atwell, E., Demetriou, G., Hughes, J., Schiffrin, A., Souter, C., & Wilcock, S. (2000). A comparative evaluation of modern English corpus grammatical annotation schemes. *International Computer Archive of Modern English Journal, 24*, 7–23.

Baldwin, T., Bannardz, C., Tanaka, T., & Widdows, D. (2003). An empirical model of multi-word expression decomposability. In *Proceedings of the ACL 2003 Workshop on Multiword Expressions: Analysis, Acquisition and Treatment* (pp. 89–96).

Berez, A. L., & Gries, S. T. (2010). Correlates to middle marking in Dena'ina iterative verbs. *International Journal of American Linguistics, 76*(1), 145–165.

Bird, S., & Liberman, M. (2001). A formal framework for linguistic annotation. *Speech Communication, 33*(1–2), 23–60.

Calzolari, N., Fillmore, C. J., Grishman, R., Ide, N., Lenci, A., MacLeod, C., & Zampolli, A. (2002). Towards best practice for multiword expressions in computational Lexicons. In *Proceedings of the 3rd International Conference on Language Resources and Evaluation (LREC 2002)* (pp. 1934–1940).

Carletta, J., McKelvie, D., Isard, A., Mengel, A., Klein, M., & Møller, M. B. (2004). A generic approach to software support for linguistic annotation using XML. In G. Sampson & D. McCarthy (Eds.), *Corpus linguistics: Readings in a Widening discipline* (pp. 449–459). London: Continuum.

Damerau, F. (1993). Generating and evaluating domain-oriented multi-word terms from texts. *Information Processing and Management, 29*(4), 433–447.

Dash, N. S., Dutta Chowdhury, P., & Sarkar, A. (2009). Naturalization of English words in modern Bengali: A corpus-based empirical study. *Language Forum, 35*(2), 127–142.

Dash, N. S., & Hussain, M. M. (2013). Designing a generic scheme for etymological annotation: A new type of language corpora annotation. In *Proceedings of the ALR-11 & 6th International Joint Conference on Natural Language Processing,* Nagoya Congress Centre, Nagoya, Japan, 14–18 Oct 2013 (pp. 64–71).

Dash, N. S. (2011). Principles of part-of-speech (POS) tagging in Indian language corpora. In *Proceedings of 5th Language Technology Conference (LTC-2011): Human Language Technologies as a Challenge for Computer Science and Linguistics.* Poznan, Poland, 25–27 Nov 2011 (pp. 101–105).

Dash, N. S., Bhattacharyya, P., & Pawar, J. (Eds.) (2017). *The WordNet in Indian languages* (pp. V–XII). Singapore: Springer.

deHaan, P. (1984). Problem-oriented tagging of English corpus data. In J. Aarts & W. Meijs (Eds.), *Corpus linguistics* (pp. 123–139). Amsterdam: Rodopi.

Demir, H., & Ozgur, A. (2014). Improving named entity recognition for morphologically rich languages using word embeddings. In *Proceedings of the 13th International Conference on Machine Learning and Applications (ICMLA 2014)*, 3–6 Dec 2014, Detroit, MI, USA (pp. 117–122).

DeRose, S. J. (1988). Grammatical category disambiguation by statistical optimization. *Computational Linguistics, 14*(1), 31–39.

Edwards, J. A., & Lampert, M. D. (Eds.). (1993). *Talking data: Transcription and coding in discourse research.* Hillsdale, NJ: Erlbaum.

Fahnestock, J. (1999). *Rhetorical figures in scientific argumentation.* New York: Oxford University Press.

Garside, R. (1987). The CLAWS word-tagging system. In R. Garside, G. Leech, & G. Sampson (Eds.), *The computational analysis of English: A corpus-based approach* (pp. 30–41). London: Longman.

Gilquin, G., & Gries, S. T. (2009). Corpora and experimental methods: A state-of-the-art review. *Corpus Linguistics and Linguistic Theory, 5*(1), 1–26.

Green, N. (2010). Representation of argumentation in text with rhetorical structure theory. *Argumentation, 24*(2), 181–196.

Greene, B., & Rubin, G. (1971). *Automatic grammatical tagging of English.* Technical Report, Department of Linguistics, Brown University, Rhode Island (a Handout).

Halliday, M. A. K., & Hasan, R. (1976). *Cohesion in English (English Language Series 9).* London: Longman.

Harris, R. A., & DiMarco, C. (2017). Rhetorical figures, arguments, computation. *Argument & Computation, 8*(3), 211–231.

Harris, R. A., Marco, C. D., Ruan, S., & O'Reilly, C. (2018). An annotation scheme for rhetorical figures. *Argument and Computation, 9*(1), 155–175.

Hymes, D. (1962). The ethnography of speaking. In T. Gladwin & W. C. Sturtevant (Eds.), *Anthropology and human behavior* (pp. 13–53). Washington: The Anthropology Society of Washington.

Hymes, D. (1964). Introduction: Toward ethnographies of communication. *American Anthropologist, 66*(6), 1–34.

Ide, N., & Romary, L. (2003). Outline of the international standard linguistic annotation framework. In *Proceedings of ACL'03 Workshop on Linguistic Annotation: Getting the Model Right* (pp. 1–5).

Ide, N., & Romary, L. (2004). An international standard for a linguistic annotation framework. *Natural Language Engineering, 10*(3–4), 211–225.

Ide, N., & Romary, L. (2007). Towards international standards for language resources. In L. Dybkjaer, H. Hemsen, & W. Minker (Eds.), *Evaluation of text and speech systems* (pp. 263–284), Springer.

Ide, N., & Suderman, K. (2014). The linguistic annotation framework: A standard for annotation interchange and merging. *Language Resources and Evaluation., 48*(3), 395–418.

Ide, N., Chiarcos, C., Stede, M., & Cassidy, S. (2017). Designing annotation schemes: From model to representation. In N. Ide & J. Pustejovsky (Eds.), *Handbook of linguistic annotation* (pp. 73–111). Dordrecht: Springer.

Johansson, S. (1995). The encoding of spoken texts. *Computers and the Humanities, 29*(1), 149–158.

Johnston, T. (2013). *Auslan Corpus annotation guidelines.* Sidney: Macquarie University.

Kupiec, J. (1992). Robust part-of-speech tagging using a hidden Markov model. *Computer Speech and Language, 6*(1), 3–15.

Leech, G., & Smith, N. (1999). The use of tagging. In H. V. Halteren (Ed.), *Syntactic word class tagging* (pp. 23–36). Dordrecht: Kluwer Academic Press.

Leech, G., & Wilson, A. (1999). Guidelines and standards for tagging. In H. van Halteren (Ed.), *Syntactic wordclass tagging* (pp. 55–80). Dordrecht: Kluwer.

Leech, G. (1993). Corpus annotation schemes. *Literary and Linguistic Computing, 8*(4), 275–281.

Leech, G. (1997). Introducing corpus annotation. In R. Garside, G. Leech, & A. McEnery (Eds.), *Corpus annotation: Linguistic information from computer text corpora* (pp. 1–18). London: Addison Wesley Longman.

Leech, G. (2005). Adding linguistic annotation. In M. Wynne (Ed.), *Developing linguistic corpora: A guide to good practice* (pp. 17–29). Oxford: Oxbrow Books.

Löfberg, L., Piao, S., Rayson, P., Juntunen, J. P., Nykänen, A., & Varantola, K. (2005). A semantic tagger for the Finnish language. In *Proceedings of the Corpus Linguistics 2005 Conference Series Online E-journal, 1*(1). 14–17 July 2005, Birmingham, UK.

McEnery, T., & Hardie, A. (2011). *Corpus linguistics: Method, theory, and practice.* Cambridge: Cambridge University Press.

McEnery, T., & Wilson, A. (1996). *Corpus linguistics.* Edinburgh: Edinburgh University Press.

Miller, G. A., Beckwith, R., Fellbaum, C., Gross, D., & Miller, K. J. (1990). Introduction to WordNet: An on-line lexical database. *International Journal of Lexicography, 3*(4), 235–312.

Mitkov, R., Evans, R., Orasan, C., Barbu, C., Jones, L., Sotirova, V., & Wolverhampton, W. S. (2000). Co-reference and anaphora: Developing annotating tools annotated resources and annotation strategies. In *Proceedings of the Discourse, Anaphora and Reference Resolution Conference (DAARC2000).* 16–18 Nov 2000. Lancaster, UK (pp. 49–58).

O'Donnell, M. B. (1999). The use of annotated corpora for new testament discourse analysis: A survey of current practice and future prospects. In S. E. Porter & J. T. Reed (Eds.), *Discourse analysis and the new testament: Results and applications* (pp. 71–117). Sheffield: Sheffield Academic Press.

Oostdijk, N., & Boves, L. (2008). Pre-processing speech corpora. In A. Lüdeling & M. Kytö (Eds.), *Corpus linguistics: An international handbook* (Vol. 1, pp. 642–663). Berlin: Walter de Gruyter.

Piao, S., Archer, D., Mudraya, O., Rayson, P., Garside, R., McEnery, A.M., & Wilson, A. (2006). A large semantic lexicon for corpus annotation. In *Proceedings of the Corpus Linguistics 2005 Conference Series Online E-journal, 1*(1), July 14–17, Birmingham, UK.

Popescu-Belis, A. (1998). How corpora with annotated co-reference links improve reference resolution. In *Proceedings of the 1st International Conference on Language Resources and Evaluation* (pp. 567–572). Granada, Spain.

Roman, I., Shipilo, A., & Kovriguina, L. (2016). Russian named entities recognition and classification using distributed word and phrase representations. In *Proceedings of the 3rd International Conference on Information Management and Big Data (SIMBig 2016),* 1–3 Sept 2016, Cusco, Peru (pp. 150–156).

Sag, I. A., Baldwin, T., Bond, F., Copestake, A., & Flickinger, D. (2002). Multiword expressions: A pain in the neck for NLP. *Lecture Notes in Computer Science, 2276*, 1–15.

Sinclair, J. M. (1996). EAGLES Preliminary recommendations on Corpus Typology. https://www.ilc.pi.cnr.it/EAGLES96/corpustyp/corpustyp.html.

Smith, N., Hoffmann, S., & Rayson, P. (2007). Corpus tools and methods today & tomorrow: Incorporating user-defined annotations. In *Proceedings of the 4th Corpus Linguistics Conference*, 27–30 July 2007, University of Birmingham, UK. Article No. 276.

Smith, N. I., & McEnery, A. M. (2000). Inducing part-of-speech tagged lexicons from large corpora. In R. Mitkov & N. Nikolov (Eds.), *Recent advances in natural language processing 2* (pp. 21–30). Amsterdam: John Benjamins.

Sperberg-McQueen, C., & Burnard, L. (Eds.) (1994). *Guidelines for electronic text encoding and interchange.* TEI P3. Text Encoding Initiative, Oxford, Providence, Charlottesville, Bergen.

Stenström, A.-B. (1984). Discourse tags. In J. Aarts & W. Meijs (Eds.), *Corpus linguistics: Recent developments in the use of computer corpora in English Language Research* (pp. 65–81). Amsterdam: Rodopi.

Thieberger, N., & Berez, A. L. (2012). Linguistic data management. In N. Thieberger (Ed.), *Oxford handbook of linguistic fieldwork* (pp. 90–118). Oxford: Oxford University Press.

Wallis, S. A. (2007). Annotation, retrieval, and experimentation or: You only get out what you put in. In A. Meurman-Solin & A. A. Nurmi (Eds.), *Annotating variation and change.* Helsinki: Varieng (ePublished).

Wallis, S. A. (2014). What might a corpus of parsed spoken data tell us about language? In L. Veselovská & M. Janebová (Eds.), *Complex visibles out there. Proceedings of the Olomouc linguistics Colloquium 2014: Language use and linguistic structure* (pp. 641–662). Olomouc: Palacký University, Czech Republic.

Wallis, S. A. & Aarts, B. (2006). Recent developments in the syntactic annotation of corpora. In E. M. Bermúdez & L. R. Miyares (Eds.), *Linguistics in the twenty-first century* (pp. 197–202). Cambridge: Cambridge Scholars Press.

Wallis, S. A., & Nelson, G. (2001). Knowledge discovery in grammatically analyzed corpora. *Data Mining and Knowledge Discovery, 5*(4), 305–336.

Webber, B., Stone, M., Joshi, A., & Knott, A. (2003). Anaphora and discourse structure. *Computational Linguistics, 29*, 545–587.

Wolfe, J. (2002). Annotation technologies: A software and research review. *Computers and Composition, 19*(4), 471–497.

Wolfe, J., & Neuwirth, C. M. (2001). From the margins to the center: The future of annotation. *Journal of Business and Technical Communication, 15*(33), 333–370.

Xiao, R. (2008). Theory-driven corpus research: Using corpora to inform aspect theory. In A. Lüdeling & M. Kytö (Eds.), *Corpus linguistics: An international handbook* (Vol. 2, pp. 987–1008). Berlin: Gruyter.

Zinsmeister, H., Hinrichs, E., Kübler, S., & Witt, A. (2008). Linguistically annotated corpora: Quality assurance, reusability, and sustainability. In A. Lüdeling & M. Kytö (Eds.), *Corpus linguistics: An international handbook* (Vol. 1, pp. 759–776). Berlin: Gruyter.

Web Links

http://ahds.ac.uk/linguistic-corpora/
http://www.comp.lancs.ac.uk/ucrel/claws/trial.html
http://www2.sal.tohoku.ac.jp/ling/corpus2/2maxims.htm
https://pynlp.wordpress.com/2014/02/03/7-corpus-processing/
http://nltk.org/book/ch02.html
http://www.gutenberg.org/
http://www.nltk.org/data
http://www.nltk.org/howto
http://www.ilc.cnr.it/EAGLES/browse.html
http://www.helsinki.fi/varieng/series/volumes/01/wallis
http://corplingstats.wordpress.com/2014/06/24/corpus-language
https://varieng.helsinki.fi/series/volumes/01/wallis/

Chapter 2
Principles and Rules of Part-of-Speech Annotation

Abstract In this chapter, we describe some principles and rules that we apply during the process of part-of-speech (POS) annotation on a written text corpus. For various practical and theoretical reasons, these principles and rules become useful and relevant for overcoming many unwanted hurdles in POS annotation. We also describe here the strategies that we apply when we formulate some algorithms for the automatic assignment of grammatical values to words in a text. Although we address theoretical and practical issues of POS annotation, we do not talk about technical and computational issues which are important when a computer system is engaged for this kind of work. Since the target readers of this chapter are students of linguistics who have limited or zero exposure to computation, we keep these technical and computational issues beyond this chapter. We primarily focus on some linguistic and theoretical aspects of the problem. We keep these issues relatively simple as an area of general inquiry, so that non-experts and common readers can get ideas about how words in a text are annotated at the POS level, and how the principles and rules are to be used during this work. This chapter has two parts: in Part I, we propose some principles that are to be followed during POS annotation; and in Part II, we define some rules which are to be adopted during the actual work of POS annotation. Supporting examples are taken from English and Bengali text corpus. This chapter imparts necessary guidance to the new generation of scholars about the nature and characteristics of POS annotation and how proper reference to these principles and rules can make the subsequent works of text processing easy and simplified.

Keywords Annotation · Part-of-speech · Tagging · Morphology · Syntax · Semantics · Context · Metadata · Tagset

2.1 Introduction

Part-of-speech (POS) annotation is considered one of the fundamental domains of natural language processing. It is normally understood as an act of assigning specific parts-of-speech value to words that are used in a piece of text. It is also known as POS tagging, grammatical annotation, and word category marking. The task primarily involves a process of marking each word with a POS value—either manually or

N. S. Dash, *Language Corpora Annotation and Processing*,
https://doi.org/10.1007/978-981-16-2960-0_2

automatically—in a piece of a written or transcribed text in accordance with the form and function of the word in the context of its use in larger syntactic frames like phrases and sentences (Brants, 2000).

In the case of a digital text corpus, the task of POS annotation is done by using a computer by a set of predefined POS tagsets and tagging rules (Ide et al., 2017a). The computer is trained to mark POS of words, terms, and other lexical items along with their linguistic properties and grammatical functions in a text. The process of assigning POS value to words, either by man or a machine, is not a straightforward and one-dimensional task (Leech, 1993). It is linked with many theoretical, practical, and technical issues which are concerned with marking lexical-cum-semantic identities as well as syntactic-cum-grammatical functions of these lexical items. Also, it includes the act of defining the basic hierarchical modalities of a tag assignment process and designing rule-based schemas that are to be used for automatic assignment of POS to words (Ide et al., 2017b). To achieve this goal, it is sensible to use a synchronized strategy designed elegantly by combining linguistic and extralinguistic knowledge and computational expertise for achieving maximum success with a minimum enterprise.

The chapter is divided into the following sections. In Sect. 2.2, we propose 12 basic principles that we suggest following during POS annotation of a written text corpus; in Sect. 2.3, we propose 12 useful rules for POS annotation. Each principle and rule is discussed in brief with examples taken from English and Bengali corpus. In Sect. 2.4, we discuss the value of a POS annotated corpus in different domains of human knowledge.

2.2 Principles of POS Annotation

For all kinds of natural language texts, we need some well-defined principles that we follow during assigning POS tags to words. These principles help to identify lexico-semantic and syntactico-grammatical functions of words in a text. These principles are available and are followed during the assignment of POS tags to words in languages like English, German, and Spanish to settle the lexico-semantic and syntactico-grammatical functions of words (Leech et al., 1994). For those languages, which are not advanced enough with regard to their use in a computer, POS annotation is still a daunting task. Since principles for annotation are not yet developed for these languages, there is a need for developing some principles that can be adopted in designing standards for POS annotation for these languages. This idea works behind the formulation of the following principles for texts of all types of these languages (Dash, 2011). Some principles are self-explanatory; they do not need examples.

Other principles require examples for explication. We describe these principles with examples to show how they are applied to texts.

Principle 1: Generic POS annotation tagset should be designed

The tagset that we develop for POS annotation should not be biased toward a particular language or a group of languages. It should be generic in the sense that it should be designed in such a manner that it works well for all languages belonging to different language families (e.g., *Indo-European*, *Indo-Aryan*, *Afro-Asiatic*, *Altaic*, *Sino-Tibetan*, *Austro-Tai*, *Dravidian*, *Caucasian*, *Uralic*, *Niger-Congo*, *Nilo-Saharan*, *Khoisan*, *Austronesian*, *and Amerindian*). It is not desired that a particular POS tagset, for instance, developed for English (a language of the Indo-European language family), does not work for Bengali (another language of the same family) or Tamil (a language of the Dravidian language family). In principle, the tagset should be appropriate for all languages with necessary recognition of language-specific unique properties and features. It is necessary to take a judicious decision in this regard keeping in mind that the primary parts-of-speech (i.e., *noun*, *pronoun*, *adjective*, *verb*, and *adverb*) are common to all languages. Therefore, annotation of words in a text with POS information should be based on the universally accepted sets of parts-of-speech.

Principle 2: Uniform POS tagset for all text types

The POS tagset should not be skewed and applicable to only one type of text of a language. A tagset should, in principle, apply to all kinds of text produced in a language. That means a tagset that is designed and developed for written texts should equally apply to spoken texts. Similarly, a tagset that is developed for scientific texts should be equally applicable to other kinds of texts (e.g., *imaginative*, *informative*, *commercial*, *legal*, *medical*, *media*, etc.). It should also work equally well for other text varieties that are available in a natural language. This principle also claims that a tagset designed for prose texts should equally apply to poetic, dialogic texts, multimodal texts, and folk texts produced in a language.

Principle 3: POS tagset should have spatiotemporal capacity

A POS tagset should not be compatible with present-day text only. It should work with texts that are produced long ago as well as with texts that are to be produced later in the language. That means a POS tagset should be designed in such a manner that it fits for present-day texts as well as for past and future texts. For instance, the POS tagset that is designed for modern Bengali texts is also compatible with old Bengali texts that were produced nearly a thousand years ago. This is the "**temporal capacity**" of a POS tagset. On the other hand, a POS tagset that is designed for a standard variety of a language should equally be compatible with texts that are produced in dialects and regional varieties. Moreover, the POS tagset should work for texts that are produced in the same language used in another province, region, state, or country. For instance, the tagset that works well for Bengali texts produced in West Bengal, India, should work well for Bengali texts produced in Tripura and Jharkhand in India as well as Bengali texts produced in Bangladesh, England, America, or any other parts of the globe. This is called the "**spatial capacity**" of a POS tagset.

Table 2.1 Multiple layers of annotation in a corpus text

No	Annotation	Domains of operation
1	Orthographic	Spoken text transcription
2	Morphological	Morphological elements of words
3	Part-of-Speech	Morphosyntactic roles of words
4	Etymological	Origin and evolution of words
5	Local word group	When two/more words form a unit
6	Chunking	Idioms, collocations, and multiword units
7	Semantic	Meanings and sense variations
8	Syntactic	Phrases, sentences, arguments
9	Anaphoric	Referential relations of words
10	Pragmatic	Pragmatic elements within texts
11	Discourse	Discourse elements within texts
12	Sociolinguistic	Socio-cultural elements in texts

Principle 4: A layered approach is better in POS annotation

It is better to adopt a layered approach in a part-of-speech annotation scheme. This is necessary because a natural language text is full of various kinds of intralinguistic and extralinguistic information. After annotation, the resultant text becomes a unique text where intralinguistic and extralinguistic information is explicit to a human and a machine. Therefore, it is desired to annotate as much information as possible in a text. However, the reality is that linguistic information annotated to a text is diverse in form and complex in nature. Since annotating all kinds of linguistic information at one layer makes an annotation process complicated, it is not sensible to annotate all information to a text both from the point of view of human use and machine learning. Therefore, it is better to divide collective linguistic information into several layers and annotate each layer separately in a text (Table 2.1).

Theoretically and practically, these layers are interrelated and interdependent to each other. During annotation, no one deals with isolated words. Everyone deals with words that are used in a sentence within a text. Everyone tries to show how these words carry out varied linguistic functions in a text. A layered approach has some advantages. In many situations, information retrieved from one layer becomes an input for another layer. For instance, information obtained from morphological annotation is useful input for POS annotation. Similarly, information retrieved from POS-level annotation becomes necessary inputs for syntactic-level annotation. This is true to the texts of all languages. The degree of interdependence may vary based on the type of a text and the nature of linguistic information to be annotated at respective layers.

Principle 5: Hierarchical POS annotation tagset is desired

It is better to design a POS annotation tagset that keeps open the scopes for annotating more than one level of POS information to words. It is possible only when a tagset

Table 2.2 Hierarchical tagset for POS annotation

SN	Category			Label	Examples
	L_1	L_2	L_3		
1	Noun			N	
1.1		Common		N_NC	lok "man"
1.2		Proper		N_NP	dilli "Delhi"
1.3		Material		N_NM	kalam "pen"
1.4		Collective		N_NL	dal "party"
1.5		Abstract		N_NA	bhay "fear"
1.6		Verbal		N_NV	grahaṇ "taking"
1.7		Location		N_NST	upare "above"

is designed in a hierarchical manner. One may, for instance, consider N (Noun) as a top level (L_1) and consider different sub-types (e.g., *proper*, *common*, *collective*, *abstract*, and *material*) as lower levels (L_2, L_3) under the top level (Table 2.2).

Similarly, one can annotate V (Verb) as a top level and V_VM (main verb), V_VAUX (auxiliary verb), V_VF (finite verb), and V_VNF (non-finite verb) as lower levels under the top level. These levels may be annotated manually or automatically. In both cases, one should start with the lowest possible level of the hierarchy for several operational and applicational advatages. Once the lower level is annotated, the higher level is automatically annotated due to hierarchical linkage. Although annotation is done with a clear focus on the POS of words, long-term applications are also kept in mind. The application of a hierarchical scheme, at later stages, becomes useful in retrieving various kinds of linguistic information from an annotated text.

Principle 6: Language-based change of POS tagset is required

The POS tagset should be modified taking into consideration the need for a language. The tagset may expand or be minimized based on language-specific requirements. It is necessary to make a POS tagset flexible, so that it can be adjusted for a particular language or a dialect. That means the POS tagset should be designed in such a manner that it includes a new POS in the existing tagset either at the top, intermediate, or lower level, as the case may be. On the contrary, if required, it removes a POS if it is not required for a language. For instance, *postposition* is a redundant POS for English. Therefore, it may be removed from the tagset designed for English. Similarly, *preposition* (e.g., *by, in, for, to, with,* etc.) and *article* (i.e., *a, an, the*) are redundant parts-of-speech for Bengali. However, they cannot be removed. In Bengali texts, there are instances of the use of English sentences in transliterated forms where the use of prepositions and articles are noted. Therefore, at the time of designing a POS tagset for Bengali, one has to consider *preposition* and *article* as necessary parts-of-speech and include them in the Bengali tagset. If a POS is never found in the text of a language, it should be discarded.

Table 2.3 Metadata with POS tagset in the TDIL Bengali corpus

Metadata information
Language: Bengali, Genre Type: Written, Category: Aesthetics, Subcategory: Literature, Text Type: Novel, Source: Book, Title: Bhut Ar Bhuto, Volume: Single, Issue: NA, Edition: First, Headline: Bhut Ar Bhuto, Author: Sudhanshu Patra, Publisher: Dey's, Place: Kolkata, Year: 1993, Index No.: B0035, Data Creator Code: 61802, Date of Creation: 12 July 2006, Collector: Anami Sarkar, Proof Reader: Aprakash Gupta, Date of Proofreading: 16 August 2007, Total Words: 5517

Principle 7: Metadata of text should be stored with POS tagset
All kinds of information (*linguistic and extralinguistic*) encoded as metadata should be stored along with a POS tagset (discussed in Chap. 4). Moreover, it should be understood and accessed by a human annotator and a machine used for POS annotation. Since a corpus is made with different kinds of text samples, it is important to preserve metadata information of each text stored in a corpus (Dash, 2011). The rudimentary information regarding *language*, *title*, *author*, *source*, *domain*, *text type*, *time*, and *creator of a digital text* should be marked on each text as metadata (Table 2.3). The information stored as metadata is useful during POS annotation when an annotator annotates different kinds of named entities. For instance, in the Bengali corpus, it is noted that many adjectives are used as named entities in texts. During POS annotation, metadata information becomes handy in the proper recognition of named entities. Metadata information is also useful in the management of extralinguistic information of texts, text documentation, record maintenance, addressing copyright issues, and research in sociolinguistics, language planning, stylistics, and discourse.

Principle 8: The POS tagset should follow a global standard
The POS tagset which is either developed or in the process of development for the less-resourced and less-advanced languages should follow and comply with the global guidelines and standards defined by agencies like the *European Languages Resource Association (ELRA), the Expert Advisory Group on Language Engineering Standards (EAGLES), the International Standards for Language Engineering (ISLE), the Text Encoding Initiative (TEI), Linguistic Annotation Framework (LAF),* and accepted by many. For example, the *Bureau of the Indian Standard (BIS)* tagset that is developed and used for the written text corpora of the Indian languages follows the standards prescribed for English and some other languages. This kind of approach is necessary to make the annotated texts comparable across languages and accessible beyond the horizon of native language users. It gives many advantages in the processing of texts that are used in translation between those languages which are structurally different (e.g., English to Bengali). In essence, the global guidelines should be followed to the highest possible extent for a language, so that an annotated text becomes globally accessible and operational (Ide & Pustejovsky, 2017).

Principle 9: Dispensability of the tagset from a text is necessary
A POS tagged corpus should be developed in such a manner that there arises no problem in removing the tags from a text easily. It is necessary to dispense with the tagset and revert to the raw text format for many non-technical linguistic studies and investigations. The format of the raw corpus has to be recovered as and when required. This is an important precondition of POS annotation of a text. Recovering the original version of the raw text is essential for many studies where the annotated text has little applicational relevance (Ide, 2017). The process of reversion from an annotated version to a raw version should be easy, so that a common text user with little technical skill can do this work. It is noted that many people use unannotated corpus texts; and for this, they do not need to be computer experts to do this work. An easy and workable solution to address this problem is, however, available now. One can keep two separate versions of the same text: one unannotated raw version, and the other one as a POS annotated version. If one can use both versions together, it will be a more useful approach to the study of a language.

Principle 10: Wide applications of a POS tagged text is needed
A POS tagset should be designed in such a manner that the annotated corpus becomes useful for a wide range of applications beyond linguistics and language technology. There is no logic to assume that only people working in linguistics and language technology are interested in annotated texts. Many people are working in allied domains like lexicography, language teaching, digital humanities, ethnography, and others who are equally interested in POS annotated corpus for studies and research. An annotated text should be potential enough to support all linguistic and non-linguistic studies that are independent of a particular application or domain. One can also visualize the direct application of a POS annotated text in language description, grammar writing, dictionary-making, language planning, ethnography, and community profile development. This is particularly relevant in case of endangered minority languages where development of digital community profile requires a large amount of language data properly annotated with POS information.

Principle 11: A user-friendly POS tagset should be designed
The POS tagset should be user-friendly as far as it is possible. It means that the tags which are designed for parts-of-speech of a language are easily understood by text users. It is an important feature because the primary purpose of a POS tagset is to assign a POS tag to a word in a text, so that one can know the actual POS of the word. If the codes used for the parts-of-speech are highly cryptic, they may not be understood by a text user. For instance, the POS "Adjective" is abbreviated as "ADJ" for ages. Everybody, who is not a linguist but has studied the grammar of his or her language, knows it. Now, some globally standard tagset (including the BIS one) uses the abbreviation "J" for "Adjective." It is a challenge for a common text user to understand the new tag for the POS. A computer system can understand and memorize it; but for a human being, it is a difficult task as he/she has to unlearn and relearn again. It has to be kept in mind that the work of POS annotation, particularly for less-resourced and less-advanced languages, is normally carried out by human annotators who are not accomplished linguists but have some knowledge to deal with the part-of-speech identity of words in a text. At the early stages of POS annotation,

even for the advanced languages, it was done by human annotators before the process was shifted to a trained computer system. A cryptic code, for these languages also, was a cognitive challenge.

Principle 12: There should be no ambiguity in the POS tagset
The task of POS annotation involves several stages of cross verification and decision making at every step of the tag assignment process. One has to look at a word, the sentence where the word is used, the grammatical role of the word, the meaning of the word, and the lexicographic identity of the word before the part-of-speech of the word is finalized and annotated. In such a complex process, it is expected that the tag for each part-of-speech should have an unambiguous and unique code with a single denotative function (e.g., *N for noun*, *V for verb*, *ADJ for adjective*, *PR for pronoun*, etc.). If a proposed POS tagset contains a tag that has a possibility for multiple interpretations, it leads to inconsistency in tag assignment and confusion in word analysis and interpretation. For instance, in the first version of the BIS tagset, the tag "PR" is used for both "Pronoun" and "Particle." In the revised version, "pronoun" is assigned with "PR," while "Particle" is assigned with "RP" to dissolve ambiguity. It is, therefore, argued that ambiguity should be removed at the time of tagset designing.

2.3 Rules for POS Annotation

The annotation of POS to words in a natural language text is not an easy task. It is full of difficulties and unforeseen challenges. The thing that has to be kept in mind that POS annotation, either it is done manually or automatically, has to be done on a language text, which contains words and terms of different origins, forms, and functions. Moreover, many of these words, when occurring in a sentence, acquire specific grammatical roles, syntactic functions, and semantic information which may not be found from their etymological history. It may also happen that these are mostly contextualized and may not be available from a grammar or a dictionary. Therefore, it is not an easy task to identify the exact part-of-speech of a word until and unless we understand, define, and refer to the actual syntactic and semantic roles of a word in a text.

There are several linguistic challenges that are directly linked with part-of-speech annotation. Earlier studies show that these are mostly related to text normalization and text standardization of a corpus developed in digital format (Dash, 2021). They include activities like pre-editing of texts, text sanitization, spelling error correction, real word-error correction, punctuation usage error correction, orthographic representation error correction, grammatical usage error correction, word tokenization, and many such issues (Dash, 2009: 40–42; Dash & Ramamoorthy, 2019, Chap. 3, pp. 35–56). These normalization works need to be carried out on a text corpus before the text is made ready for POS annotation work. Once the works relating to text normalization are completed successfully, it helps in dissolving many challenges hidden in text processing, frequency counts of words, type-token analysis of words, morphological analysis and processing of words, lemmatization of inflected words, generation of synsets, lexical sorting of words, chunking strings of multiple words, lexical database generation, dictionary compilation, WordNet compilation, language teaching, translation, and description. Keeping all these applications in view, we propose the following POS annotation rules. We also follow and apply the rules on texts before we annotate words in a corpus (Dash, 2013).

Rule 1: Apply POS annotation at the sentence level

The POS annotation of words should be executed at the sentence level only. A word, which is stored in a syntagmatic or paradigmatic distribution in a lexical database, should not be assigned with a POS tag because, in principle, a word when not used in a text, cannot be specificed with a part-of-speech idenity (e.g., *cook, call, run*, etc.). The assignment of a POS value to a word should be done only after we evaluate and confirm the linguistic role of the word in a sentence where it is used. In other words, the allocation of POS value to a word should be in accordance with the specific grammatical, semantic, and lexical role of the word in a sentence. This is necessary because, in a natural language text (here Bengali for instance), a word is often found to be used in different parts-of-speech or meanings in a sentence from the part-of-speech and meaning assigned to it in a dictionary. For instance, in Bengali, the word *sundarī* "beautiful" is stored as an adjective in a dictionary, but it is also used as a noun in a natural Bengali sentence besides being used as an adjective in another sentence.

(1) chiṛiyākhānāy sundarīke$_{[N]}$ dekhte khub bhiṛ hayechhe.

"There is a huge crowd in the zoo to see Sundari".

(2) oi sundarī$_{[Adj]}$ mahilāke se chinte pāreni.

"He could not recognize that beautiful lady".

The examples given above clearly indicate that contextual and intrasentential information is indispensable for accurate POS annotation to words.

Rule 2: Normalize words before POS annotation

All words should invariably be normalized before these are made available for POS annotation. All broken words should be joined before they are considered for POS annotation. This is known as one of the important components of **text normalization** (Sproat et al., 2001). In the Bengali text corpus, we have noted that many inflected words are broken into two parts. This phenomenon is noted because of severe irregularity practiced in the writing of Bengali texts on digital platforms. For instance, an inflected word is broken into two parts where the first part is a root or base and the second part is a suffix, case marker, enclitic, or particle(e.g., *bandar gulike* "to the ports"). This is an ungrammatical representation, and it needs to be normalized. Although written separately, the second part should be attached to the root or base, so that the final string is accepted as a single valid word (Table 2.4).

The gap between the two parts has to be removed by joining the two parts. If such errors are not repaired, all broken parts will be annotated separately. This is a real distortion of linguistic data of a language and a fatal step to decreasing the referential value of a POS annotated corpus (Dash, 2021). On the other hand, in a language like

Table 2.4 Broken words are joined together in Bengali corpus

Broken words		Joined together	Gloss
pere chhila	→	perechhila	"could do"
kathā gulo	→	kathāgulo	"words"
diye chhilen	→	diyechhilen	"had given"
chhele gulike	→	chhelegulike	"to boys"
meye der	→	meyeder	"of girls"

Table 2.5 Normalization of non-normalized words in Bengali corpus

Non-normalized		Normalized	Gloss
naukā bihār	→	naukābihār	"boating"
dekhe-śune	→	dekhe śune	"considering"
kāl krame	→	kālkrame	"in course of time"
kona-rakame	→	kona rakame	"by any chance"
ek jan	→	ekjan	"one person"
chalan-balan	→	chalanbalan	"gaits and moves"
chhele-meye	→	chhelemeye	"boys and girls"
kono-kono	→	kono kono	"some"
kare-kare	→	kare kare	"doing repeatedly"
andar-mahal	→	andar mahal	"inner house"

Bengali, many compound words, adjectives, adverbs, and reduplicated forms, due to inconsistency in writing, are written in three different ways: (a) with space, (b) without space, and (c) with a hyphen between words. Such words are also needed to be normalized as single or double word units, as the case may be, based on their lexico-syntactic identity in a sentence before these are put to POS annotation (Table 2.5).

Rule 3: Tokenize words before POS annotation

On many occasions, we have noted that some words, which are supposed to be written as separate words in a text, are written as an orthographically single word. That means two separate words are joined together due to some technical or operational reasons as a result of the removal of the white space that was supposed to be physically present between the two consecutive words. In these cases, we need to separate the words from each other before these are put to POS annotation (Table 2.6). This is a common problem of tokenization.

There is another crucial issue of tokenization relating to space management. This is another area that has drawn our attention (Huang, 2007; Schmid, 2008). In the Bengali corpus, for instance, it is an accepted norm that white space has to be provided consistently before and after a word which is considered as a separate lexical unit in a sentence. The white space ensures the separate linguistic identity of a word. A joined word, which is made with many words of different parts-of-speech should not be assigned with a POS tag without breaking the word into several valid words. It is important to split such words into two or more tokens, as the case may be

Table 2.6 Orthographically joined words are separated in Bengali corpus

Joined words		Separated	Gloss
rāmosītā	→	Rām o Sītā	"Ram and Sita"
gelennā	→	gelen nā	"did not go"
seikathā	→	sei kathā	"that word"
sārādindhare	→	sārā din dhare	"for whole day"
tinikhābennā	→	tini khāben nā	"he will not eat"
ýekonoupāye	→	ýe kono upāye	"by any means"

before a POS value is assigned to each token. For instance, the word *ýekonoupāye* "by any means" should be first broken into three separate and valid words (i.e., *ýe kono upāye*), and then, each word should be assigned with a valid POS value. The argument is that the POS value is to be assigned to a single-word unit, not to a joined word unit. This rule, however, does not apply to those compound words which are made with two words and are treated as a single-word unit. Such words should be tagged with one POS valued based on their final inflection (e.g., $mahākāśchārīrā_{[N]}$ "the astronauts," $śatabārṣikīte_{[N]}$ "on the occasion of a centenary," etc.).

Rule 4: Assign exact POS value to words

We should annotate a word at the POS level exactly in what part-of-speech it is used in a sentence. Let there be no confusion in this regard. We should not pay any attention to the lexicographic status or etymological antiquity of a word at the time of POS annotation. For instance, look at this sentence *"The difference between 'ugly' and 'lovely' is often obscured."* In this sentence, both *ugly* and *lovely* are annotated as nouns (N), and not as adjectives (ADJ). This is because the words are used as nouns in the sentence, although they are recorded as adjectives in dictionaries. Similarly, in the Bengali sentence *kheyālī gān gāite bhālobāse* "Kheyali loves to sing," the word *kheyālī* is annotated as a noun (N); not as an adjective (ADJ), even though the word is marked as an adjective in all standard Bengali dictionaries. It is quite natural that some words are morphologically marked as adjectives due to the presence of an adjectival suffix. But that should not be given maximum importance in an annotation. A word should be annotated in a POS if it is used in that particular POS in a sentence in the corpus.

Rule 5: Give optimum importance to the context in POS annotation

We should not annotate words entirely based on part-of-speech information attached to words in dictionaries and grammars. It creates problems in the proper identification of the POS value of words in texts. Annotation of words, therefore, should be contextualized and context based. It provides us necessary guidance to understand how we should annotate words in specific syntactic contexts taking lexical, semantic, and syntactic functions of words into consideration. The standard guide books of POS annotation (e.g., *grammars and dictionaries*) may provide some ideas about this. It is, however, certain that several context-specific issues lead us to modify existing POS tagsets as well as annotation guidelines. Another useful method is the application of a probability matrix that gives us ideas about the POS identity of words after analyzing POS values of neighboring words. For instance, in English, an article normally comes before a noun in a sentence (e.g., *The man bought a bicycle*). This, however, is not a full-proof method. An adjective can come after the article before a noun (e.g., *The young man…*), or one or two adjectives can be used before a noun (e.g., *…a new red bicycle*). That means the probability matrix has to be revised with new data if we want to understand the patterns of word order exhibited in a sentence.

Rule 6: We should rely on the existing POS categories
We should design a POS tagset for a language in accordance with the existing and accepted parts-of-speech of that language. The list of parts-of-speech is found in grammars, dictionaries, and other reference books. It should be kept in mind that the existing POS set is understood, applied, and taught by language users for generations. Therefore, there is no need to change it, if it is not absolutely necessary. That means a POS tagset should include only the existing parts-of-speech. In a normal situation, it should neither add any extra part-of-speech nor remove any existing one. The addition of a new part-of-speech may be considered only when it is found that the existing POS list is not enough to mark new functions of words noted in texts. Even then, we have to justify with proper evidence why we require a new part-of-speech in a language and how the new one supersedes the existing list.

Rule 7: We should identify MWUs in the text before POS annotation
We should apply a system for the identification of multiword units (MWU) in a text before the text is put to POS annotation (Sag et al., 2001). POS annotation is a word-level scheme. During POS annotation, an MWU which is made with more than one word is not treated as a single lexical block (LB). For example, multiword units like *conjunct verbs*, *idioms*, *compounds, and reduplications* are not annotated as single-word units. In the Bengali corpus, we treat multiword units as strings of several separate words and annotate accordingly.

(a) **Compounds:** bedanā\NN\ prasūta\ADJ\ "generated by pain", jīban\NN\ kalpa\ADJ\ "like life", bhramar\NN\ kṛṣṇa\ADJ\ "black as a bumblebee", bhāb\NN\ gambhīr\ADJ\ "serene with mood", raudra\NN\ dagdha\ADJ\ "burnt with the sun", sarkār\NN\ niẏukta\ADJ\ "appointed by government".
(b) **Idioms:** chokher\NN\ maṇi\NN\ "apple of the eye", āṣāṛhe\ADJ\ galpa\NN\ "cock and bull story", deoyāl\NN\ likhan\NN\ "writing on a wall", ubhay\ADJ\ saṅkaṭ\NN\ "horns of a dilemma".
(c) **Reduplication:** dine\NN\ dine\NN\ "day by day", saṅge\ADV\ saṅge\ADV\ "then and there", krame\ADV\ krame\ADV\ "gradually", pathe\NN\ pathe\NN\ "on every road".
(d) **Conjunct verb:** uṭhe\NFV\ paṛo\FV\ "rise", śuye\NFV\ paṛo\FV\ "lie down", chale\NFV\ ẏāo\FV\ "leave", phele\NFV\ din\FV\ "throwaway", dekhe\NFV\ nin\FV\ "see", gile\NFV\ phelo\FV\ "swallow".
(e) **Proverb:** kāṭā\ADJ\ ghāye\NN\ nuner\NN\ chhiṭe\NN\ deoyā\FV\ "to add insult to injury", biṛāler\NN\ galāy\NN\ ghanṭā\NN\ bādhā\FV\ "to bell a cat", telā\ADJ\ māthāy\NN\ tel\NN\ deoyā\FV\ "to carry coal to New Castle".

Before POS annotation, we use a support system to identify those multiword units which are not to be annotated as single words. In most case, we consider multiword units as **chunks** and treat accordingly. Multiword units carry highly useful lexical-cum-semantic information to be used in lexical decomposition. Therefore, multiword units ask for extra care and attention in their analysis and annotation. In fact, information retrieved from the analysis of multiword units is indispensable in chunking, lexical decomposition, and translation.

Rule 8: We should avoid the multitagging approach
A word when used in a sentence should carry only one part-of-speech value. It should never have more than one part-of-speech. Multitagging (i.e., *tagging a word with multiple POS values*) is a dangerous strategy; therefore, it should be strictly avoided. It is common and natural that a particular word can perform roles of more than one POS in a language. In reality, there are many such words in a language, and these words perform the role of several parts-of-speech depending on their use in texts. For instance, *round* performs roles of several parts-of-speech based on its use in texts.

(a) Preposition: He came *round* quite quickly.
(b) Adverb: She turned *round* and ran back to the house.
(c) Finite Verb: He *rounds* the place several times every morning.
(d) Noun: He was eliminated in the first *round.*
(e) Adjective: He placed the box on a *round* table.

Due to this particular phenomenon, a word can have more than one part-of-speech value in a dictionary. Commonly, a properly developed reference dictionary should record all possible parts-of-speech of a word. However, at the time of POS annotation, we should assign that particular POS value in which a word is used in a particular context in a sentence. For instance, if *round* occurs as a noun in a sentence, we should annotate it as a noun (not as a preposition, adjective, verb, or adverb) because, in this context, the noun value of the word is accepted and used. As a result of this **contextualization**, the word should not carry multiple POS values (e.g., round\N\,\FV\,\ADJ\,ADV\,\PP\). It should carry only one POS value (e.g., round\N\), even though it is found to be linked with different parts-of-speech in a reference dictionary.

Rule 9: We should POS annotate words in reverse hierarchical order
Most of the POS tagset developed for advanced languages are multilayered in form (Principle 5 in this chapter). Even for less-resourced Indian languages, the same kind of multilayered POS tagset is developed. When we use a multilayered POS tagset, we should do annotation in reverse hierarchical order in a step-by-step process. It has several applicational advantages. Once the lowest layer is annotated, its upper layers are also annotated because the lowest layer is linked with its upper layers by a hierarchical link. For instance, if *was*$_{[\mathrm{AUX}]}$ is marked as an auxiliary verb, its upper layer is automatically marked as a verb. The hierarchy in POS annotation is directly related to the granularity of linguistic information attached to a word.

Table 2.7 De-hyphenation of hyphenated Bengali words

Hyphenated		De-hyphenated	Gloss
ho-yāṭ	→	hoyāṭ\RP\	"what"
mā-i	→	māi\N\	"mother herself"
Kālidās-er	→	Kālidāser\N\	"of Kalidas"
pepār-e	→	pepāre\N\	"in a paper"
sombār-e	→	sombāre\N\	"on Monday"
pad-er	→	pader\N\	"of lexeme"
mā-r	→	mār\N\	"of mother"
chā-ṭā	→	chāṭā\N\	"the tea"
pā-ṭi	→	pāṭi\N\	"the leg"

Deeper is the hierarchy; more fine-grained is the linguistic information. It is better to keep the granularity of a POS tagset at the coarse level, so that less complexity is generated for text users. For instance, the hierarchy for POS categories in the Bureau of Indian Standards (BIS) tagset is kept within three levels because the primary goal of this tagset is to keep the granularity of POS annotation at a coarser level for easy application by machine and quick execution of processing tasks.

Rule 10: We should give special attention to hyphenated words
The use of hyphenated words in a natural language text is a common feature. The frequency of use of such words in a text varies based on many linguistic factors. POS annotation of hyphenated words is a real challenge for us. In the case of hyphenated words, we have to be more careful as several orthographic, morphological, syntactic, and semantic issues are involved (Dash, 2016). In the case of Bengali texts, we apply two different approaches to deal with hyphenated words. In case of those words where a word-formative component (e.g., *case, particle, or inflection*) is separated by a hyphen, we remove the hyphen and treat the whole word as a single unit. These word-formative components are dependent parts of a base or root (Table 2.7).

On other occasions, when a hyphen is used between two potentially individual words, which are capable of their independent linguistic identity, usage, and syntactic function, we annotate each word as well as hyphen as separate units. Here, hyphen works as a functional connector between words. In these cases, a hyphen is annotated separately with a different tag value meant for punctuation (Table 2.8).

Rule 11: POS annotation is different from morphological processing
Let us acknowledge that morphological processing and POS annotation are two different processes of word analysis. They have different goals, purposes, and methods of operation. Therefore, they should be considered separately. For example, the inflected Bengali verb (e.g., *dekhiteichhhilen* "he was indeed seeing") is POS annotated as a finite verb (e.g., dekhiteichhhilen\F_FV\) without any additional information. A POS annotation scheme does not ask anything more than the exact POS value of the word. On the other hand, during morphological processing, we have different expectations and operations. Here, we want to know which morphs are

Table 2.8 Annotation of the hyphen as a separate unit in Bengali text

Hyphenated		Annotation	Gloss
bhū-prakṛti	→	bhū\N\ -\PUNC\ prakṛti\N\	"Geo nature"
ku-svabhāb	→	ku\ADJ\ -\PUNC\ svabhāb\N\	"bad habit"
du-kkathā	→	du\ADJ\ -\PUNC\ kathā\N\	"two words"
bāi-pāś	→	bāi\PP\ -\PUNC\ pāś\N\	"bypass"
u-kār	→	u\N\ -\PUNC\ kār\N\	"u-allograph"
chor-ḍākāt	→	chor\N\ -\PUNC\ ḍākāt\N\	"thief and robber"
uttar-paśchim	→	uttar\N\ -\PUNC\ paśchim\N\	"North West"
rogā-moṭā	→	rogā\ADJ\ -\PUNC\ moṭā\ADJ\	"thin and thick"
man-gaṛā	→	man\N\ -\PUNC\ gaṛā\ADJ\	"fancy-made"
se-din	→	se\PN\ -\PUNC\ din\N\	"that day"
śelī-kīṭs	→	śelī\N\ -\PUNC\ kīṭs\N\	"Shelley and Keats"
ṭākā-paysā	→	ṭākā\N\ -\PUNC\ paysā\N\	"penny and pie"
kṛṣi-mantrī	→	kṛṣi\N\ -\PUNC\ mantrī\N\	"agriculture minister"
skul-māsṭār	→	skul\N\ -\PUNC\ māsṭār\N\	"school teacher"
bārlin-alimpik	→	bārlin\N\ -\PUNC\ alimpik\N\	"Berlin Olympic"

used, how these morphs are applied, what their identities are, and what kind of morphophonemic process takes place during the addition of these morphs with a root (Table 2.9).

In morphological processing, we want to retrieve all these kinds of information from a word to know its lexical identity, surface form, lexical class, syntactic function, and meaning. In most situations, we apply information extracted from a morphological analysis of a word not only in POS annotation but also in other linguistic works like lexical form generation, compiling dictionaries, machine learning of words, information extraction from inflected words, and teaching form and composition of words to learners. This shows that POS annotation should not be mixed up with morphological processing of words.

Table 2.9 Morphological information of an inflected Bengali verb

Inflected form	POS	Morphological details
dekhiteichhilen	\F_FV\	
dekh-		FV-Root
-ite-		Aspect
-i-		Particle_Emphatic
-chh-		Auxiliary
-il-		Tense_Past
-en		Person_3/2; Number_Sg./Pl

Rule 12: We should manually verify a POS annotated text
When a text is POS annotated manually (particularly during the training phase), a text should simultaneously be annotated by three linguists. The linguists should be well versed in morphology, grammar, morphosyntactic rules, semantics, and syntax of a language. This strategy may give the much-needed accuracy a POS annotated text asks for. The experts may agree on POS annotation for most of the words based on information found in standard grammars and dictionaries. They may feel confused for a few words (e.g., *demonstratives*, *non-finite verbs*, *postpositions*, *pronouns*, *particles*, *conjuncts*, etc.) where they may differ with regard to a specific POS value. In that case, they may discuss their confusions among themselves or with some external experts to come to a common agreement. It is natural that disputes will arise in POS annotation. In that case, it is sensible to agree on achieving a common goal than trying to parade morphological knowledge on the pretext of hiding syntactic ignorance. The level of accuracy in POS annotation is an ongoing debate even for well-studied languages. In reality, each new text may throw up unresolved decision-making challenges. The goal of an annotator is to maintain consistency in annotation even though decisions may show some arbitrariness with a tagset that has been defined and designed for the purpose.

2.4 Conclusion

A set of well-defined principles and rules are required for POS annotation for all natural languages. These principles and rules are needed during the time of assigning POS tags to words in a language. Because of the non-availability of such principles and rules, the POS tagset is not yet designed for many less-advanced languages. As a result, there is no manual or automatic system available for POS annotation in these languages. Therefore, there is an urgent need for designing principles and rules to be used for developing standards for POS annotation for these languages (Dash, 2011).

The process of POS annotation is usually applied to a text after the text has passed through stages of text sanitation, normalization, standardization, and lexical tokenization. After a text is made free (manually or mechanically) from various kinds of orthographic, diacritic, and typographic inconsistencies, it is made ready for POS annotation (Toutanova et al., 2003). In text normalization, for example, we need to provide a white space consistently before and after a word to ensure the separate linguistic identity of a word and to assure that the word deserves a separate POS value. Similarly, once we make a decision with regard to the number of parts-of-speech for a language, we start the work of designing a POS tagset. After developing a POS tagset, we start POS annotation. During POS annotation, we follow the principles and the rules proposed above. After marking relevant information of paragraphs, sentences, and segments in a text, we either manually annotate words or develop algorithms for a computer to do the work automatically.

After the completion of a POS annotation task, what we get is a POS annotated text. The text is now ready for verification and certification by experts. Experts may use the entire annotated text or a sample part of it to verify annotation. After this is done, a POS annotated text is made available for chunking as well as for the extraction of annotated data, lexical patterns, lexical collocations, and POS features of words to be used to train a computer system for automatic annotation. The annotated text is also available for other domains of linguistics where such texts are useful for better interpretation and application. A POS annotated text is also used for lexical processing (e.g., *lexical sorting*, *POS recognition*, *POS-based word classification*, *frequency count*, *concordance*, *lemmatization*, *type-token analysis*, and *keyword search*) to gather information of various types to be used in dictionary compilation, grammar writing, language description, language teaching, and translation.

References

Atwell, E., Demetriou, G., Hughes, J., Schiffrin, A., Souter, C., & Wilcock, S. (2000). A comparative evaluation of modern English corpus grammatical annotation schemes. *International Computer Archive of Modern English Journal, 24*(1), 7–23.

Avinesh, P. V. S. & Karthik, G. (2007). Part-of-speech tagging and chunking using conditional random field and transformation-based learning. In *Proceedings of the Workshop on Shallow Parsing for South Asian Languages (IJCAI-07)* (pp. 21–24). IIIT, Hyderabad, India.

Brants, T. (2000). TnT-a statistical POS tagger. In *Proceedings of the Sixth Applied Natural Language Processing Conference*, Seattle (pp. 37–42).

Dash, N. S. (2009). *Language corpora: Past, present, and future*. New Delhi: Mittal Publications.

Dash, N. S. (2011). Principles of part-of-speech (POS) tagging in Indian language corpora. In *Proceedings of 5th Language Technology Conference (LTC-2011): Human Language Technologies as a Challenge for Computer Science and Linguistics*, 25–27 Nov 2011, Poznan, Poland (pp. 101–105).

Dash, N. S. (2013). Part-of-speech (POS) tagging in Bengali written text corpus. *Bhasa Bijnan o Prayukti: An International Journal on Linguistics and Language Technology, 1*(1), 53–96.

Dash, N. S. (2016). Multifunctionality of a hyphen in Bengali text corpus: Problems and challenges in text normalization and POS tagging. *International Journal of Innovative Studies in Sociology and Humanities, 1*(1), 19–34.

Dash, N. S. (2021). Pre-editing and text standardization on a Bengali written text corpus. *Aligarh Journal of Linguistics, 10*(1), 1–22.

Dash, N. S., & Ramamoorthy, L. (2019). *Utility and application of language corpora*. Singapore: Springer Nature.

Garside, R. (1987). The CLAWS word-tagging system. In R. Garside, G. Leech, & G. Sampson (Eds.), *Computational analysis of English: A corpus-based approach* (pp. 30–41). London: Longman.

Garside, R. (1995). Grammatical tagging of the spoken part of the British National Corpus: A progress report. In G. Leech, G. Myers, & J. Thomas (Eds.), *Spoken English on computer: Transcription, mark-up, and application* (pp. 161–167). London: Longman.

Huang, C., Simon, P., Hsieh, S., & Prevot, L. (2007). Rethinking Chinese word segmentation: Tokenization, character classification, or word-break identification. In *Proceedings of the ACL-2007 Demo and Poster Sessions,* Prague, June 2007 (pp. 69–72). Association for the Computational Linguistics.

Ide, N. (2017). Introduction to the handbook of linguistic annotation. In N. Ide & J. Pustejovsky (Eds.), *Handbook of linguistic annotation* (Text, Speech, and Language Technology Series) (pp. 1–18). Springer.

Ide, N., & Pustejovsky, J. (Eds.) (2017). *Handbook of linguistic annotation* (Text, Speech, and Language Technology Series). Springer.

Ide, N., Calzolari, N., Eckle-Kohler, J., Gibbon, D., Hellman, S., Lee, K., Nivre, J., & Romary, L. (2017a). Community standards for linguistically-annotated resources. In N. Ide & J. Pustejovsky (Eds.), *Handbook of linguistic annotation* (Text, Speech, and Language Technology Series) (pp. 113–165). Springer.

Ide, N., Chiarcos, C., Stede, M., & Cassidy, S. (2017b). Designing annotation schemes: From model to representation. In N. Ide & J. Pustejovsky (Eds.), *Handbook of linguistic annotation* (Text, Speech, and Language Technology Series) (pp. 73–111). Springer.

Kupiec, J. (1992). Robust POS tagging using a Hidden Markov model. *Computer Speech and Language, 6*(1), 3–15.

Leech, G. (1993). Corpus annotation schemes. *Literary and Linguistic Computing, 8*(4), 275–281.

Leech, G. (1997). Introducing corpus annotation. In R. Garside, G. Leech, & A. McEnery (Eds.), *Corpus annotation: Linguistic information from computer text corpora* (pp. 1–18). London: Longman.

Leech, G., & Garside, R. (1982). Grammatical tagging of the LOB Corpus: A general survey. In S. Johansson & K. Hofland (Eds.), *Computer corpora in English language research* (pp. 110–117). Bergen: NAVF.

Leech, G., & Smith, N. (1999). The use of tagging. In H. V. Halteren (Ed.), *Syntactic word class tagging* (pp. 23–36). Dordrecht: Kluwer Academic Press.

Leech, G., Garside, R., & Atwell, E. (1983). The automatic tagging of the LOB Corpus. *International Computer Archive of Modern English News, 7*(1), 110–117.

Leech, G., Garside, R., & Bryant, M. (1994). The large-scale grammatical tagging of text: Experience with the BNC. In N. Oostdijk & P. deHaan (Eds.), *Corpus-based research into language* (pp. 47–63). Amsterdam: Rodopi.

Nguyen, D. Q., Pham, D. D., & Pham, S. B. (2016). A robust transformation-based learning approach using ripple down rules for POS tagging. *AI Communications, 29*(3), 409–422.

Sag, I. A., Baldwin, T., Bond, F., Copestake, A., & Flickinger, D. (2001). Multiword expressions: A pain in the neck for NLP. In A. Gelbukh (Ed.), *Proceedings of CICLING2002* (pp. 35–41). Verlag: Springer.

Schmid, H. (2008). Tokenizing and POS tagging. In A. Lüdeling & M. Kytö (Eds.), *Corpus linguistics: An international handbook* (Vol. 1, pp. 527–551). Berlin: Gruyter.

Sproat, R., Black, A., Chen, S., Kumar, S., Ostendorf, M., & Richards, C. (2001). Normalization of non-standard words. *Computer Speech & Language, 15*(3), 287–333.

Toutanova, K., Klein, D., Manning, C. D., & Singer, Y. (2003). Feature-rich POS tagging with a cyclic dependency network. *Proceedings of HLT-NAACL 2003* (pp. 252–259).

Web Links

http://ccl.pku.edu.cn/doubtfire/CorpusLinguistics/Corpus_Encoding/
http://ildc.gov.in/
http://take.dfki.de/C12-2103-dataset/AnnotationGuidelines_A4.pdf
http://ucrel.lancs.ac.uk/claws/
http://www.cs.vassar.edu/CES/
http://www.ilc.cnr.it/EAGLES/browse.html
http://www.tdil.mit.gov.in/
https://devopedia.org/POS-tagging
https://home.uni-leipzig.de/burr/Verb/htm/LinkedDocuments/annotate.pdf
https://nlp.stanford.edu/links/statnlp.html#Taggers
https://nlp.stanford.edu/software/tagger.shtml
https://universaldependencies.org/u/pos/
https://www.aclweb.org/anthology/L16-1684.pdf
https://www.cs.umd.edu/~nau/
https://www.nltk.org/book/ch05.html

Chapter 3
Part-of-Speech Annotation

Abstract Annotating words at the part-of-speech level, either manually or by a machine, is a tough task. It is done effectively when human annotators, as well as computer systems, are properly trained so that they can correctly identify morphological properties and syntactic functions of words in a piece of text. We discuss in this chapter some theoretical aspects and practical issues of part-of-speech (POS) annotation on a written Bengali text corpus. We deliberately avoid all those issues and aspects that are required to design and develop an automatic POS annotation tool for a text, since this is not the goal of this chapter. To keep things simple and within the capacity of those readers who are not well-versed in the application of computers, we address here some of the primary concerns and challenges involved in POS annotation. Starting with the basic concept of POS annotation, we highlight the underlying differences between POS annotation and morphological processing; define the levels and stages of POS annotation; refer to some of the early works on POS annotation; present a generic scheme for POS annotation; and show how a POS annotated text is utilized in various domains and sub-domains of theoretical, descriptive, applied, computational, and cognitive linguistics. The data and information presented in this chapter are primarily meant for the students of those less-advanced languages which still lack linguistic resources like POS annotated texts. The rudimentary ideas and information that are presented in this chapter may be treated as valuable and usable inputs for designing linguistic and computational models for POS annotation in these less-advanced languages.

Keywords Annotation · Part-of-speech · Morphological processing · Metadata · Tagset · Inflection · Syntactic annotation · Parsing · Chunking

3.1 Introduction

In corpus linguistics and language technology, part-of-speech (POS) annotation is considered as a complex type of text annotation, where we attach specific codes to words to indicate their morphological-cum-grammatical roles in a piece of text. Although complex, it is the most common type of text annotation. Also, it is considered as one of the first stages of text-based word analysis and interpretation. Each

N. S. Dash, *Language Corpora Annotation and Processing*,
https://doi.org/10.1007/978-981-16-2960-0_3

word, based on its form, function, and context of use as well as based on its relationship with its adjacent or distal words, is marked with its actual part-of-speech in a sentence. A POS annotated text is used to develop a more complex text annotation technique which is commonly known as a *syntactic annotation* (or *parsing*). Syntactic annotation involves the automatic assignment of phrase markers to the phrases used in a sentence. The process of part-of-speech annotation is also known by another name called *grammatical annotation*. The primary goals are to identify the exact part-of-speech of words as well as to disambiguate words based on their part-of-speech information. Due to such unique goals, we also recognize POS annotation as a process of *word category disambiguation* (WCD).

The process of POS annotation—either manual or automated—is a complex and error-prone task. Even then, we cannot diminish its functional importance in theoretical and applied linguistics. Many theoretical studies on words refer to information derived from POS annotation. Similarly, for many works of natural language processing and language technology, we use data and information from a POS annotated text. For instance, syntactic annotation of a sentence can be done successfully if we apply POS information of words retrieved from a POS annotated text. On the other hand, in many studies on language description and application, we use POS annotated texts to understand how words carry different parts-of-speech in different contexts of their occurrence in texts. In many situations, we fail to match the information of part-of-speech of words that we find in dictionaries with information that we gather from a piece of annotated text. Such differences as well as new findings from POS annotated texts confirm our theoretical postulations that words are free to vary in part-of-speech. They are free to take up a POS value based on their use in a text. All natural languages have a large number of words, which vary in form, meaning, function, and part-of-speech. Through POS annotation, we want to annotate part-of-speech of words based on the context of their use.

The present chapter does not speak anything about automatic POS annotation. Also, it does not speak about experiments with existing annotation technology. It speaks about the basic methods and strategies that we normally apply to texts to carry out the task. It gives some ideas for developing a usable method (even if it is not the best one) that we can apply to a text. In Sect. 3.2, we define the basic concept of POS annotation; in Sect. 3.3, we differentiate between morphological analysis and POS annotation; in Sect. 3.4, we mark different levels of POS annotation; in Sect. 3.5, we specify different stages of POS annotation; in Sect. 3.6, we refer to some earlier methods of POS annotation; in Sect. 3.7, we present a short report on POS annotation in a few Indian languages; in Sect. 3.8, we refer to the limitations of the POS tagset that we use for the Indian languages; in Sect. 3.9, we discuss the application of a POS annotated text in language technology and linguistics.

3.2 Concept of POS Annotation

Annotating words at the part-of-speech level on a piece of text is not a trivial task (Fligelstone et al., 1997). It is full of many unforeseen challenges. We have to keep in mind that POS annotation—either done manually or automatically—is carried out on a text. Typically, a text contains a large number of words, which occur in sentences with specific syntactic functions and semantic values. It is a challenge for a language user as well as a machine to identify specific POS values of words. It is argued that this cannot be done until and unless the actual morphological-cum-syntactic roles of words are properly understood and defined (Garside, 1996; Marcus et al., 1993). Also, many linguistic and technical issues need to be taken care of before a human or a machine succeeds in POS annotation. In most cases, these issues are related to the sanitation of text, normalization of words and sentences in texts, tokenization of inflected words and terms, correction or removal of orthographic errors, correction of errors in spelling, validation of real-word errors, management of white space in texts, and correction of grammatical mistakes (Dash, 2021; Toutanova & Manning 2000).

Theoretically, linguistic information relating to a word is available from its structure, meaning, syntactic role, and functional relations with other words used in a sentence (Brill, 1992). While structure refers to its morphological features, lexical properties refer to its abstract or concrete values, syntactic role refers to its subject and predicate role in a sentence, and semantics refers to its agentive or thematic function in a sentence. Based on the type of a model and method used, such information is furnished at different layers of annotation to ensure that linguistic information of a text is split rightly into different types and marked adequately in different layers of a text (Durand et al., 1996).

Variation in part-of-speech of a word is a common feature in all languages. It is equally true to an advanced language like English as well as a non-advanced language like Kurdmali. For instance, English *sound* is used in different parts-of-speech depending on its syntactic role in a sentence. It can be used as a noun (e.g., *the sound of music*), as an adjective (e.g., *a sound decision*), and as a verb (e.g., *he sounds rational*) in accordance with the context of its use in a piece of text. A native English speaker can identify when the word is used as a noun, an adjective, or as a finite verb by looking at the context of the use of the word in a text. Also, he can do the necessary analysis of grammar and meaning of the word by applying his innate knowledge and competence of the language. On the other hand, when we prepare a computer to do the same task, we need to give it proper training on linguistic rules and conditions (Abney, 1997).

It is normally argued that the number of parts-of-speech mentioned in standard grammars of a language is enough for annotating words in that language. We, however, noted that words in a text are used in more parts-of-speech than the parts-of-speech registered in standard grammars. This additional parts-of-speech need to be identified and described when we try to design a scheme for POS annotation for a language. For instance, it is stated that Bengali has eight parts-of-speech (Chakravarty

1974; Chakravarti, 1994; Chattopadhyay, 1995; Chaki, 1996; Sarkar& Basu, 1994). They include *nouns, pronouns, adjectives, adverbs, finite verbs, non-finite verbs, postpositions*, and *indeclinables*. It is stated that once we learn these parts-of-speech, we can identify the part-of-speech of a word used in Bengali texts. It is also believed that these parts-of-speech are adequate for annotating words in Bengali texts. In reality, however, we find that there are instances of parts-of-speech (e.g., *quantifiers, conjunctions, demonstratives, enclitics, particles*) that are not included in Bengali. We have to analyze, understand, and define the forms and functions of these parts-of-speech in Bengali if we want to gather better ideas about the words used in the Bengali language.

In the actual task of POS annotation, more challenges lie in those areas where we want to make a distinction between plural and singular nouns and pronouns; annotate words that are added with case makers; identify nouns and adjectives that are tagged with gender and number; annotate verbs that are attached with person, number, tense, aspect, modality, and honorification; annotate adjectives that are tagged with degree suffix; annotate adjectives that behave like nouns. These are more complex and challenging problems in POS annotation. In these cases, we make mistakes in the identification of part-of-speech of words as words are loaded with varieties of grammatical information. Annotating information of these words is necessary for developing an algorithm for POS annotation by a computer system. Else a POS annotation algorithm will fail to observe unique linguistic information of words. As a result, an annotated text will fail to show finer linguistic properties of words. The basic argument is that the information, which is indispensable in annotation, has to be annotated to a text.

3.3 Morphological Analysis Versus POS Annotation

We need to keep in mind that a POS annotation system is not a replacement for morphological analysis of words. POS annotation is characteristically different in goal and application from that of a morphological analysis. The primary goal of morphological analysis is to find out those morphs that are applied to form a word, while the primary goal of POS annotation is to recognize and mark the part-of-speech of words used in a text. A word, when used in a text, carries various kinds of information. Some information is evident from its surface form (e.g., *plurality, gender, person, tense, emphasis, honorification,* etc.*)*. These are available from specific markers attached to words. On the other hand, some information is available from the context of their use (e.g., *part-of-speech, transitivity, thematic role,* etc.). These are not available from a surface form of a word. That means different kinds of information of a word are retrieved from morphological and grammatical analysis of a word. It indicates that one should look at a word from two different levels:

1. Morphological level, and
2. Syntactic level

Table 3.1 Morphological analysis of Bengali word *bådåle*

Word	Information set: 1	Information set: 2
Surface form	bådåle	bådåle
Base form	bådål	bådåle
Suffix part	-e	Ø
Part-of-speech	Non-finite Verb $_{[VNF]}$	Postposition $_{[PSP]}$
Pronunciation	[bodle]	[bɔdole]
Meaning	"Replacing"	"In exchange for"

The information of morphological level is extracted from the morphological structure of a word through morphological analysis. In most cases, it is done on a word when the word is in an isolated situation. On the other hand, information related to part-of-speech is extracted from its grammatical function in a sentence. The first task is carried out by a morphological analyzer, and the second task is executed by a POS annotator. Thus, a morphological analyzer and a POS annotator play two different roles in providing morphological and part-of-speech information of words—one at an isolated situation and the other at a sentential frame. For instance, consider Bengali *bådåle*, which is analyzed at the morphological level in two different ways to elicit two different sets of linguistic information from the word (Table 3.1).

The information extracted from the morphological analysis shows that *bådåle*, in an isolated situation, has two morphological identities. It can be a non-finite verb or a postposition. A morphological analyzer normally intends to capture this information of a word after analyzing its morphological structure (Leech, 1997). It hardly goes beyond this level. On the other hand, a POS annotation system tries to note the grammatical roles of a word in a sentential context, as the following examples show (1a–1b). It shows that *bådåle* in (1a) is a non-finite verb, and in (1b) it is a postposition. In two different sentential contexts, the word performs two different grammatical roles. As a result, it has two different parts-of-speech identities. Thus, a POS annotation process considers the syntactic role of a word in a sentence to see if the word is used in a particular part-of-speech in a given sentential context.

POS Annotation:

(1a) cheleṭi kaleje giye anek bådåle$_{[VNF]}$ geche.
"The boy is changed much after going to college."

(1b) se sombārer bådåle$_{[PSP]}$ sukrabāre āste pāre.
"He can come on Friday instead of Monday."

We understand that a morphological analyzer looks at a word in isolation and provides all its possible morphology-related information, including multiple parts-of-speech identities. On the contrary, a POS annotator looks at a word in a sentential context (within a small window) and provides the exact part-of-speech of a word. The goal of a POS annotator, therefore, is to disambiguate part-of-speech information provided by a morphological analyzer and select the appropriate POS in a specific sentential context. Taking this observation as ground truth, the POS tagset for a language is designed with grammatical categories of words in view. Other sets of morphological information, which are obtained from a morphological analyzer, are not usually included at the POS annotation level. Before one applies morphological analysis or POS annotation on corpora, one should carry out the tasks on sample texts to gather experience, reduce errors, and save time. Prior exercise is required for achieving higher accuracy and less error when these are applied on large text corpora. Prior trial exercise can also generate the following advantages.

1. Experimental morphological analysis and annotation on words in a text throw up new issues and challenges based on which a POS tagset can be revised, modified, updated, and extended.
2. Elaborate guidelines for morphological analysis and POS annotation can be developed through trial, experiment, and analysis.
3. Morphologically analyzed words and POS annotated texts can be used to train computers for automation of the process.
4. Prior experiments provide knowledge and insights to enhance the robustness of a morphological analyzer and a POS annotator.
5. Information that is gathered from experiments can be used for other purposes such as in the description of words, making dictionaries, preparing pedagogical grammars, and teaching part-of-speech identification of words in classrooms.

3.4 Levels of POS Annotation

Scholars have described that part-of-speech annotation to words is a process of marking part-of-speech information to a word used in a piece of text after the word has passed through the stages of morphological and grammatical analysis (Garside, 1995). The process includes a set of well-designed codes, which carry the necessary morphological and grammatical information of words. These are assigned to words to indicate their parts-of-speech in accordance with their use and role in a text (Leech & Garside, 1982). In the majority of the cases, mostly for advanced languages, we have noted that scholars have developed some well-defined linguistic features and have used them to identify the POS value of a word. Based on these features, they have not only determined the grammatical roles of a word but also the lexical and syntactic roles of a word in a text. This shows that POS annotation can have advantages at several levels.

1. At the orthographic level, we can differentiate among the homographic words in a text to make note of their different semantic roles.
2. At the lexical level, we can analyze the morphological structure of words as we observe them at their surface forms.
3. At the syntactic level, we can specify grammatical as well as syntactic functions of words to assign their POS identities.
4. At the semantic level, we can determine their meanings to understand in which sense these are used in a text.

The task of POS annotation is not for single-word units only. It also covers other types of words used in a text. That means alongside single-word units, it also considers multiword units like *compound words* and *reduplicated words*. Moreover, POS annotation is not limited to non-inflected words only. It also includes all kinds of inflected words that are used in a text. For instance, the process of POS annotation on a text of the Bengali language should consider the following types of words:

1. Single non-inflected words, e.g., *ghar* "house."
2. Single inflected words, e.g., *ghare* "in the house."
3. Non-inflected compound words, e.g., *gharbāṛi* "house and others."
4. Inflected compound words, e.g., *gharbāṛite* "at residences."
5. Non-inflected reduplicated words, e.g., *ghar ghar* "all houses."
6. Inflected reduplicated words, e.g., *ghare ghare* "in every house."

In this context, we may keep in mind that POS annotation is characteristically different from chunking. In case of chunking, we usually combine two or more words together as a single lexical block (LB) and assign a chunk value to it as a phrase or a multiword unit. In many situations in a text, compound words and reduplicated words, even if these words are written separately (e.g., *hāt sāphāi* "stealing" and *mājhe mājhe* "occasionally"), are put under chunking along with phrases and idioms. We have to understand that chunking is a much higher level of text annotation which involves the assignment of phrase markers (e.g., *NP, VP, PP, etc.*) to multiword units and phrases used in a text.

After the application of a POS annotation scheme on a text, a text may look quite clumsy. As if, words are associated with some symbols, which are difficult to comprehend. Neither a human being nor a machine, if not trained adequately, can read and comprehend these. However, once a system or a human being is trained with it, a POS annotated text is a highly useful resource for them. They can extract unique linguistic information from POS annotated text and use the same for various purposes(Leech & Eyes, 1993). They can utilize a POS annotated text to increase specificity in data extraction. Moreover, they can use grammatical information in semantic annotation, discourse annotation, and parsing. From an applied perspective such a text has referential value in dictionary-making, grammar book writing, and language description.

When we annotate a text manually, particularly when we try to develop a trial database for the purpose of machine learning and annotation automation, we normally carry out the task by applying the following eight steps:

Step 1 We identify single and multiword units in a text.
Step 2 We notice the orthographic form and structure of words.
Step 3 We analyze the morphological structure and formation of words.
Step 4 We identify the grammatical functions of words in a sentence.
Step 5 We determine grammatical roles and parts-of-speech of words.
Step 6 We identify the semantic roles of words in a sentence.
Step 7 We manually assign POS value to each word in a sentence.
Step 8 We verify and validate POS values with grammar and dictionaries.

3.5 Stages of POS Annotation

While we annotate words manually, we normally execute the POS annotation process by applying the following three stages:

1. Stage I: Pre-editing of a text,
2. Stage II: POS assignment to words, and
3. Stage III: Postediting of annotated text.

3.5.1 Pre-editing Stage

In Stage I (i.e., the pre-editing stage), we convert a piece of text into a suitable format so that we can carry out the POS annotation task without much trouble. At this stage, we inspect a text from various angles to see if it contains any typographic error, orthographic irregularity, real-word error, and similar errors. If there is any mistake, we correct it according to the physical source of a text. Moreover, we put the selected text through several stages of normalization and tokenization to make the text maximally suitable for POS annotation (Dash, 2004). In essence, at the pre-editing stage, we prepare a text in such a manner that it is designed in a suitable format for an annotation task. It is the primary stage for making a text ready for POS annotation (Dash, 2016). After this, a human annotator assigns a part-of-speech value to each word in the text.

3.5.2 POS Assignment Stage

In Stage II (i.e., POS assignment stage), we begin to assign just only one part-of-speech tag to each word used in a sentence. We do this after assessing the grammatical, syntactic, and semantic role of a word in a sentence (Dash, 2015). To achieve high accuracy, we refer to lexical databases which we have already developed and stored for such purposes. In such lexical databases, each word is a separate lexical entry with a possible range of part-of-speech information. We also refer to standard dictionaries for additional information and discussion. Such lexical databases are an open-ended resource and we update them quite often with new words and information collected from various kinds of texts.

During POS annotation, we have noted that there are some new words in the texts which are not found in our lexical databases. In those cases, we normally refer to the lists of affixes, case markers, and inflections to determine the possible part-of-speech of the new words (Biber et al., 1998: 258–259). For instance, *binoṭīikaraṇ* is a new word (meaning, *demonetization*) that is found in some recent Bengali texts but not found in Bengali dictionaries. After looking at its surface form, its meaning, and the context of its use, we annotate it as a noun (e.g., binoṭīikaraṇ\NN\). This is a highly reliable and linguistically pertinent method for achieving greater accuracy in POS annotation.

3.5.3 Postediting Stage

In Stage III (i.e., postediting stage), we postedit a POS annotated text to check if we have annotated words rightly, if we have made any mistake in annotation, or if we have left some words untouched. We can check the whole data if a file contains a small amount of text. It is better if we can engage an external expert for this purpose. After an annotated text is checked and certified for its accuracy, we use it as a trial text database to develop a system that can annotate words automatically. In many languages, text annotation and verification are done manually at the early stage of POS annotation (Garrette & Baldridge, 2013). In the case of a large corpus with millions of words and sentences, manual annotation and verification are not possible. Even if we dare, it will invariably be a time-taking, monotonous, and erroneous process. In this case, a useful method is the application of a probability matrix derived from a benchmarked annotated text. It can be used to rectify errors and ambiguous tag assignments (Leech et al., 1983). Based on the information gathered from the matrix, we can determine annotation probabilities between adjacent words. For instance, in Bengali, if we annotate a word as an adjective (e.g., *sundar*\ADJ\) we can annotate its immediately following word as a noun (e.g., *ghar*\NN\) because the probability of a combination of \ADJ\ + \NN\ is much higher than other possible combinations.

A probability matrix gives a certain level of assurance with regard to the possible POS identity of a word by analyzing the POS identity of its immediately preceding and succeeding words. However, it is not a full-proof strategy. For instance, in Bengali, an adjective can be followed by another adjective before a noun takes place (e.g., *sundar*\ADJ*chaoṛā*\ADJ*rāstā*\NN\ "beautiful wide road" or *klānta*\ADJ*abasanna*\ADJ*śarīr*\NN\ "tired exhausted body"). In English, the use of three consecutive nouns in a sentence is not a rare event (e.g., *He stayed at the university*\NN\ *guest*\NN\ *house*\NN\). That means we have to revise and update a probability matrix with new information collected from corpus if we want to understand the nature of word order in a text (Leech & Wilson, 1999).

As human POS annotators, we must have good knowledge of the morphology and grammar of a language for doing this work successfully. On the other hand, if we want a computer system to do this work on our behalf, we have to feed it with the necessary information and rule with proper guidelines and instructions to do the work. That means a software developer, who is engaged in writing a program for automatic POS annotation, should be trained with elaborate linguistic knowledge and information. Only then he can try to develop a system that can assign correct part-of-speech to words in a text (Kupiec, 1992).

3.6 Earlier Methods POS Annotation

To date, several methods are proposed and applied for POS annotation. These are however mostly for written texts (Dash, 2013). Many corpora are available now which are annotated by using sets of morphological and grammatical rules followed by manual interventions. In most cases, such annotated texts are made error-free and are used as inputs to train systems for developing non-supervised models for POS annotation. Also, such texts are used as general resources for research in language technology (Atwell et al., 2000). In an early work on POS annotation on the *Brown Corpus of American English,* scholars used rule-based templates for disambiguating the POS identity of words (Greene & Rubin, 1971). They achieved more than 77% accuracy in an annotation. In the early 1980s, a team of scholars at the *Lancaster University, UK* used the CLAWS program on the *Lancaster–Oslo–Bergen Corpus of British English* to achieve 95% accuracy (McEnery & Wilson, 1996: 39). In recent times, however, most of the research teams working in this area have achieved a greater level of accuracy in the work. Following the guidelines and standards proposed in EAGLES, ISLE, and TEI, we can acquire better success in POS annotation (Ide & Pustejovsky, 2017). The following example shows how a text of the *Lancaster–Oslo–Bergen Corpus* is POS annotated (Biber et al., 1998: 258–259).

Sample English Sentence
A move to stop Mr. Gaitskell from nominating any more labour life peers is to be made at a meeting of labour MPs tomorrow.

Fig. 3.1 A sample English sentence

POS Annotated Text (Sample 1)	
A ^at++++	move ^nn++++
to ^to++++	stop ^vbi++++
Mr ^npt++++	Gaitskell ^np++++
from ^in++++	nominating ^xvbg+xvbg+
any ^dti++++	more ^ap++++
labour ^nn++++	life ^nn++++
peers ^nns++++	is ^vbz+bez+aux++
to ^to++++	be ^vb+be+aux++
made ^vpsv+agls+xvbnx+	at ^in++++
a ^at++++	meeting ^nn+xvbg+
of ^in++++	labour ^nn++++
MPs ^npts++++	tomorrow ^nr+tm+++
.^.+clp+++	

Fig. 3.2 Multidimensional POS annotation of words

POS Annotated Text (Sample 2)

^a_$_{AT}$ move_$_{NN}$ to_$_{TO}$ stop_$_{VB}$ \Mr_$_{NPT}$ Gaitskell_$_{NP}$ from_$_{IN}$ nominating_$_{VBG}$ any_$_{DTI}$ more_$_{AP}$ labour_$_{NN}$ life_$_{NN}$ peers_$_{NNS}$ is_$_{BEZ}$ to_$_{TO}$ be_$_{BE}$ made_$_{VBN}$ at_$_{IN}$ a_$_{AT}$ meeting_$_{NN}$ of_$_{IN}$ labour_$_{NN}$ \0MPs_$_{NPTS}$ tomorrow_$_{NR}$._.

Fig. 3.3 One-dimensional POS annotation of words

(Sample sentence: Fig. 3.1; Multidimensional annotation: Fig. 3.2; and One-dimensional annotation: Fig. 3.3).

The examples (Sample 1 and Sample 2) illustrate several important variations practiced in POS annotation.

Difference in Layout

1. Sample 1 has a vertical format (for space constraints, data is presented here in two columns) where each word is put on a separate line. A space is given after each word and POS information begins with ^.
2. Sample 2 applies a horizontal format. Each word is annotated with POS information in the subscript attached with an underscore. Thus, "a_$_{AT}$" refers that the word "a" is annotated as an indefinite article (AT).

Difference in the Amount of Information

1. Sample 1 uses a + sign to separate "fields" of information for each word. Sample 2 does not use a + sign. It includes information from one field only.
2. In some cases, the information given in both samples is the same and identical. For instance, in both cases, "a" is annotated as AT (indefinite article).
3. In some cases, Sample 1 includes more information. For example, look at the sequence *to be made*. In Sample 1, corresponding tags show that the word "to" is marked as an infinitive marker (to ^to ++); "be" is marked as a conjugated form of a verb (^vb). It may be marked also as a copula (+be), and as an auxiliary verb (+aux). The word "made" may be used as a passive form of a verb (^vpsv), as an agentless passive (+agls), and as a past participle form (+xvbnx). In Sample 2, information is for one field. The corresponding annotation shows that "to" is an infinitive marker (to_$_{TO}$), "be" is an infinitive form of BE (be_$_{BE}$), and "made" is a past participle verb form (made_$_{VBN}$).
4. Sample 1 carries some amount of semantic information. For instance, the word "tomorrow," in the first field is first identified as an adverbial noun (tomorrow ^nr). In the second field, it is annotated as a term that refers to the time (+tm). Sample 2 does not carry additional information relating to a word. For example, the word "tomorrow" is annotated as an adverbial noun only (tomorrow_$_{NR}$).
5. Sample 1 indicates all possibilities of a word with regard to its part-of-speech when a word is used in a text. On the other side, Sample 2 shows the real part-of-speech of a word when it is used in a sentence. POS annotated corpora thus vary in the amount of information they include.

```
^a_AT move_NN to TO stop_VB \0Mr_NPT Gaitskell_NP
from_IN nominating_VGB any_DTI more_AP labour_NN
life_NN peers_NNS is _BEZ to_TO be_BE made_VBN at_IN
a_AT meeting_NN of_IN labour_NN \0MPs_NPTS
tomorrow_NR ._.
```

Fig. 3.4 POS annotated *LOB corpus* (Barnbrook, 1998: 124)

Computer systems for POS annotation in English and some other languages are developed since the 1980s. To date, several POS annotated corpora are available in most of these languages for both commercial and academic purposes. The *LOB* corpus, for instance, is available in raw and POS annotated versions. It is POS annotated with Constituent Likelihood Automatic Word-tagging System (CLAWS) and postedited manually (Garside, 1987). We have given below a small sample of POS annotated text from the LOB corpus (Fig. 3.4). We are informed that some POS annotation schemes are revised with results retrieved from the *Lancaster–Leeds Treebank* (Leech et al., 1994). The scheme uses a system to distinguish between singular and plural noun phrases and employs skeleton parsing by using a smaller set of grammatical categories.

During grammatical annotation, a system applies linguistic and probabilistic rules to identify a word and annotates it with contextualized part-of-speech. It also tries, at the lexical level, to analyze morphological structures of words to distinguish homographic words (Leech, 1997).

We understand that POS annotation involves the assignment of specific part-of-speech to words after we realize their actual grammatical and semantic roles in a given sentence. Sometimes, we also want to attach information regarding lexical dependencies, constituent identities, named entities, argument-predicate relations in a POS annotated text. This is, however, a wrong strategy. It makes a POS annotation a complicated and cumbersome process. It mixes up with syntactic annotation, and thereby, makes a text less useful. A POS annotation scheme is a single operational process. It assigns codes with full grammatical information to words used in a text for indicating part-of-speech information of words. It has no other operation beyond this. Therefore, we should not mix it up with syntactic annotation. Syntactic annotation, in practice, marks phrases and defines dependencies among phrases (Leech & Garside, 1982).

Usually, a human text user faces severe difficulties to read and comprehend a POS annotated text. A computer, however, does not face many problems to read an annotated text. It provides the necessary information to a computer to identify part-of-speech of those words, which are identical in orthography but different in meaning and part-of-speech. A computer can be further trained with POS annotated texts to deal with problems of morphological, lexical, semantic, and syntactic ambiguities (Leech & Eyes, 1993). Even if we do not want to use a POS annotated text for other purposes, it is useful enough in retrieving lexical data from a text. Also, it offers relevant information for semantic and syntactic annotation of words.

To date, there are corpora of different types in many languages of the world. Most of these are POS annotated (either manually or automatically) by using a set of morphological and grammatical rules. Some reports and papers deal with corpus annotation, the relevance of annotated texts, and application of annotated texts in linguistics and other domains (Atwell et al., 2000; Garside 1995; Ide & Pustejovsky, 2017; Kupiec, 1992; Leech & Garside, 1982; Leech et al., 1983; Leech, 1997; Leech & Smith; 1999; Nagata et al., 2018; Naseem et al., 2009; Nguyen & Verspoor, 2018; Schulz & Kuhn, 2016; ; Wallis, 2007, 2014, 2020; Yang & Eisenstein, 2016). These works confirm that the POS annotated texts are useful for carrying out innovative linguistic research as well as devising innovative application-based tools and systems for language application.

3.7 POS Annotation: Indian Scenario

In the case of the Indian languages, perhaps, the first POS manually annotated text corpus is developed in 2004 before any attempt is made to design a system for the same purpose. In an experiment, we manually POS annotated a text of a hundred thousand words of modern Bengali prose to calculate the frequency of use of words of different parts-of-speech in Bengali (Dash, 2004). We used the existing parts-of-speech set of standard Bengali grammar to form the first POS tagset for Bengali (Table 3.2).

The actual work of POS annotation is carried out manually on a sample written Bengali text corpus (Dash, 2005: 104–108). In the Bengali corpus text, as it is shown

Table 3.2 Generic POS tagset proposed for Bengali (Dash, 2004)

No	POS categories	Tag	Example
1	Noun	[NN]	bālak, śahar, kathā, mānuṣ
2	Pronoun	[PRN]	āmi, tumi, se, tārā, tui
3	Demonstrative	[DMS]	ẏe, ei, oi, tāi
4	Finite verb	[FV]	karchi, kartām, gela, ẏābe
5	Non-finite verb	[NFV]	karle, karte, gele, giye
6	Adjective	[ADJ]	bhāla, manda, sundar,sādā
7	Adverb	[ADV]	haṭhāt, bābad, kāraṇe
8	Postposition	[PSP]	pare, kāche, āge, niche
9	Conjunction	[CNJ]	tabe, ẏadi, naile, ẏāte
10	Indeclinable	[IND]	kintu, athabā, baraṃ ār
11	Particle	[PRT]	i, o, to, nā, ne, ni
12	Quantifier	[QNT]	ek, dui, pratham, paylā
13	Punctuation	[PNC]	.,:; - / …, !, ? (), [], { }, etc
14	Symbols	[ORS]	+ , −, x, >, <, $, #, @, ^, &, * etc.

<Sentence START>
kṛṣi[NN] kāryer[NN] janya[PP] ek[ADJ] jāygāy[NN] saṅgabaddha[ADJ] haiyā[NFV] basabās[NN] karite[NFV] lāgila[FV] ebaŋ[IND] parasparer[PN] madhye[PP] kṛṣi[NN] kāryer[NN] bibhinna[ADJ] kalākauśaler[NN] biṣaye[NN] labdha[ADJ] jñān[NN] binimay[NN] dvārā[PP] kṛṣikei[NN] jībikār[NN] subidhājanak[ADJ] upāy[NN] hisābe[PP] grahaṇ[NN] karibār[NFV] siddhānta[NN] grahaṇ[NN] karila[FV] ebaŋ[IND] śikār[NN] apekṣā[PP] kṛsi[NN] kāryer[NN] sāhāyye[PP] jībikā[NN] arjaner[NN] upar[PP] mānuṣ[NN] adhik[ADJ] jor[NN] dila[FV] .[PNC]
<Sentence END>

Fig. 3.5 Sample of a POS annotated Bengali written text (Dash, 2005)

in Fig. 3.5, there is no attempt to go into the sub-classification of parts-of-speech as proposed and used in English and other languages (Barnbrook, 1998; Biber et al., 1998). Since it is the first and manual attempt, an effort is made to provide only broad part-of-speech level information to words based on their identity and role in the contexts of their use in texts.

In another experiment, with a goal to add more information at the word level, an attempt is made to provide multiple levels of POS information to words (Dash, 2005: 112). Since the occurrence of homonyms in Bengali texts is quite enormous, it is necessary to identify the scope of a word to be used in different parts-of-speech in the language. Given below is an example, where some of the Bengali words, following the model proposed in Biber et al. (1998), are annotated with multiple POS values to inform that, based on the requirement of a particular context, a word may be used in different parts-of-speech in Bengali (Figs. 3.6 and 3.7).

To make POS annotation text useful, we have taken necessary grammatical support from standard Bengali dictionaries. Here words are marked with one or more parts-of-speech. Moreover, we updated our list with information retrieved from analyzed texts. With regard to homonymous words (i.e., words which show structural similarities),

Sample Bengali Text used in POS Annotation

Sentence:

ābdul mājhi. chhũchālo tār dāṛi. gõph tār kāmāno. māthā tār neṛā. tāke chini. se dādāke padmā theke ene dita iliś māchh ār kachchhaper ḍim.

Gross Meaning:

Abdul Majhi. His beard is pointed. His mustache is shaved. His head is bald. I know him. He used to bring Hilsha fish and tortoise eggs from the Padma (river).

Fig. 3.6 Sample Bengali text without POS annotation

Fig. 3.7 Multiple POS annotation of Bengali words (Dash, 2005)

POS Annotated Text (Bengali)	
ābdul_NN ++++	chini_FV/NN ++++
mājhi_NN ++++	se_PRN/ADJ ++++
chhũchālo_ADJ ++++	dādāke_NN ++++
tār_PRN/NN ++++	padmā_NN ++++
dāṛi_NN ++++	theke_PSP/NFV ++++
gõph_NN ++++	ene_NFV ++++
tār_PRN/NN ++++	dita_FV ++++
kāmāno_ADJ/FV ++++	iliś_NN ++++
māthā_NN ++++	māch_NN ++++
tār_PRN/NN ++++	ār_IND/ADV
neṛā_ADJ/NN ++++	kachchhaper_NN ++++
tāke_PRN/NN ++++	ḍim_NN ++++

we observed that words with one orthographic form may have several possible parts-of-speech. For example, in Bengali, *chini* can be a finite verb (e.g., chini$_{_\text{FV}\backslash)}$ and a noun (e.g., chini$_{_\text{NN}).}$ Similarly, *tār* can be a pronoun (e.g., tār$_{_\text{PRN})}$ as well as a noun (tār$_{_\text{NN}}$). In these cases, we refer to a list of suffixes with their possible use with words of different parts-of-speech. This list is quite handy in determining the part-of-speech of a word.

The example (Fig. 3.7) shows that parts-of-speech are assigned to words with an underscore (_), and annotations are presented in capital letters. Most of the words are annotated with a single POS value. Some words are annotated with double POS values because, in context-free situations, these words may belong to two different parts-of-speech (e.g., tār$_{_\text{PN}\backslash\text{NN}}$). There are also possibilities for adding more information regarding morphological properties, grammatical functions, inflection, and affixation to words. This, however, needs a detailed investigation into the formal and functional properties of words. If this is done, an annotation scheme is more complex but useful for text processing.

During the last two decades, there have been attempts across India for developing POS tagset as well as POS annotated corpora in many Indian languages. These efforts are primarily computer-based as POS annotation is a computationally "easy" problem compared to attempting manually. For the Indian languages, POS annotation is no more a theoretical exercise. Some tools and systems work for many Indian language texts quite elegantly. Since giving details about these works is not the goal of the present section, we refer to only a few works that address POS annotation in Indian languages (Avinesh & Karthik, 2007). There are reports about some computer-assisted tool for POS annotation of words (Saha et al., 2004), POS annotation and chunking (Dandapat, 2007), POS annotation and shallow parsing (Rao & Yarowsky, 2007), hybrid POS annotation and chunking (Rao et al., 2007), hidden Markov model (HMM)-based POS annotation and chunking (Sastry et al., 2007), and unsupervised POS annotation (Saharia, 2009). These works use theoretical models and texts to come out with results. An attempt is also made to develop a common POS annotation framework for the Indian languages (Baskaran et al., 2008) and it contributes to developing a standard POS tagset for the Indian languages.

In the last 15–20 years, many Indian scholars have applied mathematical models, statistical tools, and computational techniques to develop POS annotation systems. These annotation tools are trained on Indian language corpora and programmed with nearest-neighbor transition probabilities to achieve a high level of accuracy. In those cases, where words are explicitly and systematically inflected, the level of accuracy is very high. To date, the POS annotation tools and texts that are developed for Indian languages, include Hindi (Shrivastava & Bhattacharyya, 2008; Ray et al., 2010; Mishra & Mishra 2011), Bengali (Ali, 2010; Chakrabarti, 2011; Dandapat, 2009; Ekbal et al., 2007), Kannada (Shambhavi et al., 2012), Tamil (Dhanalakshmi et al., 2009), Malayalam (Antoy et al., 2010), Assamese (Saharia 2009), and Bhojpuri (Singh & Jha, 2015). Attention is given to other Indian languages also (Rao et al., 2007; Pammi & Prahallad, 2007; Rao & Yarowsky, 2007; Kumar and Josan, 2010, Shambhavi & Ramakanth, 2010). One of the major milestones in this area is the generation of annotated parallel translation corpus in 23 Indian languages under the ILCI project of the Government of India (Jha, 2010). This corpus opens many possibilities of using annotated texts in various applications in Indian languages (Dash et al., 2016).

3.8 The BIS POS Tagset

The BIS (Bureau of Indian Standard) tagset is a common tagset that is designed for all Indian languages. It applies some of the principles and rules mentioned in Chap. 2. The number of POS tags for English varies within 50–160 tags, based on the requirement of a POS annotation model. For example, in an English text, we can simply use "N" for a Noun or go further to use "NN" for a singular common noun, "NS" for plural common nouns, and "NP" for singular proper nouns. Some have used more than 1000 tags for annotating parts-of-speech in a Koine Greek text (deRose, 1991; Manning, 2011). Even then some words are found to be ambiguously annotated at the part-of-speech level. The number of the tag is yet to be fixed for each Indian language, although the BIS tagset proposes a set of 45 tags for all the Indian languages. We do not know yet if this number can suffice the requirements of all Indian languages or there should be variation in number based on the requirement of individual Indian languages.

The BIS proposes a Super Tagset for all Indo-Aryan languages used in India (i.e., *Assamese, Bengali, Gujarati, Hindi, Konkani, Maithili, Marathi, Odia, Punjabi, Rajasthani, Urdu,* and *Sanskrit*). Since these languages come from the same ancestral antiquity as well as register close genealogical-cum-typological affinities, it is assumed that this Super Tagset will be enough for the languages with minimum language-specific changes. At the same time, it is argued that the Super Tagset may be considered for Dravidian, Astro-Asiatic, and Tibeto-Burman languages used in India with necessary modifications as required for each language group vis-à-vis

Table 3.3 Top-level super tag POS categories of the BIS tagset

S. No.	BIS POS tag	Label	Examples
1	Noun	\N\	bālak, ghar, śahar, kathā
2	Pronoun	\PR\	āmi, tumi, se, tārā, tui
3	Demonstrative	\DM\	ýe, ei, oi, tāi, sei
4	Verb	\V\	karchi, kartām, gela, ýābe
5	Adjective	\JJ\	bhāla, manda, sundar, sādā
6	Adverb	\RB\	kadācit, bābad, kāraṇe
7	Postposition	\PSP\	pare, kāchhe, āge, niche
8	Conjunction	\CC\	kintu, athabā, baraṃ
9	Particle	\RP\	i, o, to, nā, ne, ni, bā
10	Quantifier	\QT\	ek, dui, pratham, paylā
11	Punctuation	\PUNC\	.,:;, ?, !, (), &
12	Residuals	\RD\	Foreign words, echo words, geometric signs, mathematical signs, unknown words & characters

language (Baskaran et al., 2008). Since the top-level categories of the BIS POS tagset are generic at coarse form, only 12 basic types are considered as Super Tagset. They refer to the major parts-of-speech based on the grammar of a language. They are put at the top-level, and a special tag is assigned to each part-of-speech in the following manner (Table 3.3).

It is necessary to understand the rationale behind the decision of including only head POS categories in the **Super Tag** list. It is assumed that these are those head categories that are available in all the Indian languages; and therefore, the head categories should be uniform across all Indian languages. Taking this argument into consideration, people apply the POS annotation process to Indian languages (Kumar & Josan, 2010; Rao & Yarowsky, 2007; Shrivastava & Bhattacharyya, 2008). In the following section, we like to evaluate one of the head categories (i.e., verb) to understand why it is included and how it has to be interpreted by the POS annotators at the time of annotating a text.

3.9 The BIS Tagset and Bengali

In this section, we assess the utility of the BIS tagset with reference to Bengali and see if this POS tagset needs to be modified to address new observations obtained from the Bengali written text. In a language like Bengali, the top-level category of Verb (V), for instance, has two sub-categories. While the first level sub-category distinguishes between the main verb (VM) and the auxiliary verb (VAUX), the second level sub-category refers to verbal inflections that denote features like finiteness, non-finiteness, infiniteness, and others. The gerunds (VNG) are classified at this level as a subtype of the main verb (VM), as the following list show:

1. **Finite verb (VF)**: It includes verbs in their inflected forms with a sense of completeness of action, e.g., *karechhila* "he did," *gela* "he went," *dilām* "I gave."
2. **Non-finite verb (VNF)**: It includes those verbs that are inflected but denote a sense of incompleteness of an action, e.g., *kare* "having done," *kheye* "having eater," *bale* "having said."
3. **Infinitive verb(VINF)**: It includes those verbs which are inflected but denote a sense of starting of a continued action, e.g., *karte* "to do," *khete* "to eat," *balte* "to say."
4. **Gerund (VNG)**: It includes those verbs that occur in that position which is usually reserved for nouns. Verbs like *khāoyā* "eating," *āsā* "coming," *dekhā* "seeing" are considered gerunds as they denote a sense of a noun although the forms are originated from verbs.
5. **Auxiliary verb (VAUX)**: It includes the verbs like *chhila* "was," *āchhe* "has," *hay* "is" which are usually used after a finite verb as supporting verbs but are often used as main verbs when a finite verb is not present in a sentence.

Table 3.4 shows the subtypes of verbs and their tagsets for Bengali. What appears from this tagset is that the process of sub-classification of verbs for Bengali is quite confusing.

There is no confusion in the classification of verbs into two broad categories (i.e., main and auxiliary). It does not go against the traditional scheme of classification of the verb as found in standard Bengali grammars. However, we have to take into consideration the issue of identification and differentiation between the main verb

Table 3.4 Tagset for major sub-categories of Bengali verbs

Sl. No.	Category			Label	Tag	Examples
	Top-level	Subtype (level 1)	Subtype (level 2)			
4	Verb			V	V	
4.1		Main		VM	V_VM	
4.1.1			Finite	VF	V_VM_VF	gela, khāy, karchhi
4.1.2			Non-finite	VNF	V_VM_VNF	kare, gele, kheye
4.1.3			Infinitive	VINF	V_VM_VINF	karte, ẏete, khete
4.1.4			Gerund	VNG	V_VM_VNG	āsā, dekhā, khelā
4.2		Auxiliary		VAUX	V_VAUX	chhila, hay, āchhe

(VM) and auxiliary verb (VAUX) in Bengali as the difference between the two is quite confusing. An auxiliary verb in Bengali can take an inflection that goes with the main verb to generate a final form and to act as the main verb in a sentence. That means finiteness and other morphological properties may be present in an auxiliary verb and absent in the main verb. For illustration, consider the following examples:

(2a) tumi tāke baiṭā *diye gele.*
You to-him the-book giving went
"You went after giving him the book."
(2b) se tāke baiṭā *diye dila.*
He to-him the-book giving gave
"He gave him away the book."
(2c) āmi tomāy baiṭā *diye dite pāri.*
I to-you the-book giving to-give can
"I can give away the book to you."
(2d) baiṭā tāke *diye deoyā ẏete pāre.*
The-book to-him giving given may can
"The book may be given away to him."

In the examples given above (2a–2d), we see that in the sentence (2a), *diye* is a non-finite auxiliary verb and *gele* is a finite main verb. In sentence (2b), *diye* is a non-finite main verb and *dila* is an auxiliary finite verb. In sentence (2c), *diye* is a non-finite main verb, *dite* is a non-finite auxiliary verb, and *pāri* is a finite auxiliary verb. In sentence (2d), *diye* is a non-finite auxiliary verb, *deoyā* is the main verb in gerundial form, *ẏete* is a non-finite auxiliary verb, and *pāre* is a finite auxiliary (modal) verb. Therefore, during POS annotation, which we do at the word level, we should make clear-cut distinctions among finite, non-finite, infinitive, and gerunds for main and auxiliary verbs in Bengali and annotate these distinctions accordingly.

Although it is necessary to make distinctions between a verbal noun and a gerund in POS annotation, it is not clear if Bengali lacks in verbal noun but has gerunds (as proposed in BIS) or it has both the sub-categories. Grammatically, while verbal nouns behave more as nouns, gerunds behave more like verbs, although both can use nominal case markers. Therefore, verbal nouns should be viewed differently from gerunds on the ground that although both are nouns derived from verbs gerunds retain their verbal properties and carry arguments with grammatical case markers, while verbal nouns fail in this function as they behave like other nouns. For example, in Bengali, the verb *paṛāno* is a gerund, as it functions as a noun and takes appropriate case markers, as the following example show.

(3a) tomār paṛānor dharanṭā āmār bhāla lāge.
your of-teaching manner mine good like
"I like the manner of your teaching."

The above example (3a) shows that the verb *paṛāno* in Bengali is a gerund, as it takes arguments syntactically; that means it takes arguments and these arguments have appropriate syntactic case markings. Therefore, gerunds are conceptually different from verbal nouns because gerunds can take arguments. They are derived

Table 3.5 Difference between a gerund and verbal noun in Bengali

Root	Verb	Gerund	Verbal Noun
kar	karā	karāno	karan
chal	chalā	chalāno	chalan
bal	balā	balāno	balan
bhar	bharā	bharāno	bharan
paṛ	paṛā	paṛāno	paṛan
dekh	dekhā	dekhāna	dekhan
lekh	lekhā	lekhāno	lekhan

from verbs and their behaviors are more like verbs. For elucidation, we can cite some examples from Bengali to show how gerunds and verbal nouns are derived from the same verb roots but are different in form and function when they are used in texts (Table 3.5).

It is noted that the finiteness and non-finiteness of a verb are not often determined by its formative elements or by morphological markers. Since the same sets of inflections are added with finite and non-finite verbs in Bengali, we should be careful in using POS annotation to a verb. For instance, in Bengali, forms like *kare, karle, karte, dhuye, dhute, dhule, dekhe, dekhte, dekhle* can be finite or non-finite verbs based on the context of their use. Therefore, it is necessary to look at a sentence and the role of a verb in a sentence before a verb is annotated either as a finite or a non-finite verb. More complications will arise in the case of annotation of complex predicates for those verbs which are made with two separate words each one of which is a noun or a verb in its inflected or non-inflected form, particularly in the following cases:

1. **Conjunct verb (nām kriyā)**: The first word is a noun (or verb?) without an inflection and the second one is an inflected verb, e.g., *lābh karla* "gained," *hājir hala* "appeared," *tarka kare* "debate," *pramāṇ karbe* "will prove," *praśna karbe* "will ask," *uttar debe* "will answer," *hāi tulbe* "will yawn."
2. **Compound verb (ŷaugik kriyā)**: Both forms are verbs. The first one is a non-finite one while the second one is a finite verb, e.g., *balte thākla* "continued saying," *śunte pela* "came to hear," *lege paṛla* "started to work," *uṭhe paṛla* "got up," *ghumiye paṛbe* "will sleep," *jene rākhbe* "will know," *kāmiye nila* "earned," *bale gela* "said."
3. **Verbal compound (kriyā dvandva)**: Both forms are verbs and both are inflected. They are non-finite, finite or infinitives, e.g., *āse-ŷāy* "comes and goes," *dekhte-śunte* "seeing and hearing," *likhte-paṛte* "to write and read," *jene-śune* "knowing and hearing," *dhare-mere* "catching and beating."

At the time of POS annotation of conjunct verbs, we have to decide whether the first word should be annotated as a noun and the second word as the main verb, or the first word as the main verb and the second one as a finite auxiliary verb. Similarly, in the case of compound verbs, we have to decide whether the first one is a non-finite main verb and the second one is a finite auxiliary verb. For verbal compounds, we have to determine if both words are to be annotated as finite main verbs or inflected non-finite verbs or infinitives.

Finally, there are frequent uses of **negative verbs** in Bengali texts. These verbs are not addressed in the BIS tagset. The negative verbs are unique types of verbs in Bengali in the sense that when these are used in a sentence, they confirm the concept of "non-existence" of an object. They indicate that there is someone or something which is not present in reality as the following examples show.

(3a) āmi dāktār **nai**.
I doctor (am) not
"I am not a doctor."
(3b) tui śikṣak **nos**.
You teacher (are) not
"you (n-hon) are not a teacher."
(3c) tumi śilpi **nao**.
You artist (are) not
"You (neu) are not an artist."
(3d) āpni mantrī **nan.**
You minister (are) not.
"You (hon.) are not a minister."
(3e) se gāyak **nay.**
He singer (is) not
"He is not a singer."

The forms like *nai, nos, nay, nao, nan, nāi, nei, nahe, naha, nahen* (as shown in examples: 3a–3e) are not examples of negative particles. These are, in actuality, examples of "negative verbs" where a sense of negation is embedded within the verb (e.g., *āmi hai* "I am": *āmi nai* "I am not"). These verbs are so important that if we ignore them, we lose one of the most striking features of verbs in the Bengali language. Moreover, such forms are quite frequent in use in Bengali, and therefore, they require proper analysis and annotation. These forms should be kept under a separate sub-category of verbs in Bengali and should be annotated accordingly.

3.9.1 Utility of a POS Annotated Text

The utility of a POS annotated text is limitless. It is a kind of text that has a high value in language description, language processing, language application, and language technology. We can visualize from the following diagram (Fig. 3.8) the utility of a POS annotated text in computational linguistics, cognitive linguistics, and applied linguistics. It shows how a POS annotated text becomes a useful source of information and data for various applications.

In language description and application, we can use a POS annotated text to describe form and nature of inflection of words, record patterns of use of inflected words in texts, calculate the frequency of use of words of different part-of-speech,

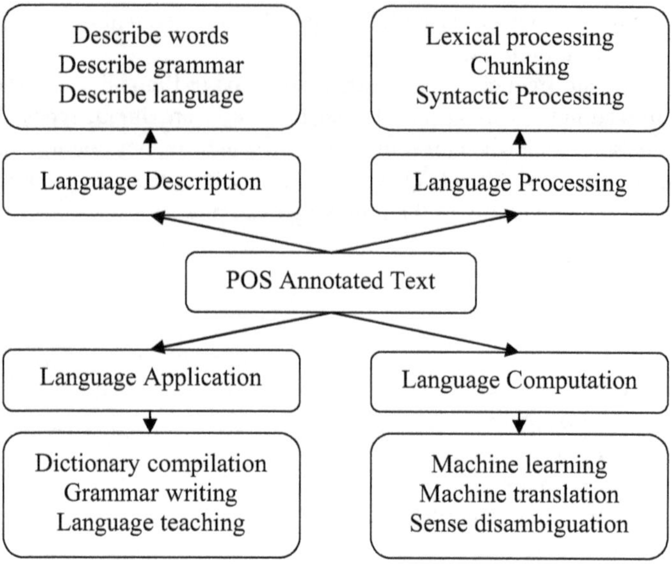

Fig. 3.8 Utilization of POS annotated text in various domains

define patterns of distribution of different lexical tokens in text, understand nature of changes words undergo during inflection, compile lexical lists of different parts-of-speech, and teach the process of formation of words of different parts-of-speech in a language.

In language computation, a POS annotated text is indispensable for developing systems for word-sense disambiguation, named entity recognition, chunking, sentence annotation, text understanding, query answering, grammar checking, e-learning, and machine translation. A POS annotated text is also applied in machine learning, extraction of linguistic properties and grammatical elements, language modeling.

Keeping multipurpose applications of POS annotated text in mind we should take initiative to develop this kind of text for all languages. And during this works, we should also keep the following four things in mind:

1. A text should invariably be pre-edited, normalized, and standardized before it is put to POS annotation.
2. The tagset should be exhaustive as much as possible keeping in view the existing parts-of-speech of a language.
3. The tagset should be designed in such a manner that it maximizes the rate of accuracy in POS annotation.
4. The POS annotation strategy should work properly on all kinds of texts covering all major and minor domains of language use.

References

Abney, S. (1997). Part-of-speech tagging and partial parsing. In S. Schreibman, R. G. Siemens, & J. M. Unsworth (Eds.), *Corpus-based methods in language & speech: A companion to digital humanities* (pp. 118–136). Blackwell.

Antony, P. J., Santhanu, P. M., & Soman, K. P. (2010). SVM-based parts-of-speech tagger for Malayalam. In *Proceedings of the International Conference on-Recent Trends in Information, Telecommunication & Computing* (ITC 2010) (pp. 339–341), Kochi, Kerala.

Atwell, E., Demetriou, G., Hughes, J., Schiffrin, A., Souter, C., & Wilcock, S. (2000). A comparative evaluation of modern English corpus grammatical annotation schemes. *International Computer Archive of Modern English Journal., 24*, 7–23.

Avinesh, P. V. S., & Karthik, G. (2007). POS tagging & chunking using conditional random field and transformation based learning. In *Proceedings of the Workshop on Shallow Parsing for South Asian Languages (IJCAI-07)* (pp. 21–24), IIIT-Hyderabad, India.

Barnbrook, G. (1998). *Language and computers*. Edinburgh University Press.

Baskaran, S., Bali, K., Bhattacharya, T., Bhattacharya, P., Chaudhury, M., Jha, G. N., Rajendran, S., Sarvanan, K., Sobha, K., & Subbarao, K. V. (2008). Designing a common POS tagset framework for Indian Languages. In *Proceedings of the 6th Workshop on Asian Language Resources, Asian Language Resources in International Joint Conference on Natural Language Processing (IJCNLP-2008)* (pp. 89–92), 11–12 January 2008, IIIT-Hyderabad.

Biber, D., Conrad, S., & Reppen, R. (1998). *Corpus linguistics—Investigating language structure and use*. Cambridge University Press.

Brill, E. (1992). A simple rule-based part of speech tagger. In *Proceedings of the Third Conference on Applied Natural Language Processing* (pp. 152–155), ACL, Trento, Italy, March 31-April 03.

Chaki, J. B. (1996). *Bangla Bhasar Vyakaran (Grammar of the Bengali Language)*. Ananda Publishers.

Chakrabarti, D. (2011). Layered parts of speech tagging for Bangla. *Language in India*. www.languageinindia.com, May 2011, *Special Volume: Problems of Parsing in Indian Languages* (pp. 1–6).

Chakravarti, N. N. (1994). *Bangla: Ki Likhben, Kena Likhben*. Ananda Publishers.

Chakravarty, B. D. (1974). *Ucchatara Bangla Vyakaran (Higher Bengali Grammar)*. Sarkar and Co.

Chattopadhyay, S. K. (1995). *Bhasa Prakash Bangla Vyakaran (Grammar of the Bengali Language)*. Rupa Publications.

Dandapat, S. (2007). POS tagging and chunking with Maximum Entropy model. In *Proceedings of Workshop on Shallow Parsing for South Asian Languages (IJCAI-07)* (pp. 29–32), IIIT-Hyd, India.

Dandapat, S. (2009). *Part-of-Speech tagging for Bengali* (Unpublished MS Thesis). Department of Computer Science and Engineering, Indian Institute of Technology, Kharagpur, India.

Dash, N. S. (2004). Text annotation: A prologue to corpus processing. *Indian Journal of Linguistics., 23*(1), 71–82.

Dash, N. S. (2005). *Corpus linguistics and language technology: With reference to Indian Languages*. Mittal Publications.

Dash, N. S. (2013). Part-of-speech (POS) tagging in Bangla written text corpus. *Bhasa Bijnan o Prayukti: An International Journal on Linguistics and Language Technology, 1*(1), 53–96.

Dash, N. S. (2015). Marking words with part-of-speech (POS) tags within the text boundary of a corpus: Problems, process, and outcomes. *Translation Today., 9*(1), 5–24.

Dash, N. S. (2016). Multifunctionality of a hyphen in Bengali text corpus: Problems and challenges in text normalization and POS tagging. *International Journal of Innovative Studies in Sociology and Humanities, 1*(1), 19–34.

Dash, N. S. (2021). Pre-editing and text standardization on a Bengali written text corpus. *Aligarh Journal of Linguistics, 10*(1), 1–22.

Dash, N. S., Arulmozi, S., & Hussain, M. M. (2016). The carriage of Indian languages corpora: And miles to go before we stop. *Indian Journal of Applied Linguistics., 42*(1 & 2), 63–92.

deRose, S. (1991). An analysis of probabilistic grammatical tagging methods. In S. Johansson & A.-B. Stenström (Eds.), *English computer corpora: Selected papers & research guide* (pp. 9–13). Mouton de Gruyter.

Dhanalakshmi, V., Kumar, A., Shivapratap, G., Soman, K. P., & Rajendran, S. (2009). Tamil POS tagging using linear programming. *International Journal of Recent Trends in Engineering,1*(2), 166–169.

Durand, D. G., DeRose, S. J., & Mylonas, E. (1996). What should mark-up really be? Applying theories of text to the design of markup systems. *In Proceedings of ALLC/ACH '96*, June 25–29, 1996, Bergen, Norway.

Ekbal, A., Mandal, S., & Bandyopadhyay, S. (2007). POS tagging using HMM and rule-based chunking. In *Proceedings of the Workshop on shallow parsing in South Asian languages (SPSAL)* (pp. 31–34), IJCAI 2007, IIIT-Hyderabad, India.

Fligelstone, S., Pacey, M., & Rayson, P. (1997). How to generalize the task of annotation. In R. Garside, G. Leech, & A. McEnery (Eds.), *Corpus annotation: Linguistic information from computer text corpora* (pp. 122–136). Longman.

Garrette, D., & Baldridge, J. (2013). Learning a part-of-speech tagger from two hours of annotation. In *Proceedings of the North American Chapter of the Association for Computational Linguistics: Human Language Technologies (NAACL-HLT-13)* (pp. 138–147) June 2013, Atlanta, GA.

Garside, R. (1987). The CLAWS word-tagging system. In R. Garside, G. Leech, & G. Sampson, (Eds.), *The computational analysis of English: A corpus-based approach* (pp., 30–41). Longman.

Garside, R. (1995). Grammatical tagging of the spoken part of the British National Corpus: A progress report. In G. Leech, G. Myers, & J. Thomas (Eds.), *Spoken English on computer: Transcription, s* (pp. 161–167). Longman.

Garside, R. (1996). The robust tagging of unrestricted text: The BNC experience. In J. Thomas & M. Short (Eds.), *Using corpora for language research: Studies in honour of Geoffrey Leech* (pp. 167–180). Longman.

Greene, B., & Rubin, G. (1971). *Automatic grammatical tagging of English.* Technical Report, Department of Linguistics, Brown University, Rhode Island (Handout).

Ide, N., & Pustejovsky, J. (Eds.). (2017). *Handbook of linguistic annotation.* (Text, Speech, and Language Technology series). Springer.

Jha, G. N. (2010). The TDIL program and the Indian language corpora initiative (ILCI). In *Proceedings of the 7th Conference on International Language Resources and Evaluation (LREC'10)* (pp., 982–985). Valletta, Malta, 19–21 May 2010.

Kumar, D., & Josan, G. S. (2010). Part-of-speech taggers for morphologically rich Indian languages: A survey. *International Journal of Computer Applications., 6*(5), 1–9.

Kupiec, J. (1992). Robust part-of-speech tagging using a hidden Markov model. *Computer Speech and Language., 6*(1), 3–15.

Leech, G. (1997). Grammatical tagging. In R. Garside, G. Leech, & A. McEnery (Eds.), *Corpus annotation: Linguistic information from computer text corpora* (pp. 19–33). Longman.

Leech, G., & Eyes, E. (1993). Syntactic annotation: Linguistic aspects of grammatical tagging & skeleton parsing. In E. Black, R. Garside, & G. Leech (Eds.), *Statistically-driven computer grammars of English: The IBM/Lancaster approach* (pp. 36–61). Rodopi.

Leech, G., & Garside, R. (1982). Grammatical tagging of the LOB Corpus: A general survey. In S. Johansson, & K. Hofland, (Eds.), *Computer Corpora in English Language Research* (pp. 110–117). Bergen: NAVF.

Leech, G., & Smith, N. (1999). The use of tagging. In H. van Halteren (Ed.), *Syntactic wordclass tagging* (pp. 23–36). Kluwer.

Leech, G., & Wilson, A. (1999). Guidelines and standards for tagging. In H. van Halteren (Ed.), *Syntactic word class tagging* (pp. 55–80). Kluwer.

Leech, G., Garside, R., & Atwell, E. (1983). The automatic grammatical tagging of the LOB corpus. *ICAME Journal: International Computer Archive of Modern and Medieval English Journal, 7*, 13–33.

Leech, G., Garside, R., & Bryant, M. (1994). The large-scale grammatical tagging of text: Experience with the British National Corpus. In N. Oostdijk & P. deHaan (Eds.), *Corpus-based research into language* (pp. 47–63). Rodopi.

Manning, C. D. (2011). Part-of-speech tagging from 97% to 100%: is it time for some linguistics? In *Proceedings of the 12th International Conference on Computational Linguistics and Intelligent Text Processing* (pp. 171–189). Vol. Part I, Tokyo, Japan, Springer, Berlin, February 20–26.

Marcus, M. P., Marcinkiewicz, M. A., & Santorini, B. (1993). Building a large annotated corpus of English: The Penn Treebank. *Journal Computational Linguistics* (Special issue on using large corpora: II), *19* (2), 313–330.

McEnery, T., & Wilson, A. (1996). *Corpus linguistics*. Edinburgh University Press.

Mishra, N., Mishra, A. (2011). Part of speech tagging for Hindi corpus. In *Proceedings of the International Conference on Communication Systems and Network Technologies* (pp. 554–558) Katra, Jammu.

Nagata, R., Mizumoto, T., Kikuchi, Y., Kawasaki, Y., & Funakoshi, K. (2018). A POS tagging model designed for learner English. In *Proceedings of the 2018 EMNLP Workshop W-NUT: The 4th Workshop on Noisy User-generated Text, Association for Computational Linguistics* (pp. 39–48). Brussels, Belgium, November 01.

Naseem, T., Snyder, B., Eisenstein, J., & Barzilay, R. (2009). Multilingual part-of-speech tagging: Two unsupervised approaches. *Journal of Artificial Intelligence Research, 36*(1), 1–45.

Nguyen, D. Q., & Verspoor, K. (2018). An improved neural network model for joint POS tagging and dependency parsing. In *Proceedings of the CoNLL 2018 Shared Task: Multilingual Parsing from Raw Text to Universal Dependencies* (pp. 81–91), Brussels, Belgium, Association for Computational Linguistics, October 31- November 1.

Pammi, S. C., & Prahallad, K. (2007). POS tagging and chunking using decision forests. In *Proceedings of the Workshop on shallow parsing in South Asian languages (SPSAL)* (pp. 33–36). IJCAI 2007, IIIT-Hyderabad, India.

Rao, D., & Yarowsky, D. (2007). Part of speech tagging and shallow parsing of Indian languages. In *Proceedings of the Workshop on Shallow Parsing for South Asian Languages (IJCAI-07)* (pp. 17–20), IIIT-Hyd, India.

Rao, P.T., Ram, S., Vijaykrishna, R., & Sobha, L. (2007). A text chunker and hybrid POS tagger for Indian languages. In *Proceedings of the Workshop on Shallow Parsing for South Asian Languages (IJCAI-07)* (pp., 9–12), IIIT-Hyd, India.

Ray, P. R., Harish, V., Sarkar, S., & Basu, A. (2010). Part of speech tagging and local word grouping techniques for natural language parsing in Hindi. In *Proceedings of the International Conference on Natural language Processing (ICON2003)* (pp. 118–125), Department of Computer Science and Engineering, IIT-Kharagpur, India.

Saha, G. K., Saha, A. B., & Debnath, S. (2004). Computer-assisted Bangla words POS tagging. In *Proceedings of (iSTRANS-2004)* (pp., 111–115), New Delhi, India.

Saharia, N., Das, D., Sharma, U., & Kalita, J. (2009). Part of speech tagger for Assamese Text. In *Proceedings of the ACL-IJCNLP-2009 Conference* (pp. 33–36). Suntec, Singapore.

Sarkar, P., & Basu, G. (1994). *Bhasa Jijnasa (Language Queries)*. Kolkata: Vidyasagar Pustak Mandir.

Sastry, G. M. R., Chaudhuri, S., & Reddy, P. N. (2007). A HMM-based part-of-speech & statistical chunker for 3 Indian languages. In *Proceedings of the Workshop on Shallow Parsing for South Asian Languages (IJCAI-07)* (pp. 13–16), IIIT-Hyd, India.

Schulz, S., & Kuhn, J. (2016). Learning from Within? Comparing POS tagging approaches for historical text. In *Proceedings of the Tenth International Conference on Language Resources and Evaluation (LREC 2016)* (pp. 4316–4322), European Language Resources Association.

Shambhavi, B. R., & Ramakanth, P. K. (2010). Current State of the art POS tagging for Indian Languages: A study. *International Journal of Computer Engineering and Technology., 1*(1), 250–260.

Shambhavi, B. R., Ramakanth, K. P., & Revanth, G. (2012). A maximum entropy approach to Kannada part of speech Tagging. *International Journal of Computer Applications, 41*(13), pp. 9–12.

Shrivastava, M., & Bhattacharyya, P. (2008). Hindi POS tagger using Naive Stemming: harnessing morphological information without extensive linguistic knowledge. In *Proceedings of the 6th International Conference on Natural Language Processing (ICON-2008)* (pp. 1–8). CDAC, Pune India, 20–22 December 2008.

Singh, S., & Jha, G. N. (2015). Statistical tagger for Bhojpuri employing Support Vector Machine. In *Proceedings of the International Conference on Advances in Computing, Communications and Informatics (ICACCI)* (pp. 1524–1529).

Toutanova, K., & Manning, C. D. (2000). Enriching the knowledge sources used in a maximum entropy part-of-speech tagger. In *Proceedings of the Joint SIGDAT Conference on Empirical Methods in Natural Language Processing & Very Large Corpora (EMNLP/VLC-2000)* (pp. 63–70).

Wallis, S. A. (2007). Annotation, retrieval, and experimentation. In A. Meurman-Solin, & A. A. Nurmi, (Eds.), *Annotating variation and change*. Helsinki: Varieng, UoH (ePublished).

Wallis, S. A. (2014). What might a corpus of parsed spoken data tell us about language? In L. Veselovská, & M. Janebová, (Eds.), *Complex Visibles Out There. Proceedings of the Olomouc Linguistics Colloquium 2014: Language Use and Linguistic Structure* (pp., 641–662). Olomouc: Palacký University, Czech Republic.

Wallis, S. A. (2020). Grammar and corpus methodology. In B. Aarts, G. Popova, & J. Bowie, (Eds.), *Oxford handbook of English Grammar* (pp. 58–83). Part I: Chapter 4. Oxford: Oxford University Press.

Yang, Y., & Eisenstein, J. (2016). Part-of-speech tagging for historical English. In *Proceedings of NAACL-HLT 2016* (pp. 1318–1328), San Diego, California, Association for Computational Linguistics, June 12–17.

Web Links

http://www.ldc.upenn.edu/Catalog/
https://www.cs.umd.edu/~nau/cmsc421/part-of-speech-tagging.pdf
https://www.geeksforgeeks.org/nlp-part-of-speech-default-tagging/
https://www.guru99.com/pos-tagging-chunking-nltk.html
https://www.nltk.org/book/ch05.html
https://www.sketchengine.eu/pos-tags/
https://www.tutorialspoint.com/natural_language_processing/
www.languageinindia.com
www.shiva.iiit.ac.in/SPSAL2007/proceedings.php.

Chapter 4
Extratextual Annotation

Abstract Extratextual annotation is an important component of corpus annotation. By using this method, we can identify a text based on metadata information of a header file rather than referring to the actual texts of the text file. When we apply this process, we put some additional information to a text included in a corpus. Extratextual annotation is relevant in those situations when a corpus includes text samples of different text types compiled from different domains of language use. A useful strategy for extratextual annotation is based on the classification of standard processes of text annotation. Normally, we embed various layers in extratextual annotation to specify applications that increase extractability and accessibility of texts from a corpus. Also, it helps in the management of text files, retrieve textual information, extract desired lexical items, and classify different kinds of texts based on contents. The technique that we suggest here can be highly useful in expanding the utility of a corpus beyond the activities of language data storage and processing. We argue that corpora of all text types should be annotated at the extratextual level in a uniform manner so that texts, as and when required, are uniformly retrieved for descriptive, theoretical, and application-based works. This is more necessary for those languages where corpora are developed haphazardly without following the standard norms and methods of corpus development. We apply this scheme to a Bengali corpus to find that we are able to extract data and information more accurately from an extratextually annotated corpus than an unannotated corpus.

Keywords Corpus · Metadata · Extratextual annotation · Intratextual annotation · Interpretative elements · Header file · Language technology

4.1 Introduction

Variation in the process of corpus generation has been instrumental in framing several critical issues in text annotation. Varieties in the quantity of text data, inclusion of different types of text samples, new criteria in text representation, new ways of corpus management, and new methods of using text data are quite responsible for designing new types of text annotation methods (Sinclair, 2004). All these factors have affected the original concept of a "corpus" (Leech, 1997). In recent times,

N. S. Dash, *Language Corpora Annotation and Processing*,
https://doi.org/10.1007/978-981-16-2960-0_4

the concept of "corpus" has undergone a conceptual change. It does not follow the predetermined matrices of text categories. It has become more open-ended with a scheme for collecting varied text types of a natural language with a provision for regular addition of texts through an undisturbed flow of data at a centrally housed electronic text archive (Archer et al., 2008). That means different types of language texts that are being collected and compiled in a regular and continuous process will be available in an electronic archive. The utility of texts will be much enhanced when these texts are extratextually annotated with additional layers of information. The corpus users will be able to access the text data as well as text-related information easily and quickly from such annotated texts (Sinclair, 1994).

When these texts are properly annotated at the intratextual and extratextual levels, they will become more user-friendly and computationally compatible. As corpus users, we can extract required text samples from the digital text archive without much trouble and utilize data in particular research we are engaged in (Johansson, 1995). This necessitates designing an advanced method for extratextual annotation even though it is known to us that some extratextual information is normally preserved as **metadata** in the **header part** of a text file during corpus generation (Baker, 1997). By definition, an extratextually annotated corpus (EAC) is furnished with additional extratextual annotation as metadata along with some basic information related to the text.

Keeping the possibility of different use of an extratextually annotated corpus in view, we describe the nature, form, and manner of extratextual annotation. We apply this scheme to a Bengali text corpus to see how the relevance of the corpus is increased in different works of applied, descriptive, and technology-based linguistics. In Sect. 4.2, we define the basic concept of extratextual annotation; in Sect. 4.3, we differentiate intratextual annotation from extratextual annotation; in Sect. 4.4, we justify the theoretical relevance of extratextual annotation; in Sect. 4.5, we refer to some early works on extratextual annotation; in Sect. 4.6, we discuss the types of extratextual annotation; and in Sect. 4.7, we specify the application of an extratextually annotated corpus in linguistics and language technology. We address all these issues with reference to a Bengali text corpus developed in 1995 in the TDIL (Technology Development for Indian Languages) project of the Govt. of India. It is the first-generation corpus in the Indian languages (Dash, 2007).

4.2 Definition of Extratextual Annotation

To date, there is no clear-cut definition of extratextual annotation. Besides, we have not come across much discussion on the methods and processes that we can use to annotate a corpus at the extratextual level. What we know so far is that extratextual information should come from outside of a text and that it should be added to a text in the form of metadata. To make the concept clear in the present context of the discussion, we can formulate a workable definition of extratextual annotation in the following way:

Definition of Extratextual Annotation:

> Extratextual annotation is a kind of text annotation by which extratextual information (i.e., *text title, author, time, gender, nativity, publisher, ethnicity, subject, text domains, register*) related to a piece of text is annotated (manually or automatically) to a text file so that subsequent identification of a text file and retrieval of textual data and information from a text file, which is stored in a large corpus database of a digital text archive, is simplified, customized, and successful.

We have to keep this definition in mind to move beyond the standard practices of language text annotation. This definition gives us a clear idea to understand the goal, nature, and importance of extratextual annotation. It is observed that extratextual annotation supplies a new kind of information that is not available from other types of text annotation. Based on the kind of information stored, we can divide extratextual annotation into two parts (i.e., header part and content part) and explain how the information of these two parts becomes relevant in the process of analyzing a sample Bengali written text. The seven maxims of part-of-speech annotation (Leech, 1993) remain valid in the scheme of extratextual annotation. Theoretically, we expand the functional validity of the seven maxims to cover different types of text annotation including the present one.

4.3 Intratextual and Extratextual Annotation

In the area of corpus annotation, scholars have already proposed some well-framed maxims for making a theoretical and applicational distinction between the two types of information added to a text (Leech, 1993).

1. Representational information and
2. Interpretative information.

Representational information is related to the orthographic representation of a text. It contains information on various linguistic properties and elements that are used in formation of a text (Leech, 2005). It includes characters (i.e., *letters, graphemes, punctuations*), words, phrases, sentences, tables, paragraphs, pictures, images, charts, and other textual and non-textual items that are available in a written or printed text. On the other hand, the set of additional information that we add to a text is called interpretative information. This is done by those people who have sound knowledge of a language and know how to add this kind of information to a text without damaging the original content and structure of a text. When we accept these schemes of annotation, we find that an annotated text actually contains four types of information under two broad types (Fig. 4.1).

An annotated corpus has two major components: (a) intratextual component and (b) extratextual component. The intratextual component primarily carries interpretative information while extratextual component carries documentative information.

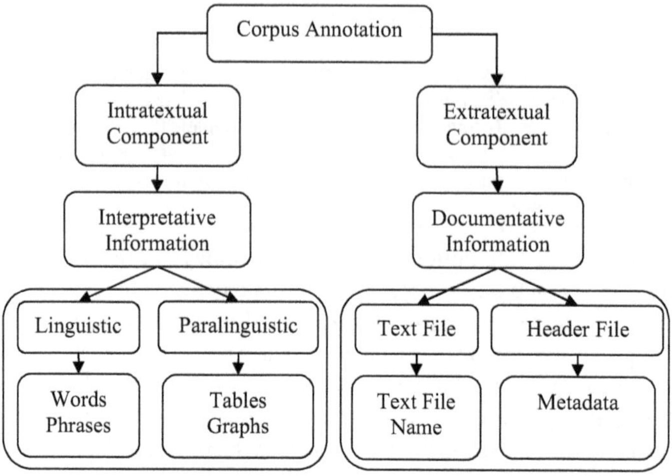

Fig. 4.1 Types of information represented in an annotated text corpus

The interpretative information has two broad parts: (a) linguistic part and (b) paralinguistic part. Both the parts are available in a written text as these are indispensable components. The linguistic part contains pure linguistic elements and information (e.g., *letters, graphemes, allographs, morphs, words, compounds, multiword units, punctuations, sentences, phrases*). We cannot construct a theoretical identity or confirm the functional relevance of a written text without these properties. On the other hand, the paralinguistic part contains those properties and elements which are not "linguistic" in nature in the true sense of the term. Primarily, these are non-textual elements (e.g., *tables, figures, pictures, images, diagrams, flowcharts*) that are used in a piece of printed or published text to make ideas and information clear to the target text users (McEnery & Wilson, 1996: 136). While developing a corpus with text samples only, all paralinguistic elements are usually removed. As a result, the corpus contains only samples of written texts. Normally, a multimodal corpus carries such paralinguistic elements as a corpus is specially designed and developed with a focus on preserving all kinds of paralinguistic elements and information along with linguistic elements and information (Dash, 2008: 66–67; Dash & Arulmozi, 2018: 58–60).

During corpus annotation, the paralinguistic elements are usually "marked-up" on a piece of text by using a set of predefined tagsets. These are annotated to a corpus by using conventional machine-readable labels which act as indicators for non-textual elements (e.g., *headings, images, diagrams, pictures, titles, tables, flowcharts chapters, paragraphs, segments*). Such non-textual items and elements are easily traced in a corpus of written text (Atkins et al., 1992). In the case of a speech corpus, on the other hand, paralinguistic elements are indicators of those properties which are considered as the salient features of spontaneous speech data. Properties like *utterance boundaries, hesitations, hedges, fillers, pauses, false starts, gaps, non-beginnings, abrupt endings, repetitions, intonation, emotional contours, suprasegmentals,* and *sentiments* are often treated as paralinguistic elements of speech (Stenström, 1984Carletta et al., 2004, Kipp et al., 2007). These properties of a spoken text are not found in a written text. These are not even found in the transcripted version of a spoken text. If we want to capture all the linguistic and paralinguistic elements and information in a text or a speech corpus, we have to depend on intratextual annotation. That means intratextual annotation is necessary for the interpretation of a corpus. Moreover, intratextual annotation helps in the identification of a text stored in a corpus. In essence, intratextual annotation is a powerful method in the retrieval of linguistic data and information from a corpus to be utilized in various works of linguistics and language processing.

The extratextual component, on the other hand, carries information relating to the form, nature, and function of a piece of text. This includes a set of properties that do not speak much about the content of a text but speak a lot about the form and manner of presentation of a text within a corpus. We require an extratextual component to identify a text file that is preclassified and preserved in a large text database of a digital text archive. Since the extratextual component carries a link with the target text domains, identification and interpretation of the extratextual component make the process of retrieval of linguistic data and information from a text corpus easy, systematic, and successful.

To increase the retrieval efficiency of a system, we design an extratextual component part of a text in an elaborate fashion. Normally, we include information related to the *title of a text, name of an author, time of publication of a text, gender of an author, nativityof an author, name of the publisher, ethnicityof an author, subject matter of a text, domains of a text, register variationsin the text* and similar information. Such information is gathered as Metadata within a header part of a text file. From an application point of view, extratextual information is useful for reference purposes in studies of *ethnolinguistics, ecolinguistics, sociolinguistics, sociology, lexicography, demography, language planning*, and *language data management*. Extratextual information is also necessary for technical, legal, and cultural interpretation of texts and various linguistic and non-linguistic studies.

4.4 Relevance of Extratextual Annotation

For various practical reasons, extratextual annotation is of high importance to those people who develop digitally encoded texts and archive texts for future applications. The variables that are considered for extratextual annotation are indispensable attributes in corpus generation, corpus management, corpus classification as well as for pulling out data and information from a corpus. The majority of the extratextual variables are characteristically non-linguistic, and we often select and determine these features impromptu before we look into the textual part of a corpus. Thus, we ensure that we do not make a priori linguistic judgment during the time of designing the tagset for extratextual annotation. We, however, keep in mind that the attributes that we consider useful for extratextual annotation are also relevant in the description of a text of a particular type and the language which is the source of the text in developing a corpus (Atkins et al., 1992). Our argument is that these characteristic features are relevant for different types of linguistic studies as well as in designing new methods for updating existing archives. These features are also essential for those new texts, which are not properly classified following the existing schemes of text classification.

We can further envisage the importance of extratextual annotation with regard to a diachronic corpus. A diachronic corpus, in principle, contains text samples that spread over a longer period of time (Kytö et al., 1994). In the case of a diachronic corpus, we can include the following types of information within the frame of extratextual annotation: (a) information of first date(s) of origin of texts, (b) information relating to the authorship of texts, (c) title of the works, (d) nationality of authors, (e) sources of texts, and (f) modification in text over the years. We store this kind of information in the header part of a text file of a corpus (Leech & Fligelstone, 1992). We refer to the extratextual information of a diachronic corpus to select a text and extract desired data from a corpus. It works betters in those situations when a corpus is put within in a very big archive along with samples of other text types in an ontologically structured manner (Archer & Culpeper, 2003).

An ontologically structured corpus with extratextual annotation is a good source of data retrieval. When we do comparative linguistic studies on text samples of different periods or all text samples of a particular period, we refer to the information of the header part of a diachronic corpus (Rissanen, 1989). We can understand variations of usage of a language across decades as well as across text types. Appropriate knowledge about extratextual information of a text is necessary for these studies as it guides us to find out relevant texts from a thematically categorized text archive. Thus with the help of characteristic features of extratextual annotation, we can go beyond language description to serve the requirements of applied linguistics, language technology, and others. We, therefore, argue that it is necessary to encode a text at the extratextual level in a corpus. This makes text file search, content search, and information retrieval from a corpus relatively easy, quick, and accurate.

4.5 Extratextual Annotation: Some Early Works

As far as we know, the first text annotation process was applied on the *Brown Corpus* (Francis, 1980) and the *LOB Corpus* (Lancaster-Oslo-Bergen) (Gerside et al., 1987). Each one contained around one million words of running English texts. The Brown Corpus contained texts of American English while the LOB Corpus contained texts of British English. At the early stage, both the corpora were grammatically annotated with minimum part-of-speech information of words used in texts. At that time, there was no effort for adding extratextual information to the texts in the corpora. This was because our knowledge of text annotation during the time, when these corpora were annotated, was not very rich. During that time we failed to realize that corpus needs extratextual annotation so that we archive texts in an organized manner when text samples in a corpus are large in volume, varied in text type, and multidimensional in content. We also failed to visualize that over the years, due to the advancement of computer science, we could be able to collect an enormous amount of language data from a wide variety of text domains and subject areas. Over the years, the scenario has changed in a large dimension. Now, there is a requirement for a systematic and user-friendly technique for data storage, data management, data retrieval, and data access from a digital corpus archive. The present scheme of extratextual annotation that is suggested in this chapter addresses all these issues. After realizing this applicational truth, we have started working in this area to develop some universal standard norms for data classification, annotation, and preservation within a broader scheme of extratextual annotation.

We have not yet been successful, despite our involvement in corpus research over the years, to develop a model or a standard that can be accepted widely and used universally for representing extratextual information in a corpus. Those who are working in the areas of corpus generation and text annotation, normally apply some not-so-elegant approaches and methods to achieve their goals. For instance, the COCOA reference, as an early computer program, was used to extract indexes of words from texts through a machine. The conventions that it followed were applied to several other programs, such as the Oxford Concordance Program(OCP). The COCOA reference was also applied to *Longman-Lancaster Corpus* and *Helsinki Corpus* (McEnery & Wilson, 1996: 26). Although it is revised later to include many new aspects and properties to be assigned to words in texts, the early version contained a set of angled brackets (< >) to represent the following two entities only:

1. A code representing the name of a particular variable and
2. A string or a set of strings to symbolize the variable.

For instance, it uses the code "A" to refer to a variable called "Author". The string "author" actually symbolizes the name of an author. Thus, the reference scheme of COCOA indicates the name of an author of a text in the following way:

<T: TEXT: Merchant of Venice>
<A: AUTHOR: William Shakespeare>
<S>: SAMPLE:>

The COCOA format header that was used in the *Helsinki Corpus* is presented below to give an idea of how extratextual information was represented inside a corpus (Table 4.1). This method is, however, not used much in later years as more advanced strategies are developed for better representation. Even then it gives an idea about how we should start the process of encoding extratextual information in a corpus text. The COCOA format header is presented on the left-hand side, and the glossary of the codes is presented on the right-hand side.

The COCOA reference is an informal format of information representation. It has the architecture to encode extratextual information relating to demographic and non-linguistic information of a text such as *title of a text, name of author, date of first publication, gender of author, type of a text, broad area of a text,* etc. In our view, this reference scheme may be revised further for representing information in a corpus keeping in mind that this reference scheme is initially applied by a human and later adopted by an automated system. The importance of the COCOA reference is that

Table 4.1 COCOA reference format used for word indexing

Code	Glossary
<BCEPRIV1>	Short descriptive code
<QE1XX CORP EBUEAM>	Text identifier
<N LET TO HUSBAND>	Name of the text
<EDA ELIZABETH>	Author's name
<C E1>	Sub-period
<O 1500–1570>	Date of composition
<MX>	Date of manuscript
<KX>	The relevance of the text
<D ENGLISH>	Dialect
<V PROSE>	Verse or prose
<T LET PRIV>	Text type
<G X>	Foreign or original
<F X>	Foreign or original
<W WRITTEN>	Written or spoken
<X FEMALE>	Sex of author
<Y X>	Age of author
<H HIGH>	Author's social status
<U X>	Audience description
<E INT UP>	Participant relationship
<J INTERACTIVE>	Interactive/non-interactive
<I INFORMAL>	Formal/informal
<Z X>	Prototypical text category
<S SAMPLE X>	Sample

it inspires to develop formalized international standards for extratextual annotation. Moreover, it helps in developing more advanced text annotation guidelines such as Text Encoding Initiative (TEI). The TEI is used to annotate both written and spoken text corpora of English and many other languages. The application of TEI on corpora has been a huge success as it provides standards for corpus annotation as well as opens ways for building text interchanging facilities in machine-readable form.

Corpus annotators now use a format known as *Standard Generalised Markup Language* (SGML-ISO 8879: 1986) for document mark-up in Text Encoding Initiative (TEI) scheme. For several years, it has been used as an international standard for text corpus annotation. It is accepted across language texts due to some functional advantages such as rigorousness in the process of encoding formalization, simplicity in the process of code implementation, and clarity in the process of text understanding (Sperberg-McQueen & Burnard, 1994). To date, we have come across several text and speech corpora in English, Spanish, German and other languages which have applied this markup system. Also, these annotated corpora are made available in machine-readable form for many new works of language description, language application, and machine learning purposes (Fierz & Grütter, 2000). In our view, the TEI has played a vital role in the advancement of the SGML markup standard (Goldfarb, 1990).

As far as we know, the TEI annotation scheme is neither adopted nor applied on written text corpora of Indian languages. In place of it, a makeshift markup method is applied on some written Indian languages corpora for intratextual and extratextual annotation. The corpus developers of Indian languages have used some indigenous ways for text annotation, which are equally useful for extracting appropriate data from text files. When compared, these ways appear old-fashioned and backdated against the modern methods of corpus annotation, which are far more advanced, robust, and computer-friendly. Even then, it is interesting to know how that old-fashioned method worked successfully for written text corpora of Indian languages before new methods were introduced and incorporated. Some ideas about this old method may be gathered from the following section (Sect. 4.6).

4.6 Extratextual Annotation Types

The most primary extratextual annotation tells us about the type of text. It provides us necessary guidance to look for a particular type of text within a digital text archive. Based on this guidance, we can identify the kind of a text we are looking for in a text file. Normally, we depend on the following two types of extratextual information, which are tagged to a corpus text file, to trace the most appropriate type of text we are searching.

1. The file name of a text file and
2. The header part of the text file

The file name of a text file provides us vital clues to know what kind of text is accumulated in a text file within a corpus archive. In most cases, a file name of a text file gives us only a limited amount of information. However, as a text user, we may be interested to know more detailed information about the type of a text which goes beyond the title of a book and the name of an author. To fulfill this requirement, we may refer to the header part of the text file. The header part, in actuality, stores exhaustive extratextual information of a text. That means both file name and header part of a file jointly serve our purpose. In essence, we may avail extratextual information of a text file partly from the file name and partly from the header part. The file name works as a gateway while header part works as metadata depository. In the following part of this section, we focus on how extratextual information is preserved in the file name and header part. In the present discussion, we have not considered the other type of annotation (i.e., *intratextual annotation*) as it involves different challenges and issues that are not related to the main theme of the chapter.

4.6.1 File Name: A Gateway

For the Indian languages corpora, text samples were stored in a computer as text files under different file names. This had been the practice during the stage when we first started developing corpora in the Indian languages in machine-readable form. File names were designed keeping in mind the subject areas of texts. Collected text samples were manually analyzed and classified based on the subject areas to which the texts belonged. These subject names were later considered and included as file names. That means the file name itself stood as a piece of extratextual annotation and provided the necessary information to us to identify the kind of text stored in the file. It also guided us to locate the file that we wanted to search out within the digital text archive. Thus, the file name became a useful gateway to track the target file in the archive.

In the corpus development part of the TDIL (Technology Development for the Indian Languages) project, the name of a text file, due to some technical reasons, was limited to 12 characters (Dash, 2007). Due to this factor, a text file name was quite confusing and deceptive. For the purpose of cross-lingual reference and comparison, it was also decided that a text file name should be consistent across all Indian language corpora and that it should carry information about the following types within its length of 12 characters:

1. Text Category (TC) information: [2 characters (all alphabets)]
2. Subject Category (SC) information: [2 characters (all alphabets)]
3. Text Title (TT) information: [4 characters (all alphabets)]
4. Division Indicator (DI) information: [1 character (symbol)]
5. Number of text files information: [3 characters (all digits)].

The name of a text file in the TDIL corpus was alphanumeric. It combined both characters and digits. Following this norm, the name of each text file was generated for each Indian language corpus in a uniform manner. It is true that this kind of naming process is quite backdated and old-fashioned. The coding system looks like an amateurish implementation process. Since there was no standard coding system available to the corpus developers during that time, we had to build our resources based on convention. It was quite useful for us as we could manage and access the text files following this method. In the present time, it is possible to adopt a different method for the same purpose.

In the present operation, when corpus file management is no more a challenge in corpus building, we as corpus researchers are more concerned with corpus design criteria and text sampling methods (Dash & Arulmozi, 2018). Rather than giving much attention to a text file name, we are more interested to focus on those common linguistic distinctions and issues, such as the followings, that may affect the overall form and content of a corpus (Wallis, 2007):

- presence versus absence of audience in a corpus
- public versus private nature of a text (possibly confidential)

- post-edited text versus spontaneously produced on-the-fly text (e.g., real-time translation, text chat)
- natural and spontaneous versus rehearsed and cooked texts, and
- rehearsed materials (e.g., broadcast interviews) versus scripted texts (e.g., speeches, soap operas).

There are also demographic issues in sampling texts for designing a corpus (e.g., *native versus non-native language users, male versus female text writers, known versus unknown authors, influential versus non-influential writers, standard versus regional languages, young versus old text writers, modern versus old texts, formal versus informal texts, printed versusdigital texts*). Demographic and ethnographic variables are important in new schemes of corpus building. These variables play crucial roles in designing technology-based language support systems and applications by industries. These are issues in *representational plurality* where modern corpus linguists are interested to be engaged.

4.6.2 Annotation of Text Categories

Taking into consideration the five types of information that are used in a file name, we have framed the file name of each text file in the following manner.

[A] $[C_1C_{2[TC]}C_3C_{4[SC]}C_5C_6C_7C_{8\,[TT]}\cdot_{[DI]}D_1D_2D_{3[Digits]}]$

(a) C_1C_2= Text Category (TC)
(b) C_3C_4= Subject Category (SC)
(c) $C_5C_6C_7C_8$= Text Title (TT)
(d) (.)= Division Indicator (DI)
(e) $D_1D_2D_3$= Digits (001–999)

The information presented above shows how a file name of a text file does not exceed the limit of 12 characters. The first 8 characters (C = character with a subscript digit signifying its number) represent the name of a text file and the dot (one character) indicates the terminal point of the name of a text file. The last 3 characters are cardinal numerals (D = digits with a subscript number signifying a numerical value). These are used to specify the number of text files belonging to a text category. We applied this method consistently across all text categories to make text files in the TDIL corpus (Dash, 2016). This was not the only method that we used for extratextual annotation of all kinds. Along with this, we also stored information in the header part, which we kept within a text file. It is however to be kept in mind that every corpus developer has the freedom to design and adopt a new strategy keeping in mind the nature of the text to be stored in a corpus and possible applications of a corpus.

We further classified the first 8 characters of a file name into three sub-groups so that we could use them to represent text category, subject category, the title of a text. The first 2 characters (C_1C_2) were used to refer to a text category; the next 2

Table 4.2 Six major text categories and their codes in TDIL corpus

Domains	Text categories of the TDIL Corpus	Codes
1	Texts procured from Literature	LT
2	Texts procured from social sciences	SS
3	Texts procured from natural sciences	NS
4	Texts procured from business and commerce	BC
5	Texts procured from mass media	MM
6	Texts procured from other domains	OR

characters (C_3C_4) were used to refer to a subject category, and the last 4 characters ($C_5C_6C_7C_8$) were used to refer to a title of a text (TT). The following example shows how we constructed a file name after embedding several kinds of information into it.

[B] Text file name: LTFCKLBL.005

The above example has 12 characters. The first 2 characters (LT) stand for a text category called "Literature"; the next 2 characters (FC) stand for a subject category called "Fiction", and the last 4 characters (KLBL) represent the title of the fiction. This strategy was quite successful in putting names of major text categories that were selected for building a written corpus. Moreover, it helped us to divide texts of different subjects into six categories. After classification, it was easy for us to encode extratextual information in a minimized form. This was crucial in searching out a text file for a particular study (Table 4.2).

Depending on the text domain, a text was put in one of the 6 text categories stated above (Table 4.2). We designed each text category in such a manner that we were able to include several subject categories under a single text category. We framed this model following the ontology of text classification where texts of different sub-domains/sub-disciplines are put under different head categories (Davidson, 1974).

1. Literature (LT): fiction, short story, essay, painting, drawing, music, sculpture, and others.
2. Social Science (SS): political science, history, philosophy, education, religion, and others.
3. Natural Science (NS): physics, chemistry, biology, mathematics, geography, and others.
4. Business & Commerce (BC): accountancy, banking business, and others.
5. Mass Media (MM): newspapers, periodicals, advertisements, notices, magazines, and others.
6. Others (OR): Texts that do not belong to the above categories. It takes texts from administrative, legal, legislative, and government documents.

The text classification scheme that we used had some functional advantages. First, it served our primary purpose of representing a text in a corpus (Biber, 1993). By looking at the diagram present below (Fig. 4.2), we could find a text file from the name of a text file itself. Also, we could identify to which text category a text actually belonged.

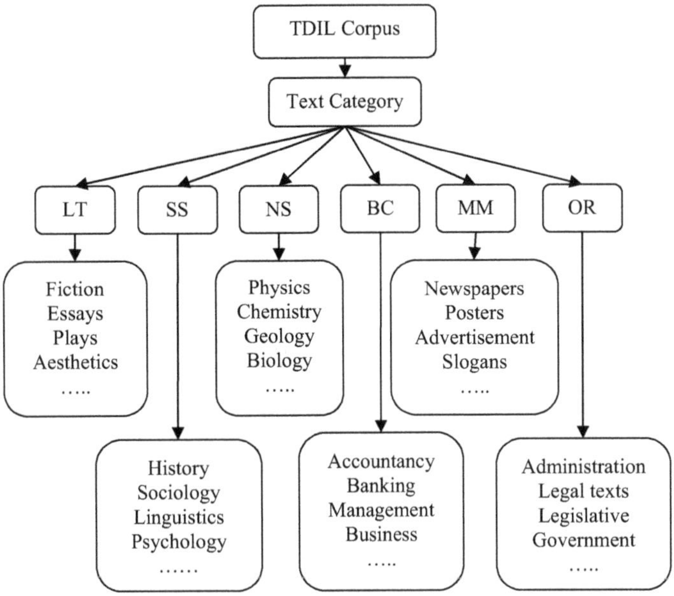

Fig. 4.2 Text classification model used in the TDIL corpus

An important aspect is to be noted here. The names of text categories were put within two characters. Therefore, our challenge was to abbreviate names of text categories into 2-letter code in such a manner that no code was replicated. If it did, it would lose its unique code identity and generate identical codes for subject categories. This could create confusion in the activities relating to text identification, corpus utilization, text processing, and data retrieval.

4.6.3 Subject Category Annotation

Following the method proposed above, we assigned a unique 2-letter code to each subject category immediately after we assigned codes to the text category. It made a file name of a text referentially unique and different from other codes. Also, due to this process, we could handle text files easily during corpus processing. We present below the process of subject category encoding to show how we could store texts in the TDIL corpus (Table 4.3).

Table 4.3 Subject category encoding in the TDIL corpus

Discipline	Code	Discipline	Code	Discipline	Code
Accountancy	AC	Administrative	AD	Advertisement	AV
Aesthetics	AE	Agriculture	AG	Anthropology	AN
Archaeology	AR	Architecture	AT	Astrology	AS
Astronomy	AM	Ayurveda	AV	Banking	BK
Biography	BG	Biology	BL	Botany	BT
Business	BM	Chemistry	CH	Child literature	CL
Cinematography	CG	Computer science	CS	Criminology	CR
Criticism	CT	Dance	DN	Diary	DR
Drama/play	DP	Drawing	DW	Ecology	EL
Economics	EC	Education	ED	Essay	ES
Fiction	FC	Folk text	FT	Games and sports	GS
Geography	GR	Geology	GL	History	HS
Hobby	HB	Humour	HR	Journalism	JL
Law and order	LW	Legal texts	LL	Legislative texts	LT
Letters	LP	Library science	LS	Linguistics	LN
Magazine	MZ	Mathematics	MT	Medicine	MD
Mythology	MY	News texts	NT	Pamphlets	PP
Philosophy	PH	Photography	PG	Physics	PH
Political science	PL	Pornography	PR	Printing technology	PT
Psychology	PS	Public Admin	PA	Religion	RL
Sculpture	SC	Sexology	SX	Short story	ST
Sociology	SL	Song/Music	SM	Statistics	ST
Travelogue	TL	Veterinary	VT	Zoology	ZO

4.6.4 Annotating Title of a Text

The subject domain that we selected for data input had its representation in the file name itself. Due to this reason, we could easily understand, after looking at a file name, to which subject domain a text belonged. For many reasons, it was not possible to preserve the full title of a text in a file name. For us, the best option was to abbreviate the title in such a manner that we could embed it within 4 characters. At the same time, we kept in mind that a corpus user, after looking at a file name, could get information to understand that a particular type of a text was kept in the file. A possible way to overcome this problem was to create an **acrostic** term by using 4 characters allotted for a title. For instance, in the Bengali text corpus, we used the code "GMGH" to refer to the title of a fiction named *Gharer Madhye Ghar* (a house inside a house), a famous novel written in Bengali by Shankar.

This kind of technique of encoding the title name of a text was, however, not a very good practice. Rather, it was a naive, back-dated, and old-fashioned one. A corpus user could derive a wrong or different name from this kind of code. We had experienced this problem several times during the time of retrieving texts from the TDIL corpus. A possible solution to this problem was to record each title and its respective code at the time of data input or corpus generation. In fact, due to several logistic and technical constraints, we had no other option but to follow this process. We stored the titles in a separate file and provided a link with the file name in the archive. Thus, it was easy for a text user to refer to the code for a particular title of a text he wanted to access from the corpus archive.

The 3-digit unit, which we used after a dot (.), determined further specification of a file name (Dash & Chaudhuri, 2000). The digits indicated the number of files generated from a text. We noted that even from a text that contained one million words, we could produce 100 files if each file contained ten thousand words (Dash, 2007). It was, therefore, rational that we allowed three digits for the number of files to be generated from a single text. It also worked for those texts that contained more amounts of data. It never exceeded the limit of 100 files from a single text. Theoretically, however, it was not a safe strategy as this could fail if there were texts containing more than one million words. In that case, our unspecified logic was to increase the number of words in each file from ten thousand to twenty thousand words or more.

Looking at the last three digits we could tell how many files were made from a particular source text. Also, it provided necessary information with regard to a text file that was under our scrutiny. For instance, .020 referred to the serial number of a file that was generated from a particular text. In a reverse manner, it had another advantage. If we were interested to access data from the last part of a text, we could do it by accessing files tagged with higher numbers.

4.6.5 Header Part: Metadata Depository

The header part of a text file in the TDIL corpus contained a detailed stock of extratextual information as metadata. In general, the extratextual information contained the following types of data: name, age, nationality and gender of the author of a text, genre of a text, year of first publication of a text, name of the publisher, place of publication of a text, edition of the text used for building a corpus, type of text considered, and other information that might be useful in future reference purposes. It was necessary to store this kind of information in a text file for various academic and non-academic purposes. This kind of data and information were applied in sociolinguistic and demographic analysis of texts as well as for addressing questions relating to legal claims on texts by copyright holders. We may get some ideas from Table 4.4 to understand how extratextual information of different kinds was represented in the header part of a text file in the TDIL corpus.

Table 4.4 Extratextual information stored in the header part of a text file

Header file	Metadata information
Title	Gharer Madhye Ghar
Language	Bengali
Genre	Written Text
Text category	Literature
Subject category	Fiction
Text type	Imaginative
Source type	Book
Publication year	1991
Edition	First
Volume	Single
Issue	Not applicable
Publisher	Dey's publication
Publication place	Kolkata, India
Author	Shankar
Gender	Male
Age	71+
Nationality	Indian
Total words	8973
Actual data	Sample text

The table above shows that the header part of a text file contained some basic information relating to a piece of text that is included in the file (McEnery & Wilson, 1996: 30). As text users, we found necessary information from the header part about the kind of text we were looking for in the corpus archive. The basic information was stored in an elaborate fashion than just giving the name of an author or the title of a text. In most cases, it also informed us about the content of a text file and supplied necessary information about the age of an author, sex of an author, date of publication of a text, variety of language used in the text, broad subject domain of a text, type of a text (*informative* or *imaginative*), and much other information. On several occasions, we used data and information from the header part in language description, addressing queries of sociolinguistic studies, and documentation of titles of texts in chronological order. We also used this information in discourse and stylistic analysis of some texts. Data was also used to address copyright conflicts and the right to use data for research and development purposes. Looking at the metadata of a header file one could retrieve extratextual information, which was not available from the text itself (Table 4.5).

The header part was accessed as it was full of different types and domains of information. Reference to this information was required for retrieving proper data from a text based on specific extratextual attributes (deHaan, 1984). In the case of automatic access of data by machine, we could use a computer to find and extract

Table 4.5 Metadata in the header part of a text file of TDIL corpus

Header part	<Doc id>B0037</doc id> <Language>Bengali</language> <category>Aesthetics</category> <subcategory>Literature-Novel</subcategory> <text>Book</text> <title>Arundhuti Tarar Rat</title> <vol></vol> <issue><issue> <headline>Arundhuti Tarar Rat</headline> <author>Amar Mitra</author> <gender>Male</gender> <words>8840</words> <pubPlace>India-Kolkata</pubPlace> <publisher>Karuna Prakashani</publisher> <pubDate>2000</pubDate> <Text ID code>65,180</Text ID code> <index>B0037</index> <date>14-Sep-2006</date> <inputter>ABC</inputter> <proof>XYZ</proof>
Text	<p>ār tārā ýena niśāchar, tāi jege āche. ei ghare konodin rod ḍhokeni, konodin rod āloo nā. ālo āchamkā nibhe gele ei ghare ýena maraṇer andhakār. bhāblei tār bhay hay. ei gharer māthāy kono ākāś nei ýe tārār ālo thākbe.</p>

a file based on information provided here. It was indeed easy for us to search and sort files in the corpus archive with reference to the data stored in the header part. For instance, if we wanted to refer to the texts composed by female writers in the archive, we could do it by referring to the information found in the header part of a file. It included a variable where the gender of an author was encoded as "Female". Thus, various kinds of data and information provided in the header part of a text file were quite useful in activities relating to text and information retrieval from the corpus archive. We could easily engage a system to access all extratextual variables included in the header part to retrieve a file we want to access. In a similar way, we could retrieve data of a particular year, text type, genre, and author from a large number of text files of the corpus archive based on extratextual information of the header part of a text file.

4.7 Conclusion

When we first developed the TDIL corpus for the Indian languages in the digital version in the last decade of the last century, we had an expectation that this corpus would contain thousands of text files made from varieties of written texts that would be used in research and development works of Indian languages (Dash, 2007). Therefore, it was necessary to design a workable method that could be handy in the storage, management, and retrieval of texts from the archive. It was not only the question of referring to the text files but also related to extraction of intralinguistic and extralinguistic data and information from files. Our simple argument was that if we could have a useful method for accessing information and data from a digital corpus archive, it would enrich the observational, descriptive, and explanatory abilities of corpus users. This was the importance of a text file name as well as the header part of a text file (Oostdijk & deHaan, 1994). When combined, these two aspects formed the basic concept of extratextual annotation; and we proposed to attach this property to each text file in the digital corpus archive.

A text file, by virtue of its composition, contains a large amount of language data. Apart from data, it contains information that is linked with intralinguistic and extralinguistic aspects of a language text. We all know that information relating to these areas varies on many aspects and features, and therefore, it is rational to devise a workable strategy through which we can store and retrieve both types of information from a text file. A well-designed text file name and the header part of a text file are able to save us from taking extra labour for searching through the entire archive for the appropriate data we are looking for. If a system is trained properly with these two aspects, it will be a useful gateway for investigators who are engaged in quick and accurate retrieval of texts from a large digital corpus archive (Leech et al., 1997).

Extratextual annotation is a workable strategy that can be effectively used for the identification, classification, and retrieval of texts based on some predefined parameters. By referring to extratextual annotation we can increase the precession of a system in both text identification and information retrieval (Zinsmeister et al., 2008). It is a quick, easy, and accurate method in the identification of a text and extraction of data from it. It also works well in description, analysis, and application of a text. This method, although was quite useful at the early stage of corpus development, is used no more in the TDIL corpus. Some new techniques are adopted for this purpose, and these are more precise, robust, and accurate in corpus file storage, management, and retrieval. Reference to an old-fashioned method of this kind, in the new world of corpus management tools and techniques, give us an idea of how, nearly thirty years ago, Indian languages text corpora were generated, stored, managed, and accessed.

References

Archer, D., & Culpeper, J. (2003). Sociopragmatic annotation: New directions and possibilities in historical corpus linguistics. In A. Wilson, P. Rayson, & T. McEnery (Eds.), *Corpus linguistics by the Lune: Studies in honour of Geoffrey Leech* (pp. 37–58). Peter Lang.

Archer, D., Culpeper, J., & Davies, M. (2008). Pragmatic annotation. In A. Lüdeling & M. Kytö (Eds.), *Corpus linguistics: An international handbook* (pp. 613–642). Gruyter.

Atkins, S., Clear, J., & Ostler, N. (1992). Corpus design criteria. *Literary and Linguistic Computing, 7*(1), 1–16.

Baker, P. (1997). Consistency and accuracy in correcting automatically tagged corpora. In R. Garside, G. Leech, & A. McEnery (Eds.), *Corpus annotation: Linguistic information from computer text corpora* (pp. 243–250). Longman.

Biber, D. (1993). Representativeness in corpus design. *Literary and Linguistic Computing, 8*(4), 243–257.

Carletta, J., McKelvie, D., Isard, A., Mengel, A., Klein, M., & Møller, M. B. (2004). A generic approach to software support for linguistic annotation using XML. In G. Sampson & D. McCarthy (Eds.), *Corpus linguistics: Readings in a widening discipline* (pp. 449–459). Continuum.

Dash, N. S. (2007). Indian scenario in language corpus generation. In N. S. Dash, P. Dasgupta, & P. Sarkar, (Eds.), *Rainbow of linguistics* (Vol. 1, pp. 129–162). T. Media Publication.

Dash, N. S. (2008). *Corpus linguistics: An introduction.* Pearson Education-Longman.

Dash, N. S. (2016). Some corpus access tools for Bengali corpus. *Indian Journal of Applied Linguistics, 42*(1–2), 7–31.

Dash, N. S., & Arulmozi, S. (2018). *History, features, and typology of language corpora.* Springer Nature.

Dash, N. S., & Chaudhuri, B. B. (2000). The process of designing a multidisciplinary monolingual sample corpus. *International Journal of Corpus Linguistics, 5*(2), 179–197.

Davidson, D. (1974). On the very idea of a conceptual scheme. In *Proceedings and Address of the American Philosophical Association* (Vol. 47 (1973–1974), pp. 5–20).

deHaan, P. (1984). Problem-oriented tagging of English corpus data. In J. Aarts & W. Meijs (Eds.), *Corpus linguistics* (pp. 123–139). Rodopi.

Fierz, W., & Grütter, R. (2000). The SGML standardization framework and the introduction of XML. *Journal of Medical Internet Research.* Published online 2000 Jun 30. [https://doi.org/10.2196/jmir.2.2.e12]

Francis, W. N. (1980). A tagged corpus: problems and prospects. In S. Greenbaum, G. Leech, & J. Svartvik, (Eds.), *Studies in English linguistics: In Honour of Randolph Quirk.* Longman.

Garside, R., Leech, G., & Sampson, G. (Eds.). (1987). *The computational analysis of English: A corpus-based approach* (pp. 30–41). Longman.

Goldfarb, C. F. (1990). *The SGML handbook.* Clarendon Press.

Johansson, S. (1995). The encoding of spoken texts. *Computers and the Humanities, 29*(1), 149–158.

Kipp, M., Neff, M., & Albrecht, I. (2007). An annotation scheme for conversational gesture: How to economically capture timing and form. *Language Resources and Evaluation, 41*(3/4), 325–339.

Kytö, M., Rissanen, M., & Wright, S. (Eds.). (1994). *Corpora across the centuries.* Rodopi.

Leech, G. (1993). Corpus annotation schemes. *Literary and Linguistic Computing, 8*(4), 275–281.

Leech, G. (1997). Introducing corpus annotation. In R. Garside, G. Leech, & A. McEnery (Eds.), *Corpus annotation: Linguistic information from computer text corpora* (pp. 1–18). Longman.

Leech, G. (2005). Adding linguistic annotation. In M. Wynne (Ed.), *Developing linguistic corpora: A guide to good practice* (pp. 17–29). Oxbow Books.

Leech, G., & Fligelstone, S. (1992). Computers and corpora analysis. In C. S. Butler (Ed.), *Computers and written texts* (pp. 115–140). Blackwell.

Leech, G., McEnery, T., & Wynne, M. (1997). Further levels of annotation. In R. Garside, G. Leech, & T. McEnery (Eds.), *Corpus annotation: Linguistic information from computer text corpora* (pp. 85–101). Longman.

McEnery, T., & Wilson, A. (1996). *Corpus linguistics.* Edinburgh University Press.

Oostdijk, N., & deHaan, P. (Eds.). (1994). *Corpus-based research into language.* Rodopi.

Rissanen, M. (1989). Three problems connected with the use of diachronic corpora. *International Computer Archive of Modern English Journal, 13*(1), 16–19.

Sinclair, J. M. (2004). *Trust the text: Language, corpus, and discourse.* Routledge.

Sinclair, J. M. (1994). Trust the text. In M. Coulthard (Ed.), *Advances in written text analysis* (pp. 12–25). Routledge.

Sperberg-McQueen, C. M., & Burnard, L. (Eds.). (1994). *Guidelines for electronic text encoding and interchange.* ACH, ALLC, and AC.

Stenström, A.-B. (1984). Discourse tags. In J. Aarts & W. Meijs (Eds.), *Corpus linguistics: Recent developments in the use of computer corpora in English language research* (pp. 65–81). Rodopi.

Wallis, S. A. (2007). Annotation, retrieval, and experimentation. In A. Meurman-Solin, & A. A. Nurmi, (Eds.), *Annotating variation and change.* Varieng, University of Helsinki, Finland (ePublished).

Zinsmeister, H., Hinrichs, E., Kübler, S., & Witt, A. (2008). Linguistically annotated corpora: Quality assurance, reusability, and sustainability. In A. Lüdeling, & M. Kytö, (Eds.), *Corpus linguistics: An international handbook* (Vol. 1, pp. 759–776). Gruyter.

Web Links

http://ftp.cis.upenn.edu/pub/treebank/doc/tagguide.ps.gz
http://helsinki.fi/varieng/CoRD/corpora/HelsinkiCorpus/HC_XML.html
http://ilc.pi.cnr.it/EAGLES96/corpustyp/corpustyp.html
http://ucrel.lancs.ac.uk/claws/
http://ucrel.lancs.ac.uk/corpora.html
http://workshare.com/solutions/what-is-metadata
https://www.ilc.pi.cnr.it/EAGLES96/corpustyp/corpustyp.html
https://github.com/TEIC/Stylesheets/tree/master/cocoa
https://sites.ualberta.ca/~dmiall/Brazil/Brazil_cocoa.htm

Chapter 5
Etymological Annotation

Abstract Etymological annotation of a corpus is a new kind of text annotation. Here, our primary goal is to annotate the source of origin of those words that are used in a piece of text. It is a crucial scheme of corpus annotation as lexical borrowing is a common and frequently applied linguistic phenomenon of all natural languages. Through lexical borrowing, every natural language is enriched over the years with a new set of words that help that language grow with time and assimilate new ideas and concepts. Since lexical borrowing is a regular and recurrent linguistic process in all natural languages, it is necessary to annotate the origin of words in a corpus, so that we can know how words are borrowed from other languages at different points in time to enrich the lexical stock of a language. Keeping the issue in mind, we introduce in this chapter a new kind of corpus text annotation, which we call etymological annotation (EA). We propose and design a usable method of annotating the source of origin of words that are used in a piece of text in a language, so that we can identify, record and document the *mother languages* from where these words are borrowed, assimilated, and naturalized in another language. Etymological annotation not only enhances the referential value of a corpus but also contributes toward the development of systems that are able to classify words based on the source of origin as well as record patterns of changes these words might have undergone while these are borrowed into another language. A real application of an etymologically annotated corpus may be realized in counting the frequency of occurrence of words of different origins in a text vis-à-vis their place in the dictionary of a language.

Keywords Etymological annotation · Lexical borrowing · Mother language · Assimilation · Naturalization · Portmanteau words · Machine learning

5.1 Introduction

When we look at the vocabulary list of any modern language, we can see that a large number of words are obtained and assimilated from many languages. For instance, when we look at a vocabulary list prepared from a corpus of modern Bengali, we find that the list contains a large number of words that the users have borrowed from foreign languages (e.g., *Arabic*, *Persian*, *Portuguese*, *Dutch*, *Spanish*, *French*,

N. S. Dash, *Language Corpora Annotation and Processing*,
https://doi.org/10.1007/978-981-16-2960-0_5

English, *German*, *Russian*, *Chinese*, *Japanese*, and others). It has also inherited and borrowed from many Indian languages (e.g., *Odia, Assamese*, *Sanskrit*, *Hindi*, *Gujarati*, *Tamil*, *Malayalam*, *Marathi*, and others) besides having its own words inherited from native and local sources (Acharya, 1985; Amin, 2012; Basu, 2015; Das, 2010; Datta, 2008; Sarkar, 2015). While we do a linguistic analysis of these words, we find that most of the words are naturalized into Bengali to such an extent that it is now difficult for us to trace their actual source of origin or etymological antiquity. In the majority of cases, these words are naturalized into Bengali through various word formation processes (e.g., *adoption, adaptation, assimilation*, *inflection*, *compounding*, *analogy*, etc.) which are quite active in Bengali over the centuries (Sarkar & Basu, 1994; Chakravarti, 1994; Chakravarty, 1974; Chattopadhyay, 1995; Chaki, 1996). Most of these word formation processes are still active and productive in this language (Dash et al., 2009). Due to this factor, many so-called "foreign words" are no more "foreign" to us; they are on the verge of losing their original identity. This leads us to explore the phenomena of naturalization in a language as well as introduce the concept of etymological annotation. Here, our primary goal is to annotate etymological information to the words used in the corpus, so that we can identify which words have entered in the language and are regularly used in the borrower language texts. Also, we plan to utilize this information for future reference and application purposes.

Etymological annotation (EA) on a corpus becomes necessary for the analysis of the vocabulary of a language. It also becomes necessary when a large number of words of a language are obtained from various other languages and when these words are assimilated with indigenous lexical stock. Also, the etymological source of words has to be marked in a text because such texts become useful for the linguistic description of words, compiling reference dictionaries, source-based lexical classification, and language-specific synset generation for WordNets (Dash et al., 2017). Keeping these requirements in view, in this chapter, we have carried out the following tasks:

- Classified the present Bengali vocabulary based on etymology
- Defined an elaborate tagset for annotating words,
- Used the tagset to annotate the source of origin of words,
- Discussed the methods and strategies we have adopted for annotating words,
- Addressed the challenges involved in annotation of portmanteau words (i.e., words that are made with two or more parts taken from different languages),
- Discussed applicational relevance of etymologically annotated corpus in linguistic studies and technological engineering, and
- Justified the scheme of work in a wider frame of text annotation and machine learning.

From a theoretical point of view, the present chapter is visualized as an attempt for correcting the tendency that desires to see a language as "natively pure" and considers "borrowing" as an external event. We also desire to spread the message during the future engagement of scholars to understand "annotation as an event of theory building and validation" (i.e., building a knowledgebase on annotation) as well as "annotation as a process of adding information to texts" (i.e., building an annotated corpus).

In this chapter, we discuss different stages of etymological annotation covering activities like vocabulary classification, tagset design, implementation of the annotation process, and others. In Sect. 5.2, we present a short sketch on the global scenario of lexical borrowing; in Sect. 5.3, we focus on vocabulary classification with reference to the etymology of words; in Sect. 5.4, we define an elaborate language-based tagset for etymological annotation; in Sect. 5.5, we discuss strategies that we have adopted for etymological annotation; in Sect. 5.6, we discuss the actual process of etymological annotation we have applied, in Sect. 5.7, we identify the most frequently used English words in an etymologically annotated Bengali text; in Sect. 5.8, we record the major findings from an etymologically annotated text; in Sect. 5.9, we highlight the concept of *system adoption* as an outcome of etymological annotation; and in Sect. 5.10, we discuss the application of an etymologically annotated corpus in linguistics and other domains.

5.2 Lexical Borrowing: Some Scenarios

Lexical borrowing is a common linguistic process for all natural languages. The etymological analysis of borrowed words shows how words are borrowed into a language. It also shows how words undergo structural changes while they are borrowed, how original forms and meanings of borrowed words are affected due to borrowing, and how borrowed words are used in speech and writing in borrower language. Most of the advanced languages (e.g., *English, French, Spanish, Italian, Portuguese, German, Russian, Japanese, Chinese,* and others) are rich with a large number of words that are borrowed from other languages. For instance, English has borrowed words from many languages over the centuries. In a recent study, it is reported that words from as many as 350 languages are represented in English vocabulary and it makes up nearly 80% of the present vocabulary of the language (Stamper, 2017). Several Web sources have also informed us that a major part of the English vocabulary has come from the following languages (alphabetically): *Anglo-Saxon, Australian Aboriginal, African origin, Arabic, Balinese, Bengali, Chinese, Czech, Danish, Dayak, Dutch, Etruscan, Finnish, French, Gaelic, Gaulish, German, Greek, Hawaiian, Hebrew, Hindi, Hungarian, indigenous languages of the Americas, Indonesian, Irish, Italian, Japanese, Korean, Latin, Malaya, Maori, Papuan, Norwegian, Old Norse, Persian, Philippine, Polish, Portuguese, Romani, Romanian, Russian, Sami, Sanskrit, Scots, Scottish, Serbo-Croatian, Slovak, Spanish, Sumatran, Sudanese, Swedish, Tamil, Turkic, Ukrainian, Urdu, Welsh, Yiddish, Zulu*, and many others.

Similar to English, the modern Bengali language has a large number of words that are borrowed from other languages over many centuries. Most of the words are assimilated and naturalized into its present vocabulary. From a rough estimate, we may claim that Bengali has borrowed words from near about 30 Indian and foreign languages. These languages include (alphabetically) *Arabic, Assamese, Bihari, Burmese, Chinese, Dutch, English, German, Gujarati, Hindi, Japanese,*

Kannada, Kashmiri, Kurdmali, Malayalam, Mundari, Nepali, Odia, Pali, Persian, Portuguese, Prakrit, Punjabi, Russian, Sanskrit, Santali, Spanish, Tamil, and Urdu. When we scrutinize the present vocabulary more closely, we find traces of some other languages also (e.g., *aboriginal languages and regional dialects*) into its vocabulary (Basu, 2015; Das, 2010; Datta, 2008; Sarkar, 2015).

The striking fact is that, in most cases, there is no scientific documentation except one or two etymological dictionaries, to know which words are directly inherited from ancestral languages and which words are borrowed from neighboring and foreign languages. It is, therefore, a challenge for us to find out how the present Bengali vocabulary has evolved over the centuries and how these words have undergone structural changes and semantic modifications due to the influence of indigenous, neighboring, and foreign languages. Here, we notice the theoretical importance of etymological annotation on a corpus. We understand that etymological annotation becomes theoretically and practically significant when words in a corpus are properly annotated with information of their origin and evolution.

(a) Theoretically, information of lexical borrowing gives us enough insight to formulate methods for language description for recognition of the impact of neighboring and foreign languages in building up the vocabulary of a language.
(b) Practically, etymological annotation helps us in compiling dictionaries of word origin for building structured knowledge texts for empowering speech communities and providing linguistic support in the development of knowledge-based societies.

From a practical angle, in the area of language technology, an etymologically annotated corpus is useful in lexical search, machine learning, word-sense disambiguation, and machine translation as the diagram shows (Fig. 5.1).

The annotation method and strategy that we propose here have some advantages. It helps to solve problems of etymological indeterminacy as we can document proper etymological information of each word used in a corpus. Here, each word is annotated with a tag referring to its source language of origin. At the initial stage, the

Fig. 5.1 Theoretical and practical relevance of etymological annotation

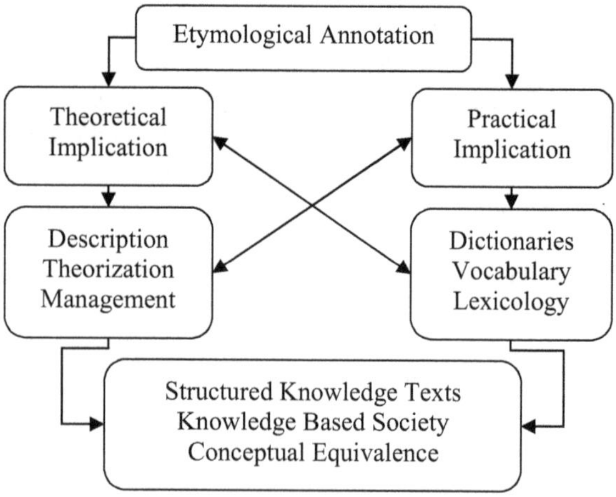

work is carried out manually to generate a trial corpus. We plan to utilize this trial corpus to train scholars and systems to annotate future Bengali corpora with accurate etymological information. Later these corpora may be used for designing a supervised or semi-supervised annotation system (Leech & Fligelstone, 1992). The annotated corpus can also be used as training data for machine learning and annotation automatization in later phases. The final goal is to make a tool or system that can automatically annotate a corpus at the etymological level by using information and data from a machine learning system. Keeping this goal in mind, we have developed a strategy for etymological annotation and have discussed this in this chapter. On an experimental basis, we have annotated the sources of origin of words in a Bengali corpus and marked the languages these words are borrowed from.

5.3 Vocabulary Classification

Vocabulary classification is a useful process for vocabulary analysis, lexical type description, and lexical record generation in a language. In language engineering, it is an important part of language-specific lexical information retrieval, knowledge representation, and machine learning (Jha et al., 2011). After classifying the vocabulary of a language, we identify the source of origin of words and mark them in that order. For instance, in Bengali, we classify the naturalized word $iskul_{\backslash ENG\backslash}$ "school" as an English word because although the word is a part of the present Bengali vocabulary, the immediate source of origin of the word is English. Therefore, we classify and annotate it as an English word. By applying this method, we not only identify words and terms that belong to other languages but also understand how such words are evolved and naturalized in Bengali. For instance, in the above example, we show that the original English word (i.e., *school*) is naturalized in modern Bengali through a phonological process called "prosthesis." Thus, we gather information of morphophonemic changes the words undergo through naturalization (Rissanen, 1989).

Another purpose of vocabulary classification is to gather information about the source of origin of a word that has come to be used in another language. For instance, according to different surveys carried out at different points in time, the percentages of English words that are taken from different language group are as follows: Latin (29%), French (29%), Germanic (26%), Greek (6%), and others (10%). That means about 84% of English words are borrowed from Germanic, French, and Latin (Finkenstaedt & Wolff, 1973). Moreover, 12% of words are taken from Greek, and other languages, i.e., Chinese, Spanish, and Japanese (Williams, 1986) (Fig. 5.2).

In a similar manner, it is found that a large section of the present Bengali vocabulary is borrowed from several languages including *Arabic, Persian, English, Hindi, Portuguese*, *Russian, Dutch,* and others although it has words inherited from Sanskrit and taken from many indigenous sources (Sarkar & Basu, 1994; Chaki, 1996; Shaw, 1999; Basu, 2015; Sarkar, 2015). At present, due to naturalization, most of the words that are borrowed from foreign languages have become a part of the modern Bengali vocabulary. These words are in regular use in speech and writing of native Bengali

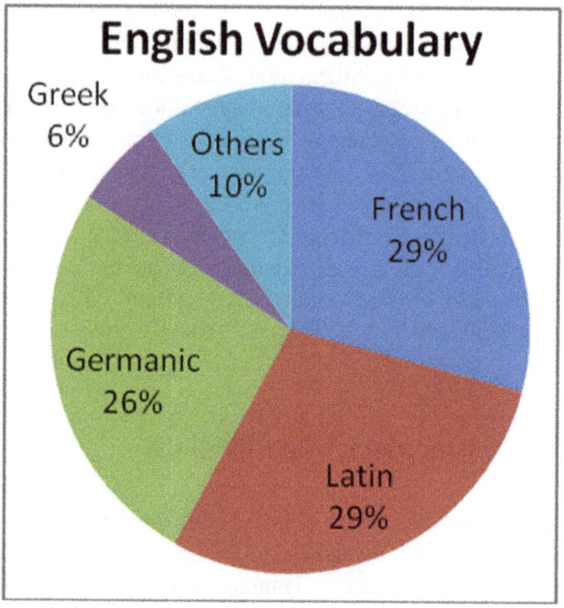

Fig. 5.2 Distribution of words in modern English vocabulary

Table 5.1 Word of different origin in the Bengali vocabulary

Native/National words	Usage (%)	Foreign words	Usage (%)
Tatsama words	40.17	English words	14.05
Tadbhava words	16.12	Arabic words	6.04
Deśi words	10.08	Persian words	5.03
Others	5.45	Others	3.06
Total	71.82	Total	28.18

speakers. The following list (Table 5.1) presents a tentative percentage of words in the modern Bengali vocabulary with regard to their source of origin. It reveals that the percentage of *Tatsama* words in modern Bengali is the highest followed by that of *Tadbhaba, Deśi, English, Persian,* and *Arabic* words. It shows that a combination of native and national words (71.82%) is higher than that of all foreign words put together (28.18%). Most of the native words belong to *Tatsama* and most of the foreign words belong to English (Dash, 2007).

In some earlier studies, it is observed that the number of Arabic and Persian words is higher than English in fifteenth- to eighteenth-century Bengali vocabulary (Musa & Elias, 2003). This is quite natural because Bengali people used to use these words to interact with Muslim rulers and their associates, who ruled Bengal for nearly 600 years before the British people came to rule (Chatterji, 1926; Majumder, 1993; Maiick et al., 1998; Shaw, 1999; Sen, 1992). After the beginning of the British regime in Bengal, Arabic and Persian words started to lose their use in Bengal to give place to English words due to several sociopolitical reasons. At present, the number of Arabic and Persian words is frozen due to increasing use of English words in modern Bengali life. A recent study on modern Bengali texts shows that the majority of English words that came into Bengali vocabulary nearly a century ago are now naturalized (Dash et al., 2009). Due to this reason, it has become a challenge to trace their origin and mark their etymology. This is one of the factors for introducing the concept of etymological annotation of a corpus.

We argue that etymological information should be annotated to words within a piece of text in accordance with their source of origin. It will help us, at the later stages, to know which languages these words have come from into our language. To achieve this goal, following the standard method of vocabulary classification, we divide words used in modern Bengali into three types:

(a) **Inherited vocabulary:** It includes words that we inherit from our mother language. It also includes words that we collect from indigenous sources. For example, Bengali words inherited from *Sanskrit, Tatsama, Tadbhaba, Deśi,* and dialects are put into this category.
(b) **National vocabulary:** It includes words that we obtain from regional and national languages. For Bengali, it covers words taken from *Hindi, Assamese, Odia, Marathi, Kashmiri, Urdu, Tamil, Malayalam, Telugu,* and other Indian languages.
(c) **Foreign vocabulary:** It includes words that we borrowed from foreign languages. For Bengali, words borrowed from *English, French, Persian, Arabic,* and others are kept in this category.

We present below an etymology-based classified list of words that we have collected from a corpus of written Bengali texts. It shows how modern Bengali vocabulary is formed with words of different languages (only three or fewer words are given from each language, as examples).

(a) Inherited Vocabulary

Bengali	kāl "time," rāstā "road," ghar "house"
Indigenous	ḍiṅgi "canoe," jhā̃ṭā "broom," jhol "broth"
Tadbhaba	āj "today," āṭ "eight," unun "oven"
Tatsama	aṅga "body," akṣi "eye," agni, "fire"

(b) National Vocabulary

Hindi	kāmāi "income," bātābaraṇ "climate," lāgātār "constant"
Odia	dālmā "mixed veg curry," meṛa "idol," pādā "barren land"
Santali	kurāṭ "axe," khā̃ṛi "lagoon," biṛā "bundle"
Tamil	curuṭ "cigar," khokā "boy," pile "kid"

(c) Foreign Vocabulary

African	jebrā "Zebra," bhubhujelā "vuvuzela"
Arabic	ārji "request," kisyā "story," jilā "district"
Australian	kyāṅgāru "Kangaroo," koyālā "koala"

Burmese	ghughni "spicy curry," luṅgi "lungi"
Chinese	chā "tea," chini "sugar," ṭāiphun "typhoon"
Dutch	hartan "harten," ruitan "ruhiten," iskāban "skophen"
English	āpil "appeal," āpel "apple," kamiṭi "committee"
French	ā̃tāt "entate," ā̃tel "intellectual," byāle "ballet"
German	jār "Tsar," nātsi "Nazi," gārḍen "garten"
Hybrid	slibhhīn "sleeveless," oṣṭhagrāphi, "art of kissing"
Italian	kompāni "company," gejeṭ "gazette," phyāsist "Fascist"
Japanese	hārākiri "hara-kiri," hāiku "haiku," bansāi "bonsai"
Persian	kāmān "canon," kharid "purchase," cāmac "spoon"
Peruvian	kuināin, "quinine"
Portuguese	ālmāri "almirah," gudām "go-down," cābi "key"
Russian	spuṭnik "sputnik," glāsnast "glasnost," istāhār "manifesto"
Spanish	kamreḍ "comrade," ārmāḍā "armada"
Tibetan	iyāk "yak," lāmā "Llama"
Unknown	harpoon "harpoon"

This kind of scheme for classifying words in a language is, however, open for revision based on the name of a source language from where words are either inherited or borrowed. English, for instance, includes *Scandinavian, Greek, Latin, French, German, Spanish, Italian,* and other languages into its list, while Tamil (a Dravidian language) includes *Sanskrit, Malayalam, Telugu, Kannada,* and other languages as primary sources of words.

5.4 Defining Etymological Annotation Tagset

Etymological annotation is a kind of corpus annotation where information about the origin of words is attached to words within a piece of text. The primary purpose of this annotation is to collect information about the source of origin of words that have been used in a text, vis-a-vis language. It is known to us that words that are used in a text come from various sources—indigenous sources, neighboring languages, regional languages, national languages, and foreign languages. This phenomenon, for linguistic and non-linguistic reasons, carries high importance in many studies related to languages and people. In principle, it is necessary to record etymological information of words that are regularly used in the generation of texts in a language. It helps us to know how words have come into a language and how they are evolving over a long period through usage. For instance, most of the Indian languages have inherited words from Sanskrit and borrowed words from neighboring and foreign languages besides using their indigenous sources. At the time of etymological annotation, we want to mark this information to words in a corpus. To serve this purpose for Bengali, we use the following tagset for words of different origins. After we apply these tags to words, it becomes easy for us to know the actual source of origin of words (Table 5.2).

Table 5.2 Tagset and examples of vocabulary tagging in Bengali

Language	Tag	Examples
Bengali	\BNG\	kāl, rāstā, ghar, samay, ẏeman, kathā, dhuti, śāṛi, meye, chele, bābā, kākā, māmā
Sanskrit	\SKT\	aṅga, akṣi, agni, aśva, indu, īśvar, kānti, krodh, charaṇ, jīban, nakṣatra, śakti, śubhra
Tadbhaba	\TDV\	āj, āṭ, unun, kāṭh, kāj, kayā, gā, cākā, jāmāi, jhi, pākhi, bhāi, māchi, māch, hāti
Native	\NTV\	ḍiṅgi, jhā̃ṭā, jhol, ḍhil, ḍhol, jhiṅgā, ḍheu
English	\ENG\	āpil, āpel, rel, bās, kamiṭi, ḍāktār, brāś, myān, sṭriṭ, sṭeśan, haspiṭāl, ṭāim, aphis, belṭ, halṭ
Hindi	\HND\	roṭi, puri, miṭhāi, baṭuyā, tarkāri, kāmāi, samjhotā, bātābaraṇ, lāgātār, hāṅgāmā, selām, ostād, mastān, jādughar, hāl, hartāl, bakoyās
Arabic	\ARB\	aku, ākkel, ākher, ārji, kisyā, khāś, khāsi, gost, imārat, jilā, dābi, bāki, muhuri, rāji, sipāhi, suphi, hāsil, hisāb, hukum
Persian	\PRS\	āmdaj, āmir, iyār, ujir, kām, kāmān, kārdāni, kārsāji, kharac, kharid, khub, khuśi, kitab, khorāk, garam, gardān, carbi, caśmā, cākar, cāmac, cālāk
Foreign	\FRN\	ātā, ālkātrā, ālmāri, ālpin
Hybrid	\HRB\	nārsāyā (nurse + ayah), myānochit (man + uchit), bā̃kademi (Bangla + akademi), slibhhīn (sleeve + hīn), ciyārkanyā (cheer + kanyā), citiṃbāj (cheating + bāj), biṭrebāj (betray + bāj), siniktama (cynic + tama), parnokuṭīr (porn + kuṭīr), oṣṭhagrāphi (oṣṭha + grāphy), relgāṛi (rail + gāṛi), phāṅgāmā (fun + hāṅgāmā), udhāolyānḍ (udhao + land), meṭrobāsī (metro + bāsī)
Unknown	\UNN\	jār, nātsi, kamreḍ, ārmāḍā, kompāni, gejeṭ, phyāsisṭ, spuṭnik, glāsnast, istāhār, hārpun, cā, cini, licu, sāmpān, ṭāiphun, ghughni, luṅgi, jebrā, kuināin, kyāṅgāru, riksā, hārākiri, bansāi,kimono, hāiku, iyāk, iyeti, lāmā

Annotating etymological information to words in a corpus is not a trivial task. An annotator requires sound knowledge about the etymological history of words to be successful in this kind of work. Therefore, it is wiser to engage those people who know about this area of study and have an interest in etymology in this work. When trained scholars are not available, we gather information from structured knowledge texts (e.g., *etymological dictionary*, *dialect dictionary*, *dictionary of word origin*, *foreign word dictionary*, *historical dictionary*, *grammar*, and *encyclopedia*) to serve purposes. These resources are consulted to check, verify, and authenticate the source of origin of words before words are annotated. Most of the advanced languages use words from other languages along with words of their own vocabulary. We argue that during etymological annotation, information about the source of words is marked in such a way that it becomes easily accessible to both man and machine. To achieve this goal, we should develop a well-formed tagset, which we can uniformly apply to all kinds of corpora of a language. For the Indian languages, we have proposed the following tagset considering the fact that the majority of the Indian languages have words that have come from other languages (Table 5.3).

Table 5.3 Etymological tagset for the Indian languages

No.	Language	Tag	No	Language	Tag
1	African	\AFR\	16	Japanese	\JPN\
2	Arabic	\ARB\	17	Native	\NTV\
3	Assamese	\ASM\	18	Odia	\ODI\
4	Australian	\AUS\	19	Persian	\PRS\
5	Bengali	\BNG\	20	Peruvian	\PRV\
6	Burmese	\BRM\	21	Portuguese	\PRG\
7	Chinese	\CHN\	22	Russian	\RSN\
8	Dialectal	\DLT\	23	Santali	\SNT\
9	Dutch	\DTH\	24	Spanish	\SPN\
10	English	\ENG\	25	Tadbhaba	\TDV\
11	French	\FRN\	26	Tamil	\TAM\
12	German	\GMC\	27	Tatsama	\TSM\
13	Hindi	\HND\	28	Telugu	\TLG\
14	Hybrid	\H RB\	29	Tibetan	\TBT\
15	Italian	\ITL\	30	Unknown	\UNN\

There are many applicational advantages of a corpus, which is annotated with etymological information.

(a) It helps us to know which words in the corpus are of native origin and which words are of non-native origin.
(b) It supplies elaborate information to know what kind of native affixes are used with foreign words (and vice versa) to produce new kinds of words in a language.
(c) It supplies information to know which indigenous words have combined with foreign words to generate compounds and portmanteau words.
(d) Information derived from the above areas becomes useful in frequency calculation of words of various origins as well as language teaching and compilation of general and foreign word dictionaries.

In this context, it is to be noted that the levels of annotation that are considered to be added to words are realized in terms of the nature of their *integration*. That means etymological information may be annotated to a *root morpheme, a word without inflection, an inflected word, affixed word, multiword unit, or an inflected multiword unit*. This assists us to integrate etymological annotation into a lemmatizer, part-of-speech annotator, or a morph analyzer. This issue will also arise in the speech-act analysis and parsing as well as semantic analysis and parsing, etc.

5.5 Defining Annotation Strategy

The tagset that we propose (Table 5.3) is primarily designed for annotating first-level information to words of different language sources. We can also prepare a plan for elaborate annotation based on the nature and range of vocabulary of a language. Encoding an extra layer of information to words is, however, a far more challenging task. It can be initiated once the first layer of an annotation is over.

5.5.1 Annotating Borrowed Words

In this section, we propose only language-level tags. It primarily marks the source language a word is borrowed from. We may, however, include a second layer (in hierarchical order) to mark information of morphophonemic changes a word has undergone. It might happen that at the time of use in a text, a word has passed through the process of inflection, derivation, compounding, and others in a borrower language. Due to such operations, a word might have changed in surface form, meaning, and usage. For instance, consider the Bengali word *bālti* "bucket." Etymologically, it is perhaps derived from English *balty* (Campos), which is again derived from Portuguese *bālde* (cf. Hindi *bālṭī,* Gujarati *bāldī*). In this case, the word has undergone a phonological change after it is borrowed into Bengali. This information is annotated explicitly with the word through a process called **sequential annotation**.

- bālti\ENG_PRG\

The process of sequential annotation indicates an etymological hierarchy of a word under annotation. It indicates that the word is borrowed into Bengali from English, while English has borrowed it from Portuguese. Therefore, English is the primary source for Bengali, while Portuguese is the secondary source. This kind of sequential annotation is necessary in case of those words which have come into a language through another language as an intermediate source. For instance, words like *resṭurenṭ, kindārgārḍen,* and *myāṭāḍor* have come into Bengali from English, while English has borrowed these words from French, German, and Spanish, respectively. Therefore, in the Bengali corpus, these words are annotated in the following manner:

- resṭurenṭ\ENG_FRN\
- kindārgārḍen\ENG_GER\
- myāṭāḍor\ENG_SPN\

One may, however, argue if this kind of sequential annotation is at all necessary in a corpus text because the goal of this annotation is to mark the immediate source of origin of the word. There is no need to specify all those languages a word has passed through to reach to a borrower language. In that case, for instance, if only the immediate source language is annotated, the basic goal of this annotation is achieved. Further information may be available from an etymological dictionary.

Table 5.4 Etymological annotation of portmanteau words

Portmanteau	Annotation	Gloss
hukumdātā	\ARB + BNG\	"order giver"
selāikal	\PRS + BNG\	"sewing machine"
magajdholāi	\PRS + BNG\	"brainwash"
sinemākhor	\ENG + BNG\	"cinema addict"
klāśghar	\ENG + BNG\	"classroom"
noṭbai	\ENG + BNG\	"notebook"
bhoṭdātā	\ENG + BNG\	"voter"
hātbyāg	\BNG + ENG\	"handbag"
dukalam	\BNG + ENG\	"two columns"
chārlāin	\BNG + ENG\	"four lines"

5.5.2 *Annotating Portmanteau Words*

The portmanteau words are those words which are made with two separate words and these two words have come from two different languages. In the case of portmanteau words, words of two different languages are put together to make a compound word. For example, look at the examples given in the list (Table 5.4). It shows that in the Bengali corpus, there are many compound words which are made with two separate words—one word belongs to Bengali, while the other word belongs to a foreign language.

The process of annotation of such words is a tricky challenge. We follow a very simple process that partially serves our purpose. We put the annotation at the end of the word within the slash bracket keeping information of both the languages in sequential order with a + sign in the following manner (e.g., *bhoṭdātā\ENG + BNG\ "voter"*). It indicates that this is a portmanteau word where the first part is an English word (i.e., *bhoṭ\ENG\ "vote"*), and the second part is a Bengali word (i.e., *dātā\BNG\ "giver"*). Both the parts are combined to generate a compound portmanteau word in the language.

5.5.3 *Annotating Affixed Words*

In the case of affixed words, annotation is done in a slightly different manner. During this process, it is noted that there are four types of affixed words in Bengali and they need different ways of annotation.

(a) Foreign words with foreign affix written in Bengali orthography, e.g., *ḍyānsiṃ* "dancing," *peinṭiṃ* "painting," *sāikliṃ* "cycling," etc.
(b) Bengali words with Bengali affix written in Bengali orthography, e.g., *mahilārā* "ladies," *lokera* "people," *pākhiguli* "birds," etc.

Table 5.5 Annotation of affixed words with the nixed formation

Affixed forms	Annotation	Gloss
leḍijrā	\ENG + BNG\	"ladies"
jenṭsrā	\ENG + BNG\	"gentlemen"
aṭooyālā	\ENG + BNG\	"auto-driver"
ṭichārgiri	\ENG + BNG\	"teachership"
sāikelgulo	\ENG + BNG\	"cycles"
khepchuriās	\BNG + ENG\	"angry"
sāmājikyāli	\BNG + ENG\	"socially"
ḍākiṃ	\BNG + ENG\	"calling"

(c) Foreign words with Bengali affix written in Bengali orthography, e.g., *leḍijrā* "ladies," jenṭsrā "gents," *sāikelgulo* "cycles," etc.
(d) Bengali words with foreign affix written in Bengali orthography, e.g., *khepchuriās* "angry," *sāmājikyāli* "socially," *ḍākiṃ* "calling," etc.

The annotation of the words of group (a) is not a problem. These are uniformly annotated as English words (e.g., *ḍyānsiṃ\ENG*). The annotation of the words of the group (b) is also not a problem. These are uniformly annotated as Bengali words (e.g., *lokera\BNG*). The annotation of words of the group (c) and (d) are quite challenging as these words are made in a complex process. The words of the last two groups are annotated in the following manner (Table 5.5).

5.5.4 *Annotating Inflected Words*

In the case of the inflected words, the typical trend in Bengali is that the borrowed foreign words are attached with Bengali inflections without any change in the structure of English words. The only change that is noted is that these English words are transliterated into Bengali before the Bengali inflections are added to them (e.g., *pener* "of a pen," *ṭrene* "in train," *bāser* "of a bus," etc.). These words also need sequential annotation—one for the base form (or stem) and the other for the inflection. Following the same strategy used for the affixed words, these words are also annotated in the following manner (Table 5.6).

5.6 Process of Etymological Annotation

In this section, we present a small sample text to give an idea about how we have annotated words in a written Bengali text corpus with their etymological information (Dash & Hussain, 2013). When we look at the annotated text, we understand that it has many linguistic applications which can be realized after the annotated corpus

Table 5.6 Annotation of inflected words with the nixed formation

Inflected words	Annotation	Gloss
māiler	\ENG + BNG\	"of a mile"
chānse	\ENG + BNG\	"in a chance"
sṭeśane	\ENG + BNG\	"at a station"
haler	\ENG + BNG\	"of a hall"
sṭore	\ENG + BNG\	"in a store"
ṭrāme	\ENG + BNG\	"in a tram"
bāser	\ENG + BNG\	"of a bus"

is put into a computer system for machine learning and text processing. We can do etymological annotation manually or automatically. At a trial stage, we did it manually to make the output text open for expert verification and necessary modification. Once an annotated text is checked and certified, it may be used as a benchmarked text for designing an automated tool. By using the tagset (Table 5.3), we have manually annotated a small Bengali text sample. For simplification, the Bengali text is rendered into Roman with diacritics. The text is further supported by a literal translation into English (Fig. 5.3).

When a piece of text is ready after normalization, the process of etymological annotation starts. Each word of a sentence is manually annotated with its basic etymological information. For each word, necessary reference and information are drawn from etymological dictionaries or other structure knowledge texts that are available in Bengali. Given below is an example that shows how words in a Bengali text mentioned above are annotated with etymological information derived from various sources (Fig. 5.4).

For automatic etymological annotation, we have to design and develop a tool for this specific purpose. The tool will work in such a manner that it is able to annotate every single and multiword unit in a text with a proper etymological tag. For this, we have to empower the tool with a digitized lexical database that contains relevant information. We call it a machine-readable etymological dictionary (MRED), which stores words arranged alphabetically with detailed etymological information. The tool has to be trained in such a manner that it can collect necessary etymological information from MRED to apply the same on words to mark their source language information. This is a challenging task as a high rate of accuracy has to be represented in the MRED with accurate and valid information retrieved from structured knowledge texts and verified by experts of a language. The first part of the preparation for developing an automatic etymological annotation system includes the following stages:

(a) Build an MRED with detailed etymological information for each word used in language.
(b) Integrate MRED with an etymological annotation tool as a supporting resource.
(c) Apply etymological annotation tool on a normalized text corpus.

Bengali Text in Roman script with diacritics

kṛṣṇa ebār mādhyamik parīkṣā debe. kṛṣṇer mā balechhen, āmār keṣṭa myāṭrik pāś karle moṭar sāikel kine debo, kaleje paṛte ýābe. kṛṣṇer bāp bhuṣimāler kārbāri. tini balechhen, osab habe nā. pāś karle dokāne basiye debo. jami jiret nei, dokān nā dekhle khābe kī ? kaleje paṛe ki chākri karbe? pāś karle chārṭe jāmā, duṭo phatuyā, ār chārṭe luṅgi kine debo. otei habe. baṛa jor ekṭā sāikel. tāi śune kṛṣṇer man khub khārāp. kṛṣṇer ṭhākumā śune balechhen, ore keṣṭā, bhābis nā. pāś karle tor ekṭā be debo. sukhe saṃsār karbi ār bāper dokān sāmlābi.

English translation

Krishna is going to appear for the secondary examination this year. His mother has said, when my Krishna passes this exam, I shall buy him a motorbike. He will go to college. Krishna's father is a grocery shop owner. He has said, nothing of this sort is going to happen. I shall put him into my shop after he passes out. Is he going to get a service after going to college? We have no land and others. What will he eat if he does not take care of the shop? I shall give him four shirts, four phatuyas, and four lungis. That will do. At best a bicycle. Krishna is mentally very upset hearing this. His grandmother said to Krishna, dear Krishna, don't worry. I shall get you married after you pass out. You will live happily and take care of your father's shop.

Fig. 5.3 Sample Bengali text and its translation into English

After the trial stage is over, a tool becomes robust and powerful with a limited chance for errors. The process of automatic annotation of words on a large raw corpus may be carried out in accordance with the following steps.

Step 1: Encounter a word in a text in the corpus.
Step 2: Match the word with words stored in MRED.
Step 3: Extract etymological information from MRED.
Step 4: Mark the word with a relevant etymological tag.
Step 5: Generates the annotated output.

An expert etymologist may monitor the whole process when the tool works on a text in a corpus. The annotation tool will work on all kinds of words found in a text. That means all affixed, non-affixed, inflected, non-inflected, naturalized, compound, reduplicated, multiword, and hybrid words are put to annotation without any discrimination (Rayson et al., 2006). In the beginning, we consider only surface-level information for annotation. We may increase the layers and amount of information if we find this information inadequate at later stages.

ST0001	kṛṣṇa\SKT\ ebār\BNG\ mādhyamik\SKT\ parīkṣā\SKT\ debe\BNG\.
ST0002	kṛṣṇer\SKT\ mā\TDV\ balechhen\BNG\, āmār\BNG\ keṣṭā\TDV\ myāṭrik\ENG\ pāś\ENG\ karle\BNG\ moṭar\ENG\ sāikel\ENG\ kine\BNG\ debo\BNG\.
ST0003	kaleje\ENG\ paṛte\BNG\ ýābe\BNG\.
ST0004	kṛṣṇer\SKT\ bāp\TDV\ bhuṣimāler\PRS\ kārbāri\ARB\.
ST0005	tini\BNG\ balechhen\BNG\, osab\BNG\ habe\BNG\ nā\BNG\.
ST0006	pāś\ENG\ karle\BNG\ dokāne\PRS\ basiye\BNG\ debo\BNG\.
ST0007	jami\ARB\ jiret\ARB\ nei\BNG\, dokān\ARB\ nā\BNG\ dekhle\BNG\ khābe\TDB\ kī\TDV\?
ST0008	kaleje\ENG\ paṛe\BNG\ ki\TDV\ chākri\PRS\ karbe\BNG\ ?
ST0009	pāś\ENG\ karle\BNG\ chārṭe\TDV\ jāmā\ARB\, duṭo\TDV\ phatuyā\PRS\, chārṭe\TDV\ luṅgi\UNN\ kine\TDV\ debo\BNG\.
ST0010	otei\BNG\ habe\BNG\.
ST0011	baṛa\TDV\ jor\ARB\ ekṭā\TDV\ sāikel\ENG\.
ST0012	tāi\TDV\ śune\BNG\ kṛṣṇer\SKT\ man\SKT\ khub\PRS\ khārāp\PRS\.
ST0013	kṛṣṇer\SKT\ ṭhākumā\TDV\ śune\BNG\ balechhen\BNG\, ore\NTV\ keṣṭā\TDV\, bhābis\BNG\ nā\BNG\.
ST0014	pāś\ENG\ karle\BNG\ tor\BNG\ ekṭā\TDV\ be\TDV\ debo\BNG\.
ST0015	sukhe\SKT\ saṃsār\SKT\ karbi\BNG\ ār\BNG\ bāper\TDV\ dokān\ARB\ sāṁlābi\BNG\.

Fig. 5.4 Sample Bengali text annotated at etymological level

To overcome problems of disputes in annotation, we have to decide the origin of words with specific information collected from authoritative knowledge texts (e.g., *etymological dictionary*) of a language. By referring to knowledge texts, we can solve doubts about the origin of words. In case of ambiguity also, we can refer to etymological or historical dictionaries. In the case of those words, which are found unannotated in a corpus, we need to further verify data and information in MRED. If required, we have to augment new data and information in the MRED. That means we have to modify and upgrade MRED regularly to succeed in the annotation of all words in a corpus. After this process, an annotated text will offer new insights and information to man and machine. For a human, an annotated corpus presents a ratio of the use of words of different origins in a text. For a machine, it helps a tool to identify the major patterns of use of words of different origin in a text. Based on this, a software engineer can develop a prediction method on the patterns of use of words of different origins in a language. It can also help to determine the type of a text or diachronic stage of a language.

5.7 Findings of an Etymologically Annotated Text

For a pilot study, we have etymologically annotated all words in a modern Bengali newspaper text corpus. This corpus was randomly prepared with texts collected from several domains. It contained a hundred thousand Bengali words. The results that we obtained from this pilot study gave some new information. We found that the percentage of use of words of different language origins varies quite largely in Bengali newspapers. Also, it sheds some light on the present status of the Bengali language and the patterns of use of words of different origins in newspaper texts (Table 5.7).

We may not like to consider this annotated corpus as a faithful representative of the modern Bengali language. However, the findings from this text have some values and linguistic implications. The use of words of indigenous origin is the highest in modern Bengali followed by *Tadbhaba* and English words. They form the largest part of the modern Bengali vocabulary (73.48%). It also shows that the percentage of English words in Bengali is quite high (15.13%). It is more than the percentage of *Tatsama* words in modern Bengali. It is a clear indication of the change in the distribution of words in modern Bengali vocabulary. The Arabic and Persian words are not entirely lost in Bengali even though their use is notably reduced over the years due to excessive use of English. The use of words of other languages in Bengali is very small. Their presence in a text does not affect the vocabulary of the language.

We can find out the reasons behind the overhauling impact of English on Bengali vocabulary. The use of English is increased over the years in all spheres of Bengali life. Incorporation of English culture and practices into Bengali life, the use of English in primary and secondary education, exchange of local news and information in English, and international interaction in English are some of the primary factors. Also, the long use of English in higher academic spheres has been instrumental in the increased use of English words in modern Bengali vocabulary. Moreover, we can notice several changes that are taking place in various domains of Bengali life and society (e.g., *science, technology, politics, culture, foreign affairs, entertainment, administration, media, communication,* etc.). In most cases, the exchange of information is done in English, and it inspires common Bengali people to use English

Table 5.7 Frequency of words of different origin in a Bengali news text

Words in a Bengali newspaper text	Percentage (%)
Indigenous words	39.17
Tadbhava words	19.18
English words	15.13
Tatsama words	11.13
Arabic words	07.11
Persian words	05.16
Other words	03.12
Total	100.00

words, terms, idioms, and phrases in their speech and writing. As a result, the number of English words is gradually increasing in modern Bengali vocabulary.

The naturalization of English words into Bengali takes place at three linguistic levels: phonology, morphology, and lexicon. It operates in two ways: lexical adoption and lexical adaptation (Dash et al., 2009).

(a) **Lexical adoption:** English words are borrowed, transliterated, and incorporated into Bengali lexicon without changing their phonological and morphological properties.
(b) **Lexical adaptation:** Borrowed and transliterated English words undergo phonological and morphological changes to be naturalized with the existing lexical stock of Bengali.

Lexical adoption works for those words where existing Bengali phonological and morphological processes are not applied (e.g., *ball, club, cycle, cricket, politics, party, pool, naughty, arts, game, car, road*, etc.). These words are easy and simple in form and meaning. Bengali speakers can speak, read, write, and understand these words without much trouble. Therefore, they directly adopt these words into Bengali without change. These words are mostly transliterated and used.

Lexical adaptation works in those English words which undergo phonological and morphological changes when they are used in Bengali (e.g., *bench* > *beñchi, table* > *ṭebil, lamp* > *lampha, bolṭ* > *bolṭu, aunt* > *ānṭi, school* > *iskul*, etc.). These words pass through some processes of morphophonemic change to be naturalized into Bengali. It is noted that phonological and morphological adaptations are quite robust, frequent, and productive in naturalizing English words into Bengali. The other process (i.e., *adoption*) is also frequent and robust, but not much productive. It fails to percolate beyond the level of lexical transfer from English to Bengali. It can simply show how some English words have entered into Bengali vocabulary without changing their surface forms at the time of their entry into the language.

The table (Table 5.7) also presents some statistical information about the possible contribution of foreign languages to modern Bengali vocabulary. However, this information is not much praiseworthy because the corpus that we have used for this study is made with newspaper texts where information of text domains is removed. It is, however, known that the stock of words of a language varies based on subject domains. For instance, texts from science and technology have more English words than texts from literature. Similarly, texts from philosophy and religion have more Sanskrit words than medical and legal texts. To verify this hypothesis, we propose to carry out some frequency calculations on corpora of different subject domains and sub-domains. In a similar way, we should carry out frequency studies on multitext corpora to find the difference in the percentage of words in texts, measure **lexical proximity** (structural and semantic proximity of words in two or more languages), and identify cognate word distributions across languages. We also plan to do some case-based studies to measure how annotation information at the etymological level helps in NLP application.

The information that we are able to collect from the table (Table 5.7) can be used in dictionary-making, language education, and language planning. In dictionary-making, we may consider the percentage of use of words of different origin in a language to select words to be used as headwords in a dictionary. In language education, we may look at the percentage of use of words of different origin to design graded vocabularies for different levels of language education. In language planning, we may gather data to decide how we should design different types of text materials with a reference to the percentage of use of words of different origins in a language.

5.8 Frequently Used English Words in Bengali

The following table (Table 5.8) contains an interesting result. We present a list of English words, which are most frequently used in a Bengali text corpus. A simple look at the list shows the kinds of English words that are in use in modern Bengali texts due to their wide acceptability among common Bengali people. It also reveals some interesting features of the modern Bengali life which are hardly understandable by any other means.

From a sociolinguistic and ethnographic point of view, words such as *police, power, party, union, vote,* and *committee* refer to the continuous interference of party, politics, and administration in Bengali life and living. On the other hand, words like *ball* and *cricket* refer to the impact of games and sports like football and cricket on Bengali life. Words like *bus, train, ticket, mile,* and *line* refer to the basic means of the transport system, without which the Bengali people can hardly move from place to place. Since the traditional means of transport of Bengal (e.g., *bullock carts, horse-drawn carts, palanquins,* and *boats*) have become redundant in modern Bengali life, people are completely dependent on the new means of transport run by machine and automation. The self-driven cycles and man-pulled rickshaws are also being replaced by advanced items of transportation like *motorbikes, cars, buses, trams, taxies, planes,* and *trains*. The recurrent use of these transport items in the regular day-to-day life of people is distinctly reflected in the language they use.

Table 5.8 Most frequently used English words in a Bengali corpus

English words	English words	English words
Police (748)	Company (585)	Bank (433)
Ball (663)	College (526)	Line (431)
Bus (655)	Mile (514)	Hospital (411)
No. (620)	kg (495)	Train (402)
Ok (617)	Power (490)	Party (399)
Sir (614)	Office (483)	Record (398)
Pass (611)	School (474)	Cricket (393)
Staff (602)	Degree (466)	Ticket (382)
Doctor (592)	Committee (455)	Union (375)
Minute (591)	Cinema (438)	Vote (365)

The frequent use of words like *doctor, hospital*, and *nurse* indicates their total dependence on medical science and allied domains. The use of *school, college, degree, and record* refers to the importance people give to processes of succeeding in various examinations to become *staffs* in *offices* and *companies*. The word *cinema* refers to their regular dependence on it as a source of entertainment. The word *minute* refers to a system of managing time, and *bank* refers to their dependence on the banking system for financial management. Similarly, words like *number, kg, meter, foot, and liter* refer to the dependence of Bengali people on English words relating to measurement because traditional Bengali systems of measurement are obsolete for ages. Finally, words like *ok* and *sir* reveal some interesting aspects with regard to their attitude when Bengali people interact with seniors or strangers. The frequent use of *sir* implies that Bengali people have not yet been successful to overcome the colonial hangover imposed upon them by the British rulers. The frequent use of *ok*, on the other hand, reflects on the overall inertia and callousness of the mass despite the acute troubles they face in their daily life and living. For them, everything is *ok*, even though they are inflicted with man-made troubles or nature-made calamities.

5.9 System Adoption at Lexical Level

Etymological annotation highlights an interesting phenomenon of the modern Bengali language which we call "System Adoption" (Dash et al., 2009). This phenomenon is understood when all the words in a text corpus are annotated at the level of their etymology. After analyzing the annotated corpus we find that it is not individual words but the entire lexical stock that belongs to a system of the denotation of a particular domain is absorbed in the Bengali vocabulary from English. The followings are the domains where the total or near-total stock of English words is borrowed into Bengali.

(1) **Education:** *school, college, university, syllabus, student, teacher, aunty, sir, school-bus, peon, staff, madam, holiday, summer camp, homework, private tuition, tutor, hostel.*
(2) **Months:** *January, February, March, April, May, June, July, August, September, October, November, December.*
(3) **Measurement:** *minute, second, meter, kg, gram, foot, inch, gauge, yard, mile, kilogram, kilo, liter, dozen.*
(4) **Transport:** *bus, tram, train, taxi, car, rail, plane, auto, cycle, rickshaw, bike, motor, metro, scooter, launch, steamer, boat.*
(5) **Toiletries:** *snow, cosmetics, powder, lipstick, shampoo, gloss, blusher, mascara, ribbon, eye-liner, eye-shadow.*
(6) **Medicine:** *doctor, medicine, hospital, nurse, nursing home, saline, bed, injection, treatment, prescription, patient.*

A scrutiny into the list of English words borrowed into Bengali shows that almost all the English words belonging to a domain are incorporated into Bengali. In case of education, there are a few Bengali words (e.g., *śreṇī, chhātra, śikṣak, śikṣikā, chhātrī, chhātrābās*, etc.) which are gradually replaced with semantically equivalent words of English (e.g., *class, student, teacher, master, education, hostel*, etc.). Moreover, many English words, which have no equivalent Bengali forms, are included in the Bengali vocabulary to represent new concepts and ideas.

In case of referring to months, Bengali people normally use the English names of months in their day-to-day life. Only on special occasions with cultural and religious significance (e.g., *marriage, pujās, social,* and *family festivals*), they tend to refer to Bengali months. In the case of measurement, Bengali people have no other alternative but to depend on English words as their traditional words of measurement along with their traditional ways of measurement, have been obsolete for years. It is a rare incidence if someone uses Bengali words like *poyā, ser, gaṇḍā, siki, ānā, chhaṭāk*, etc., to refer to some units of measurement. As a result, the Bengali people, to serve their purposes, have adopted the entire stock of English words.

In earlier years, the Bengali people used only a few means of transport both on land and water. Moreover, they had hardly any means for long-distance travel on land except walking or by using a palanquin. After the introduction of the modern land transport system like *car, bus, tram,* and *train*, they have adopted this new system along with those words that refer to those means of transport. The beautification spheres of the Bengali ladies and gentlemen have undergone a sea change both at a cosmetic and linguistic level. In practice, they hardly use their traditional toiletries except on specific occasions like marriage and others. In most cases, they use toiletries that are primarily purchased from the "English world." It is therefore not surprising that the entire lexical stock relating to this domain comes from English, although the ancient Indian culture was very rich with items and words related to this domain.

Finally, the lexical stock relating to traditional Indian medicine and medication has largely shrunk with a rejection of traditional Indian medicine in Bengali life. As a result, words of this domain are either lost or on the verge of loss. This has opened ways for modern English medical terms and words to come into the Bengali vocabulary along with modern Western medicines. The present Bengali vocabulary has a huge list of English medical terms that are directly borrowed from English and used in transliterated forms in Bengali texts. As exceptions, we find a few Bengali terms (e.g., *peṭbyathā* "stomach ache," *māthābyathā* "headache," *jar* "fever," etc.) that are used in modern Bengali texts. Gradually, such terms are also giving away their places to equivalent English terms.

5.10 Conclusion

Etymological annotation is a new type of corpus annotation which is discussed briefly in this chapter. In the last four decades, we have come across various types of corpus annotation—both spoken and written (Atkins et al., 1992; Biber, 1993). We, however, have never come across suggestions regarding etymological annotation on a corpus. Nobody has ever argued that words that are included in a text also need to be annotated at the etymological level based on which we extract information relating to the origin of words in a language. For the first time in the history of corpus annotation, we have tried to address this issue. In this chapter, we present a brief sketch of it with a focus on its character, nature, relevance, and application.

The utilities of an etymologically annotated corpus are many. It is utilized in language description, dictionary compilation, language teaching, and language planning. In a dictionary, headwords are presented with information about their etymological history and lexicological changes they pass through to take new forms and usage in a language. An etymologically annotated corpus is used to know many other aspects, such as the followings:

(1) Recognize words of native, national, and foreign origin.
(2) Know native words that combine with foreign words to make compounds and hybrid words.
(3) Find out those native affixes that combine with foreign words.
(4) Find out foreign affixes which combine with native words.
(5) Identify morphophonemic changes foreign words undergo in the process of naturalization.
(6) Calculate frequency of use of foreign words in a language.
(7) Identify patterns of use of foreign words in language texts.
(8) Identify domains where foreign words are frequently used.
(9) Understand nature of change in the meaning of foreign words.
(10) Count number of foreign words in vocabulary of a language.
(11) Compile databases and dictionaries of foreign words.
(12) Identify affixes that are productive in word formation.

All advanced languages possess a large number of words, which are borrowed from other languages. Identification of sources of origin of words carries some relevance in a part-of-speech annotation (Rayson et al., 2006), morphological analysis of words, lexical database generation, dictionary-making, language description, language documentation, language teaching (Hunston, 2002), and language planning. We keep all these applications in view to propose a method and a tagset for etymological annotation of words in a corpus. It expands the applicational relevance of a corpus beyond the realms of language engineering and information technology. It establishes theoretical and functional relevance in applied, descriptive, comparative, and historical linguistics also. Studies of these domains can earn extra credit due to the use of information and data from an etymologically annotated corpus.

References

Acharya, P. B. (1985). *Shabdasandhan Shabdabhidhan (Word inquiry: Word dictionary)*. Bikash Grantha Bhaban.

Amin, M. (2012). *Bangla Shabder Pauranik Utsa (Ancient sources of the Bengali word)*. Puthi Nilay.

Atkins, S., Clear, J., & Ostler, N. (1992). Corpus design criteria. *LiTerary and Linguistic Computing, 7*(1), 1–16.
Basu, A. (2015). *Shabdagalpadrum: Bangla byutpatti abhidhan (Bengali etymological dictionary).* Gangchil.
Biber, D. (1993). Representativeness in corpus design. *Literary and Linguistic Computing, 8*(4), 243–257.
Chaki, J. B. (1996). *Bangla Bhasar Byakaran (Grammar of the Bengali language).* Ananda Publishers.
Chakravarti, N. N. (1994). *Bangla: Ki Likhben, Kena Likhben (Bengali: What to write).* Ananda Publishers.
Chakravarty, B. D. (1974). *Ucchatara Bangla Vyakaran (Higher Bengali Grammar).* Sarkar and Co.
Chatterji, S. K. (1926). *The origin and development of the Bengali language.* Calcutta University Press.
Chattopadhyay, S. K. (1995). *Bhasa Prakash Bangla Vyakaran (Grammar of the Bengali language).* Rupa Publications.
Das, B. (2010). *Bangla Shabder Utsa Sandhane (In search of the origin of the Bengali words).* Jogomaya Prakashani.
Dash, N. S., Dutta Chowdhury, P., & Sarkar, A. (2009). Naturalization of English words in modern Bengali: A corpus-based empirical study. *Language Forum., 35*(2), 127–142.
Dash, N. S. (2007). Frequency-based analysis of words and morphemes in Bengali text corpus. *Indian Journal of Linguistics, 25–26*, 223–253.
Dash, N. S., & Hussain, M. M. (2013). Designing a generic scheme for etymological annotation: A new type of language corpora annotation. In *Proceedings of the ALR-11 & 6th International Joint Conference on Natural Language Processing,* (pp. 64–71). Nagoya Congress Centre, Nagoya, Japan, 14–18 October 2013.
Dash, N. S., Bhattacharyya, P., & Pawar, J. (Eds.). (2017). *The WordNet in Indian languages.* Springer Nature
Datta, M. (2008). *Chalti Islami Shabdakosh (Colloquial islamic vocabulary).* Gangchil.
Finkenstaedt, T., & Wolff, D. (1973). *Ordered profusion: Studies in dictionaries and the English lexicon.* C. Winter.
Hunston, S. (2002). *Corpora in applied linguistics.* Cambridge University Press.
Jha, G. N., Nainwani, P., Banerjee, E., & Kaushik, S. (2011). Issues in annotating less-resourced languages: The case of Hindi from Indian Languages Corpora Initiative. *Proceedings of 5th LTC.* Poznan, Poland, 25–27 Nov 2011.
Leech, G., & Fligelstone, S. (1992). Computers and corpora analysis. In C. S. Butler (Ed.), *Computers and written texts* (pp. 115–140). Blackwell.
Majumder, P. C. (1993). *Bangla Bhasa Parikrama (Survey on Bengali)* (Vol. II). Dey's Publishing.
Mallik, B. P., Bhattacharya, N., Kundu, S. C., & Dawn, M. (1998). *Phonemic and morphemic frequency in the Bengali language.* The Asiatic Society.
Musa, M., & Elias, M. (2003). *Banglay Pracalita Ingreji Shabder Abhidhan (Dictionary of English words used in Bengali).* Mouli Prakashani.
Rayson, P., Archer, D., Baron, A., Smith, N. (2006). Tagging historical corpora—the problem of spelling variation. In *Proceedings of digital historical corpora, Dagstuhl-seminar 06491.* International Conference and Research Center for Computer Science, Schloss Dagstuhl, Wadern, Germany, 3–8 Dec 2006.
Rissanen, M. (1989). Three problems connected with the use of diachronic corpora. *International Computer Archive of Modern English Journal, 13*(1), 16–19.
Sarkar, I. (2015). *Bangla shabder utsa sandhane (In search of the origin of the Bengali words).* Tuhina Prakashani.
Sarkar, P., & Basu, G. (1994). *Bhasa Jijnasa (Language queries).* Vidyasagar Pustak Mandir.
Sen, S. (1992). *Bhashar Itivrittva (History of language).* Ananda Publishers.

Shaw, R. (1999). *Sadharan Bhasabijnan O Adhunik Bangla Bhasa (General linguistics and modern Bengali language)*. Pustak Bipani.
Stamper, K. (2017). *Word by word: The secret life of dictionaries*. Pantheon.
Williams, J. M. (1986) (1975) *Origins of the English language. A social and linguistic history*. Free Press.

Web Links

http://arxiv.org/pdf/1501.03191v1.pdf
http://www.amazon.com/etymological-Annotations-Classical-Criticism-selections/dp/7020026877
https://en.wikipedia.org/wiki/Lists_of_English_words_by_country_or_language_of_origin
https://en.wikipedia.org/wiki/Machine-readable_dictionary
https://www.academia.edu/10856518/Etymological_Annotation
https://www.dictionary.com/e/borrowed-words/
http://citeseerx.ist.psu.edu/viewdoc/summary?doi=10.1.1.401.1617

Chapter 6
More Types of Corpus Annotation

Abstract In this chapter, we define the basic concepts of some non-conventional types of text annotation which are, due to several reasons, not frequently used on corpus texts. This discussion gives readers some preliminary ideas about the ways and means of annotating a text at various levels, beyond the grammatical and syntactic level of annotation, for making a text useful in various domains of linguistics and language engineering. The availability of different types of annotated texts is a blessing for various academic and commercial applications. The primary goals and objectives of each type of corpus annotation are characteristically different. Goals vary depending on the type of a text and scopes for possible utilization in a customized and object-oriented application. Because of marked differences in goals, the processes of corpus annotation vary. Besides, the kind of text considered for annotation plays a decisive role in the selection of annotation type. The non-conventionally annotated texts are not always useful for all kinds of linguistic investigation and studies. They are useful in those contexts where non-standard analysis and interpretation of texts are required for a specific application. That means the application of non-conventional annotation processes on text generates a kind of outputs which are not frequently applied in traditional schemes of language description and analysis. However, such texts become significantly relevant in many advanced areas of applied linguistics and language data management. On the other hand, non-conventional annotation techniques require a different kind of capability in understanding a text, which in return generates a new kind of expertise in text interpretation and information processing and management. Keeping all these aspects in view, in this chapter, we focus on some of the non-typical and non-conventional text annotation types which are not so frequently applied in corpus annotation.

Keywords Orthography · Figure-of-speech · Semantics · Prosody · Discourse · Rhetoric

6.1 Introduction

In the present global scenario, the number of common and conventional types of annotated corpora of advanced languages is quite large and varied. The same kind

N. S. Dash, *Language Corpora Annotation and Processing*,
https://doi.org/10.1007/978-981-16-2960-0_6

of situation is not observed in less-advanced languages. To date, some of the less-advanced languages have been able to develop one or two POS annotated corpora for specific research and application purposes. It will take a long time before these less-advanced languages are able to produce standard, common, and conventional types of annotated corpora to address their linguistic and technological needs. It is indeed a long journey for most of these languages.

With regard to non-conventional annotation, the number of corpora of this type, even in advanced languages, is quite less. For less-advanced languages, such a corpus is yet to be envisaged. That means except for a few conventional annotation types, non-conventional annotations have a low presence in languages. There are several reasons behind this. The non-availability of necessary guidelines, tagsets, rules, principles, methods, tools, and trained manpower are some of the reasons. Also, there is a lack of vision and insight to realize the theoretical importance and application relevance of such an annotated corpus in linguistic research and development works. In most cases for example, we fail to visualize how a text, when annotated at the discourse level, is to be utilized by a human being or a computer system, which is engaged in the analysis of the discourse of a text. Such limitations often restrain us from annotating a corpus at the discourse level, and for years, we roam around grammatical and syntactic annotation only. Limited availability of corpora of different text types is another factor that forces us to concentrate only on grammatical and syntactic annotations.

The grammatical annotation, when compared to other types of text annotation, appears to be comparatively an easy process—linguistically and technologically. With a working knowledge of part-of-speech of words of a language, we can do this—manually or using a tool designed for this—on a corpus without heavy trouble. At the initial stage, we may require some training and fine grammatical information to identify the part-of-speech of a word for assigning a tag. At a later stage, we have a fair chance to improve our knowledge with the addition of new information gathered from the analysis of new texts. Acquiring high success in the grammatical annotation is not impossible even though it is full of trials, errors, and modifications.

The non-conventional annotations are far more complex and challenging tasks. These annotation processes require specialized knowledge of different domains of linguistics for achieving an even marginal amount of success. For instance, if we want to do proper orthographic annotation of a text, we must have (a) clear ideas about the kinds of orthographic characters, symbols, and signs used in a written text, (b) patterns of use of these characters and symbols in texts, and (c) linguistic and extralinguistic functions they perform in a text. In the same way, if we want to annotate a spoken text successfully, we need to have strong knowledge in phonetics, phonemics, transcription, suprasegmental features, tonal variations, stress, accent, intonation patterns, and other features of speech that we observe in isolated, continuous, and sequential speech events of monologues, dialogues, and conversations. That means we require specialized linguistic knowledge and information to execute non-conventional corpus annotation processes. We need good knowledge and information about word meanings to execute semantic annotation, special discourse information for discourse annotation, and a strong understanding and knowledge of figures-of-speech for rhetoric annotation.

The present stage and practice of text annotation is rapidly changing. We come across many new methods that are being incorporated effectively in many non-conventional types of text annotations. This indicates that we are moving toward a better state where existing methods are being revised, new methods are being applied, new types of text annotations are envisaged, and new techniques of text annotation are being introduced. The requirements for annotated corpus by new commercial applications are leading scientists in this new direction. They are now developing new ways of text annotation that address the requirements of IT industries. This is a new age with new possibilities and new applications. Keeping this phase in view, in Sect. 6.2, we present a small discussion on orthographic annotation; in Sect. 6.3, we present a short sketch of prosodic annotation; in Sect. 6.4, we highlight some of the basic aspects of semantic annotation; in Sect. 6.5, we briefly address some essential traits of discourse annotation; and in Sect. 6.6, we introduce some of the rudimentary ideas of rhetoric annotation.

6.2 Orthographic Annotation

Through orthographic annotation, we encode orthographic information to a text of a written corpus (Leech & Wilson 1999). It is not a representational type of annotation. It is an interpretative type of annotation (Leech, 1993: 276). Here, we try to identify textual functions and linguistic relevance of the orthographic symbols (e.g., *punctuation marks, diacritics, italics*) used in a written text. The basic aim is to represent a text on a digital platform in a similar fashion as the text is found in its natural printed form, even though we attach multiple extra-textual and intratextual codes and tags to it (McEnery & Wilson, 1996:34). Before annotating a text at the orthography level, we decide whether the scheme of an annotation is meant to represent a language as unaffected by any external aspect of typography or to represent the text, as fully as possible, with all its aspects. Representing a text in the latter way means, we need to account for various aspects of the original form of a text. They include the formal layout of a text (e.g., *page breaks, paragraph breaks, line breaks*), use of different types of font for emphasis (e.g., *bold, underlined, italic,* etc.), use of subscript and superscript for reference and notes, and use of non-textual elements and materials (e.g., *flowcharts, figures, tables, diagrams,* etc.). At the early stages of orthographic annotation, these aspects are handled in different ways. For instance, asterisk marks are used in the Lancaster-Oslo/Bergen (LOB) corpus to indicate a change in typography. In recent times, *the Text Encoding Initiative* (TEI) guideline suggests standard ways of representing these phenomena, based on the concept of start and end page.

From an applicational point of view, we classify orthographic annotation into two broad types: structure annotation and string annotation. During structure annotation, we encode the external structure of a text. Keeping the external structure of a written

<p>				
	<sg>	Handling the IPR issues	<sg>	
	<s>	The IPR issue is not yet solved, as far as I understand.	<s>	
	<s>	I approached them but they did not respond to my request (as usual, you know the problem better than anybody else).	<s>	
	<s>	Therefore, we just crawled the data from some open-source archives and took a small percentage of data (around 10%) from each day of the month.	<s>	
	<s>	We broke paragraphs into separate sentences, assigned a unique ID to each sentence, and broke each sentence into words for application purposes.	<s>	
				<p>

Fig. 6.1 Structure annotation of a written text sample

text in mind, we record and encode the following types of annotation: (a) paragraph annotation, (b) sentence annotation, and (c) segment annotation. In paragraph annotation, a text constituting a paragraph is marked with <p> both at the beginning and the end to indicate the start and endpoint of a paragraph. In sentence annotation, each sentence of a text is encoded with a start-and-end sentence marker <s> to indicate its separate syntactic identity. In segment annotation, the same process is followed where each segment is encoded with a segment marker <sg> (Fig. 6.1).

In string annotation, on the other hand, we encode those unique characters that require interpretative information in understanding a text. In most cases, such strings require additional interpretation to resolve identity crises and functional ambiguities in texts. In a typical sample of a text, string annotation is required for encoding capital letters, hyphenated strings, punctuation marks, numerals and digits, non-standard orthographic symbols, and characters of different scripts (e.g., the *Roman characters used in Bengali text*). The orthographic symbols which are annotated to dissolve issues of text representation and ambiguities include the followings:

- Sentence-initial capital letters (needed for English texts)
- Capital letters of proper names (e.g., *person, place, item names*)
- Spelling representation variations in words
- Quotations from other languages, poems, songs, dialects
- All punctuation marks and diacritic symbols
- Hyphenation in compounds and proper names
- Numbers, numerals, digits, and fractions
- Geometric equations, mathematical expressions, chemical formulae
- Symbolic representations, pictures, tables, and diagrams
- Abbreviations of proper names (e.g., MKG, KBS)
- Titles of address (e.g., Mr. = Mister, Dr. = Doctor, St. = Saint)

- Short forms of organization (e.g., RAF = Rapid Action Force)
- Postcode (e.g., St. = Street, St. = Station)
- Units of measurement (e.g., kg = kilogram)
- Day of week (e.g., Sat. = Saturday)
- Name of festivals (e.g., X' mas = Christmas)
- Name of months (e.g., Jan. = January).

A good number of the orthographic symbols are annotated following a simple technique of **string matching** and character recognition. Since these are not very large in frequency of their use in a text, a system can annotate these quite fast, based on the information provided to a system. After annotation, a text is reviewed to rectify false and omitted annotation as well as to see if contextual sense is captured through annotation (Atkins et al., 1992: 11).

In the case of those languages like English and others who use Roman script, the guideline proposed by the *Text Encoding Initiative* (TEI) is sufficient (Sperberg-McQueen & Burnard, 1994). It contains detailed instruction for annotating characters in texts at different levels based on requirements of text access and utilization. It has codes for open-quote (“) and close-quote (”) irrespective of typographical devices used in texts. Also, it provides guidance for encoding the non-canonical orthographic symbols, which are used to resolve ambiguities at the sentence level. For instance, it has codes to denote the function of a sentence-initial capital letter, as well as the function of a full stop and an apostrophe. For those languages, which use additional characters with the Roman script, there are many challenges in an orthographic annotation (Hepburn & Bolden, 2013). To overcome such challenges, text annotators use different strategies and methods. For example, the French text annotators omit accents entirely; the German text annotators introduce an additional letter *e* for umlaut (*für* > *fuer*) and replace *ß* with Roman *ss* (*scharfeß* > *schaefess*) and so on (McEnery & Wilson, 1996:33). The TEI guideline has also devised some standard codes to encode special characters in texts.

Since most of the text analysis and processing devices are meant for the texts produced with Roman scripts, they have limited applicability to those Indian language texts which use non-Roman scripts. As a result, for those Indian languages that use non-Roman scripts, different solutions are envisaged by text annotators. One of the major problems is the use of Roman characters in Indian language texts. For example, the use of words in Roman characters inside a Bengali text is a very common feature. Such entries require special treatment in an orthographic annotation. A common strategy that we use is a transliteration of Roman texts into Bengali so that the text is successfully processed. This makes the exchange and analysis of texts simplified as Roman characters are removed from texts. Also, it simplifies the process of designing common text processing systems (e.g., *lexical sorting, concordance, stemming, local word grouping*) for a corpus of these languages. However, it has some limitations. Although it helps to normalize a text through the use of non-Roman characters in a text, it removes an important piece of information. It removes the information that the use of Roman characters in Bengali text is a common practice in wring.

In this context, there is an urgent need for developing a uniform standard for orthographic annotation for written texts for the Indian languages. If we want to adopt TEI guidelines, we have to modify some of its formats and standards to make it suitable for the Indian languages. Also, we have to solve problems of ambiguity caused by single-character strings, onomatopoeic words, fillers, ejectives, and echo strings which are quite frequent in written texts (Fink et al., 1995). Ambiguities may also arise due to indiscriminate use of punctuations and spaces within and across words in texts in these languages. Application of orthographic annotation on Indian language texts will enhance retrieval scope from texts, identify words and special orthographic units, dissolve ambiguities caused by strings, and address challenges caused by the indiscriminate use of punctuation marks. Such problems have to be dissolved to make the Indian languagecorpora useful for language technology works. It is observed that due to practiced inconsistencies in the traditional writing system, many orthographic strings are used haphazardly. Once these are solved, extraction of the right kind of information from texts will become systematic, error-free, and reliable.

6.3 Prosodic Annotation

We can apply prosodic annotation on a spoken text after the text is transcribed into written form (Johansson, 1995). Normally, here we encode different kinds of prosodic information, prosodic features, and suprasegmental properties, which are considered as primary attributes of a speech (Grice et al., 2000). It is a far more complex and difficult type of text annotation because prosody is more impressionistic than realistic in nature. A successful prosodic annotation requires careful listening by a trained ear for proper interpretation of an audio text. We undertake prosodic annotation of a spoken text to make explicit all the aspects of spontaneous speech. In a wider sense, these aspects include a temporal grouping of syllables, accents in speech sequence, variations in emotion, and others which are not considered in orthographic transcription (Knowles, 1991). The analysis of a spontaneous spoken text is incomplete if its prosodic features are not properly interpreted. Similarly, a prosodic annotation is incomplete if prosodic properties of a spoken text are not captured and represented in its transcripted version (Grover et al., 1998). To make a spoken text really useful for research and application, we have to apply prosodic annotation on a spoken text. The prosodic annotation should be independent of any specific linguistic theory or model. Moreover, it should reveal those aspects of prosody that we recognize and understand easily. It is rational to design a perception-based prosodic annotation scheme (Grover et al., 1998; Portele & Heuft, 1995 than using a more complex method of annotation that minimizes the application value of an annotated speech corpus (Gussenhoven et al. 1999). The elements that we normally annotate through prosodic annotation are the followings.

(a) **Prominent syllables:** Syllables which carry clear prominence.
(b) **Pauses:** Between-words and within-words interruptions in speech.
(c) **Lengthening:** Lengthening of those sounds that do not carry prominence but carry emotion or represents a filled pause like hesitation.
(d) **Pitch variation:** The quality of a sound governed by a rate of vibrations producing it relating to the degree of highness or lowness of a tone.
(e) **Accent variation:** Marking distinctive ways of pronouncing words of an individual to locate his/her country, area, or social class.
(f) **Loudness:** Marking a sound produced with a high magnitude of auditory sensation due to emotional exuberance.
(g) **Tonal variation:** Marking variations in tone for distinguishing lexical or grammatical meaning and capturing emotional and paralinguistic information (*emphasis, contrasts*)
(h) **Juncture:** Marking a cue by which one can distinguish between the two otherwise identical sequences of sounds having different meanings.
(i) **Silence:** Marking the cues as an interactive locus of turn-taking and "allocating the floor" in conversation.

Since the objective of prosodic annotation is to allow listeners with a limited phonological or prosodic background to perform the task, listeners are usually asked to mark prosodic properties on orthographically transcripted texts than on original spoken texts (Sinclair, 1994). Moreover, annotators are discouraged from using annotation on phonetically transcripted texts. Such texts are usually less comprehensible to native language users. In essence, the process for prosodic annotation should be independent of the availability of phonetic transcriptions.

During prosodic annotation, a common practice is that all punctuation marks are removed from an orthographically transcripted text before the text is put to annotation. The goal is to avoid any bias toward putting a break at sentence terminal positions. An orthographically transcripted text without punctuations is presented to annotators. To facilitate the annotation process, annotators are trained to use PRAAT (Boersma & van Heuven) or similar tools by which they annotate prosodic features. Texts are annotated independently by annotators who have the liberty to decide which annotations they think appropriate for a particular prosodic feature. An annotation scheme usually indicates stress, pauses, and patterns of intonation in a speech. An interesting example of a prosodically annotated corpus is the annotated version of the *London-Lund Speech Corpus (*LOB) of British English (Fig. 6.2). Another good example is the *Lancaster /IBM Spoken English Corpus*, which is annotated on several levels. In this corpus, stressed syllables (with and without independent pitch movement) are marked with symbols, while unstressed syllables (whose pitch is predictable from tone marks of nearby accented syllables) are left unmarked.

Linguistic and phonetic expertise are necessary qualifications of an annotator for prosodic annotation. Annotators need trained ears for careful listening and comprehension of prosodic features of spoken texts (Milde & Gut, 2002). A piece of a spoken text should be transcribed and annotated separately by two or more annotators (ideally by three annotators) so that differences that arise in transcription and annotation are resolved through discussion. For instance, a small part of the *Lancaster/IBM Spoken*

Transcripted text

Well, very nice of you to come and spare the time and come and talk. Tell me about the - problems. And incidentally, do do tell me anything you want about the college in general. I mean, it doesn't have to be confined to the problems of English and the horrors of living in this part of the college or anything like that (laugh)

An annotated version of the text

well ^ very nice of you to ((come and))_spare the !tVime and# ^come and !t\alk#-
^tell me a'bout the - !pr\oblems# and ^inci\dentally#.
^| [@:] ^do ^do t\ell me#
^anything you 'want about the :college in "!g\eneral#
I ^mean it !doesn't "!h\ave to be {con^f\ined#}#
to the ^problems of !\English#
[@:@:] and the ^horrors of :living in :this 'part of the c/ollege# or ^anything like th\at# *(-laugh)*

Keys used in the prosodic annotation

^ ' ! " _	are features of stress, including boosters
\ / V	are tones (fall, rise, and fall-rise)
. –	are pauses
#	is a tone unit boundary
@ :	is a pause filler '*er*'
{ }	enclose a subordinate tone unit
*( ) *	enclose contextual comments
(( ))	enclose uncertain material

Fig. 6.2 Prosodic annotation on the London-Lund Speech Corpus

English Corpus has been transcribed and annotated by two annotators and the rest is done by one annotator (Leech, 1993). Because of the complexities involved in prosodic annotation, the number of prosodically annotated speech corpora is very few even in advanced languages. The number of speech corpora and the number of prosodically annotated speech corpora in the Indian languages are few (Dash & Ramamoorthy, 2019: 237–248). Most of these are developed at an individual level for personal research and system development works (Dash, 2009).

6.4 Semantic Annotation

Semantic annotation (also known as *word-sense tagging*) is another innovative process of text annotation. We apply it to a piece of a text to annotate the most appropriate sense a word denotes in the context of its use(Löfberg et al., 2003). The basic goal of semantic annotation is to distinguish among lexicographic senses of words. This helps to understand if recorded lexicographic senses are represented in the use of words or new senses are generated due to new contexts of use. Semantic annotation is one of the most useful methods applied in the sense disambiguation of words as well as in assigning semantic domains to words based on their use in texts (Löfberg et al., 2004). It is a kind of text annotation, which is independent in its own right and is different from other types of text annotation in goal and modes of operation. The process of semantic annotation emphasizes the following three basic purposes.

(a) Identification of semantic information of words used in texts
(b) Marking semantic relationships underlying between words in a text
(c) Specifying agent–patient relations of words denoting thematic roles

During semantic annotation, our aim is to annotate the exact sense of a word in a given context. If the exact sense is not annotated, then the meaning of a word vis-a-vis a sentence is affected. The failure in marking the exact sense of a word results in wrong interpretation and retrieval of wrong information from a text (Löfberg et al., 2005). A piece of text is not made with a set of single words only. It is made with a large number of multiword units which also perform similar kinds of lexical, semantic, syntactic, and extralinguistic roles as single-word units. In such a situation, it is necessary to annotate both single words and multiword units (e.g., *word groups, collocations, phrases, reduplications,* and *idioms*) at the grammatical and semantic level so that their lexical identity and semantic roles are captured. During syntactic annotation, those lexical blocks which are marked as multiword units, are considered as constituent units and are parsed accordingly (Piao et al., 2015).

A semantic annotation scheme takes a POS annotated corpus as an input text and assigns specific semantic information to words to represent the general sense field of words. In most cases, this task is done with reference to a lexicon of single words and multiword units where major senses of words are previously defined. In some rare cases, it also takes idioms into consideration to specify senses idioms generally signify in a language (Rayson & Stevenson, 2008). In the course of semantic annotation, however, it is noted that the general sense of a word that is recorded in a lexicon does not often match with the sense that a word implies in a sentence where it is used. In such a situation, it is necessary to annotate the sense which is noted in the context of its use. Even then, some words create confusions due to several linguistic and extralinguistic factors—the multiplicity of meanings is one of them. Such words are reassessed to see if these words are polysemous in sense denotation. If they are, a lexical database is updated with new information found from corpora.

The storage and management of senses of words in a lexicon is a challenge. It is not yet defined how multiple meanings of words are to be stored in a lexical database. What we understand is that information of contextualized senses of words is procured from processed corpora and stored in a lexical database as a standard class of information. Sometimes entries in a lexical database are put based on their frequency rank in use in a language. In most cases, the frequency rank of senses is obtained from a corpus through a concordance-based sense classification scheme (Table 6.1). The information is further checked to find which senses are dominant in use in texts.

Table 6.1 Frequency-based sense information stored in a lexical database

Frequent senses of "move" (first 4 senses)			
No.	Frq.	Sense	Example
1	[130]	(travel, go, move, locomote) {change location; move, travel, or proceed}	"How fast does your new car go?"; "We travelled from Rome to Naples by bus"; "The policemen went from door to door looking for the suspect"; "The soldiers moved toward the city in an attempt to take it before night fell"
2	[60]	(move, displace) {cause to move, both in a concrete and in an abstract sense}	"Move those boxes into the corner, please"; "I'm moving my money to another bank"; "The director moved more responsibilities onto his new assistant"
3	[52]	(move) {move so as to change position, perform a non-translational motion}	"He moved his hand slightly to the right"
4	[20]	(move) {change residence, affiliation, or place of employment}	"We moved from Idaho to Nebraska"; "The basketball player moved from one team to another"

The table (Table 6.1) shows that codes for senses are entered into a text. Also, words are promoted to the maximum frequency level in the list. A combination of the general frequency of words and the domains of their occurrence, supported with heuristics, is used to identify the senses of words to remove false annotation. After completion of the sense assignment, we do postediting to ensure that each word carries a correct semantic classification code. An example of semantic annotation is UCREL Semantic Analysis System (USAS) which uses a well-designed framework for semantic analysis and annotation of senses of words (Piao et al. 2015). The semantic tagset that is used here is built on the *Longman Lexicon of Contemporary English* (McArthur, 1981). It has a multitier frame with 21 semantic fields (Table 6.2) with a possibility for subdivision.

This annotation framework has been greatly revised, modified and extended further to make it applicable to many other languages, viz. Chinese, Spanish, Italian, Portuguese, Dutch, Finnish, Indonesian, Swedish, Turkish, French, Malay, Urdu, and Welsh (Piao et al., 2016). We have presented below an example of sense annotation of words. The example is adapted from the USAS annotation system of the Lancaster University, UK (Fig. 6.3).

The figure (Fig. 6.3) shows that we can annotate a text in two different ways. When we annotate a text at the horizontal level, annotation information is minimized with

Table 6.2 Major semantic domains of semantic annotation of USAS

Semantic domains	Code	Semantic domains	Code
General and abstract terms	A	The body and the individual	B
Arts and crafts	C	Emotional actions states and processes	E
Food and farming	F	Government and the public domain	G
Architecture, buildings, houses and the home	H	Money and commerce in industry	I
Entertainment, sports, and games	K	Life and living things	L
Movement, location, travel, and transport	M	Numbers and measurement	N
Substances, materials, objects, and equipment	O	Education	P
Linguistic actions, states, and processes	Q	Social actions, states, and processes	S
Time	T	The World and our environment	W
Psychological actions, states, and processes	X	Science and technology	Y
Names and grammatical words	Z		

specific cues referring to further details that are preserved in a semantic tagset stored within a system. Since detailed information is difficult to annotate at this level, only some hints are provided. We can refer to the preserved semantic tagset to retrieve full information for further processing. On the other hand, when we annotate words at the vertical level, we normally give each word a much wider space on both sides to annotate more information. We put each word in a separate line for this purpose. In this case, one has to read words in a downward direction. Grammatical information is annotated at the left side of a word, and semantic information is annotated at the right side of the word. The semantic annotations are composed in upper case letters indicating a general semantic domain. It is followed by a numeral that indicates the first subdivision of a semantic field. After that, there is a decimal point which is followed by a digit. The digit is used to indicate finer subdivisions of the sense. Finally, there are "plus" and "minus" signs which are used to indicate a positive or a negative position of sense of the words on a generic semantic scale. For instance, we can look at the word *view* given below (Table 6.3) to understand how it is annotated at the vertical level in a text.

There are many other attempts for semantic annotation of a text. However, due to the many complexities involved in the process, not much success is reported. First, the number of semantic tagset is open. Second, there is no benchmarked process of selection of features to be annotated to words to recognize the full range of semantic information to be assigned to words. Some scholars (Rayson & Wilson, 1996; Wilson & Thomas 1997; Archer et al., 2003) use semantic categories loosely based on the *Longman Lexicon of Contemporary English* (McArthur, 1981). Others follow the conceptual categories that are available in *Roget's Thesaurus*. In this thesaurus, all

Input Text

The main sources of knowledge are natural language texts, in which humans express how they view and conceptualize the world.

Horizontal Semantic Annotation

The_Z5 main_A11.1+ sources_T2+ of_Z5 knowledge_X2.2+ are_A3+ natural_A6.2+ language_Q3 texts_Q1.2 ,_PUNC in_Z5 which_Z8 humans_S2mf express_Q1.1 how_Z5 they_Z8mfn view_X2.1 and_Z5 conceptualize_Z99 the_Z5 world_W1 ._PUNC

Vertical Semantic Annotation

0000003	01	AT	The	Z5
0000003	02	JJ	main	A11.1+ N5+++
0000003	03	NN2	sources	T2+ Q1.1 X2.2 W3/M4
0000003	04	IO	of	Z5
0000003	05	NN1	knowledge	X2.2+ S3.2/B1%
0000003	06	VBR	are	A3+ Z5
0000003	07	JJ	natural	A6.2+ A9+ A5.4+ W3 W5 B1 K2
0000003	08	NN1	language	Q3 Y2
0000003	09	NN2	texts	Q1.2 Q4.1
0000003	10	II	in	Z5
0000003	11	DDQ	which	Z8 Z5
0000003	12	NN2	humans	S2mf
0000003	13	VV0	express	Q1.1 B1%
0000003	14	RRQ	how	Z5 A13.3
0000003	15	PPHS2	they	Z8mfn
0000003	16	VV0	view	X2.1 X3.4 X2.4
0000003	17	CC	and	Z5
0000003	18	VV0	conceptualize	Z99
0000003	19	AT	the	Z5
0000003	20	NN1	world	W1 S5+c A4.1 N5+
0000003	21	.	.	PUNC

Fig. 6.3 Sample from UCREL semantic analysis system (USAS)

Table 6.3 Semantic information annotated to *view* in USAS

Word	view	Semantic domain Information
No	16	Position of the word in the sentence
Part-of-speech	VV0	Base form of lexical verb (e.g., "*give*," "*work*")
Sense annotation	X2.1 X3.4 X2.4	X2.1 (Thought, belief), X3.4 (Sensory: Sight), X2.4 (Investigate, examine, test, search)

words are conceptually classified and grouped into categories based on semantic features (Garside & Rayson, 1997; Garside et al., 1997). We can think of applying an alternative framework to divide the open class and closed class of words as well as mark proper nouns as a separate class as it deserves special attention due to its unique nature of reference and linguistic functions. During the last few years, both techniques and tagsets for semantic annotation have been modified to a large extent. As a result, the rate of success in semantic annotation has improved remarkably. However, most of these efforts are confined to English and a few other languages. We need to test if these methods are applicable to other languages.

One of the notable applications of a semantically annotated corpus is visualized in the management of meanings of words. Using information from this kind of corpus it is possible to develop semantic ontologies, design systems for sense disambiguation of words, develop semantic webs for representing underlying semantic relations among words, and develop lexical profiles of words for capturing the wider semantic range a word denotes. It is not possible to capture a wide range of semantic information of a word from a dictionary or thesaurus. We have to depend on texts where words are used. A corpus is a good source of information of word meaning. It shows how our views and conceptions are realized through words in texts. Since the extraction of the meaning of words from a text is a tough task, we use semantically annotated text as a useful means for meaning extraction. A text with elaborate semantic annotation offers vital clues to trace underlying relations between concepts and words.

6.5 Discourse Annotation

The term "discourse" refers to events of written and spoken interactions under particular settings. Due to its polysemous nature, the term is used to refer to different ideas in different disciplines. In semantics and conversation analysis, it refers to a conceptual generalization of conversation within varied modalities and contexts of communication. On a different scale, the term is used to refer to the totality of vocabulary used in a given field of intellectual inquiry and of social practice (e.g., *legal discourse, political discourse, cultural discourse, religious discourse, medical discourse*, etc.) (Rastier, 2001).

In corpus linguistics and language processing, we use the expression "discourse annotation" for explicitly marking discourse properties in a text. It involves the works of identification and marking of discourse elements, sociolinguistic cues, conversational features, and extralinguistic properties that are embedded within a piece of written or spoken text and hardly visible at the surface level of a text (Edwards & Lampert, 1993). The presence of various discourse elements, structures, and properties in a text is understood when a text is put to discourse analysis and interpretation (Archer & Culpeper, 2003). A text, when annotated at the discourse level, becomes a unique resource for studying discourse information manifested by linguistic elements used in a text (O'Donnell, 1999). For instance, a dialogic text is marked with unique discourse elements which we analyze to identify and understand the conversational cues deployed in dialogic interaction. In discourse annotation, unlike grammatical, syntactic, and semantic annotation, we adopt a different route to annotate discourse elements and structure of a text. Since the objectives, applications, and importance of discourse annotation are yet to be finalized, we have not been able to develop a standard framework for discourse annotation. As a consequence, we come across various efforts at the grass-root level for producing texts annotated with a wide variety of discourse phenomena (Carlson et al., 2003).

(a) Annotating attributive expressions and coreferences in texts which are normally included in anaphora annotation.
(b) Marking spatiotemporal expressions and identifying discourse relations among these expressions.
(c) Marking elliptic expressions and their dependence on discourse structure of a text.
(d) Identification of discourse units (markers and discourse particles) as well as defining their relations to one another.
(e) Information structure used in the presentation of themes and **rhemes** (the part of a sentence that provides new information regarding the current theme) that license them.
(f) Identification and marking of discourse connectives and elements what they connect with.
(g) Identification of contexts and contextualized elements in the interpretation of texts (particularly of dialogic texts).
(h) Identification of cognitive accessibility scales of a text (e.g., *animacy, polarity, countability*, etc.).
(i) Determining types of speech used in a spoken text (e.g., *direct, indirect, dialogic, monologic, continuous, broken, interrupted,* etc.).
(j) Recognizing and marking ethnographic information embedded in a text (e.g., *SPEAKING: Setting and Scene, Participants, Ends, Act sequence, Key, Instrumentalities, Norms, Genre*) (Hymes 1962, 1963).
(k) Marking register variations (i.e., *Field, Tenor*, and *Mode)* in language use (Halliday & Hasan 1976, 1989).
(l) Marking primary functions of a text (i.e., *Emotive, Referential, Conative, Poetic, Metalingual,* and *Phatic*) (Jakobson 1959, 1960).
(m) Marking stylistic variations in texts (e.g., *Frozen, Formal, Consultative, Casual,* and *Intimate*) or language in action (Joos, 1962).

Those who are engaged in language processing works need corpora annotated at the discourse level for a wide range of applications (Teufel et al., 1999). We use a discourse annotated corpus to empirically test accepted theoretical claims and hypotheses. We also use it as a supporting resource to train learners about noticing discourse-sensitive linguistic elements in second-language acquisition (Webber, 2005). Also, we apply this corpus to train a computer system to solve the issues of coreferring expressions and anaphors in texts (Miltsakaki et al., 2004). This kind of corpus is applied as a training text for annotating new texts and designing text processing tools for information extraction (Polakova et al., 2013), question answering (Prasad et al., 2017), sentiment analysis and emotion detection (Lee et al., 2006), text summarization, new text generation, and text-domain recognition (Wolf & Gibson, 2005).

The discourse annotation is still an open area of corpus annotation. There are debates if a standard annotation guideline is possible to develop for every type of discourse information or phenomenon observed in different types and genres of texts. To address this issue from a wider perspective, the present discourse annotation practices tend to focus on several areas such as the followings:

(a) It brings in a fuller range of discourse annotation activity to the attention of text researchers who are working on other domains of text annotation.
(b) It proposes to engage those people who are already involved in other text annotation tasks and who can work on different discourse phenomena and their usefulness for language applications.
(c) It suggests developing sound theoretical frameworks and models for discourse annotation based on the type of text (e.g., *spoken, written, poetic, dialogic, monologic,* etc.).
(d) It proposes developing tools and systems that are used in discourse annotation for further upgradation of their quality and effectiveness.
(e) It desires to highlight the challenges and obstacles faced in all forms and types of discourse annotation.
(f) It proposes to identify the gaps and limitations in discourse annotation, such as genre or text types that are being annotated.
(g) It proposes to make discourse annotated corpus available for developing information technology tools to be used in non-advanced languages.
(h) It suggests stimulating a new generation of researchers to be engaged in this kind of text annotation and analysis.
(i) It encourages the identification of domains, areas, and applications in language technology where discourse annotated texts are used.
(j) It proposes to create a significantly large and reusable corpus annotated at multiple discourse levels for making theories and building better tools.

Despite potential applications of discourse annotated texts in linguistics and language technology (and some other areas like *sociology* and *ethnography*), discourse annotation, across all languages, is never a widely used practice due to the following reasons.

(a) Identification of discourse features, elements, and categories in a text is primarily context-dependent.
(b) Identification of specific discourse and pragmatic function of units used in a text is a source of disputes than other forms of linguistic phenomena.
(c) Functional analysis of discourse properties in a text is context-based and context-controlled.
(d) Extralinguistic information and insights are required to understand the linguistic significance of discourse elements present in a text.

In discourse annotation, it is necessary to understand how a spoken text is built up with several discourse elements and cues. Theoretically, a typical dialogic text is made with six parts of a discourse:

(a) **Introduction (Exordium):** It makes the audience attentive, receptive, and well disposed of.
(b) **Statement of Facts (Narratio):** It sets forth events that have occurred or might have occurred.
(c) **Division (Partition):** It makes clear what matters are agreed upon, what is contested, and what points are intended to be taken up.
(d) **Proof (Confirmatio):** It presents arguments together with appropriate corroborations and supporting evidence.
(e) **Refutation (Refutatio):** It destroys adversaries' arguments and makes counterarguments that may come to the mind of interactants.
(f) **Conclusion (Peroratio):** It summarizes arguments to establish the need to believe and act upon arguments through summation, amplification, and appeal to pity (Crowley & Hawhee,).

Keeping these factors in view, Stenström (1984) proposes discourse annotation on *London-Lund Speech Corpus* to identify the categories of discourse signals. These categories are considered capable to indicate the conversational structure of a normal speech sequence. The annotation scheme that Stenström suggests includes the following discourse categories (Stenström, 1984).

(a) Apologies: e.g., *sorry, excuse me,* etc.
(b) Hedges: e.g., *kind of, sort of,* etc.
(c) Greetings: e.g., *hello, hi,* etc.
(d) Politeness: e.g., *please, dear,* etc.
(e) Responses: e.g., *really, that's true,* etc.
(f) Emphasis: e.g., *okay, right, sure,* etc.
(g) Permeation: e.g., *dear, honey, darling,* etc.
(h) Verification: e.g., *really, absolutely*, etc.
(i) Evaluation: e.g., *well, enough*, etc.,
(j) Confirmation: e.g. *yeah, innit, sure,* etc.

In a later attempt, a simplified version is outlined for discourse transcription of a spoken text (duBois et al., 1992). This scheme is further modified to annotate another set of the text of the *London-Lund Speech Corpus* with sixteen types of discourse markers to observe the trends of speech patterns of London teenagers (Stenström & Andersen, 1996).

There is an interest in analyzing language data at the discourse level (beyond lexical and syntax levels) in language technology, psycholinguistics, ecolinguistics, sociolinguistics, ethnography, pragmatics, and language teaching. To address their needs, we have to invite researchers from various domains of linguistics and social sciences to work on different aspects of discourse annotation (Webber et al., 2003). We have noted that formal pragmatics provides empirical linguistic support for research on **dialogues** and discourse structure to produce multilayered discourse annotation (Prasad et al., 2017). Such efforts can solve some of the challenges of discourse annotation. Even then, there are challenges with regard to designing protocols for discourse annotation. Some challenges that are still pending are as follows.

(a) Defining methodological issues of discourse annotation (e.g., *manual, automated, or supervised*).
(b) Automatic discourse annotation of texts using computational approaches, methods, and algorithms.
(c) Designing tools for discourse annotation (e.g., *assist manual annotation or a semi-automated process*).
(d) Developing systems for verification and authentication of corpora that are annotated at the discourse level.
(e) Evaluating various discourse annotation schemes and verification of the reliability of such annotation schemes across text types.
(f) Crowd-sourcing annotation works to trained and partly trained corpus text annotators.
(g) Supporting discourse annotation of some aspects for larger datasets.
(h) Marking discourse relations to various computational frameworks and applicable for argumentation mining.
(i) Marking the information structural concepts in texts (i.e., *topics, focuses, givenness, and questions under discussion*).
(j) Document the current state of the art for preparing a blueprint for future direction in discourse annotation.

The development of tools that can be used in discourse annotation is the need of the time. There is also a need for starting research to bridge up gaps existing between qualitative linguistic analysis of texts and empirically broad analysis of discourse properties on ecologically and ethnographically valid databases. It is also necessary to design tools for integrating different layers of annotation in a single piece of text (e.g., *different types and use of words, different sentence types, various discourse types, and elements,* etc.). Experiments for integrating different layers of information (i.e., *from word to discourse level*) to text can be an agenda in discourse annotation. The immediate applications of discourse annotation include the utilization of annotated text in language description, critical discourse analysis, machine interpretation of a text, and ethnography. Future use of this corpus, along with other types of annotated corpora, in various domains of human knowledge, is a far more workable incentive (O'Donnell, 1999).

6.6 Rhetoric Annotation

Rhetoric annotation (also called a figure-of-speech annotation) is another type of corpus annotation. In this scheme, we annotate various rhetorical features and properties (e.g., *similes, metaphors, metonymies, zeugmas, idioms, hyperboles, foregrounding, aphorisms,* and others) in a spoken or written text (Cuddon, 1998) manually or automatically. Rhetorical annotation is necessary because we want to mark out those rhetorically designed sentences which are characteristically different from typical syntactic constructions. Such sentences usually differ in lexical choice, lexical ordering, syntactic form, grammatical formation, semantic information, stylistic implication, discourse reference, and linguistic significance from typical normal sentences. Theoretically, we argue that the use of figures-of-speech in a written or spoken text is actually a kind of deviation from ordinary and accepted manners of linguistic expression. In highly stylized sentences, words are used in different orders from their typical permitted orders in a text to evoke a new sense to enhance the ways the thoughts are being expressed. Therefore, rhetoric annotation becomes a crucial strategy for capturing hidden information that is otherwise not possible to derive from a simple syntactic analysis of sentences. Rhetoric annotation is a useful strategy based on which we understand how various figures-of-speech, which are used in a text, contribute to the construction of information in the text.

Aristotle has defined *rhetoric* as "the faculty of understanding in any given case the available means of persuasion" (Aristotle, 1982). There are five canons of rhetoric (i.e., *invention, arrangement, style, memory,* and *delivery*) that are implicitly present in a text. We require a text annotator to capture these canons and mark them in a text so that the text becomes easier for comprehension, linguistic analysis, and extralinguistic interpretation (Crowley & Hawhee, 2004). It is noted that the figures-of-speech that are used in texts often change the form and texture of an ordinary expression. The use of such devices generates many new shades of meaning and implications which are different from the literal senses of a text. Thus, they enhance the quality of a text and modify the ways our thoughts are represented. Given below a few quotes to show how rhetorics in texts are indeed important in understanding a text.

(a) "The figures of speech reveal to us the apparently limitless plasticity of language itself. We are confronted, inescapably, with the intoxicating possibility that we can make language do for us almost anything we want. Or at least a Shakespeare can" (Quinn, 1995:15).
(b) "Figures of speech change the ordinary language through repetition, substitution, sound, and wordplay. They mess around with words—skipping them, swapping them, and making them sound different" (Heinrichs, 2007: 31).
(c) "But instead of being inventions of art, they are the natural, and therefore necessary and universal forms, in which excited imagination and passion manifest themselves. The young and the old, the barbarous and the civilized, all employ them unconsciously. Languages in their earlier state are highly figurative; as they grow older they lose their natural picturesqueness and become collections of lifeless symbols. These abstract forms are regarded by rhetoricians and grammarians as the natural and ordinary forms of speech, and so they describe figures as departures from the usual forms of expression." (Hepburn, 1875: 93)
(d) "The vast pool of terms for verbal ornamentation has acted like a gene pool for the rhetorical imagination, stimulating us to look at language in another way. The figures have worked historically to teach a way of seeing." (Lanham, 1991).

From the language processing perspective, rhetorical devices are critical items that play crucial roles in the understanding of a text. Rhetorical devices deserve attention and annotation for the following reasons.

(a) Rhetorical devices are frequently used in natural language texts. We find that different figures-of-speech are used in all kinds of texts, although in a different frequency, to make a text more interesting, more penetrative, and more impactful.
(b) Rhetorical devices often become an area of central focus in cognitive linguistics, literary studies, stylistics, and developing semantic ontologies like FrameNets and WordNets.
(c) Rhetorical devices epitomize argument structure, which is increasingly becoming a prime concern for advanced language processing researches. Figures-of-speech epitomize analogic argumentation of a proposition, yet these are largely unrecognized and unattended in machine learning.
(d) There are figures-of-speech (especially the *schemes*) which have formal patterns and which are detected through surface analysis by algorithms. An analysis of these *schemes* helps us to understand how information, arguments, and sentiments are mixed together in construction.

Rhetorical devices are tough computational challenges. They are still elusive and enigmatic, despite the careful attention they have drawn from stylistics, literary criticism, linguistics, cognitive science, and artificial intelligence (Harris et al., 2018). In this context, we argue for applying novel computational methods for rhetoric annotation on digitally accessible texts of various types. We propose to assign annotation to those rhetorical devices (e.g., *metaphors, metonymies, idioms, foregrounding, hyperboles, zeugmas, proverbs, similes,* etc.) which are frequently used to convey an extra amount of information in a text. We argue for annotating these devices in a different way in a text because these are structurally, functionally, and characteristically different from the normal form, function, and character of phrases and sentences used in a text.

The use of figure-of-speech in a text is a willful and deliberate event. The text composer consciously tries to deviate from the standard manners of expression. A text composer uses words and multiword units in a text in different senses to enhance the way their thoughts are molded for manifestation. Therefore, it is necessary to annotate figurative expressions through rhetoric annotation for understanding the multidimensional implication of a text. Rhetoric annotation can help to know how different figures-of-speech are used in a text and how they help in the construction of information in different shades and layers within a text. Successful application of rhetoric annotation on a piece of text is a more complex and tedious process of text annotation. We are yet to develop a full set of tagset for rhetoric annotation. It is, therefore, an open area of research and application in the wider frame of text annotation.

6.7 Conclusion

A corpus annotated with different kinds of non-conventional information is a unique linguistic resource. It is useful for several works of mainstream linguistic and information technology. Such corpora have multiple applications in language engineering, textual analysis of a language, cognitive linguistics, computational linguistics, and allied domains. Multiple application potentials are the incentives that can motivate us to generate annotated corpora of various types and make them available for use in academic and commercial works. New kinds of corpus annotation demand new applicational foresight, new linguistic knowledge, and new text analysis skills with the serious involvement of annotators and system designers. It asks for developing benchmarked standards which may be adopted across languages for producing annotated corpora of different types. However, any corpus that is annotated with non-conventional linguistic information has to answer the following questions:

(a) What kind of linguistic information is annotated in a text?
(b) Why this kind of linguistic information is required to be annotated?
(c) How this linguistic information is to be annotated into the text?
(d) What are the short- and long-term benefits of such annotations?

To address these questions, we need to come up with innovative schemes and plans of work. It will allow to annotate various kinds of linguistic information on a text. Information may be related to orthography, transcription, meaning, anaphora, discourse, pragmatics, sociolinguistics, rhetorics, and other domains. During annotation, we may annotate only one type of information in a text at a time and preserve other types of information for other types of text annotation. Mixing information of different types in one annotation is not sensible. It makes an annotated corpus clumsy in representation and cumbersome in information retrieval and text data management.

It is to be understood that all types of information that are annotated in a text are not necessary for all kinds of applications and utilization of a corpus. We are free to add additional levels of annotation to a corpus even if it is already annotated with other levels of information. It is expected that the annotation scheme of a particular type should be designed and developed in such a manner that it does not put up barriers to other annotation types. To make it feasible, however, there should be no curtailment with the amount of information that is to be annotated at each level of a text. The final realization is that the more levels of information annotated to a corpus, the utility of a corpus is more enhanced across domains and disciplines. A corpus, which is annotated at different levels with different types of information, is indeed a treasure island that is ready to serve the needs of text users coming from different walks of life.

References

Archer, D., & Culpeper, J. (2003). Socio-pragmatic annotation: New directions and possibilities in historical corpus linguistics. In A. Wilson, P. Rayson, & A. McEnery (Eds.), *Corpus linguistics by the Lune: A festschrift for Geoffrey Leech* (pp. 37–58). Peter Lang.

Archer, D., McEnery, T., Rayson, P., & Hardie, A. (2003). Developing an automated semantic analysis system for Early Modern English. In Archer, D., Rayson, P., Wilson, A., and McEnery, T. (Eds.). *Proceedings of the corpus linguistics 2003 conference.* UCREL technical paper number 16 (pp. 22–31). UCREL, Lancaster University.

Aristotle. (1982). *The art of rhetoric* (Trans. John Henry Freese). Loeb Classical Library.

Atkins, S., Clear, J., & Ostler, N. (1992). Corpus design criteria. *Literary and Linguistic Computing, 7*(1), 1–16.

Boersma, P., & van Heuven, V. (2001). Speak and unSpeak with PRAAT. *Glot International., 5*(9/10), 341–347.

Carlson, L., Marcu, D., & Okurowski, M. E. (2003). Building a discourse-tagged corpus in the framework of rhetorical structure theory. In Kuppevelt, J. V. & Smith, R. W. (Eds.) *Current and new directions in discourse and dialogue* (pp. 85–112). Springer.

Crowley, S., & Hawhee, D. (2004). *Ancient rhetorics for contemporary students.* Pearson Education.

Cuddon, J. A. (1998). *The Penguin dictionary of literary terms and literary theory.* Penguin Books.

Dash, N. S. (2009). *Language corpora: Past, present, and future.* Mittal Publications.

Dash, N. S., & Ramamoorthy, L. (2019). *Utility and Application of Language Corpora.* Springer Nature.

DuBois, J. W., Cumming, S., Schuetze-Coburn, S., & Paolino, D. (Eds.) (1992). *Discourse transcription.* Santa Barabara papers in linguistics (vol. 4). University of California.

Edwards, J. A., & Lampert, M. D. (Eds.). (1993). *Talking data: Transcription and coding in discourse research.* Erlbaum.

Fink, G. A., Johanntokrax, M., & Schaffranietz, B. (1995). A flexible formal language for the orthographic transcription of spontaneous spoken dialogues. In *Proceedings of the 4th European conference on speech communication and speech technology (Eurospeech'95)* (vol. 1, pp. 871–874). Madrid, Spain, 18–21 Sept 1995.

Garside, R., & Rayson, P. (1997). Higher-level annotation tools. In R. Garside, G. Leech, & A. McEnery (Eds.), *Corpus annotation: Linguistic information from computer text corpora* (pp. 179–193). Longman.

Garside, R., Leech, G., & McEnery, A. (Eds.). (1997). *Corpus annotation: Linguistic information from computer text corpora.* Longman.

Grice, M., Leech, G., Weisser, M., & Wilson, A. (2000). Representation and annotation of dialogue. In: Dafydd, G., Mertins, I. and Moore, R.K. (eds.) *Handbook of multimodal & spoken dialogue systems. Resources, terminology,* and *product evaluation* (pp. 1–101). Kluwer Academic Publishers.

Grover, C., Facrell, J., Vereecken, H., Martens, J. P., & Coile, B. V. (1998). Designing prosodic databases for automatic modelling in 6 languages. In *Proceedings of the 3rd ESCA/COCOSDA workshop on speech synthesis (SSW3–1998)* (pp. 93–98). Jenolan Caves House, Blue Mountains, Australia, 26–29 Nov 1998.

Gussenhoven, C., Rietveld, T., & Terken, J. (1999). *ToDI: Transcription of Dutch intonation.* http://todi.let.kun.nl/ToDI/home.htm

Halliday, M. A. K., & Hasan, R. (1976). *Cohesion in English (English language series 9).* Longman.

Halliday, M. A. K., & Hasan, R. (1989). *Language, context, and text: Aspects of language in a social-semiotic perspective.* Oxford University Press.

Harris, R. A., Marco, C. D., Ruan, S., & O'Reilly, C. (2018). An annotation scheme for rhetorical figures. *Argument & Computation, 9,* 155–175.

Heinrichs, J. (2007). *Thank you for arguing.* Three Rivers Press.

Hepburn, A., & Bolden, G. B. (2013). The conversation analytic approach to transcription. In J. Sidnell & T. Stivers (Eds.), *The handbook of conversation analysis* (pp. 57–76). Blackwell.

Hepburn, A. D. (1875). *Manual of English rhetoric*. American Book Company.
Hymes, D. (1962). The ethnography of speaking. In T. Gladwin & W. C. Sturtevant (Eds.), *Anthropology and human behavior* (pp. 13–53). The Anthropology Society of Washington.
Hymes, D. (1964). Introduction: Toward ethnographies of communication. *American Anthropologist, 66*(6), 1–34.
Jakobson, R. (1959). On linguistic aspects of translation. In R. A. Brower (Ed.), *On translation* (pp. 232–239). Harvard University Press.
Jakobson, R. (1960). Linguistics and poetics. In T. Sebeok (Ed.), *Style in language* (pp. 350–377). MIT Press.
Johansson, S. (1995). The encoding of spoken texts. *Computers & the Humanities, 29*(1), 149–158.
Joos, M. (1962). The five clocks. *International Journal of American Linguistics, 28*, 9–62.
Knowles, G. (1991). Prosodic labelling: The problem of tone group boundaries. In S. Johansson & A.-B. Stenström (Eds.), *English computer corpora: Selected papers and research guides* (pp. 149–163). Mouton de Gruyter.
Lanham, R. (1991). *A handlist of rhetorical terms* (2nd ed.). University of California Press.
Lee, A., Prasad, R., Joshi, A., Dinesh, N., & Webber, B. (2006). Complexity of dependencies in discourse. In *Proceedings of the 5th Workshop on Treebanks and Linguistic Theory (TLT'06)*.
Leech, G., & Wilson, A. (1999). Guidelines & standards for tagging. In H. van Halteren (Ed.), *Syntactic wordclass tagging* (pp. 55–80). Kluwer.
Leech, G. (1993). Corpus annotation schemes. *Literary and Linguistic Computing, 8*(4), 275–281.
Löfberg, L., Archer, D., Piao, S., Rayson, P., McEnery, A., Varantola, K., & Juntunen, J. P. (2003). Porting an English semantic tagger to the Finnish language. In: Archer, D., Rayson, P., Wilson, A., & McEnery, T. (Eds.) In *Proceedings of the corpus linguistics 2003 conference*. UCREL technical paper number 16 (pp. 457–464). UCREL, Lancaster University.
Löfberg, L., Juntunen, J. P., Nykanen, A., Varantola, K., Rayson, P., & Archer, D. (2004). Using a semantic tagger as a dictionary search tool. In: Williams, G., & Vessier, S. (Eds.) *Proceedings of the 11th EURALEX (European association for lexicography) International congress (Euralex 2004)* (vol. I, pp. 127–134). Université de Bretagne Sud, 6–10 July 2004.
Löfberg, L., Piao, S., Rayson, P., Juntunen, J.P., Nykänen, A., & Varantola, K. (2005). A semantic tagger for the Finnish language. In *Proceedings of the corpus linguistics 2005 conference series online e-journal* (vol. 1, no. 1.). 14–17 July 2005.
McArthur, T. (Ed.). (1981). *Longman lexicon of contemporary English*. Longman.
McEnery, T., & Wilson, A. (1996). *Corpus linguistics*. Edinburgh University Press.
Milde, J. T., & Gut, U. B. (2002). A prosodic corpus of non-native speech. In: Bel, B., & Marlien, I. (Eds.) *Proceedings of the speech prosody 2002 conference* (pp. 503–506). Laboratoire Parole et Language, 11–13 April 2002.
Miltsakaki, E., Prasad, R., Joshi, A., & Webber, B. (2004). *Annotating discourse connectives and their arguments*. In NAACL/HLT Workshop on Frontiers in Corpus Annotation.
O'Donnell, M. B. (1999). The use of annotated corpora for New Testament discourse analysis: A survey of current practice and future prospects. In S. E. Porter & J. T. Reed (Eds.), *Discourse analysis and the new testament: Results and applications* (pp. 71–117). Sheffield Academic Press.
Piao, S., Archer, D., Mudraya, O., Rayson, P., Garside, R., McEnery, A.M., & Wilson, A. (2006). A large semantic lexicon for corpus annotation. In *Proceedings of the corpus linguistics 2005 conference series online e-journal* (vol. 1, no. 1). July 14–17.
Piao, S., Bianchi, F., Dayrell, C., D'Egidio, A., & Rayson, P. (2015). Development of the multilingual semantic annotation system. In *Proceedings of the 2015 conference of the North American chapter of the association for computational linguistics—human language technologies (NAACL HLT 2015)* (pp. 1268–1274).
Piao, S., Rayson, P., Archer, D., & McEnery, A. M. (2005). Comparing and combining a semantic tagger and a statistical tool for MWE extraction. *Journal of Computer Speech & Language., 19*(4), 378–397.
Piao, S., Rayson, P., Archer, D., Bianchi, F., Dayrell, C., El-Haj, M., Jiménez, R., Knight, D., Kren, M., Löfberg, L., Nawab, R. M. A., Shafi, J., Teh, P., & Mudraya, O. (2016). Lexical coverage

evaluation of large-scale multilingual semantic lexicons for twelve languages. In *Proceedings of the 10th International language resources and evaluation conference (LREC2016)* (pp. 2614–2619).

Polakova, L., Mirovsky, J., Nedoluzhko, A., Jinova, P., Zikanova, S., & Hajicova, E. (2013). Introducing the Prague discourse treebank 1.0. In *Proceedings of the Sixth International joint conference on natural language processing (IJCNLP)* (pp. 91–99). 14–18 Oct 2013.

Portele, T., & Heuft, B. (1995). Two kinds of stress perception. In *Proceedings of the 13th international congress of phonetic sciences (ICPhS 95)* (pp. 126–129). 13–19 August 1995.

Prasad, R., Forbes-Riley, K., & Lee, A. (2017). Towards full-text shallow discourse relation annotation: Experiments with cross-paragraph implicit relations in the PDTB. In *Proceedings of the 18th Annual SIGdial meeting on discourse and dialogue* (pp. 7–16).

Quinn, A. (1995). *Figures of speech: 60 ways to turn a phrase.* Routledge.

Rastier, F. (ed.) (2001). *A little glossary of semantics. Texts* and *cultures (electronic glossary)* (Larry Marks Trans.). Retrieved on 26 June 2020.

Rayson, P., & Stevenson, M. (2008). Sense and semantic tagging. In A. Lüdeling & M. Kytö (Eds.), *Corpus linguistics: An international handbook* (pp. 564–579). Gruyter.

Rayson, P., & Wilson, A. (1996). The ACAMRIT semantic tagging system: progress report. In Evett, L. J., & Rose T. G. (Eds.) *Language engineering for document analysis and recognition, LEDAR, AISB96 workshop proceedings* (pp. 13–20).

Sinclair, J. M. (1994). Spoken language: Phonetic-phonemic and prosodic annotation. In Calzolari, N., Baker, M., & Kruyt, P. G. (Eds.) *Towards a network of European reference corpora* (pp. 129–132). Giardini.

Sperberg-McQueen, C. M., & Burnard, L. (Eds.) (1994). *Guidelines for electronic text encoding and interchange.* The Association for Computers and the Humanities/The Association for Literary and Linguistic Computing and The Association for Computational Linguistics.

Stenström, A.-B., & Andersen, G. (1996). More trends in the teenage talk: A corpus-based investigation of the discourse items 'cos' and 'init.' In C. Percy, C. F. Meyer, & I. Lancashire (Eds.), *Synchronic corpus linguistics: Papers from the 16th International conference on english language research on computerized corpora* (pp. 189–203). Rodopi.

Stenström, A.-B. (1984). Discourse tags. In J. Aarts & W. Meijs (Eds.), *Corpus linguistics: Recent developments in the use of computer corpora in English language research* (pp. 65–81). Rodopi.

Teufel, S., Carletta, J., & Moens, M. (1999). An annotation scheme for discourse-level argumentation in research articles. In *Proceedings of the 9th European conference of the ACL (EACL-99)* (pp. 110–117).

Webber, B., Stone, M., Joshi, A., & Knott, A. (2003). Anaphora and discourse structure. *Computational Linguistics, 29*(4), 545–587.

Webber, B. (2005). A short introduction to the Penn discourse treebank. In *Copenhagen working papers in language and speech processing.*

Wilson, A., & Thomas, J. A. (1997). Semantic annotation. In R. Garside, G. Leech, & A. McEnery (Eds.), *Corpus annotation: Linguistic information from computer text corpora* (pp. 53–65). Longman.

Wolf, F., & Gibson, E. (2005). Representing discourse coherence: A corpus-based study. *Computational Linguistics, 31*, 249–287.

Web Links

http://lands.let.kun.nl/todi

http://lands.let.ru.nl/cgn/doc_English/topics/version_1.0/annot/prosody/info.htm

http://users.ox.ac.uk/~eets/Guidelines%20for%20Editors%2011.pdf.

http://www.fon.hum.uva.nl/praat/

http://www.helsinki.fi/varieng/series/volumes/10/diemer/
http://www.ling.upenn.edu/hist-corpora/annotation/index.html.
http://www.tei-c.org/release/doc/tei-p5-doc/en/Guidelines.pdf.
http://www.helsinki.fi/varieng/CoRD/corpora/CEEM/MEMTindex.html.
http://www.uis.no/getfile.php/Forskning/Kultur/MEG/Corpus_manual_%202011_1.pdf.
http://www.uis.no/research-and-phd-studies/research-areas/history-languages-and-literature/the-middle-english-scribal-texts-programme/meg-c/.
https://tei-c.org/release/doc/tei-p5-doc/en/html/CC.html
https://www.ling.upenn.edu/hist-corpora/annotation/index.html
http://phlox.lancs.ac.uk/ucrel/semtagger/chinese
http://phlox.lancs.ac.uk/ucrel/semtagger/dutch
http://phlox.lancs.ac.uk/ucrel/semtagger/italian
http://phlox.lancs.ac.uk/ucrel/semtagger/portuguese
http://phlox.lancs.ac.uk/ucrel/semtagger/spanish
http://ucrel.lancs.ac.uk/usas/
http://ucrel-api.lancaster.ac.uk/usas/tagger.html
http://www.revue-texto.net/Reperes/Glossaires/Glossaire_en.html
https://www.seas.upenn.edu/~pdtb/
http://www.wlv.ac.uk/~le1825/anaphora_resolution_papers/state.ps

Chapter 7
Morphological Processing of Words

Abstract The morphological processing of words is a lexical analysis process which is used to retrieve various kinds of morphological information from affixed and inflected words. The concept of morphological processing, in the general linguistic discussion, is often mixed up with part-of-speech annotation and syntactic annotation. To make things clear, we define the core concept of morphological processing and discuss some of the methods and approaches that are so far developed and used for processing words across languages. Also, we briefly describe how a morphological processing system is actually applied to analyze affixed and inflected words used in texts. Moreover, we show how processing of inflected words of different parts-of-speech usually put up strong challenges in the generation of right outputs; how orthographic irregularities and inconsistencies posit strong barriers in proper recognition of inflected words; and how detached words and lexical ambiguities can mar the robustness of a morphological processing system in analysis and generation of right outputs. The success of a morphological processing system largely depends on two basic components: (a) its ability in dealing with the inherent morphological complexities of inflected words, and (b) its ability in the management of linguistic data, information, and grammatical mapping rules. We address all these issues in this chapter with reference to Bengali—one of the highly inflected Indian languages.

Keywords Inflected words · Paradigm-based approach · Lemma · Grammatical mapping · Detached words · Delayed processing · Isolated ambiguity · Sequential ambiguity

7.1 Introduction

Morphological processing of words involves the analysis of the elements that are used to form a word. It is done manually or automatically based on the grammar of a language (Goldsmith, 2001). Technically, it refers to a process of knowing the internal structures to words by performing some decomposition operations on them to find out formative elements, patterns of their distribution, nature of their use, method of their composition, and nature of their function in the act of formation of words in a language. It also involves the generation of patterns and rules

N. S. Dash, *Language Corpora Annotation and Processing*,
https://doi.org/10.1007/978-981-16-2960-0_7

from analysis of inflected and affixed words and application of the same in lexical composition and decomposition, lexical identification, and part-of-speech (POS) annotation. Morphological processing is different from POS annotation on many grounds. In morphological processing, we try to retrieve grammatical information of morphemes to understand their functional roles in the formation of words. In POS annotation, on the other hand, we try to assign explicit part-of-speech value to words in a text after considering their morphological structures and function in the context of their use.

From a processing point of view, words are, with regard to their structure and composition, strings of continuous characters with approved surface representation. The morphemes that are combined to form words are the building blocks. Following the word formation rules (WFRs) of a language, morphemes are used in an organized manner to generate final forms of words (Selkirk, 1983: 7). For a word analysis tool, the ground method of morphological processing involves automatic extraction of morphemes with their full grammatical, syntactic, and semantic information to be used at higher levels of text processing. A tool that is used in morphological processing is also trained to learn about the functional role(s) of morphemes in generating words. Also, it explores morphophonemic representation and extracts grammatical, syntactic, and semantic information from words. To achieve success, it analyzes surface structures of words based on lexical, syntactic, morphophonemic, and semantic properties and information.

A morphological processing system in most cases, operates at the word level. At this stage, a word is presented either as a unit of a sentence bound with contextualized information or as a separate lexical unit isolated from any context of use. In both cases, a morphological processing system never tries to look beyond the word. In morphological processing, a word is a single composite unit which is made with one or more than one morpheme as formative elements. Once it is understood, a system extracts morphological, grammatical, and semantic information from words by using some methods of information extraction. Thus, it differs from syntactic processing (i.e., *parsing*) which operates at the sentence level and where words are treated as members of a larger construction (i.e., *phrase, clause,* and *sentence*). Syntactic processing involves a context-based analysis of syntactic roles of words and phrases by using information obtained from morphological processing.

Keeping this information in view, we organize this chapter in the following way. In Sect. 7.2, we summarize different methods used in morphological processing of words (e.g., *two-level morphology-based approach, paradigm based approach, stemmer based approach, acyclic graph-based approach, morph based approach, corpus-based approach, and suffix stripping based approach*); in Sect. 7.3, we focus on the issues in morphological processing with reference to word formation rules; in Sect. 7.4, we present a short sketch of the process of information storage in lemma and inflection database; in Sect. 7.5, we describe the basics of morphological processing; in Sect. 7.6, we propose a new method for processing detached words; in Sect. 7.7, we discuss possible outputs of morphological processing; in Sect. 7.8, we focus on the challenges of ambiguity in morphological processing; and in Sect. 7.9, we discuss applications of morphological processing in linguistics and other domains.

7.2 Models and Approaches

The efforts for analyzing morphological structures of words have been a part of linguistics for ages. Starting from the early ages of language study, we come across discussions of various types with regard to methods and approaches in analyzing form and meaning of words. Efforts are also made to understand their forms and functions when they are compiled in a lexical database as well as when they are used in a piece of text. Great grammarians of every age provided us with new insights for analyzing and understanding words, which, however, is not the topic of this chapter. Here our goal is to understand models and approaches scholars have used to analyze words automatically by a tool or system or through partial human intervention.

Analyzing the morphological structure of words through a computer system is not a trivial task. In the last fifty years, various models, methods, approaches, and strategies are proposed and applied for this purpose. Even then, we cannot claim that a morphological processing system for a language is ready (a) which works with hundred percent accuracy, (b) which can be used by any individual interested in this kind of work, and (c) which can be modeled and customized for any other language. The reality is that we have to go a long way before we can make a morphological processing system which is robust and useful for all kinds of words available in a language or all languages. Keeping this factor in mind, in the remaining part of this section, we present a brief outline of a few approaches that are used to develop automated or semi-automated morphological processing systems for English and some other languages.

A morphological processor, from a technical point of view, is a computer program that analyzes the morphological information of an input word and generates some results relating to the input word and its formative components. Guided by some linguistic rules and information, it detects morphemes used in a word and defines the roles of these morphemes. If we keep the basic requirements of a language in mind, a morphological processor, based on the area of its operation, may be divided into two broad types:

(a) **Single-word processor:** Works for single-word units—both inflected and non-inflected, e.g., *balechhilen* "said," *diner* "of days," *śaktiśālī* "powerful."
(b) **Double-word processor:** Works for words made of two words that are written separately, e.g., *biśeṣ bhābe* "specially," *niden pakṣe* "at least," *bale dilen* "said."

There are three primary methods for analyzing morphs of words in a language. Each one tries to capture the distinctions of morphs in different ways.

(a) Morph-based morphology (Item-and-Arrangement approach). Here words are looked into and analysed as arrangements of morphemes. For instance, the word, *internationally* is considered to be made with 'inter-', 'nation', '-al', and '-ly' where 'nation' is a free morph (base), while others are bound morphs (derivational affixes). In this process of analysis, we normally treat words as if they are made of with some morphemes which are put with each other to produce the final form (Beard, 1995: 2).

(b) Lexeme-based morphology (Item-and-Process approach). Here, instead of analysing a word as a set of morphemes arranged in a sequence, we consider a word as an outcome of application of some rules that alter the word or stem to produce a new word. For instance, during derivation, we invoke a derivational rule that takes a stem, changes it as per its requirement, and generates a new form which is different from the input form (Bybee, 1985: 11).

(c) Word-based morphology (Word-and-Paradigm approach). It takes paradigms as a central notion and instead of stating rules to combine morphemes into words or generating words from stems, it states about some generalizations that hold between the forms of inflectional paradigms. It considers words as 'whole words' that are related to each other by analogical rules. Words are categorized based on the pattern they fit into. The analogical rules apply both to existing words and to new words (Singh, 2003; Bhattacharja, 2007).

Keeping these three methods in view, morph analysis approaches are devised with a focus on the structure and formation of words used in languages. Some descriptions of the commonly used approaches are presented in the following subsections.

7.2.1 Two-Level Morphology-Based Approach

This approach is proposed by Koskenniemi (1983). It takes into account the phonological features in morphological processing. It introduces the concept of **concatenation** at the morpheme level based on language-specific processes of morphotactics and morphophonemics. The two levels which this system takes into operation are "surface-level" and "lexical level". It considers a word as a representation which has a direct and letter-for-letter correspondence between these forms (i.e., lexical and surface). Due to this factor, it is called a "two-level morphological analysis scheme" (also KIMMO system) (Koskenniemi, 1984). The "two-level morphology" approach is based on three rubrics:

(a) Rules are symbol-to-symbol constraints. These are applied in parallel and not in sequential order, like the rewrite rules.

(b) Constraints can refer to lexical context, surface context, or both contexts at the same time.

(c) Lexical lookup and morphological analysis are performed at the same time in tandem.

This approach uses regular expressions of a language to accept or reject a word. It follows a special system based on "finite-state machinery (automata)", which skims through morphological components used in a word. Within this system, letters are realized to have two levels: surface level and lexical level. Each letter belonging to the surface level is mapped with more than one symbol at the lexical level. Thus, for instance, character <t> converts into <c> at lexical level when it occurs before <i> . It remains <t> at surface level when it does not occur before <i> (i.e., t + i = ci, but t + u = tu). When the system starts to analyze words, it considers phonological rules with due emphasis on contexts of phonological change or conversion of characters, which determines the link between surface level and lexical levels of words. The structure in which this information is encoded in a system is "finite-state transducer"—an important part of "finite-state machinery". This approach is further modified to generate more robust outputs in the processing of Finnish words (Koskenniemi and Church 1988). It is also used by Karttunen and Wittenburg (1983) to process German and English words. Lun (1983) adopts this approach to develop an algorithm for the processing of French words. However, at present, this approach is no more used due to several constraints at concatenation and rule operation.

7.2.2 Paradigm-Based Approach

In this approach, an effort is made to process words based on a paradigm to which a word belongs. For a particular language, each word category is classified into certain types of paradigms (e.g., *noun, pronoun, verb, adjective, adverb, postposition*). Based on morphological properties and features of morphs, an algorithm is developed for a word paradigm for designing a morphological processor. In a morphologically productive language like Bengali, it is possible to form multiple words by applying word formation rules (WFRs) that are appropriate to a particular word paradigm. For instance, by using nominal affixes and inflections, we can generate more than a hundred nouns in Bengali (Dash, 2015: Chap. 5). Also, following this model, we can classify Bengali words into different paradigms (e.g., *noun paradigm, verb paradigm, adjective paradigm, adverb paradigm, and postposition paradigm*). Moreover, based on the nature of similarity in word formation processes and morphological operations, we can combine words of a particular paradigm with another paradigm. For instance, we can merge the Bengali pronoun paradigm with the Bengali noun paradigm as both the paradigms follow almost the same morphological processes in word formation.

A paradigm defines all the words that are generated from a given stem along with the grammatical features set that is associated with each word (Baxi et al., 2015). For constructing a paradigm, it is better to collect a large number of inflected words from a corpus and prepare a list of all possible suffixes from the data. The words which take a similar set of suffixes may be grouped into a single paradigm. For instance, for Bengali nouns, *rāstā* "road" and *darjā* "door" take the same markers for pluralization and inflection. So they are grouped under the same paradigm. Similarly, for Bengali verbs, *deoyā* "to give" and *neoyā* "to take" undergo the same types of morphophonological change during verbal conjugation. So they are grouped under the same paradigm. The argument is that rules to form words are the same for the words belonging to the same paradigm. The sets of suffixes that are used to generate inflected words are also the same.

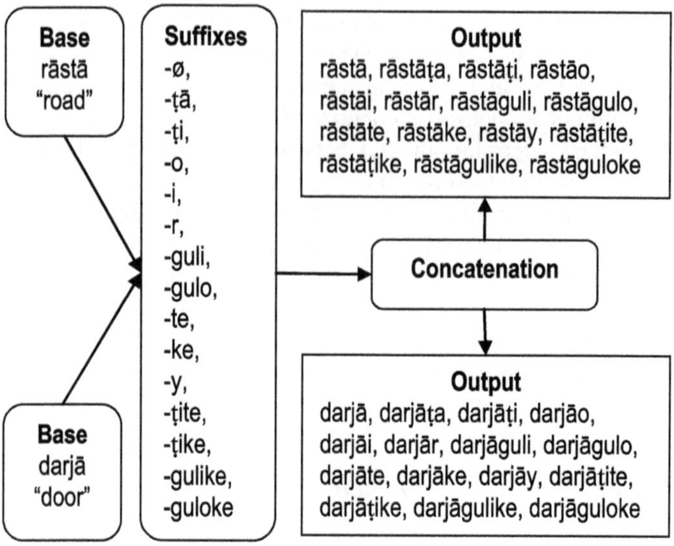

Fig. 7.1 Information processing in paradigm based approach

During the paradigm building phase, each paradigm is prepared with rules that help to obtain roots (and bases) and suffixes and inflections that go with the words of a paradigm. For instance, *rāstā* "road" and *darjā* "door" are put in the same paradigm because they behave similarly in word formation. The following diagram shows how information is processed and stored in a paradigm-based approach (Fig. 7.1). It works in two ways: (a) morphological decomposition and (b) morphological generation.

Once an inflected word is given as an input, it finds the suffixes to determine a matching paradigm. The paradigm may be one or many based on the nature of inflections used with an input word. The same rule and similar suffixes may be present in more than one paradigm. For each token, the system applies rules to break the token and generate a base as an output. If there are situations where a single inflected word is mapped with more than one base or root, it takes the support of linguistic rules, heuristics, and statistics to record multiple outputs. For example, the Bengali word *kamala* is mapped into noun paradigm as a noun without suffix (i.e., $kamala + \phi > kamala$ *"lotus"*) as well as into the verb paradigm as a verb with $-la$ suffix (i.e., $kam + la > kamla$ *"lessened"*).

7.2.3 Stemmer-Based Approach

In this approach, one uses a stemmer, which operates with a set of lexical rules containing a list of stems and a set of replacement rules that can strip affixes from inflected words. It is primarily a program-based automated approach where one has to specify all possible affixes that can go with a word with a set of replacement rules. The Porter algorithm (Porter, 1980) is one of the most widely used algorithms that is heavily used for stemming and morphological analysis of words in English and many other languages.

This algorithm is useful for stemming words. However, it is not much robust for lemmatization of words of many inflected languages. It is far less useful for morphological processing as it hardly tries to address the primary goals of a morphological processing system. Breaking a word into a few valid morphs is not the only goal of a morphological processing system. It has to identify the morphological identity of each morph as well as show the grammatical role each morph plays in the formation of a word. A stemmer is not a good candidate for fulfilling all the tasks that we expect from a morphological processing system. In our view, the Porter algorithm is not useful for creating a morphological processing system for highly agglutinative Dravidian languages as well as for highly inflectional Indian languages like Bengali, Odia, and Assamese.

7.2.4 Acyclic Graph-Based Approach

For processing inflected Bengali verbs, scholars used the acyclic graph-based approach (AGBA), which managed to process only a specific set of inflected verbs with marginal success (Sengupta & Chaudhuri, 1993). This approach is further modified to generate trie-structure-based approach (TAB), which is a little more robust and accurate in processing inflected words in Bengali (Dash et al., 1997). Despite its robustness, simplicity, and easy computability, it has not been successful to process many inflected verbs which are differently inflected or which do not fall under any existing paradigm of inflection. Also, it records very limited success in the act of processing of inflected nouns and affixed adjectives. Besides, it is not tested much with large varieties of inflected words taken from the modern Bengali corpus. Therefore, its claim of its applicability in other inflectional Indian languages like Hindi, Assamese, Marathi, and Odia is not beyond question.

7.2.5 Morph-Based Approach

This approach tries to process words in an inflected language like Bengali by considering the roles of graphemes (i.e., *orthographic symbols or characters*) used in the formation of words. Based on this approach, it is called a graphemestructure-based morph analysis (GS_Morph) system (Sengupta, 1997). The basic criteria of this approach are as follows:

(a) It is primarily based on graphemes and orthographic symbols used in writing words in a language.

(b) It takes input data in the conventional spelling of words rather than in their phonemic transcripted forms.
(c) Phonological features of characters are ignored as these are not possible to implement fruitfully within a morph analyzer.
(d) The spelling system of a language like Bengali is not always phonemic. Phonological rules are applicable to a few words in phonemic form.

This approach shows some advantages that are not found in other approaches proposed for Bengali. It uses simple linguistic algorithms the implementation of which is straightforward with minimum programming skill. The method is further modified and fine-tuned after analysis of resultant outputs generated by an earlier version of the system. However, this approach is used for processing only Bengali verbs (Sengupta, 1999). It is not known if this approach works equally efficiently for words to other parts-of-speech such as nouns, pronouns, and adjectives.

7.2.6 Corpus-Based Approach

This approach is based on corpus data and the use of statistics (Wicentowski, 2005). In most cases, large corpora are used as training databases. Moreover, machine learning algorithms are used to collect necessary information and features from corpus data to train a system. The difficulty of this approach, however, is to find out a corpus that is annotated at the part-of-speech (POS) level and is made ready for use by a system. For advanced languages like English and Spanish, it is not a problem as many corpora are annotated at the part-of-speech level. But for less-known languages like Santali, Mundari, or Kurdmali, this is a bottleneck as these languages do not have a corpus where words are annotated at the part-of-speech level.

In English, after the introduction of digital text corpora, many approaches are experimented with and developed within a very short period of time. In most cases, the emphasis is given on initial manual analysis of words and the use of information as inputs in the development of an automated morphological processing system. For instance, using information from *Brown Corpus*, *Lancaster-Oslo-Bergen Corpus*, *British National Corpus*, *Survey of English Usage*, *American National Corpus*, and others, the morphological processing system is developed for English. The performance of corpus-based systems is far better than rule-based systems as corpus-based systems use knowledge and information from corpus data.

A corpus works as a source of information regarding the morphological structure of words. It also works as a testbed for the evaluation of the performance of a system. Information about how corpus data are used, how systems are developed, how new approaches are applied, how new techniques are implemented, and how better results are achieved are available in Greene and Rubin (1971), de Haan (1984), Garside (1987), Church et al. (1991), deRose (1991), Meyer and Tenney (1993), Merialdo (1994), Barnbrook (1998), Bosch and Daelemans (1999), Yarowsky and Wicentowski (2000), Oflazer et al. (2001), Creutz (2003), Wicentowski (2004), Creutz and

Lagus (2005), Freitag (2005), Nicolas and Francaois (2005), and others. Many of the systems are not only interested in the morphological processing of words but also concerned with grammatical, semantic, and syntactic annotation of texts.

7.2.7 *Suffix Stripping-Based Approach*

This is another approach which is useful for agglutinative Dravidian languages (Viswanathan et al. 2003; Idicula and David 2007; Rajeev et al., 2008, Jayan et al., 2011). The primary advantage of this approach is that, for languages like Tamil and Malayalam, words are usually formed by adding suffixes to the root parts of words. This aspect of word formation is well suited for using in suffix stripping-based approach. It is believed that once the suffix part is identified, a stem of a word is obtained by removing that suffix part and applying *sandhi* rules that help in the removal of the suffix from the root. This approach may work equally well in the case of inflectional languages like Bengali and Odia where the suffix part is stripped from an inflected word to separate root and suffix. Interestingly, in many such cases, the application of *sandhi* rules is not required.

A major part of the following section is related to an experimental process that we propose for morphological processing of Bengali words (not suffix stripping alone). Our discussion assimilates ideas and information from all the approaches mentioned above. Our approach is a combination of a paradigm-based approach, corpus-based approach, and suffix stripping-based approach. It is, therefore, better to call it a **multimodal morphological processing system** (MMPS).

7.3 Issues in Morphological Processing

Most of the inflected words used in a language belong to nouns and verbs than other parts-of-speech (Maxwell, 2002). In Bengali, the use of inflection is more frequent in verbs and pronouns followed by nouns, adjectives, and adverbs. It is observed that almost all Bengali verbs and pronouns, barring a few, are inflected (Dash, 2015, Chap. 2). During nominal and pronominal declension and verbal conjugation, word-formative elements are attached to nominal/pronominal bases and verb roots, respectively, to produce inflected forms. The primary tasks of a morphological processing system, therefore, include the followings:

(a) Identification of inflected words from a text.
(b) Detection of a part-of-speech or lexical class of an inflected word.
(c) Identification of the inflection part of a word.
(d) Segmentation of inflection part from base or root.
(e) Extraction of morpho-grammatical information of inflection.

(f) Produce this information as an output when needed.
(g) Supply this information and data for parsing and word-sense disambiguation.

The extraction of information of part-of-speech of a word and representation of information relating to inflection (e.g., *singularity, plurality, gender, case, person, tense, aspect, modality, honorificity, emphasis, degree*) are necessary tasks of a morphological processing system. It enables one to analyze non-inflected, inflected, compound, and reduplicated words of a language. It helps in the management of a large amount of morpho-grammatical and lexico-syntactic information which are indispensable in works like word retrieval from texts, machine translation, spelling checking, lexical categorization, lexical database generation, language teaching, and lexicography. A morphological processing system thus contributes to understanding the form, identity, and function of a word of a language. It is an indispensable system in online language education, cognition, and application.

A morphological processing system, as stated above, is primarily concerned with a study of the internal morphological structure of a word. It is a stage where surface structure, lexical type, grammatical property, formation, and functional role(s) of a word are empirically analyzed. For an inflectional language like Bengali, a morphological processing system reduces lexical ambiguities by increasing compactness in the process of lexical representation of a word. At the first stage, manual analysis of inflected words is necessary to understand how an inflected word is formed in a language. Analysis of a large number of inflected words shows that there are two types of morphs which are used in an inflected word.

(a) **Root or stem** (the primary part of a word). The inflection part is added to the root and stem to generate an inflated form. Roots and stems are free to be used as independent words with an explicit or implicit meaning.
(b) **Inflection** (the secondary part of a word). It is attached to a root or stem to form an inflected word. It is a covert term that includes all word-formative elements that are added to roots and stem to generate additional linguistic information of words.

After structural analysis of inflected words of all parts-of-speech, we find that Bengali inflected words are generated as a result of the following processes (Table 7.1).

In the processes noted above, each constituent morph contributes toward the overall linguistic form of a word. Based on this formation, morphs are divided into several subclasses, and each one discharges a specific and unique linguistic function. In word formation in Bengali, morphs are usually governed by the following two rules:

(i) **Rules of morphosyntax**. Works to restrict random conjoining of various morpheme subclasses.
(ii) **Rules of generativity**. Controls orthographic restructuring of characters at the boundary of two conjoining morphs.

The rules of morphosyntax generate a final form of a word with constituent morphs. These rules are, therefore, known as **word formation rules** (WFR). In

Table 7.1 Generation of inflected words in Bengali

No	Parts	Example	Gloss
1	Stem + Inflection	kāler	"of time"
2	Inflection + Stem	ākāl	"famine"
3	Inflection + Stem + Inflection	ākāler	"of famine"
4	Stem + Stem + Inflection	dinkāler	"of days"
5	Inflection + Stem + Stem	sudinkāl	"good days"
6	Inflection + Stem + Stem + Inflection	sudinkāler	"of good days"
7	Root + Inflection	balchhe	"is saying"
8	Root + Root + Inflection	bale phelechhe	"has said"

Bengali, a morph is not usually embedded in another morph during word formation. However, due to some spelling rules, the final orthographic forms of some words are not the results of a simple linear combination of constituent morphs. Sometimes spelling rules control the selection of rules that are to operate at morph boundaries. Therefore, a big challenge in Bengali word processing is the detection of morph boundaries, which are not as explicit as a boundary existing between words. Therefore, for extracting an inflected part from an inflected word, we must have good knowledge of Bengali grammar as knowledge of grammar helps one to find out the right inflection part.

The identification of part-of-speech of an inflected word, when it is not used in a text, is done with help of inflection. For instance, in Bengali, *balgulo* "balls" is a noun, and *balechhila* "said" is a verb based on inflection (-$gulo_{[\text{NN\_NUM\_PRL}]}$ and –$echhila_{[\text{FV\_TN\_PST}]}$) they are attached with. On the other hand, the determination of part-of-speech of an inflected word, when it is used in a text, depends on the role it plays in a sentence. By analyzing the syntactic and semantic role of an inflected word in a sentence, we identify if a word is used as a verb or a noun. For example, *bale* (< bal + -e) can be a verb or a noun based on the context of its use. Therefore, the determination of part-of-speech of an inflected Bengali word depends on its structure and function in a sentence.

During morphological processing, an inflected finite verb is treated as a string where a root is tagged with an inflection. The inflection part includes aspect marker, auxiliary marker, tense marker, person marker, and particle in a fixed sequential order. That means all the elements are grammatically arranged in a fixed linear order following a sequence of their permitted use in Bengali. For instance, *ghumāiteichhilen* "was indeed sleeping" is an inflected finite verb in Bengali which has a root (i.e., √ghumā) followed by an aspect (i.e., –*ite*), an emphatic particle (i.e., −*i*), an auxiliary (i.e., −*ch*), a tense marker (i.e., −*il*), and a person + honorific marker (i.e., −*en*). The final processed output of this verb is as follows (Table 7.2).

In a similar manner, the word *dokānguloteo* "in the shops also" is an inflected noun which has a stem (i.e., *dokān*) followed by a plural (i.e., −*gulo),* a locative case (i.e., −*te*), and an emphatic particle (i.e., −*o*). The word *tomāderkei* "to you indeed" is an

Table 7.2 Morphological processing of a Bengali inflected finite verb

Input word	ghumāiteichhilen
Root	√ghumā)
Inflection Part	−āiteichhilen
Number	Sing + Plural
Aspect	−ite-
Particle_Emphatic	−i-
Auxiliary	−ch-
Tense_Past	−il–
Person_3rd	−en–
Honorific	−en–
Part-of-Speech	Finite Verb
Meaning	"was indeed sleeping"

inflected pronoun which has a stem (i.e., −*tomā*) followed by a plural (i.e., −*der*), an accusative case (i.e., −*ke*), and an emphatic particle (i.e., −*i*). The word *buddhimān* "intelligent" is an adjective which has a nominal stem (i.e., *buddhi*) followed by an adjective suffix (i.e., −*mān*). In each case, the word-formative elements are used following the word formation rules (WFRs) applicable to Bengali.

7.4 Method of Information Storage

Before starting morphological processing of inflected words, it is necessary to develop a lexical database, which is to be used at subsequent stages of processing. For Bengali, a digital lexical database (DLD) is compiled with inflected words of all types collected from a text corpus. The DLD is different from a standard dictionary in many aspects and features. It has two major parts.

(a) **Lemma Database (LD)**: It contains regular and allomorphic variants of verb roots, nominal stems, pronominal bases, adjectival stems, adverbial stems, postpositions, and indeclinables.
(b) **Inflection Database (ID)**: It contains all kinds of inflections and their allomorphic variations belonging to words of all parts-of-speech in the language.

At the training phase, LD and ID are compiled in sequential order following the frame stated (Table 7.3).

The following stages are followed to form DLD, LD, and ID (Table 7.4).

The lemma database and inflection database are divided into several subgroups based on part-of-speech of words. For instance, lemma database has seven subgroups each one of which stores lemmas of specific part-of-speech. Thus, 1st one (LD1) stores nominal stems; 2nd one (LD2) stores pronominal bases; 3rd one (LD3) stores

Table 7.3 Proposed structure of DLD with LD and ID

Digital lexicaldatabase (DLD)			
Lemma database (LD)		Inflection database (ID)	
LD1 (NN)	Nominal stem	ID1 (NN)	Nominal suffix
LD2 (PN)	Pronominal base	ID2 (PN)	Pronominal suffix
LD3 (FV)	Verbal root	ID3 (FV)	Verbal suffix
LD4 (AJ)	Adjectival stem	ID4 (AJ)	Adjectival suffix
LD5 (AV)	Adverbial stem	ID5 (AV)	Adverbial suffix
LD6 (PP)	Postposition		
LD7 (IND)	Indeclinables		–

Table 7.4 Preparatory stages for morphological processing

Stage 1	All non-inflected and inflected words are compiled from a corpus and sorted out in alphabetical order
Stage 2	After tokenization, all repetitively used words are allowed to have only one entry in the list
Stage 3	Sorted words are classified into inflected and non-inflected forms based on the use of inflection
Stage 4	Non-inflected words are directly put into the appropriate subgroup of lemma database (LD) based on their part-of-speech (e.g., non-inflected nouns are sent to LD1)
Stage 5	Inflected words are further classified according to their part-of-speech. Necessary information is taken from dictionaries and grammars to assign a part-of-speech to the words
Stage 6	Inflected words are split into Lemma and Inflection. Lemmas are put in LD subgroups according to their primary part-of-speech
Stage 7	Inflections are classified based on their part-of-speech and stored within the respective subgroups of IL
Stage 8	Representative samples of the inflected word of different parts-of-speech are manually analyzed to find rules of grammatical mapping that underlie behind their surface forms
Stage 9	Based on information obtained from Stage 8, a schema is prepared to identify the inflections that are tagged to a lemma to generate a valid surface form
Stage 10	Identified grammatical mapping rules are converted into an algorithm for designing a morphological processing system

verb roots; 4th one (LD4) stores adjectival stems; 5th one (LD5) stores adverbial stems; 6th one (LD6) stores postpositions; and 7th one (LD7) stores indeclinables. Similarly, inflection database has five subgroups of which 1st one (ID1) stores nominal inflections, 2nd one (ID2) stores pronominal inflections, 3rd one (ID3) stores verbal inflections, 4th one (ID4) stores adjectival inflections, and 5th one (ID5) stores adverbial inflections. Inflections are collected from analysis of inflected words of different parts-of-speech from Bengali. The lemma database and inflection database are often updated and grammatical mapping rules are modified to deal with

Table 7.5 (Prefix) + lemma + (suffix) + (case) combination for nouns

(NP)	+	NL	+	(NS)	+	(NC)	→	Output
Set_1	+	Set_1	+	Set_1	+	Set_1	→	Set_1
Set_2	+	Set_2	+	Set_2	+	Set_2	→	Set_2
Set_3	+	Set_3	+	Set_3	+	Set_3	→	Set_3
Set_4	+	Set_4	+	Set_4	+	Set_4	→	Set_4

new words, which are found in the corpus but not in the dictionary. These databases and sets of grammatical rules are indispensable resources for the morphological processing of words. The information presented above is not found in the dictionary. What makes it relevant in the present context is its elaborate analysis of the structure of words. This is an elaborate set of information required for designing a morphological processing system. The system with lemmas, inflections, and grammatical mapping rules processes inflected words and produces outputs with relevant morphological information.

The information collected from inflected words is stored in a unique manner in subgroups for processing words. For instance, nominal prefixes are stored in Noun Prefix (NP), nominal lemmas are stored in Noun Lemma (NL), nominal suffixes are stored in Noun Suffix (NS), and nominal case markers are stored in Noun Case (NC) in sequential order. This felicitates root–suffix mapping for the generation of valid inflected nouns. The following list shows how (NP) + NL + (NS) + (NC) information of nouns are stored in a noun database (Table 7.5). In the case of inflected nouns, NL is a mandatory component while NP, NS, and NC are optional components.

Similarly, for inflected pronouns, lemmas are stored in Pronoun Lemma (PL), suffixes are stored in Pronoun Suffix (PS), and case markers are stored in pronoun case (PC). Since Bengali pronouns do not use prefixes, there is no pronoun prefix group. For adjectives, adjectival prefixes are stored in adjective prefix (AP), adjectival lemmas are stored in adjective lemma (AL), and adjectival suffixes are stored in adjective suffix (AS). As adjectives never use case markers, it is absent here. In the case of verbs, verb roots are stored in verb root (VR) and verbal suffixes are stored in verb suffix (VS). Similarly, adverbial lemmas are stored in adverb lemma (AvL) and adverbial suffixes are stored in adverb suffix (AvS).

The above method of information storage is supported by another dictionary called general dictionary (GD). It contains compound and reduplicated words collected from the Bengali corpus and other sources. It is modeled after a standard Bengali dictionary so that all kinds of lexicographic features of words (e.g., *spelling, part-of-speech, etymology, meaning, synonym, usage, lexical association*) are preserved for further application. All variations in the spelling of words are represented in the General Dictionary, so that a word, due to different spelling, is not analyzed differently. However, it has no inflected compound words and reduplicated words, as these words are not possible to analyze by using the rules that are applied for inflected single words.

7.5 Method of Morphological Processing

In morphological processing, an inflected word is treated as an unbroken string of characters with a space on both sides. Keeping this condition in view, once an inflected word is given as an input, our system tries to process it with the sets of information available to it. In general, the processing task is done in two phases.

(a) Phase I: It processes an inflected word considering it a single-word unit.
(b) Phase II: It modifies results after considering information taken from a dictionary and other sources.

Inflected words in Bengali are found in nouns, pronouns, adjectives, verbs, and adverbs. Words belonging to these parts-of-speech follow a uniform pattern of using inflections. Due to this feature, the processing is regular and systematic for most of the inflected words. The system takes the necessary information from LD and ID as well as grammatical rules that work between a lemma and inflection pair belonging to a part-of-speech. Words of each part-of-speech have unique ways of preserving morphological and lexical information. This is because the formation of inflected words of each part-of-speech follows different types of morphological operation. Therefore, the arrangement of lemma and inflection of each part-of-speech differ from others. For instance, analysis of an inflected noun is done by using the following 8 rules (Table 7.6).

The method of processing inflected valid nouns, in reality, is not as simple as it appears. Each noun subgroup has lemmas, which are selected based on their mapping with nominal inflections of different subgroups. That means analysis of an inflected noun depends on valid concatenation between a particular lemma with a particular inflection. We make sure that a lemma is allowed to concatenate with an appropriate inflection at a linear level to get valid output. In actuality, it does not produce all valid forms since all inflections do not concatenate with all lemmas. The combinations that are presented in the list (Table 7.6) are the only acceptable combinations for Bengali. Thus, the processing of inflected nouns involves a combination of sets of character strings with rules that control valid grammatical matching for accepted outputs.

Table 7.6 Rules applied for processing inflected Bengali nouns

No	(NP)	+	NL	+	(NS)	+	(NC)	→	Output
1	–	+	din	+	–	+	-	→	din
2	–	+	din	+	–	+	– er	→	diner
3	–	+	din	+	– guli	+	–	→	dinguli
4	–	+	din	+	– guli	+	– r	→	dingulir
5	su–	+	din	+	–	+	–	→	sudin
6	su–	+	din	+	–	+	-er	→	sudiner
7	su–	+	din	+	-guli	+	-	→	sudinguli
8	su–	+	din	+	-guli	+	-r	→	sudingulir

In sum, the method of processing inflected words includes identification of an inflected word, separation of lemma and inflection, understanding patterns of morphological agreement between lemma and inflection, and generation of processed results. For this, a system follows many steps in sequential order. After taking an inflected word, a system breaks it into lemma and inflection by using information from LD and ID. Next, it applies rules of lemma–inflection matching to process further. When lemma and inflection are matched, the system obtains relevant grammatical information from GD to present information as an output. The following flowchart shows how inflected nouns are processed with information from LD, ID, and GD (Fig. 7.2).

The most complex task in the entire process is splitting. It means the separation of inflection from an inflected word. For this, we apply the "trial-and-error" method based on heuristics. Success depends on the robustness of a system. The system proceeds from left to right direction following the sequence of characters used in an inflected word. With each character, it forms a subset and verifies it with a string stored in LD. It goes on adding one more character at each time until it finds out an appropriate match (details in Chap. 9, Sect. 9.10). After a lemma and an inflection are matched with strings in LD and ID, the system applies rules of grammatical agreement to approve the combination. After validation, it declares a word as a valid one and retrieves information from GD for the final presentation. To make the system work faster, we put LD and ID in a Trie-structure format so that we can link information easily. Segmentation of an inflected word into lemma and inflection part is not the complete work. It generates information relating to lemma and inflection. If a word has different parts-of-speech due to orthography, our system generates multiple results. For instance, words like *bale, kare, pare, mate, māri, pāli, ḍāke, tār* have more than one result based on their part-of-speech and morpho-syntactic functions.

Fig. 7.2 Flowchart for automatic processing of inflected Nouns

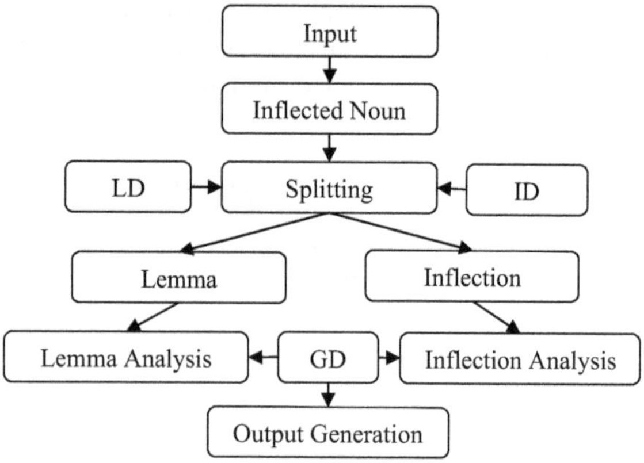

7.6 Processing Detached Words

The processing of detached words is a more challenging task. These words are normally made with two words: W_1 and W_2. **Detached words** include those compound words, reduplicated words, adjectives, and adverbs which are made with two separate words with space in between. Although these are considered as "single-word units" for their lexical, grammatical, and semantic functions, the words are detached from each other due to orthographic inconsistencies practiced in Bengali writing. Therefore, finding out words like *klāś ghare* "in class room," *khabar kāgaje* "in the newspaper," *mājhe mājhe* "sometimes," *hāte hāte* "by hands," *biśvās bhājan* "reliable," *grahaṇ ýogya* "acceptable," *biśheṣ bhābe* "specially," *niden pakṣe* "at least" in Bengali written texts is not a rare and unique event.

In a wider spectrum, detached words include multiword units of various types (e.g., *idioms, phrases, proverbs*) which ask for special treatment in annotation and processing. Processing these words is a far more complicated task as it requires lexical information from the analysis of morphemic and orthographic structures of these words as well as syntactic information from the contexts of their use. Morphological processing of inflected detached words is also a stiff challenge. In most cases, these words appear in the following forms.

(a) The first word is not inflected. The second word carries inflection, e.g., *baṛa loker* "of a rich man," *mājh dariyāy* "at mid-ocean," *tele bhājār* "of oil-fried fitters," *biye pāglāke* "to whom who is mad to marry."
(b) Both words are inflected, e.g., *dine rāte* "in day and night," *kathāy bārtāy* "in speech," *hāte kalame* "in practice," *hāṭe bājāre* "at many places," *bale dila* "said," *dekhe phella* "saw," *ghumiye paṛla* "slept."

Processing of detached words needs elaborate analysis of formative elements. In these cases, one of the words can have multiple processing outputs. For example, in *kare phella* "did," *kare* has four identities (i.e., *finite verb, non-finite verb, noun, and indeclinable*), while *phella* has one identity. Variations in suffix create problems when a system tries to collect information from the members of detached words. To process these words, our system follows many stages of cross-reference and cross-verification to analyze constituent words with reference to LD and ID. Once it is confirmed that W_1 and W_2 combine to form a detached word, our system analyzes further to see if there is any hidden lexical interface between the two words. Also, it analyzes the co-occurrence of the two words to see if they carry any **collocation relation**. If a positive reply is found, our system declares it as an instance of a valid detached word where the combination of two words carries a special implication. It helps to process the inflected compounds, reduplicated words, adjectives, and adverbs which have two consecutive words with unique linguistic significance. The following steps are followed for processing detached words in Bengali.

Stage 1: Start processing the first word (W_1).

Step 1.1: Verify the lemma of W_1 with data stored in LD.

Step 1.2: Verify inflection of W_1 with data stored in ID.

Step 1.3: Validate lemma–inflection pair with GD.

Stage 2: Start processing the second word (W_2).
Step 2.1: Verify the lemma of W_2 with data stored in LD.
Step 2.2: Verify inflection of W_2 with data stored in ID.
Step 2.3: Validate lemma–inflection pair with GD.
Stage 3: Verify co-occurrence of $W_1 + W_2$ as a valid one.
Step 3.1: If positive, collect information from GD.
Stage 4: Present the final output.

To overcome challenges involved in detached word processing, we apply an approach called **delayed processing** (DP) where the result of the first word (W_1) is withheld until we receive the result of the second word (W_2). This process is comparatively slow but helpful for processing detached words and multiword units. Moreover, it helps to dissolve ambiguity at the lexical level itself. For instance, consider two detached words: *niye* (W_1) *nila* (W_2) "took," and *niye* (W_1) *dila* (W_2) "gave after taking." In the first example, W_1 and W_2 combine to form a compound verb with a collocational sense. In the second example, W_1 and W_2 occur by chance without any collocational sense. Similarly, for words with two consecutive identical forms (e.g., *bāire bāire* "outside," *madhye madhye* "in-between," *dike dike* "in all directions," *kāle kāle* "over the years," etc.), our system combines them as instances of detached words. In essence, information obtained from neighboring words helps our system to process the detached words quite successfully.

7.7 Results of Morphological Processing

After morphological processing on inflected words, the outputs are verified by experts. The experts check if outputs are valid; if there are errors in outputs; if reclassification of mapping rules is required; if algorithms need modifications; and if existing databases are enough. The verification of processed outputs generates four types of results:

(a) Rightly processed words,
(b) Wrongly processed words,
(c) Doubly processed words, and
(d) Non-processed words.

To make processing accurate, our system asks for augmentation of data stored in LD and ID as well as modifies linguistic rules for valid mapping. Both works are done by experts who are engaged in output analysis, rule formation, and rule modification. The deficiency of a system is mostly caused due to a crude set of linguistic rules used in a system. Lack of adequate and sophisticated linguistic knowledge also makes a system perform below expectation. It is, therefore, necessary to fine-tune linguistic rules for robust processing. It is also noted that verification of grammatical rules depends on part-of-speech information stored in LD and ID. Information about unacceptable subsets of lemma–inflection pairs helps a system avoid errors in analysis and processing.

7.7.1 Rightly Processed Words

In the Bengali corpus, most of the inflected nouns, pronouns, verbs, adjectives, and adverbs are rightly processed. The reasons are as follows:

(a) Inflected nouns and pronouns are rightly processed because LD contains required lemmas while ID contains necessary inflections. Also, matching algorithms between lemmas and inflections are approved by grammatical agreement rules of word formation. The system searches a lemma in LD, searches an inflection in ID, and a matching rule between the two. Once a match is found, the match is processed with information from GD.
(b) Most of the finite and non-finite verbs are rightly processed as LD has a full list of roots and ID contains full verbal inflections. The system is supported with matching rules between a root and an inflection. The system first separates inflection from a verb, matches inflection in ID, matches root in LD. When both are matched, the relevant information is extracted from GD to produce the final result.
(c) A similar process is used for inflected adjectives and adverbs. Since a large number of adjectives and adverbs are stored in LD, finding out a suitable match for inflected adjectives and adverbs is not a big problem. Besides, adjectival and adverbial inflections are unique in nature. Due to this reason, the mapping of lemma and inflection is simpler.
(d) Doubly inflected words are also rightly processed. For instance, words like *śaktimāner* "of powerful," *maraṇśīlder* "to mortals," *jayīrā* "the winners" are rightly processed. These are processed as nouns because the final inflection is a nominal inflection.
(e) The postpositions are easy to process. The system finds matches from LD. Postpositions are further processed with information obtained from GD. Thus *āge* "before," *pare* "after," *upare* "above," *kāche* "near," *nice* "under," *mājhe* "middle," *dike* "towards," *pāśe* "beside," *sāmne* "in front of" are rightly processed.

7.7.2 Wrongly Processed Words

Morphological processing generates some wrong outputs also. In the Bengali corpus, there is a small list of inflected words which are wrongly processed. This has happened due to orthographic similarities and the wrong application of mapping rules. The mistakes are as follows.

(a) The part-of-speech identity of a word changes due to the use of inflection. This is a crucial factor in the wrong processing of words. In Bengali, some verbs are processed as nouns due to this factor. For instance, *kare* "in tax," *bale* "on a ball," *pāte* "on a plate" are processed as nouns as $-e$ is considered as a locative case marker.

(b) Some non-inflected words are processed as inflected ones. For instance, *nāgar* "lover," *sāgar* "ocean" are processed as inflected words, because the system considered the last character (-r) as an inflection marker (i.e., nāg + (å)r = nāgar, sāg + (å)r = sāgar). Similarly, some postpositions are processed as inflected nouns (e.g., *dike, dūre*) and verbs (e.g., *pare, dhāre*).

(c) The negative particle *nei* "is not" is identified as a finite verb because the lemma *ne* is stored in LD (for inflected verbs like *nebo, nebe, neben* "will take"') and inflection $-i$ is stored in ID. The sense of negation, which the word denotes, is not captured in processed output.

Such outputs arise when lemmas and inflections are valid forms in respective LD and ID and grammatical mapping rules are properly applied between the two. Such errors cannot be avoided at the lexical level unless multiple outputs are generated and analyzed.

7.7.3 Double Processed Words

Some inflected words have more than one processing output. It is a common phenomenon in Bengali. An inflected verb looks like an inflected noun due to orthographic similarities. As a result, while the majority of inflected words have single processing output, some have more than one output.

(a) When an inflected word shows more than one output, it is possible that the word is used in two different parts-of-speech in texts. For example, *ghore* is an inflected noun where $-e$ is a locative case marker attached to *ghor* (e.g., $\text{ghor}_{[\text{NN}]} + -\text{e}_{[\text{Case}]}$). The word *ghore* is also an inflected verb in which $-e$ is 3rd person singular/plural present tense marker tagged to root *ghor* (e.g., $\text{ghor}_{[\text{Root}]} + -\text{e}_{[\text{3P-PRS-Case}]}$) to generate the final inflected form.

(b) The possibility of double processing is high for inflected words. Chance of finding identical lemma–inflection pairs and their valid grammatical agreement is quite common across different part-of-speech in Bengali. For instance, *karāte* is possible to process in two different ways: (a) as an inflected verb (i.e., $\sqrt{\text{kar}}_{[\text{Root}]}$ + $\text{-āte}_{[\text{NFV-Sfx}]}$) and (b) as an inflected noun (i.e., $\text{karāt}_{[\text{NN}]} + -\text{e}_{[\text{Loc-Case}]}$). Similarly, *pāre* has two results: (a) a finite verb (i.e., $\sqrt{\text{pār}}_{[\text{Root}]} + -\text{e}_{[\text{3P-PRS-Case}]}$) and (b) an inflected noun (i.e., $\text{pār}_{[\text{NN}]} + -\text{e}_{[\text{Loc-Case}]}$).

In the case of double outputs, both the outputs are accepted as valid forms. A morphological processing system does not determine which alternatives are to be considered for further processing. The selection of appropriate candidates depends on POS annotation and syntactic processing that consider contexts of use of inflected words in texts. In the context-free situation, double processing of inflected words is not restricted because it gives important insights regarding the nature of the lexical association of words in neighboring situations. It helps to dissolve processing problems of compounds, reduplicated words, and detached words where words are written separately with space. In essence, at the time of morphological processing, more than one processing output is a quite normal feature. The final selection of one output from two alternatives is a different task where information of the sentential environment of words is considered.

7.7.4 Non-Processed Words

There are some inflected words in the Bengali corpus which are not processed. The possible reasons for non-processing are as follows:

(a) Inflected verbs like *pete* "laying," *geye* "singing," *here* "losing," *rekhe* "keeping" are not processed due to structural change in the root. The roots have undergone changes, and these changes are not marked in mapping rules. For instance, √rākh, √pāt, √gā, and √hār change into √rekh, √pet, √ge, and √her when inflections like *−e, −te,* and *−ye* are tagged to these roots. To avoid complications, we should better preserve all the allomorphic variants of these verbs in LD. The disadvantage of this method is that the number of roots is increased as some verb roots have two or more allomorphic variants. For instance, √yā, √gi, √ge, and √ýe are stored in LD as allomorphic variants of √gam "to go."

(b) Some finite and non-finite verbs are not processed due to the non-availability of roots in LD and lack of inflections in ID.

(c) Some nouns, pronouns, and adjectives are not processed due non-availability of inflection or root.

(d) The proper names, which are not stored in LD, are not processed even if they are inflected.

(a) Some inflected adverbs are not inflected due to space between a lemma and inflection.

(b) Some nouns, which are used as inflected verbs, are not processed. For instance, *hātiyeche* "has stolen" is not processed, because it is formed by adding a verb inflection (i.e., *−iyeche*) with a noun (i.e., *hāt* "hand"). It is a new kind of word formation where verb inflection is tagged to a noun lemma to generate an inflected finite verb.

(c) Many foreign words, scientific and technical terms, abbreviated forms, acrostic words, dialectal words, and slang are not processed due to their absence in respective lists.

The problems of non-processed inflected words are mostly linguistic and technical. The linguistic problems can be solved by augmentation of data in respective LD and ID as well as by modification of mapping rules. The technical problems, on the other hand, may be solved by a few trial runs of the system and modifying algorithms used.

7.8 Ambiguity in Morphological Processing

The lexical ambiguity in morphological processing is a common feature in all natural languages. A word, due to many reasons and factors, conveys multiple items, senses, ideas, or objects based on the context of its use. This inspires Leech (1993: 280) to argue, "... experience with corpora suggests that uncertainties of a category (e.g., *part-of-speech*) assignment are quite frequent: not merely because of failures of human understanding, but because of the prototypical, or fuzzy, nature of most linguistic categories." A corpus, due to its large collection of texts from the sources of actual language use, supplies a large number of ambiguous words. The success of a morphological processing system is measured by the way it handles lexical ambiguity in processing.

In general, lexical ambiguity is caused because words generate more than one reading. Readings differ due to categorization features, selectional features, morphological makeup, semantic identity, grammatical properties (i.e., *tense, aspect, modality, case, number, etc.*), syntactic role, discoursal impact, cultural relevance, idiomatic readings, figurative usage, and so on (Sinclair, 1991: 104). For instance, *khāoyā* "to eat," *māthā* "head" *mukh* "face," *kā̃cā* "raw", *pākā* "ripe", *path* "way," *karā* "to do," *kāṭā* "to cut," *dharā* "to catch," *pātā* "leaf" is associated with more than twenty different senses when their contexts of use are considered (Dash, 2004; Dash & Chaudhuri, 2002). Representing these issues in morphological processing is not desired. For this purpose, we require **lexical profiling**—a more complex strategy for lexical processing.

After morphological processing on Bengali corpus, we come across two types of ambiguities: (a) isolated ambiguity and (b) sequential ambiguity. The isolated ambiguity is caused for those inflected words which are not dependent on their preceding or following words. They are single, isolated, and complete in structure. They belong to various word classes. In context-free processing, they duplicate or triplicate their word classes and meanings based on their usage. Consider the following examples which are ambiguous even if these are not used in varied texts. Due to their forms, they are ambiguous by nature. Their ambiguity is reported in dictionaries also (Table 7.7).

The sequential ambiguity, on the other hand, is caused due to the presence of an immediately following word (W_2). It combines with the preceding word (W_1) to produce a sense which is different from their individual senses. For instance, if *biśeṣ* and *bhābe* are processed separately, *biśeṣ* is an adjective "specific" and *bhābe* is a noun "mood" or a verb "thinks." However, when *biśeṣ* is combined with *bhābe*, they become an adverb "specially." This is a unique word game that puts a morphological processing system under strong challenges. To resolve problems of sequential ambiguity we apply delayed processing. It applies information from immediate contexts or local word grouping. For instance, when *niden* and *pakṣe* are processed together, it means "at least" where individual POS and meanings are superseded to acquire a new POS and meaning.

Lexical ambiguity is also linked to other ambiguities (e.g., *attachment ambiguity, assignment ambiguity, and referential ambiguity*). These are mostly addressed

Table 7.7 Isolated ambiguity of inflected words in Bengali

Word	Part-of-speech	Meaning
tār	Pronoun	"his"
tār	Noun	"wire"
kāmāno	Adjective	"shaved"
kāmāno	Verb	"to earn"
neṛā	Adjective	"bald"
neṛā	Noun	"bald man"
tāke	Pronoun	"to him"
tāke	Noun	"on a shelf"
chine	Noun	"Chinese"
chine	Verb	"knowing"
theke	Postposition	"from"
theke	Verb	"staying"
chhõṛā	Adjective	"thrown"
chhõṛā	Verb	"to throw"
chõṛā	Noun	"urchin"

through analysis of lexical association, occurrence probabilities, analysis of internal structures of words, and reference to contextual frames of words (Biber et al., 1998: 261). These are also solved through the application of second language monolingual corpus (Dagan and Itai 1994: 76) and following a schema of principled disambiguation (Justeson and Kats 1995: 15). In all these methods, a morphological processing system is likely to wait until the results of the processing of both the words are considered and combined together.

A morphological processing system also uses probabilistic information to dissolve lexical ambiguities. Information is normally taken from a previously POS annotated corpus where words are already annotated with part-of-speech. Probabilistic information tells us how likely a given word belongs to one POS or other. For instance, although *kar* is used as a verb and a noun, the frequency information collected from the corpus shows that it has much higher use as a verb than as a noun in Bengali. A morphological processing system also makes use of other information taken from a dictionary to deal with ambiguous words.

7.9 Conclusion

A morphological processing system is built upon information of grammatical uniformity of words used in a language. Non-inflected words are processed easily and accurately as these are comparatively less complex in formation. Processing non-inflected nouns or verbs, for instance, is easy as these words are free from inflectional complexities. But processing inflected words is a challenging task as these words are complex in the process of formation and are characterized by several inflectional complexities. Moreover, these words change their orthographic identities and grammatical roles in a text based on the contexts of their use. We have to be far more careful and cautious in generating their actual morphological information.

Morphological processing is an important system of language processing. A robust morphological processing system fulfills the requirements of many domains of descriptive and applied linguistics and language technology. Developing a morphological processing system requires a connection between dictionaries, grammatical mapping rules, and computation. Since the success of a system is controlled by methods of lexicon access, there is a need for lexicon generation, storage, and management. Making a morphological processing system useful for inflectional languages, a system needs regular modification with new information about the morphological structure of words. Moreover, inflected words, compounds, and reduplicated inflected words need to be analyzed to augment the lexical database and to enhance grammatical mapping rules.

Based on the complexity of a language, a morphological processing system tries to generate results for part-of-speech, meaning, and morphological information of words. Accuracy varies based on the amount of information included in the lexicon. It is easier to identify a word within a piece of text than to present its full morphological information. Occasional errors in morphological processing are a common feature. It should not be taken as a major deficiency. An interactive morphological processing system, which can be designed to check processing results and suggest corrections, is a more reliable option in the generation of better processing outputs.

References

Barnbrook, G. (1998). *Language and computers.* Edinburgh University Press.

Baxi, J., Patel, P., & Bhatt, B. (2015). Morphological analyzer for Gujarati using paradigm based approach with knowledge-based and statistical methods. In *Proceedings of the 12th International Conference on Natural Language Processing* (pp. 178–182), 15–17 December 2015, Trivandrum, India

Beard, R. (1995). *Lexeme-morpheme base morphology: A general theory of inflection and word formation.* Albany, NY: State University of New York Press.

Bhattacharja, S. (2007). *Word formation in Bengali: A whole word morphological description and its theoretical implications.* München: Lincom Europa.

Biber, D., Conrad, S., & Reppen, R. (1998). *Corpus linguistics—Investigating language structure and use.* Cambridge University Press.

Bosch, A., & Daelemans, W. (1999). Memory-based morphological analysis reference. In *Proceedings of the 37th Annual Meeting of the Association for Computational Linguistics, ACL'99* (pp. 285–292). University of Maryland, USA, June 20–26, 1999.

Bybee, J. L. (1985). *Morphology: A study of the relation between meaning and form.* Amsterdam: John Benjamins.

Church, K., Gale, W., Hanks, P., & Hindle, D. (1991). Using statistics in lexical analysis. In U. Zernik (Ed.), *Lexical acquisition* (pp. 115–164). Erlbaum.

Creutz, M., & Lagus, K. (2005, March). Unsupervised morpheme segmentation and morphology induction from text corpora using Morfessor 1.0. Published in *Computer and Information Science*, Report A81, Helsinki University of Technology.

Creutz, M. (2003, July). Unsupervised segmentation of words using prior distributions of morph length and frequency. In *Proceedings of the 41st Annual Meeting of the Association for Computational Linguistics* (pp. 280–287).

Dagan, I., & Itai, A. (1994). Word sense disambiguation using a second language monolingual corpus. *Computational Linguistics, 20*(4), 563–596.

Dash, N. S., & Chaudhuri, B. B. (2002). Using text corpora for understanding polysemy in Bengali. In *Proceedings of IEEE Language Engineering Conference* (pp. 99–109). Department of Computer Science and Engineering, Central University, Hyderabad, 13–15 November 2002.

Dash, N. S. (2004). Corpus-based study of lexical polysemy in Bengali for application in language technology. In *Symposium on Indian Morphology, Phonology* and *Language Engineering (SIMPLE-2004)* (pp. 70–74), Department of Computer Science and Engineering, Indian Institute of Technology, Kharagpur, 19–21 March 2004.

Dash, N. S. (2015). *A descriptive study of Bengali words.* Cambridge University Press.

Dash, N. S., Chaudhuri, B. B., & Kundu, P. K. (1997). Computer parsing of Bangla verbs. *Linguistics Today., 1*(1), 64–86.

deHaan, P. (1984). Problem-oriented tagging of English corpus data. In J. Aarts & W. Meijs (Eds.), *Corpus linguistics* (pp. 123–139). Rodopi.

deRose, S. (1991). An analysis of probabilistic grammatical tagging methods. In S. Johansson & A.-B. Stenström (Eds.), *English computer corpora: Selected papers and research guide* (pp. 9–13). Mouton de Gruyter.

Freitag, D. (2005). Morphology induction from term clusters. In *Proceedings of the Ninth Conference on Computational Natural Language Learning (CoNLL-2005)* (pp. 128–135). Ann Arbor, MI, June 2005.

Garside, R. (1987). The CLAWS word-tagging system. In R. Garside, G. Leech, & G. Sampson (Eds.), *The computational analysis of English: A corpus-based approach* (pp. 30–41). Longman.

Goldsmith, J. (2001). Unsupervised learning of the morphology of a natural language. *Computational Linguistics., 27*(2), 153–198.

Greene, B., & Rubin, G. (1971). *Automatic Grammatical Tagging of English.* Technical Report. Department of Linguistics. Brown University, RI, USA.

Idicula, S. M., & David, P. S. (2007). A Morphological processor for Malayalam language. *South Asia Research, 27*(2), 173–186.

Jayan, J. P., Rajeev, R. R., & Rajendran, S. (2011). Morphological analyzer and morphological generator for Malayalam—Tamil machine translation. *International Journal of Computer Applications, 13*(8), 15–18.

Justeson, S. J., & Katz, S. M. (1995). Principled disambiguation: Discriminating adjective senses with modified nouns. *Computational Linguistics, 21*(1), 01–27.

Karttunen, L., & Wittenburg, K. (1983). A two-level morphological description of English. In *23rd Annual Meeting, Proceedings of Advanced Computational Linguistics (ACL-83)* (pp. 217–228).

Koskenniemi, K., & Church K. W. (1988). Complexity, two-level morphology, and Finnish. In *Proceedings of Conference on Computational Linguistics (COLING-88)* (pp. 335–340). Hungary, Budapest.

Koskenniemi, K. (1983). Two-level model for morphological analysis. *Proceedings of the International Joint Conference on Artificial Intelligence (IJCAL-83)* (pp. 683–685).Germany, Karlsruh.

Koskenniemi, K. (1984). A general computational model for word-form recognition and production. In *Proceedings of Conference on Computational Linguistics* (COLING-84) (pp. 178–181). Stanford, CA.

Leech, G. (1993). Corpus annotation schemes. *Literary & Linguistic Computing, 8*(4), 275–281.

Lun, S. (1983). A two-level morphological analysis of French. *Texas Linguistic Forum, 22*(3), 271–278.

Maxwell, M. (2002). Resources for morphology learning and evaluation. In: Rodriguez, G. M., Araujo, S., & Paz, C. (Eds.), *Third International Conference on Language Resources and Evaluation* (Vol. III., pp. 967–974), LREC 2002, Paris.
Merialdo, B. (1994). Tagging English texts with a probabilistic model. *Computational Linguistics, 20*(2), 155–171.
Meyer, C. F., & Tenney, R. (1993). Tagger: An interactive tagging program. In C. Souter & E. Atwell (Eds.), *Corpus-based computational linguistics* (pp. 25–36). Rodopi.
Nicolas, S., & Francois, Y. (2005). An analogical learner for morphological analysis. In *Proceedings of the Ninth Conference on Computational Natural Language Learning (CoNLL-2005)* (pp. 120–127. Ann Arbor, Michigan.
Oflazer, K., Nirenburg, S., & McShan, M. (2001). Bootstrapping morphological analyzers by combining human elicitation and machine learning. *Computational Linguistics, 27*(1), 59–86.
Porter, M. F. (1980). An algorithm for suffix stripping. *Program, 14*(3), 130–137.
Rajeev, R. R., Rajendran, N., & Sherly, E. (2008). A suffix stripping based morph analyzer for the Malayalam language. *Indian Science Congress, 2008*, 482–484.
Selkirk, E. O. (1983). *The syntax of words*. MIT Press.
Sengupta, G. (1997). Three models of morphological processing. *South Asian Language Review., 7*(1), 1–26.
Sengupta, G. (1999). GS_Morph: a grapheme-oriented structuralist morphological processor. In *Presented at the 2nd International Conference on the South Asian Linguistics (ICOSAL-II)*, Punjabi University, Patiala, 9–11 January 1999.
Sengupta, P., & Chaudhuri, B. B. (1993). Natural Language Processing in an Indian Language (Bangali)-I: Verb Phrase Analysis. *Institute of Electronics and Telecommunication Engineers Technical Review, 10*(1), 27–41.
Singh, R. (2003). *Explorations in seamless morphology*. New Delhi: Sage India.
Sinclair, J. (1991). *Corpus, concordance, collocation*. Oxford University Press.
Viswanathan, S., Ramesh Kumar, S., Kumara Shanmugam, B. Arulmozi, S., & Vijay Shanker, K. (2003). A Tamil morphological analyzer. In *Proceedings of International Conference on Natural Language Processing*, Mysore.
Wicentowski, R. (2004). Multilingual noise-robust supervised morphological analysis using Word-Frame model. In *Proceedings of Seventh Meeting of the ACL Special Interest Group on Computational Phonology (SIGPHON)* (pp. 70–77).
Wicentowski, R. (2005). Improving statistical MT through morphological analysis. In *Proceedings of the Conference on Empirical Methods in Natural Language Processing (EMNLP)*, Vancouver.
Yarowsky, D., & Wicentowski, R. (2000). Minimally supervised morphological analysis by multimodal alignment. In *Proceedings of the ACL-2000* (pp. 207–216). Morgan Kaufmann, San Francisco/CA.

Web Links

http://ltrc.iiit.ac.in/showfile.php?filename=onlineServices/morph/index.htm.
http://reports-archive.adm.cs.cmu.edu/anon/2003/CMU-CS-03-147.pdf.
http://www.cis.hut.fi/morphochallenge2005/results.shtml.
https://code.google.com/p/foma/wiki/MorphologicalAnalysisTutorial.
https://en.wikipedia.org/wiki/Morphological_analysis.
https://tdil-dc.in/index.php?option=com_vertical&parentid=60&lang.

Chapter 8
Lemmatization of Inflected Nouns

Abstract In this chapter, we describe a process of lemmatization of inflected nouns in Bengali as a part of lexical processing. Inflected nouns are used at a very high frequency in Bengali texts. We first collect a large number of inflected nouns from a Bengali corpus and compile a noun database. Then we apply a process of lemmatization to separate inflections from nominal bases. There are several intermediate stages in lemmatization which are applied following grammatical mapping rules (GMRs). These rules isolate inflections from nominal bases. The GMRs are first designed manually after analyzing a large set of inflected nouns to collect necessary data and information. At subsequent stages, these GMRs are developed in a machine-readable format so that the lemmatizer can separate the inflections from inflected nouns with the least human intervention. This strategy is proved to be largely successful in the sense that most of the inflected Bengali nouns, which are stored in a noun database, are rightly lemmatized. This multilayered process also generates an exhaustive list of nominal inflections and a large list of lemmatized nouns. At the subsequent stage, nouns are semantically classified for their use in translation, dictionary compilation, lexical decomposition, and language teaching. We have also applied this method to lemmatize inflected pronouns and adjectives which follow a similar pattern of inflection and affixation in Bengali.

Keywords Bengali · Lemma · Base · Lemmatization · Stemming · Morphology · Word · Inflection · Corpus · Language processing · Lexical database

8.1 Introduction

We describe a process of noun lemmatization, which we apply to a large set of inflected Bengali nouns to produce a database of noun lemmas. Here, the term "inflected" is used in a covert sense to include particles, plural markers, case markers, and other word-formative elements (WFE) that are attached to Bengali nouns to produce final inflected forms. The inflected nouns are collected from a multidisciplinary modern Bengali text corpus which contains texts from sixty-five subject domains (Dash, 2007a). We do this as there is no separate database available for Bengali nouns. Moreover, such a noun database has many applications in

N. S. Dash, *Language Corpora Annotation and Processing*,
https://doi.org/10.1007/978-981-16-2960-0_8

various development works of computational, descriptive, and applied linguistics. The present noun database is used for other academic and development works also.

Lemmatization requires a representative lexical database, which is standard, Unicode compatible, error-free, machine-readable, normalized, processed, and formatted (Leech, 2007). These are indispensable features because the application of lemmatization on non-formatted and non-normalized texts produces many hurdles and failures. For the Bengali language—the script of which is not much computer-compatible—it is bound to create more troubles. We may have to abort the task before we produce acceptable results. Therefore, before we start lemmatization in Bengali, we apply text normalization to remove orthographic and textual inconsistencies found in texts (Airio, 2006).

The first step of text normalization is splitting paragraphs into sentences and splitting sentences into words (and multiword units). The next steps involve alphabetical sorting of words; lexical classification of words based on parts-of-speech; and classification of words into non-inflected and inflected types. The lemmatization process starts after this. It operates on inflected words only to produce separate lists of lemmas and inflections. Both the lists pass through tokenization to prepare final lists of word types, which are subclassified based on linguistic and semantic features. After these steps of text preparation are complete, we apply lemmatization on inflected nouns to produce lemmas. Although not exhaustive, the lemma database records maximum coverage of nouns used in the language. The lemma database is used in morphological analysis, machine learning, language teaching, dictionary compilation, and some other works of application-based linguistics.

In this chapter, we discuss all issues related to the lemmatization of inflected nouns in Bengali. In Sect. 8.2, we explain the concept of lemmatization, its goal, and its use in language; in Sect. 8.3, we draw a line of distinction between stemming and lemmatization; in Sect. 8.4, we refer to some early works done in English and other languages; in Sect. 8.5, we describe the structure of inflected Bengali nouns and the processes of using inflections by nouns; in Sect. 8.6, we describe stages of lemmatization that includes identification of nouns from a POS annotated text, alphabetical sorting of nouns, and separating inflected nouns from non-inflected ones; in Sect. 8.7, we describe the actual process of lemmatization where our system strips inflection from an inflected noun and stores base and inflection in a separate list. In this section, we also show how our system validates base and inflection through type-token analysis and generates lemmas; in Sect. 8.8, we highlight the importance of lemmatization in various linguistic and non-linguistic tasks.

8.2 Lemma(-tization)

For centuries the term *lemma* is used in logic, philosophy, and mathematics. According to the *Oxford English Dictionary* (2008), in earlier centuries, a *lemma* is used to denote the following two concepts:

(a) An assumed or demonstrated proposition that is used in an argument or a proof, and
(b) A heading that indicates the subject or argument of literary composition.

The term has changed its sense in linguistics and lexicography. It has acquired a new sense to refer to "an entry word or a headword of a dictionary." In corpus linguistics, natural language processing, and language technology, it refers to the basic form of a word disregarding its grammatical properties (e.g., *tense, aspect, modality, number, gender,* etc.) (Biber et al., 1998: 94). The term *lemmatization* is derived from *lemma* to denote a process that creates base forms from inflected words (Fligelstone, 1994). In those languages where words appear in various inflected forms in a piece of text, the base forms, which are obtained from inflected forms, are considered nuclei because all inflected forms are produced by adding inflections to the base forms (Federici & Pirelli, 1992). The base form, which we usually look up in a dictionary, is called a *lexeme.* We normally attach inflection of various types and forms with the lexemes to generate new words that may vary in surface structure, usage, grammatical role, and semantic denotation (Savoy, 1993). For instance, after lemmatization of *learns, learning, learners, learned, learnt,* and *learnable,* we get the following two sets: base forms and inflections (Table 8.1):

A preliminary idea of lemmatization may be derived from the following diagram (Fig. 8.1).

By lemmatization, we assemble structurally transformed but grammatically related words under one base form. For instance, we put *go, went,* and *gone* under *GO; do, did* and *done* under *DO; write, wrote,* and *written* under *WRITE.* Since words of a language are not always found in a simple form to be tagged with inflections to generate final inflected forms, all structurally transformed forms are put under a single base form. For instance, *am, is, are, was, were, be, been* are put under *BE* as variants. Although they are different in form, they are morpho-semantically linked to the base form *BE* (Fig. 8.2). However, in those situations, where we lemmatize *am, is, are, was, were* under *BE*, but the base form *BE* is not present in a text, we

Table 8.1 Generation of base forms and inflections after lemmatization

Inflected Words	learns, learning, learners, learned, learnt, learnable, learnability, learnabilities
Base form	Inflections
learn	-s
	-ing
	-er
	-ers
	-ed
	-t
	-able
	-ability
	-abilities

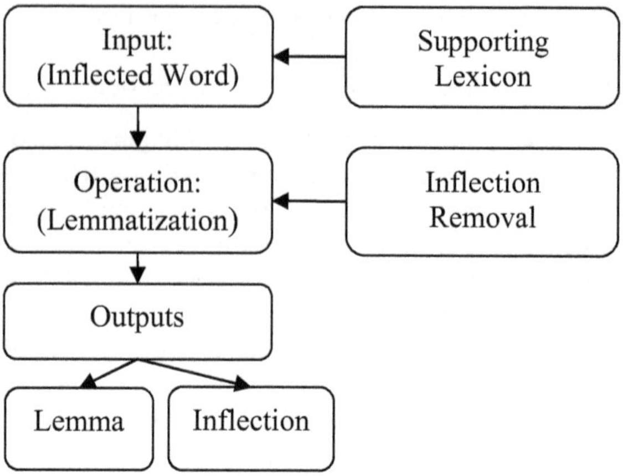

Fig. 8.1 Primary idea of lemmatization of inflected words

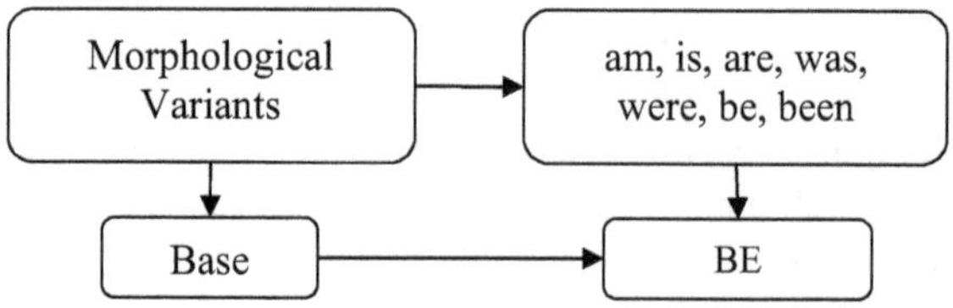

Fig. 8.2 All morphological variants under a single base form

consider *am, is, are, was, were* as separate lemmas in the list. This is necessary because morphological variants normally show more frequent usage in texts than their original source form.

We apply lemmatization also on conceptually related words, which are broadly categorized under a single theme. It helps to compile all conceptually related words (i.e., Synsets) of a language under one LEMMA. We group together all conceptually similar words to specify their usage in a specific area of human interest. For instance, we put words relating to *death* under a single lemma to signify that these words, individually or collectively, refer to a state which is related to death (Fig. 8.3).

The figure (Fig. 8.3) indicates that all words related to death are put under one head DEATH so that we conceptualize how a concept is expressed by different words

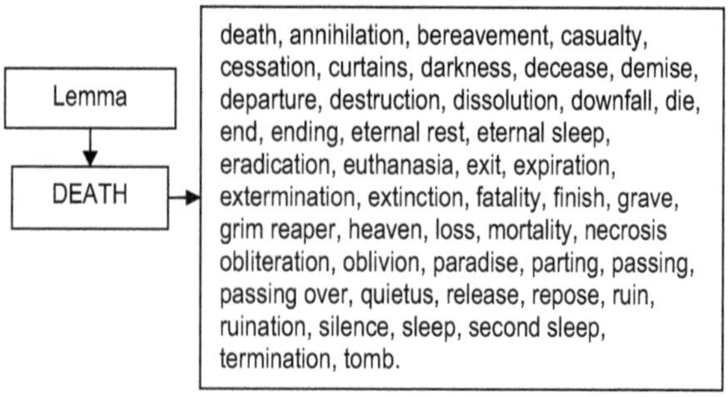

Fig. 8.3 Conceptually related words under the single lemma

in a language. To achieve this, we apply **lexical clustering** on different thematic layers in a wide ontological frame, since the information available from words varies characteristically even though words conceptually relate to a theme or idea of a language (Lovins, 1971). We call this **thematic lemmatization** in which we assemble conceptually linked words under a lemma. Clustering of semantically linked words helps in language education, lexical classification, dictionary compilation, discourse mapping, and thesaurus development. Also, it contributes to word-sense disambiguation, lexical association, information mapping, translation, synset generation, and WordNet building (Dash, 2017).

The process of lemmatization is a computer-based program which can be supervised or semi-supervised. It is based on a set of predefined morpho-grammatical rules and citations. It works to strip inflection from an inflected word to retrieve the lemma and store it in a lemma database (Creutz, 2003). Since lemmatization involves the conversion of inflected words into their respective lexemes, it extracts all variants of a lexeme. Words which change their surface forms due to morphological change are also put to lemmatization (Sanchez & Cantos, 1997). Words that do not usually follow a paradigm but belong to the same base are lemmatized even if they show grammatical and semantic distance, e.g., *beauty: beautification and night: nocturnal.* These forms, however, require a more sophisticated strategy to trail back to the base form.

Lemmatization has an important place in lexicography, language processing, and language teaching. Some of the major works of these areas are dependent on lexical information collected from inflected words through lemmatization (Dawson, 1974). It gives good results when used on words collected from large and widely representative language corpora built with varied texts. Inflected words with different types of inflections are better inputs for testing robustness and accuracy of lemmatization (Xu & Croft, 1998). Lemmatization is also useful for the cognitive processing of words (Ulmschneider & Doszkocs, 1983). While we deal with a lexicon of a language, we want to know the following things about the words used in a language.

(a) Words on which inflections are used,
(b) The number of inflections attached to a word, and
(c) Rules behind joining inflections with words.

We address these questions when we apply lemmatization to words. However, running this lemmatization process on words is not an easy task. It requires a clear understanding of the process and grammatical mapping rules (GMRs). Also, it asks for the proper application of several computational strategies in a systematic order for yielding valid and expected outputs (Reichel & Weilhammer, 2004). Sometimes, a lemmatization process is backed up by a POS annotation system for disambiguating homonyms (Kornilakis et al. 2004). The WordNet builders use lemmatizer supported with POS information to assign proper parts-of-speech to words (Table 8.2).

This method is also applied to Bengali words because many inflected Bengali words are ambiguous in part-of-speech. A POS annotated corpus helps a lemmatizer to focus on the part-of-speech assigned to words before lemmatization. Given below

Table 8.2 POS information used in lemmatization

Word	dove	saw	dove	saw
POS	FV	FV	NN	NN
	↓	↓	↓	↓
Lemmatization	application of derivation rule	Application of derivation rule		
	↓	↓	↓	↓
Lemma	dive	see	dove	saw

Table 8.3 Different lemmatization based on POS of words

Part-of-speech	Structure	Meaning	Lemma
hāre$_{[ADV]}$	hāre + ø	"in that rate"	hāre
hāre$_{[FV]}$	hār + -e	"loses"	hār
hāre$_{[NN]}$	hār + -e	"on necklace"	hār
tāke$_{[PN]}$	tā + -ke	"to him"	tā
tāke$_{[NN]}$	tāk + -e	"on the shelf"	tāk
pāne$_{[ADV]}$	pāne + ø	"towards"	pāne
pāne$_{[FV]}$	pān + -e	"in a betel roll"	pān
karāte$_{[NN]}$	karāt + -e	"in saw"	karāt
karāte$_{[FV]}$	karā + -te	"for doing"	karā
galāy$_{[NN]}$	galā + -y	"in throat"	galā
galāy$_{[FV]}$	gal + -āy	"melts"	gal

are some Bengali examples where inflected words, due to their part-of-speech, are lemmatized differently (Table 8.3).

It is pragmatic to apply lemmatization on POS annotated words as many unwanted hurdles can be avoided in this manner. The success and effectiveness of a lemmatizer are greatly enhanced when it rightly breaks an inflected word into base and inflection based on POS information.

8.3 Lemmatization and Stemming

It is good to understand the difference between stemming and lemmatization in this context. We often confuse the two types of lexical processing due to their close conceptual and operational similarities (Frakes & Fox, 2003). It is also necessary to know that stemming is different from lemmatization in several aspects and operations. A comparative study between the two gives us better knowledge and helps us to realize how the two processes work. Stemming is a process of "normalizing tokens" in which the tool (known as *stemmer*) yields a standard form for tokens (i.e., *lexical items*) by looking at their prefixes or suffixes if any, and removing these elements (or occasionally rewriting) from a stem (Korenius et al., 2004). The operation takes place through several short phases, as the followings:

(a) It first looks for an inflected lexical item to deal with one set of suffixes.
(b) When it is dealt with them, it looks for another set of suffixes.
(c) In the end, what remains as a part of a token is called a "stem."

The basic assumption of stemming is that tokens with the same stems tend to have the same meaning. Based on this assumption, a stemmer improves accuracy in lexical search (Lovins, 1968). This assumption is, however, not always true. If we accept it, forms like *general, generous, generate, generosity,* and *generative* are assumed to have the same meaning because they have the same (stem!): **gener.* However, in many situations, it is useful for some applications (Fig. 8.4).

The usefulness of a stemmer depends on morphological complexities involved in words as well as on the number and frequency of prefixes and suffixes used in a language (Paice, 1996). It is not required for Chinese, as Chinese hardly uses a prefix or suffix in the formation of words. It is, however, indispensable for those languages which have complex inflectional and conjugational systems. Such systems obscure the surface forms of final outputs when the same words are used more than once in different inflected and affixed forms (Porter, 1980).

We refer to the **Porter Stemmer** which is frequently used in English (Porter, 1980). It is also used in many other languages like French, Italian, Spanish, Portuguese, Romanian, Dutch, German, Swedish, Norwegian, Danish, Russian and Finnish (http://snowball.tartarus.org). There are at least five major steps in Porter Stemmer each one of which consists of a set of rules, which operate in "clipping and

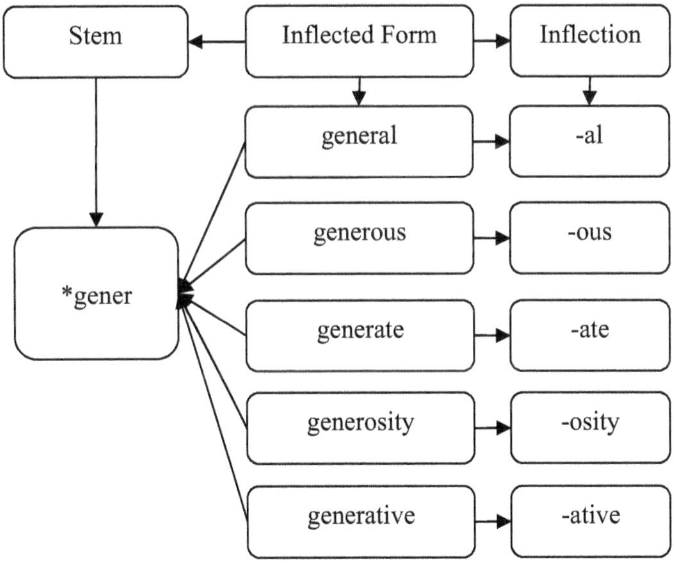

Fig. 8.4 Stemming of inflected words having a structural affinity

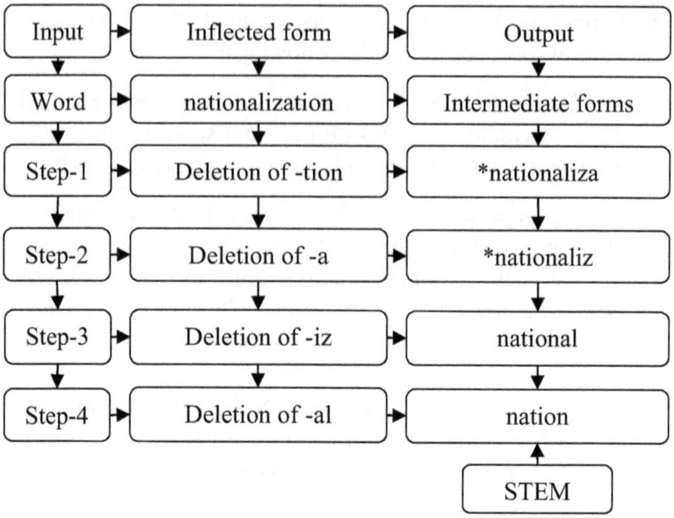

Fig. 8.5 Step-by-step operation of stemming for suffix stripping

feeding order." Each step is designed in such a manner that it deletes certain types of suffixes and then the output becomes the input for the rules of the next step, as shown below with the English word "nationalization" (Fig. 8.5).

The suffixes that are deleted include inflectional endings (e.g., *-s, -ed, -er, -ing*) as well as derivational endings (e.g., *-full, -able, -ism, -ize, -tion, -ment*). The output of the final step is the "stem." Most of the time, it produces acceptable results, particularly in those cases where words with similar meanings are possible to map onto the same stem (Table 8.4):

It is to be carefully noted that a stem which is generated through stemming is not always a "real word." For example, the form "*beauti," which is derived as a stem from the words *beauties, beautiful, beautifully, beautify, beautified, beautification, beautificated* is not a stem in a true linguistic sense, although it makes sense in machine learning, lexical clustering, and information retrieval (Paice, 1990). There are also instances where words with different meanings are assigned to the same stem. For example, *general, generally, generation, generations, generative, generous, generously,* and *generals* are assigned to stem "gener." Similarly, *sever,*

Table 8.4 Stemming affixed words with similar meanings

Inflected surface forms in English	Stem
car, cars	car
care, cared, careful, cares (not *caring*)	care
time, timer, timely, timed, times (not *timing*)	time
joy, joyful, joyous, joyed, joys	joy
form, forms, formal, formed, former, forming	form

several, severally, severe, severed, severely, severing, severity, and *severs* are put under "sever." Such stemming **collisions** are not accepted in linguistics, lexicography, lexical analysis, and language teaching even if such collisions are considered as exceptions than regular outputs of stemming (Kanis & Skorkovská, 2010).

A pragmatic approach is needed to avoid such lapses in stemming. We have to retrieve lexical and grammatical information of words from dictionaries to eliminate false members from a list of orthographically competent candidates (Savoy, 1993). Also, we can use statistical information to refer to the co-occurrence of words in texts to achieve success (Xu & Croft, 1998). What we understand is that stemming is different from lemmatization even though we find some functional similarities between the two.

8.3.1 Lemmatization is Similar to Stemming

Lemmatization and stemming appear to have close functional relations. It is, therefore, necessary to sum up similarities between the two methods:

(a) Lemmatization and stemming are methods of lexical processing. They try to identify a canonical representative for a set of related words.
(b) The goal of both the processes is to reduce inflectional/affixed forms (and sometimes derivationally related forms) to a common base form.
(c) The purpose of both the processes is to reduce morphological variations observed in case of a single base/stem.

Thus lemmatization and stemming jointly stand in contrast to a more general process called *term conflation* (Frakes, 1984) through which we try to explore lexico-semantic, syntactic, and orthographic variations of a lexical item in a language (Lennon et al., 1981). In information retrieval, documents are indexed by "uniterms," which sometimes generate ambiguity as a system fails to isolate only the pertinent information. One solution to this problem is to work with "multiterms" (i.e., *multi-word terms and phrases*). In this context, the idea of *term conflation* may be functionally useful as the idea is rooted in the concept of "linguistic variants" that are defined as conceptually related items to an original term. The process of conflation involves segmentation of words and elimination of affixes, or lexical searches through thesauri (Galvez et al., 2005).

8.3.2 Lemmatization is Different from Stemming

On the other hand, differences between lemmatization and stemming are many. Some of these are summarized below.

(a) Stemming is a function that removes inflectional components of words from stems or bases by using rules and lists of known suffixes (Minnen et al., 2001).

Lemmatization, on the other hand, is a function that does the same kind of removal but uses a comprehensive dictionary with grammatical rules and an inflection database so that it can deal with the irregularities in inflected words (Erjavec & Dzeroski, 2004).

(b) Stemming reduces word forms to pseudo-stems. It works in a heuristic process that chops off the ends of words to achieve its goal (Kraaij & Pohlmann, 1996). Lemmatization, on the other hand, reduces inflected words to linguistically valid lemmas. It carries out a proper linguistic operation with vocabulary and morphological information of words with an aim of removing inflectional endings and suffixes to return to the base of a word known as a lemma.

(c) Stemming deals with derivational variants besides inflected and suffixed variants. Lemmatization primarily deals with inflectional variations. It hardly deals with derivational forms (Liu et al., 2012).

(d) Stemming, by removing inflectional (and sometimes derivational) suffix, wants to reach to a base to which all original words are probably related to (Harman, 1991). On the other hand, lemmatization wants to obtain a single base that allows to group together a bunch of related inflected forms.

(e) Stemming is largely crude in implementation. Lemmatization is more sophisticated (especially for morphologically complex languages). Good success is achieved in stemming with simple rule-based approaches. On the other hand, lemmatization usually requires lexicons in the form of suffix and inflection databases.

(f) Stemming is simpler, smaller, and faster than lemmatization. Results obtained from stemming are good enough for many language processing applications (Hull, 1996). Using lemmatization for that purpose is a waste of resources. Dimensionality reduction is common in stemming where we replace *drive, driving, driven, driver* by "driv" in searched documents. It is not necessary to know if it is *drive, driver, driven, driving,* or *driv* as long as it forms a cluster of inflectionally related words together.

(g) Stemming considers the surface forms of words and ignores information of other domains. Lemmatization, on the other hand, takes surface forms of words into account along with information of their parts-of-speech, orthographic form, morphological structure, meaning, and contexts of use in a piece of text (Popovic & Willett, 1992).

(h) Scopes of application of stemming and lemmatization are also different. These are mostly function-dependent and application-oriented methods. When we develop an information retrieval system for billions of text documents where 99% of our queries range within 1–3 words, we settle for stemming. On the contrary, when we develop a machine translation system, design an interface for computer-assisted language teaching, and develop an interface for compiling headwords for a dictionary, we want a lemmatization tool as it yields linguistically appropriate stems/bases for translation, dictionary compilation, language teaching, and test modules generation.

Table 8.5 Difference in output between a lemmatizer and a stemmer

Stemmer		Lemmatizer	
Input	Output	Input	Output
have, having	hav	have, having	have
true, truth, truly	tru	true, truth, truly,	true
like, likes, liking	lik	like, likes, liking	like
mate, mating, mated	mat	mate, mating, mated	mate

Based on the observations, we argue that lemmatization is essentially a higher (and more sophisticate) version of stemming. The present state of language processing (specifically for English) has reached to a stage where stemmer is an "archaic technology" when a lemmatizer is available. It is because while a stemmer changes the surface form of a word into a meaningless stem, a lemmatizer produces valid bases out of all inflected forms (Table 8.5).

8.4 Lemmatization in English and Other Languages

Lemmatization is one of the most useful word processing tools from the early days of digital text generation. Scholars have developed lemmatizer for English and other languages once digital texts are made available in these languages (Krovetz, 1993). In the last few years, lemmatizer is developed and used semi-automatically with marginal human intervention (Beale, 1987). For instance, Dawson (1974) uses a scheme for suffix removal for word conflation. It derives lemma from inflected words. An almost similar approach is used by Frakes (1984) on some English texts. A part of the *Brown Corpus* is lemmatized to separate lemma with full lexico-grammatical information for second-language teaching and translation (Francis & Kucera, 1982; Hundt et al., 1999). Lemmatizer is also applied on *Frankenstein Text Corpus* (Barnbrook, 1996), *CRATER Corpus* (McEnery & Wilson, 1996), *SUSANNE Corpus* (Biber et al., 1998), and *CUMBRE Corpus* (Sánchez & Cantos, 1997). Lemmas obtained from these corpora are used in dictionary-making, computer-assisted language teaching, teaching materials development, graded vocabulary development, spelling errors detection and correction, morphological analysis of words, and lexical description (Fligelstone, 1994). Automatic training of lemmatizer is done to handle morphological changes in affixes (Jongejan & Dalianis, 2009). In sum, lemmatizer is designed, developed, and used in many advanced languages (Hafer & Weiss, 1974, Kamps et al., 2004). It generates lemmas which are further classified and marked with different linguistic information and are used in several studies and research (McEnery & Hardie, 2006). Lemmatizer is yet to be developed for many Indian languages although some amount of primary training datasets and rules are available for this work (Dash, 2006). The resources, in our view, can be used to develop a lemmatizer for the Indian languages (Dash 2007b).

In the following sections, we use a new method to lemmatize inflected Bengali nouns. For this purpose, we use data from a Bengali written text corpus (Dash 2007a). The corpus passes through several stages of text normalization to make it maximally useful for part-of-speech annotation, lemmatization, concordance, and other text processing works. We use this corpus to collect inflected nouns for lemmatization described in Sects. 8.6 and 8.7. Before this, we briefly discuss the nature of inflection of Bengali nouns (Sect. 8.5).

8.5 Surface Structure of Bengali Nouns

From the orthographical point of view, there are four types of nouns in Bengali. These are quite frequently used in all kinds of Bengali text.

(a) Nouns with zero inflection: *bālak* (bālak + ø) "boy," *jal* (jal + ø) "water," *ākāś* (ākāś + ø) "sky," *ghar* (ghar + ø) "house," *din* (din + ø) "day," *magaj* (magaj + ø) "brain," *chālak* (chālak + ø) "driver," *basanta* (basanta + ø) "spring."
(b) Nouns with one inflection: *bālakṭi* (bālak + -ṭi) "the boy," *jale* (jal + -e) "in water," *ākāśer* (ākāś + -er) "of sky," *ghare* (ghar + -e) "in house," *dinguli* (din + -guli) "days," *magaje* (magaj + -e) "in brain," *chālakerā* (chālak + -erā) "drivers," *basanter* (basanta + -er) "of spring."
(c) Nouns with two inflections: *bālakṭike* (bālak + -ṭi + -ke) "to the boy," *jaleo* (jal + -e + -o) "in water also," *ākāśṭāo* (ākāś + -ṭā + -o) "the sky also," *gharṭāte* (ghar + ṭā + -te) "in the house," *dingulite* (din + -guli + -te) "in days," *magajeo* (magaj + -e + -o) "in brain also," *chālakerāi* (chālak + -erā + -i) "drivers indeed," *basanteo* (basanta + -e + -o) "in spring also."
(d) Nouns with three inflections: *bālakṭikei* (bālak + -ṭi + -ke + -i) "to the boy indeed," *dinguliteo* (din + -guli + -te + -o) "in the days also," *meyederkei* (meye + -der + -ke + -i) "to the girls indeed," *chhelederkeo* (chhele + -der + -ke + -o) "to the boys also," *śaharṭātei* (śahar + -ṭā + -te + -i) "in the city indeed"

We take only the last three types (i.e., (b), (c), and (d)). These are used as single-word units in texts. Nouns with zero inflection (i.e., (a)) are disqualified as these are already in their base forms. We also ignore the two-word and multiword nouns which are written with space in between the first and second words. These nouns require a separate strategy for lemmatization. The nominal inflections that are attached to nominal bases in Bengali are of different types, nature, and function. Given below is a list of nominal inflections that are normally attached to Bengali nouns to generate final inflected forms.

Type I: Single Marker (Total: 24)

[1] Emphatic (2): -i, -o
[2] Singular (5): -ṭā, -ṭi, -khānā, -khāni, -ṭuku

[3] Plural (7): -rā, -erā, -gulo, -guli, -gulā, -der, -diga
[4] Case (10): -e, -er, -ke, -ete, -te, -re, -ār, -r, -yer, -āy.

Type II: Double Marker (Total: 76)

[1] Singular + Emphatic (10): -ṭii, -ṭio, -ṭāi, -ṭāo, -khānāi, -khānāo, -khānii, -khānio, -ṭukui, -ṭukuo
[2] Plural + Emphatic (14): -rāi, -rāo, -erāi, -erāo, -gulii, -gulio, -guloi, -guloo, -gulāi, -gulāo, -deri, -dero, -digai, -digao
[3] Singular + Case (17): -ṭāke, -ṭāte, -ṭār, -ṭāy, -ṭike, -ṭite, -ṭir, -khānāke, -khānāte, -khānār, -khānāy, -khānike, -khānite, -khānir, -ṭukuke, -ṭukute, -ṭukur
[4] Plural + Case (15): -gulike, -gulite, -gulir, -guloke, -gulote, -gulor, -guloy, -gulāke, -gulāte, -gulār, -gulāy, -derke, -digake, -diger, -digere
[5] Case + Emphatic (20): -ei, -eo, -kei, -keo, -etei, -eteo, -tei, -teo, -āri, -āro, -āyi, -āyo, -ri, -ro, -eri, -ero, -yeri, -yero, -āyi, -āyo.

Type III: Triple Marker (Total: 66)

[1] Singular + Case + Emphatic (36): -ṭākei, -ṭākeo, -ṭātei, -ṭāteo, -ṭāri, -ṭāro, -ṭāyi, -ṭāyo, -ṭākeri, -ṭākero, -ṭikei, -ṭikeo, -ṭitei, -ṭiteo, -ṭiri, -ṭiro, -khānākei, -khānākeo, -khānātei, -khānāteo, -khānāri, -khānāro, -khānāyi, -khānāyo, -khānikei, -khānikeo, -khānitei, -khāniteo, -khāniri, -khāniro, -ṭukukei, -ṭukukeo, -ṭukutei, -ṭukuteo, -ṭukuri, -ṭukuro,
[2] Plural + Case + Emphatic (30): -gulikei, -gulikeo, -gulitei, -guliteo, -guliri, -guliro, -gulokei, -gulokeo, -gulotei, -guloteo, -gulori, -guloro, -guloyi, -guloyo, -gulākei, -gulākeo, -gulātei, -gulāteo, -gulāri, -gulāro, -gulāyi, -gulāyo, -derkei, -derkeo, -digakei, -digakeo, -digeri, -digero, -digerei, -digereo.

It is not mandatory that each inflection is attached to every noun. In Bengali, there are (56.42%) nouns, which are used without any inflection (Dash 2015: 94). Since these words are not attached to any inflection, they are removed from lemmatization. This does not mean that these nouns cannot use inflection. They are capable of using inflection, if required. When they are inflected, they are put to lemmatization. On the other hand, in case of inflected nouns, there are rules and sequences for valid grammatical arrangement between a noun and an inflection. It becomes evident during attaching an inflection to a noun. It follows certain rules for valid grammatical concatenation between a noun and an inflection (Harman, 1991). The elements that are attached to Bengali nouns include articles, number markers, case markers, gender markers, and particles. Due to their bound nature, they never occur as independent words in texts. Person markers are never used with Bengali nouns since nouns are considered to belong to a third person only. Inflections are usually attached at the end of nouns to generate the final inflected form. The arrangement of inflections behind a noun follows the following patterns (Table 8.6).

Table 8.6 Order of arrangement of Bengali noun and inflection

Noun	Markers	Final form	Gloss
lok	-Ø$_{\text{[Null Suffix]}}$	Lok	man
lok	-i$_{\text{[Particle]}}$	Loki	the man himself
lok	-er$_{\text{[Case]}}$	loker	of man
lok	-guli$_{\text{[Num]}}$	lokguli	the men
lok	-ke$_{\text{[Case]}}$ + -i$_{\text{[Particle]}}$	lokkei	to the man
lok	-erā$_{\text{[Num]}}$ + -i$_{\text{[Particle]}}$	lokerāi	men indeed
lok	-guli$_{\text{[Numr]}}$ + -ke$_{\text{[Case]}}$	lokgulike	to the men
lok	-guli$_{\text{[Num]}}$ + -ke$_{\text{[Case]}}$ + -i$_{\text{[Particle]}}$	lokgulikei	to the men also

Inflections are usually attached to the end of nouns to generate inflected nouns. Based on this observation, we classify "single-word nouns" into the following four types to see how nouns are made with or without formative elements (Details are presented in Appendix I at the end of the chapter):

Type 1: Nouns Without Word-Formative Element (WFE)

(a) Noun + Ø marker: (1)

Type 2: Nouns with One Word-Formative Element (WFE)

(a) Noun + Emphatic Particle: (2)
(b) Noun + Singular Marker: (5)
(c) Noun + Plural Marker: (3)
(d) Noun + Case Marker: (4).

Type 3: Nouns with Two Word-Formative Elements (WFEs)

(a) Noun + Singular + Particle: (10)
(b) Noun + Plural + Particle: (6)
(c) Noun + Singular + Case: (13)
(d) Noun + Plural + Case: (11)
(e) Noun + Case + Particle: (6).

Type 4: Nouns with Three Word-Formative Elements (WFEs)

(a) Noun + Singular + Case + Particle (28)
(b) Noun + Plural + Case + Particle (22).

8.6 Stages for Noun Lemmatization

There are at least five stages which we execute before the act of lemmatization of inflected nouns begins. The stages are presented graphically in the flowchart (Fig. 8.6). Each stage is explained in a separate subsection.

Stage 1 POS annotation (Conversion of a raw text into a POS annotated text)
Stage 2 Noun identification (Identification of nouns from POS annotated text)
Stage 3 Alphabetical sorting (Arrangement of nouns in alphabetical order)
Stage 4 Noun classification (Division of inflected and non-inflected nouns)
Stage 5 Tokenization (Removal of multiple tokens and storing a single type)

8.6.1 Stage 1: POS Annotation

The first stage is the conversion of a raw Bengali text into a POS annotated text. How a text is POS annotated is discussed in Chapter 3. For Bengali, it is necessary to have a POS annotated text where each noun is annotated so that it is identified and

Fig. 8.6 Stages and steps to be executed before noun lemmatization

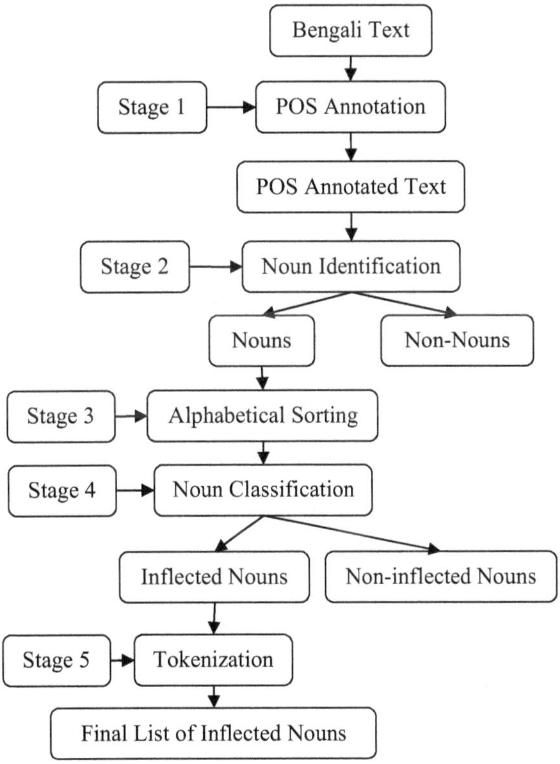

Table 8.7 Sample of a Bengali text transliterated into Indic Roman

Raw Bengali text: In Indic Roman
Nandādebīke uttarākhaṇḍer kumāun elākār nibāsī debī pārbatīr svarūp bale mānā hay. ei himācchhanna śikharkeo okhāne ekṭā pabitra śikhar bale mane karā hay. jānen ki, koṭer artha hala dūrga o paurāṇik ākhyāne ei parbat nandādebī arthāṯ pārbatīr ābās chhila. nandākoṭ śṛṅger ek dike piṇḍārgaṅgā nadīr upatyakā ebaṃ anya dike gaurīgaṅgā nadīr upatyakā āchhe. ei upatyakā duṭo juṛe ýe giripath āchhe, seṭāke dānā dūrā giripath balā hay

Table 8.8 Example of a POS annotated Bengali text

POS annotated Bengali text
nandādebīke\N_NNP uttarākhaṇḍer\N_NNP kumāun\N_NNP elākār\N_NN nibāsī\N_NN debī\N_NN pārbatīr\N_NNP svarūp\N_NN bale\V_VM_VNF mānā\V_VM_VNG hay\V_VAUX.\RD_PUNC ei\DM_DMD himācchanna\JJ śikharkeo\N_NN okhāne\DM_DMR ekṭā\QT_QTC pabitra\JJ śikhar\N_NN bale\V_VM_VNF mane\V_VM_VNF karā\V_VM_VNG hay\V_VAUX.\RD_PUNC jānen\V_VM_VF ki\PR_PRQ,\RD_PUNC koṭer\N_NNP artha\N_NN hala\V_VAUX dūrga\N_NN o\CC_CCD paurāṇik\JJ ākhyāne\N_NN ei\DM_DMD parbat\N_NN nandādebī\N_NNP arthāṯ\CC_CCS pārbatīr\N_NNP ābās\N_NN chila\V_VAUX.\RD_PUNC nandākoṭ\N_NNP śṛṅger\N_NN ek\QT_QTC dike\PP piṇḍārgaṅgā\N_NNP nadīr\N_NN upatyakā\N_NN ebaṃ\CC_CCD anya\JJ dike\PP gaurīgaṅgā\N_NNP nadīr \N_NN upatyakā \N_NN āche\V_VAUX.\RD_PUNC ei\DM_DMD upatyakā\N_NN duṭo\QT_QTC joṛe\V_VM_VNF ýe\RP_RPD giripath\N_NN achhe\V_FV seṭāke\DM_DMR dānā\N_NNP dūrā\N_NNP giripath\N_NN balā\V_VM_VNG hay\V_VAUX.\RD_PUNC

separated for lemmatization. For instance, let us consider the following Bengali text (Table 8.7).

The same Bengali text is annotated at the POS level following the BIS tagset designed for this purpose (Table 8.8).

8.6.2 Stage 2: Noun Identification and Isolation

The second stage is the identification of those words in the POS annotated texts which are marked as nouns. Since we are concerned only with nouns, we ignore words that are annotated with other parts-of-speech in the text. Given below is an example to show how nouns are identified and separated in the POS annotated Bengali text corpus (Table 8.9).

8.6.3 Stage 3: Alphabetical Sorting of Nouns

The third stage is an arrangement of the nouns in alphabetical order in a separate list. Once we get the entire list of nouns from a POS annotated text, we start the third

Table 8.9 List of nouns complied from a POS annotated corpus

List of noun annotated words	
nandādebīke\N_NNP	uttarākhaṇḍer\N_NNP
kumāun\N_NNP	elākār\N_NN
nibāsī\N_NN	debī\N_NN
pārbatīr\N_NNP	svarūp\N_NN
śikharkeo\N_NN	śikhar\N_NN
koṭer\N_NNP	artha\N_NN
dūrga\N_NN	ākhyāne\N_NN
parbat\N_NN	nandādebī\N_NNP
pārbatīr\N_NNP	ābās\N_NN
nandākoṭ\N_NNP	śṛṅger\N_NN
piṇḍārgaṅgā\N_NNP	nadīr\N_NN
upatyakā\N_NN	gaurīgaṅgā\N_NNP
nadīr\N_NN	upatyakā\N_NN
upatyakā\N_NN	giripath\N_NN
dānā\N_NNP	dūrā \N_NNP
giripath\N_NN	

stage. We pass the list of nouns through alphabetical sorting so that all nouns are arranged in alphabetical order. The list is made in such a way that each noun gets an entry in a separate line. The list contains all inflected and non-inflected nouns as well as all tokens included in the annotated text. This is done by a simple computation of lexical sorting, as the table (Table 8.10) shows. (To save space nouns are arranged in three columns here).

Table 8.10 Alphabetically sorted nouns from a Bengali text

artha\N_NN	ākhyāne\N_NN	ābās\N_NN
uttarākhaṇḍer\N_NNP	upatyakā\N_NN	upatyakā \N_NN
upatyakā\N_NN	elākār\N_NN	koṭer\N_NNP
kumāun\N_NNP	giripath\N_NN	giripath\N_NN
gaurīgaṅgā\N_NNP	dānā\N_NNP	debī\N_NN
dūrga\N_NN	dūrā\N_NNP	nadīr \N_NN
nadīr\N_NN	nandākoṭ\N_NNP	nandādebī\N_NNP
nandādebīke\N_NNP	nibāsī\N_NN	parbat\N_NN
pārbatīr\N_NNP	pārbatīr\N_NNP	piṇḍārgaṅgā\N_NNP
śṛṅger\N_NN	śikhar\N_NN	śikharkeo\N_NN
svarūp\N_NN		

8.6.4 Stage 4: Noun Classification

The fourth stage is related to finding out inflected nouns from the list. Since the list contains nouns with and without inflection, the resultant output has two lists: (a) non-inflected nouns and (b) inflected nouns. The lemmatization is done on inflected nouns only. We classify nouns into two types and store them in separate lists to be added later with a final lexical database after lemmatization is run on inflected nouns and final lemmas are obtained. The following table shows how non-inflected and inflected nouns are stored into two separate lists in the database (Table 8.11).

8.6.5 Stage 5: Tokenization

The fifth stage is type-token analysis and division of nouns. Since the list has multiple entries of the same form (i.e., *tokens*), we remove identical nouns after preserving one of the variants as a token of the type. For instance, this list contains two tokens of *nadīr* "of a river" in it along with other inflected forms (Table 8.11). Our task is, therefore,

Table 8.11 Separate list of non-inflected and inflected nouns

Non-inflected nouns	Inflected nouns
artha\N_NN	ākhyāne\N_NN
ābās\N_NN	uttarākhaṇḍer\N_NNP
upatyakā\N_NN	elākār\N_NN
upatyakā \N_NN	koṭer\N_NNP
upatyakā\N_NN	nadīr \N_NN
kumāun\N_NNP	nadīr\N_NN
giripath\N_NN	nandādebīke\N_NNP
giripath\N_NN	pārbatīr\N_NNP
gaurīgaṅgā\N_NNP	pārbatīr\N_NNP
dānā\N_NNP	śṛṅger\N_NN
debī\N_NN	śikharkeo\N_NN
dūrga\N_NN	
dūrā\N_NNP	
nandākoṭ\N_NNP	
nandādebī\N_NNP	
nibāsī\N_NN	
parbat\N_NN	
piṇḍārgaṅgā\N_NNP	
śikhar\N_NN	
svarūp\N_NN	

Table 8.12 Tokenization of inflected nouns in the lexical database

Non-tokenized nouns	Tokenized nouns
ākhyāne\N_NN	ākhyāne\N_NN
uttarākhaṇḍer\N_NNP	uttarākhaṇḍer\N_NNP
elākār\N_NN	elākār\N_NN
koṭer\N_NNP	koṭer\N_NNP
nadīr \N_NN	**nadīr\N_NN**
nadīr\N_NN	nandādebīke\N_NNP
nandādebīke\N_NNP	**pārbatīr\N_NNP**
pārbatīr\N_NNP	śṛṅger\N_NN
pārbatīr\N_NNP	śikharkeo\N_NN
śṛṅger\N_NN	
śikharkeo\N_NN	

to preserve only one of the tokens as a type and remove other tokens. Other tokens are removed because they are identical to the type stored in the list. By applying this process, a large list of inflected noun is turned into a small and manageable set on which lemmatization works. The following list (Table 8.12) shows how the tokenization process is operated on the list of inflected nouns (boldfaced).

Thus, following the five stages and steps mentioned above, we finalize the list of inflected Bengali nouns from a POS annotated Bengali corpus. After we identify and store inflected nouns in a separate lexical list, the list is applied to lemmatization. The next stage is the actual process of lemmatization, which is described in the following section.

8.7 Operation of Lemmatization Process

The lemmatization works as per our instruction to remove the inflection part from inflected nouns to retrieve the nominal bases. We apply a simple process of removing the inflection part so that the bare nouns are compiled together to generate a list of nominal bases. The list is further classified based on linguistic and extralinguistic features (e.g., *orthographical form, semantic relations, conceptual proximity, cultural alignment*, *etymology, ontology, typology,* etc.). The task of lemmatization involves three primary stages.

(a) Stripping-off inflection part from inflected nouns.
(b) Storing base forms in a nominal base database.
(c) Storing inflections in nominal inflection database.

Following a simple process of computation empowered with sufficient input from word formation rules and strategies used to generate inflected nouns in Bengali,

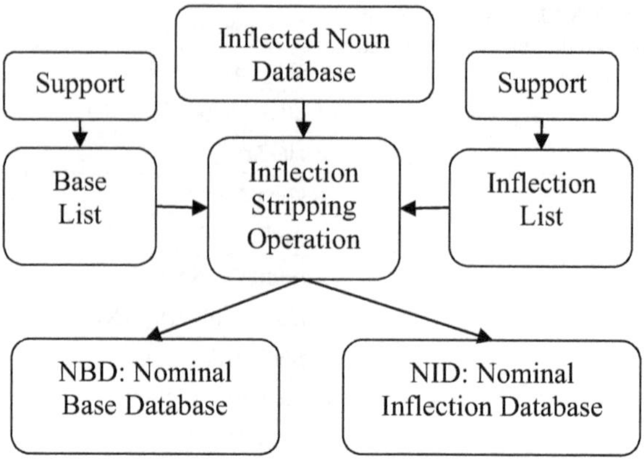

Fig. 8.7 Lemmatization process on Bengal inflected nouns

we develop a tool to remove inflection parts from nouns. The process works in the following manner (Fig. 8.7).

Given an inflected noun, the tool first identifies the base part of an inflected noun with the nouns which are stored in nominal base database (NBD). Then it identifies the inflection part with inflections stored in the nominal inflection database (NID). Once the required pairs are identified, the tool breaks an inflected noun into two parts: (a) nominal base and (b) nominal suffix. Next, it sends the nominal base to NBD and nominal inflection to NID.

Before the application of the inflection stripping process on inflected nouns, it is necessary to understand how these inflections are arranged in sequential order and how they combine with nominal bases to generate the final inflected nouns. It is understood from the list and order of use of inflection (given in Sect. 8.5) that these inflections, although observe a strict order of occurrence, their use is not always uniform with all noun bases. That means, for some nouns, only one inflection is used (Type I), and for some other nouns, two inflections are attached to nouns (Type II). For the remaining nouns, three inflections are combined and used (Type III). This implies that an inflected noun in Bengali can have either one, two, or three inflections as the situation and context require (Table 8.13).

This particular feature makes the process of noun lemmatization a highly complex operation. The system has to identify first if an inflected noun is made of any of the three types of inflections stated above (Table 8.13). Since it is not easy for a system to understand this, we invoke the inflection stripping algorithm as proposed in Porter Stemmer (Porter, 1980). It works elegantly for separating inflections from

Table 8.13 Type and order of inflections used with Bengali nouns

Base	Inflections in NID	
Nominal base	Type 1 (Total: 24)	Emphatic, Singular, Plural, Case
	Type 2 (Total: 76)	Singular + Emphatic, Plural + Emphatic, Singular + Case
	Type 3 (Total: 66)	Singular + Case + Emphatic, Plural + Case + Emphatic

Algorithm

1 Enter an inflected noun to be lemmatized
2 Invoke inflection stripping rules
3 Invoke inflections in Type 3
  (a) Apply a string from Type 3 to identify the inflection part
  (b) If a match is found, strip matched part from inflected form
  (c) Store the stripped part in NID and base part in NBD
4 If no match is found, invoke Type 2
  (a) Apply a string from Type 2 to identify the inflection part
  (b) If a match is found, strip matched part from inflected form
  (c) Store the stripped part in NID and base part in NBD
5 If no match is found, invoke Type 1
  Apply a string from Type 1 to identify the inflection part
  If a match found, strip matched part from inflected form
  Store the stripped part in NID and base part in NBD
6 Update NBD and NID with new entries
7 Display NBD and NID

Fig. 8.8 Suffix stripping algorithm for Bengali nouns

inflected nouns. However, we adopt a new strategy, which is notably different from the Porter stemmer. Rather than breaking an inflection into two or more short parts, we consider each inflection as a composite unit that carries several sets of information. This is required because, in case of Bengali nouns, at the time of joining an inflection with a noun base, there is hardly any morphophonemic change during base-inflection concatenation. Also, our process of suffix stripping works in reverse order, i.e., inflections stored in Type 3 are first invoked, followed by that of Type 2 and Type 1, respectively, as the following algorithm and example show (Fig. 8.8).

Example

Step 1 Noun: *gharguli* "the houses."
Step 2 Apply a string from Type 3 to identify a match.
Step 3 No match (matching fails).
Step 4 Apply a string from Type 2 to identify a match.
Step 5 No match (matching fails).
Step 6 Apply a string from Type 1 to identify a match.
Step 7 Match found (matching successful).
Step 8 Separate matched part (i.e., -guli) from the noun.
Step 9 Separate nominal base [ghar].
Step 10 Display base [ghar] and inflection [-guli].

According to our simplified strategy, W_N is a valid inflected noun. It has two parts: $W_{NB} + W_{NI}$, where W_{NB} is the front substring representing a noun base and W_{NI} is the back substring representing a nominal inflection. Based on the word formation rules of Bengali, W_{NB} and W_{NI} grammatically agree to form a valid inflected noun (Dash and Chaudhuri, 1997). A valid base part implies that the string is a noun base while a valid inflection part signifies that the string is a nominal inflection. That

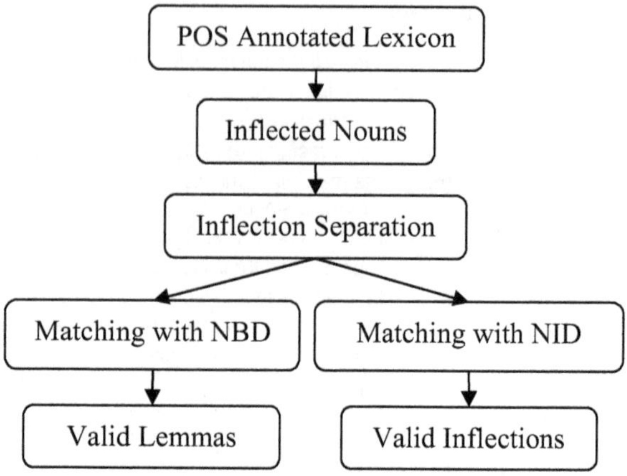

Fig. 8.9 Frame for generating lemmas from inflected Bengali nouns

means segmentation of W_N into valid noun base and valid inflection part, satisfying the above conditions above, is an accepted stage of valid lemmatization.

For instance, consider *hātiyārer* "of weapons" as a valid inflected noun. Our algorithm works as follows: it opens the in-built NID and searches for *-er* that matches maximally with the inflection part of the word. When a valid match is found, it breaks the word into two parts: *hātiyār* + *-er*. Then it stores the first part in NBD and the second part in NID. In most situations, this method is used to break inflected nouns with a list of nominal inflections that are stored in NID. According to our simple logic, since W_N is a valid inflected noun, it has an inflection part, the perfect match of which is available in NID, if NID is exhaustive. Therefore, the selection of an appropriate match for an inflection from NID is not a tough task. The following frame presents a conceptual framework which is adapted to collect lemmas from inflected Bengali nouns (Fig. 8.9).

We use this method to lemmatize successfully more than one hundred thousand inflected nouns obtained from a Bengali corpus. Our method runs into trouble only in a few cases due to paucity of data in NID or alternation in surface form of an inflection due to morphophonemic change during concatenation with a nominal base. However, such alternation is a rare phenomenon and noted for a few nouns, e.g., *mā* + *-rā* = *māyerā* "mother" (not *mārā*), *bhāi* + *-rā* = *bhāyerā* "brothers" (not *bhāirā*), *pā* + *-er* = *pāyer* "of leg" (not *pāer*), etc.

All compound nouns, which are written as single-word units, are lemmatized in the same manner. When these words are attached to inflections, they are put to lemmatization. For instance, *uttarākhaṇḍer* "of Uttarakhand" and *nandādebīke* "to Nandadevi" are successfully lemmatized and their nominal bases are stored as *uttarākhaṇḍ* and *nandādebī*, respectively in the NID. Also, all single-word compounds, after separation from inflections, are put under **lexical clustering** so that they are linked to the **lexical profile** of headwords. Compound words like *kathākali, kathārambha, kathāntar, kathābārtā, kathāmukh, kathāmṛta, kathāśilpa, kathāśilpi, kathārūp, kathāsāgar, kathāsāhitya, kathāsāhityik,* and *kathopakathan* are linked up with *kathā* through a lexical clustering. We link these words to the lexical profile of *kathā* to inform that these are generated from *kathā* by compounding—a highly productive word formation process in Bengali. Thus, we use information derived through lemmatization to reflect on the nature and range of lexical generativity of nouns in Bengali. It is possible to develop a lexical profile for each noun in this manner to measure its width and span of lexical generativity as well as lemmatize the variants through thematic lemmatization. Thus, by lemmatization, we store all nominal bases extracted from inflected nouns in NBD. This enables us to assemble all noun lemmas in one place so that we can access this word stock without searching at various other sources. The list of lemmas is also available for a morphological generation process as well as subclassification of nouns into different groups and classes with a network of a lexical cluster to show how these are collectively displayed under one head (Barnbrook, 1996).

8.8 Conclusion

Lemmatization is an important word processing technique in corpus-based research and application in languages. In vocabulary study and lexicography, it produces a distinct set of lemmas along with information of their patterns of distribution (Sánchez & Cantos, 1997) in different contextual frames. It facilitates our understanding about the nature of affixation of lemmas while they undergo the word formation process in a language (Harmann 1991). Moreover, it allows one to compile databases of lemmas, which have applications in digital lexical resource generation and language teaching. In computational linguistics and language technology, lemmatization has utilities in developing systems for lexical subclassification, lexical clustering, word formation pattern analysis, word-sense disambiguation, WordNet building, information retrieval and other activities.

Keeping these applications in view, we have briefly discussed here how we lemmatize inflected Bengali nouns and how we achieve our goal through a combination of linguistic knowledge and computation. We understand that knowledge about the nature and pattern of inflection of Bengali nouns is necessary for developing a method for lemmatizing inflected Bengali nouns. The rules for combining noun bases and inflections are essential inputs based on which a system can generate expected outputs. The format of the resources that we use may vary based on the nature of a tool and the nature of input data in question. We expect that the method that we have applied here can be useful for looking into the external form and internal structure of Bengali words of other parts-of-speech to generate lexical lists for various theoretical, descriptive, and applied linguistic works.

Appendix

Bengali nouns formed with or without formative elements.

Type 1: Noun Without Word-Formative Element (WFE)

(a) **Noun + Ø marker: (1)**

Ghar	[ghar-Ø]	"house"

Type 2: Noun with one Word-Formative Element (WFE)

(b) **Noun + Emphatic Particle: (2)**

Ghari	[ghar-i]	"house indeed"
Gharo	[ghar-o]	"house also"

(c) **Noun + Singular Marker: (5)**

gharṭi	[ghar-ṭi]	"the house"
gharṭā	[ghar-ṭā]	"the house"
gharkhānā	[ghar-khānā]	"the house"
gharkhāni	[ghar-khāni]	"the house"
gharṭuku	[ghar-ṭuku]	"the house"

(d) **Noun + Plural Marker: (3)**

Gharguli	[ghar-guli]	"houses"
Ghargulo	[ghar-gulo]	"houses"
Ghargulā	[ghar-gulā]	"houses"

(e) **Noun + Case Marker: (4)**

Ghare	[ghar-e]	"in house"
Gharer	[ghar-er]	"of house"
Gharke	[ghar-ke]	"to house"
Gharete	[ghar-ete]	"in house"

Type 3: Noun with Two Word-Formative Elements (WFEs)

(a) **Noun + Singular + Particle: (10)**

gharṭii	[ghar-ṭi-i]	"the house indeed"
gharṭio	[ghar-ṭi-o]	"the house also"
gharṭāi	[ghar-ṭā-i]	"the house indeed"
gharṭāo	[ghar-ṭā-o]	"the house also"
gharkhānāi	[ghar-kānā-i]	"the house indeed"
gharkhānāo	[ghar-kānā-o]	"the house also"
gharkhānii	[gharkhāni-i]	"the house indeed"

gharkhānio	[ghar-khāni-o]	"the house also"
ghartukui	[ghar-ṭuku-i]	"the house indeed"
ghartukuo	[ghar-ṭuku-o]	"the house also"

(b) **Noun + Plural + Particle: (6)**

ghargulii	[ghar-guli-i]	"houses indeed"
ghargulio	[ghar-guli-o]	"houses also"
gharguloi	[ghar-gulo-i]	"houses indeed"
gharguloo	[ghar-gulo-o]	"houses also"
ghargulā	[ghar-gulā-i]	"houses indeed"
ghargulā	[ghar-gulā-o]	"houses also"

(c) **Noun + Singular + Case: (13)**

ghartike	[ghar-ṭi-ke]	"to the house"
ghartite	[ghar-ṭi-te]	"in the house"
ghartir	[ghar-ṭi-r]	"of the house"
ghartāke	[ghar-ṭā-ke]	"to the house"
ghartāte	[ghar-ṭā-te]	"in the house"
ghartār	[ghar-ṭā-r]	"of the house"
ghartāy	[ghar-ṭā-y]	"of the house"
gharkhānāi	[ghar-kānā-ke]	"the house indeed"
gharkhānāo	[ghar-kānā-te]	"the house also"
gharkhānii	[gharkhāni-ke]	"the house indeed"
gharkhānio	[ghar-khāni-te]	"the house also"
ghartukui	[ghar-ṭuku-ke]	"the house indeed"
ghartukuo	[ghar-ṭuku-te]	"the house also"

(d) **Noun + Plural + Case: (11)**

ghargulike	[ghar-guli-ke]	"to the houses"
ghargulite	[ghar-guli-te]	"in the houses"
ghargulir	[ghar-guli-r]	"of the houses"
gharguloke	[ghar-gulo-ke]	"to the houses"
gharguloté	[ghar-gulo-te]	"to the houses"
ghargulor	[ghar-gulo-r]	"of the houses"
ghargoy	[ghar-gulo-y]	"houses also"
ghargulāke	[ghar-gulā-ke]	"houses also"
ghargulāte	[ghar-gulā-te]	"houses indeed"
ghargulār	[ghar-gulā-r]	"houses also"
ghargulāy	[ghar-gulā-y]	"houses also"

(e) **Noun + Case + Particle: (6)**

gharei	[ghar-e-i]	"in the house indeed"
ghareo	[ghar-e-o]	"in the house also"
gharkei	[ghar-ke-i]	"to the house indeed"
gharkeo	[ghar-ke-o]	"to the house also"
gharetei	[ghar-ete-i]	"in the house indeed"
ghareteo	[ghar-ete-o]	"in the house also"

Type 4: With three Word-Formative Elements (WFEs)

(a) **Noun + Singular + Case + Particle (28)**

ghartikei	[ghar-ṭi-ke-i]	"to the house indeed"
ghartikeo	[ghar-ṭi-ke-o]	"to the house also"
gharṭitei	[ghar-ṭi-te-i]	"in the house indeed"
gharṭiteo	[ghar-ṭi-te-o]	"in the house also"
gharṭākei	[ghar-ṭā-ke-i]	"to the house indeed"
gharṭākeo	[ghar-ṭā-ke-o]	"to the house also"
gharṭātei	[ghar-ṭā-te-i]	"in the house indeed"
gharṭāteo	[ghar-ṭā-te-o]	"in the house also"
gharṭiri	[ghar-ṭi-r-i]	"of the house indeed"
gharṭiro	[ghar-ṭi-r-o]	"of the house also"
gharṭāri	[ghar-ṭā-r-i]	"of the house indeed"
gharṭāro	[ghar-ṭā-r-o]	"of the house also"
gharṭāyi	[ghar-ṭā-y-i]	"of the house indeed"
gharṭāyo	[ghar-ṭā-y-o]	"of the house also"
gharkhānākei	[ghar-khānā-ke-i]	"to the house indeed"
gharkhānākeo	[ghar-khānā-ke-o]	"to the house also"
gharkhānātei	[ghar-khānā-te-i]	"to the house indeed"
gharkhānāteo	[ghar-khānā-te-o]	"to the house also"
gharkhānāyi	[ghar-khānā-y-i]	"to the house indeed"
gharkānāyo	[ghar-khānā-y-o]	"to the house also"
gharkhānikei	[ghar-khāni-ke-i]	"to the house indeed"
gharkhānikeo	[ghar-khāni-ke-o]	"to the house also"
gharkhānitei	[ghar-khāni-te-i]	"to the house indeed"
gharkhāniteo	[ghar-khāni-te-o]	"to the house also"
gharṭukukei	[ghar-ṭuku-ke-i]	"to the house indeed"
gharṭukukeo	[ghar-ṭuku-ke-o]	"to the house also"
gharṭukutei	[ghar-ṭuku-te-i]	"in the house indeed"
gharṭukuteo	[ghar-ṭuku-te-o]	"in the house also"

(b) **Noun + Plural + Case + Particle (22)**

ghargulikei	[ghar-guli-ke-i]	"to the houses indeed"
ghargulikeo	[ghar-guli-ke-o]	"to the houses also"
ghargulitei	[ghar-guli-te-i]	"in the houses indeed"
ghargulitco	[ghar-guli-te–o]	"in the houses also"
ghargulokei	[ghar-gulo-ke-i]	"to the houses indeed"
ghargulokeo	[ghar-gulo-ke-o]	"to the houses also"
ghargulotei	[ghar-gulo-te-i]	"in the houses indeed"
gharguloteo	[ghar-gulo-te-o]	"in the houses also"
ghargulākei	[ghar-gulā-ke-i]	"to the houses indeed"
ghargulākeo	[ghar-gulā-ke-o]	"to the houses also"
ghargulātei	[ghar-gulā-te-i]	"in the houses indeed"
ghargulāteo	[ghar-gulā-te-o]	"in the houses also"
gharguliri	[ghar-guli-r-i]	"of the houses indeed"
gharguliro	[ghar-guli-r-o]	"of the houses also"
ghargulori	[ghar-gulo-r-i]	"of the houses indeed"
gharguloro	[ghar-gulo-r-o]	"of the houses also"
ghargulori	[ghar-gulā-r-i]	"of the houses indeed"
gharguloro	[ghar-gulā-r-o]	"of the houses also"
gharguloyi	[ghar-gulo-y-i]	"of the houses indeed"
gharguloyo	[ghar-gulo-y-o]	"of the houses also"
ghargulāyi	[ghar-gulā-y-i]	"of the houses indeed"
ghargulāyo	[ghar-gulā-y-o]	"of the houses also"

References

Airio, E. (2006). Word normalization and decompounding in mono- and bilingual IR. *Information Retrieval, 9*, 249–271.

Barnbrook, G. (1996). *Language and computers*. Edinburgh University Press.

Beale, A. D. (1987). Towards a distributional lexicon. In R. Garside, G. Leech, & G. Sampson (Eds.), *The computational analysis of English: A corpus-based approach* (pp. 149–162). Longman.

Biber, D., Conrad, S., & Reppen, R. (1998). *Corpus linguistics: Investigating language structure and use*. Cambridge University Press.

Creutz, M. (2003). Unsupervised segmentation of words using prior distributions of morph length and frequency. In *Proceedings of the 41st Annual Meeting of the Association for Computational Linguistics*, July 2003 (pp. 280–287).

Dash, N. S., & Chaudhuri, B. B. (1997). Computer parsing of Bengali verbs. *Linguistics Today., 1*(1), 64–85.

Dash, N. S. (2006). The process of lemmatization of inflected and affixed words in Bengali text corpus. In Presented in the*28th All India Conference of Linguists (28-AICL)*. Varanasi: Department of Linguistics, Banaras Hindu University, November 2–5, 2006.

Dash, N. S. (2007a.) Indian scenario in language corpus generation. In: N. S. Dash, P. Dasgupta, & P. Sarkar (Eds.) *Rainbow of linguistics* (Vol. I, pp. 129–162). Kolkata: T. Media Publication.

Dash, N. S. (2007b). Toward lemmatization of Bengali words for building language technology resources. *South Asian Language Review, 17*(2), 1–15.
Dash, N. S. (2015). Marking words with part-of-speech (POS) tags within the text boundary of a corpus: The problems, the process, and the outcomes. *Translation Today, 9*(1), 5–24.
Dash, N. S. (2017). Defining Language-Specific Synsets in IndoWordNet: Some theoretical and practical issues. In N. S. Dash, P. Bhattacharyya, & J. Pawar (Eds.), *The WordNet in Indian languages* (pp. 45–64). Springer.
Dawson, J. L. (1974). Suffix removal for word conflation. *Bulletin of the Association for Literary and Linguistic Computing., 2*(3), 33–46.
Erjavec, T., & Dzeroski, S. (2004). Machine learning of morphosyntactic structure: Lemmatizing unknown Slovene words. *Applied Artificial Intelligence, 18*(1), 17–40.
Federici, S., & Pirelli, V. (1992). A bootstrapping strategy for lemmatization: Learning through examples. In: Kiefer, et al. (Eds.) (pp. 123–135).
Fligelstone, S. (1994) JAWS: Using lemmatization rules and contextual disambiguation rules to enhance CLAWS output. In *Lancaster database of linguistic corpora: Project report*. UK: Linguistics Department, Lancaster University.
Frakes, W. B., & Fox, C. J. (2003). Strength and similarity of affix removal stemming algorithms. *SIGIR Forum., 37*, 26–30.
Frakes, W. B. (1984). Term conflation for information retrieval. In *Proceedings of the 7th Annual International ACM SIGIR'84 Conference on Research and Development in Information Retrieval* (pp. 383–389).
Francis, N., & Kucera, H. (1982). *Frequency analysis of english usage: Lexicon and grammar*. Houghton Mifflin Company.
Galvez, C., de Moya-Anegon, F., & Solana, V. H. (2005). Term conflation methods in information retrieval: Non-linguistic and linguistic approaches. *Journal of Documentation., 61*(4), 520–547.
Hafer, M. A., & Weiss, S. F. (1974). Word segmentation by letter successor varieties. *Information Processing and Management., 10*(11/12), 371–386.
Harman, D. (1991). How effective is suffixing? *Journal of the American Society for Information Science., 42*(1), 7–15.
Hull, D. A. (1996). Stemming algorithms—A case study for detailed evaluation. *Journal of the American Society for Information Science., 47*(1), 70–84.
Hundt, M., Sand, A., & Skandera, P. (1999). *Manual of Information to accompany The Freiburg-Brown Corpus of American English (Frown)*. Albert-Ludwigs-Universität Freiburg.
Jongejan, B., & Dalianis, H. (2009). Automatic training of lemmatization rules that handle morphological changes in pre-, in-, and suffixes alike. In *Proceeding of the ACL-2009, Joint conference of the 47th Annual Meeting of the Association for Computational Linguistics and the 4th International Joint Conference on Natural Language Processing of the Asian Federation of Natural Language Processing*, Singapore, August 2–7, 2009 (pp. 145–153).
Kamps, J., Monz, C., Rijke, M., & Sigurbjörnsson, B. (2004). Language dependent and language-independent approach to cross-lingual text retrieval. In C. Peters, J. Gonzalo, M. Braschler, & M. Kluck (Eds.), *Comparative evaluation of multilingual information access systems* (pp. 152–165). Springer.
Kanis, J., & Skorkovská, L. (2010). Comparison of different lemmatization approaches through the means of information retrieval performance. In *Proceedings of the 13th International Conference on Text, Speech and Dialogue TSD'10* (pp. 93–100).
Korenius, T., Laurikkala, J., Järvelin, K., & Juhola, M. (2004). Stemming and lemmatization in the clustering of Finnish text documents. In *Proceedings of the 13th ACM International Conference on Information and Knowledge Management, CIKM'04* (pp. 625–633).
Kornilakis, H., Grigoriadou, M., Galiotou, E., Papakitsos, E. (2004). Using a lemmatizer to support the development and validation of the Greek WordNet. In *Proceedings of the 2nd Global WordNet Conference* (pp. 130–135). Brno, Czech Republic, January 20–23, 2004.

Kraaij, W., & Pohlmann, R. (1996). Viewing stemming as recall enhancement. In: H. P. Frei, D. Harman, P. Schauble, & R. Wilkinson (Eds.), In *Proceedings of the 17th ACM SIGIR Conference*, Zurich, August 18–22 (pp. 40–48).

Krovetz, R. (1993). Viewing morphology as an inference process. In *Proceedings of ACM-SIGIR93, 16th International ACM/SIGIR '93 Conference on Research and Development in Information Retrieval*, Pittsburgh, PA, USA, June 27–July 01, 1993 (pp. 191–203).

Leech, G. (2007). New resources or just better old ones? The Holy Grail of representativeness. In M. Hundt, N. Nesselhauf, & C. Biewer (Eds.), *Corpus linguistics and the web* (pp. 133–149). Rodopi.

Lennon, M., Pearce, D. S., Tarry, B. D., & Willett, P. (1981). An Evaluation of some conflation algorithms for information retrieval. *Journal of Information Science., 3*, 177–183.

Liu, H., Christiansen, T., Baumgartner, W. A., & Verspoor, K. (2012) BioLemmatizer: a lemmatization tool for morphological processing of biomedical text. *Journal of Biomedical Semantics*. 1–29.

Lovins, J. B. (1968). Development of a Stemming algorithm. *Mechanical Translation and Computational Linguistics., 11*, 22–31.

Lovins, J. B. (1971). Error evaluation for stemming algorithms as clustering algorithms. *Journal of the American Society for Information Science., 22*, 28–40.

McEnery, T., & Hardie, A. (2006). *Corpus linguistics: Method, theory, and practice*. Cambridge University Press.

McEnery, T., & Wilson, A. (1996). *Corpus linguistics*. Edinburgh University Press.

Minnen, G., Carroll, J., & Pearce, D. (2001). Applied morphological processing of English. *Natural Language Engineering., 7*, 207–223.

Paice, C. D. (1990). Another stemmer. *SIGIR Forum., 24*(3), 56–61.

Paice, C. D. (1996). Method for evaluation of stemming algorithms based on error counting. *Journal of the American Society for Information Science., 47*(8), 632–649.

Popovič, M., & Willett, P. (1992). The effectiveness of stemming for natural-language access to Slovene textual data. *Journal of the American Society for Information Science., 43*(5), 384–390.

Porter, M. F. (1980). An algorithm for suffix stripping. *Program, 14*(3), 130–137.

Reichel, U. D., & Weilhammer, K. (2004). Automated morphological segmentation and evaluation. In *Proceedings of LREC 2004*, Lisbon.

Sánchez, A., & Cantos, P. (1997). Predictability of word forms (types) and lemmas in linguistic corpora, a case study based analysis of the CUMBRE corpus: An 8-million-word corpus of contemporary Spanish. *International Journal of Corpus Linguistics., 2*(2), 259–280.

Savoy, J. (1993). Stemming of French words based on grammatical categories. *Journal of the American Society for Information Science., 44*(1), 1–9.

Ulmschneider, J. E., & Doszkocs, T. (1983). A practical stemming algorithm for online search assistance. *Online Review., 7*(4), 301–318.

Xu, J., & Croft, W. B. (1998). Corpus-based stemming using co-occurrence of word variants. *ACM Transactions on Information Systems., 16*(1), 61–81.

Web Links

http://khnt.hit.uib.no/icame/manuals/frown/index.htm
http://snowball.tartarus.org
http://www.ncbi.nlm.nih.gov/pmc/articles/PMC3359276/
https://blog.bitext.com/what-is-the-difference-between-stemming-and-lemmatization/
https://nlp.stanford.edu/IR-book/html/htmledition/stemming-and-lemmatization-1.html
https://towardsdatascience.com/stemming-lemmatization-what
https://www.datacamp.com/community/tutorials/stemming-lemmatization-python

https://www.geeksforgeeks.org/python-lemmatization-with-nltk/
https://www.machinelearningplus.com/nlp/lemmatization-examples
https://www.quora.com/What-is-lemmatization-in-NLP
https://www.twinword.com/blog/what-is-lemmatization/

Chapter 9
Decomposition of Inflected Verbs

Abstract We apply an analytical method to decompose inflected verbs in Bengali. We treat these verbs as autonomous and isolated linguistic units that are physically free from their contextualized frames of occurrence in sentences. The basic goal behind applying this strategy is to retrieve various kinds of morphological information from inflected Bengali verbs. Other goals are to develop a verb root database, a verb suffix database, and a semi-supervised verb analysis system. To achieve these goals, we apply a rule-based suffix stripping method based on knowledge and information obtained from a manual analysis of a large number of inflected verbs that are used in the Bengali written corpus. Our system first accepts an inflected verb as a lexical input, treats it as a word of an unbroken string of characters, applies stripping rules for root and suffix segmentation, matches segmented parts with respective roots and suffix lists, extracts relevant information from a machine-readable inbuilt dictionary, and displays outputs with information about the constituents that are used to generate the final inflected form. The outputs are root lists, suffix lists, morph lists, grammatical rules, and matching algorithms all of which are necessary for developing a morphological analyzing system for Bengali. The lexical database, morph lists, and metadata that are produced through this method are also useful for developing systems which work for lexical information retrieval and lexical teaching. The method that we use here can be applied for decomposing inflected verbs of other Indian languages by replacing the respective root and suffix databases and concatenation rules.

Keywords Bengali verb · Morphology · Morphological analysis · Root · Suffix · Mapping · Negative verb

9.1 Introduction

A sentence, in some sense, is an orthographic representation of our thoughts. The whole message in a sentence revolves around the notion of an "action" which is embedded in the sentence. The verb is an orthographic representation of an action performed in a sentence. Other than the action being performed, a sentence also contains a whole range of thematic information such as subject, object, goal, place,

N. S. Dash, *Language Corpora Annotation and Processing*,
https://doi.org/10.1007/978-981-16-2960-0_9

and time information of an action. These thematic properties, both theoretically and functionally, center around a verb. A verb usually takes a conjugated form based on the nature of these dimensions. In order to understand the information conveyed by a verb in a sentence, we have to analyze the form of a verb as well as its relation with other words used in a sentence (Bharati et al., 1995: 12).

The primary items of our present interest are inflected verbs that are used in the Bengali language—a member of the Indo-Aryan language family, spoken in the eastern part of India and Bangladesh (Islam & Khan, 2006). It is an inflectional language where verbs are inflected during conjugation according to tense, mood, person, and honorificity. The analysis of an inflected verb used in a sentence reveals much more information than an isolated verb (Dabre et al., 2012). We gather morpho-lexical information of inflected verbs from decontextualized frames, which we apply to build up metadata to cut short long, and cumbersome ways of analysis of sentences. To achieve this goal, we apply a decomposition process to the inflected verbs. We call it a "structural-cum-functional analysis" of inflected Bengali verbs.

In Sect. 9.2, we shed some light on differences between part-of-speech annotation and lexical decomposition; in Sect. 9.3, we report on early works on Bengali morphological analysis; in Sect. 9.4, we analyze morphological structure of Bengali verbs; in Sect. 9.5, we describe conjugation pattern of Bengali verbs in general; in Sect. 9.6, we categorize Bengali verb roots based on their surface orthographic representation; in Sect. 9.7, we highlight major issues involved in lexical decomposition of Bengali inflected verbs; in Sect. 9.8, we discuss the process of information storage; in Sect. 9.9, we describe the method of decomposing non-conjugated Bengali verbs with examples; in Sect. 9.10, we describe a process of decomposing conjugated Bengali verbs; in Sect. 9.11, we discuss the method of data creation and storage; in Sect. 9.12, we refer to special instances of Bengali verbs that stand as exceptions; in Sect. 9.13, we present results received from application of the method on verb database; in Sect. 9.14, we evaluate the performance of the system; and in Sect. 9.15, we highlight the advantages and limitations of the system and suggest for modification and upgradation of the system with new set of data and rules to make it more robust and accurate.

9.2 Lexical Decomposition

The process of lexical decomposition is different from part-of-speech (POS) annotation in the sense that while POS annotation aims at assigning explicit POS information to words, lexical decomposition aims at retrieving all kinds of grammatical information of morphemes that are used in the formation of words to understand the specific functional roles of the formative elements. Similar to morphological processing, it analyzes the structure of a word with a focus on its part-of-speech, components, composition, function, and meaning (Abu Zaher & Tyers, 2009). It, however, differs from morphological processing in the sense that in morphologial processing we do not pay attention to the semantic aspects of morphs used to form a word, in lexical decomposition we pay attention to the semantic information that are embedded with the components used to form a word. The primary goal of lexical decomposition is to identify and extract grammatical, syntactic, information from words by using an expanded lexicon as a separate part of grammar (Chomsky, and semantic1972: 36). For achieving this goal, it analyzes surface structures of words and records their lexical, syntactic, morphophonemic, and semantic properties that are embedded within their surface structures. It also aims at studying the functional roles of morphemes that are used to form words. From a computational point of view, lexical decomposition involves the extraction of grammatical, syntactic, and semantic information from words to be used at higher levels of word analysis and application.

In this chapter, we discuss a method for the lexical decomposition of Bengali verbs. For this, we refer to detailed lexico-grammatical information of verbs as these are useful in part-of-speech annotation, information retrieval, machine learning, query answering, stemming, lemmatization, language teaching, and dictionary-making. This method generates information about the form and function of morphs of verbs indispensable in teaching, cognition, and utilization of Bengali verbs (Bapat et al., 2010). We decompose the Bengali verbs as decontextualized autonomous lexical units by developing a strategy supported with verb roots and verb suffixes. To carry out the task, we apply a rule-based suffix stripping method on a large list of Bengali verbs. The outputs are generated through a gradual scheduled process. Finally, we analyze the outputs to gather insights about their process of formation and the nature of function in the language.

The decomposition of Bengali inflected verbs involves following the existing grammar and word formation rules of the language, identification, and analysis of the constituents used to form inflected verbs (Das & Bandyopadhyay, 2010). Technically, it refers to the process of analyzing internal structures of verbs by performing screening operations on them to find out components, patterns of composition, and functions in the formation of final verbs (Dasgupta & Khan, 2004). Within this scheme, Bengali inflected verbs are treated as sets of constructions where morphemes are used as building blocks to generate final forms following the existing word formation rules (WFRs) applicable to the language (Selkirk, 1983: 7).

At the initial stage, we consider an inflected verb as an independent lexical unit which is made with a sequence of chained characters. After referring to a suffix list, we apply a suffix stripping method to separate the suffix part from an inflected verb. Finally, we preserve the suffix part in the suffix database and the root part of the root database. Once the process is complete, the outputs are used as inputs for further processing. The outputs are mainly root list, suffix list, morph list, grammatical rules, and matching algorithms. To develop this model, we analyze every part of a Bengali verb and capture all information a Bengali verb provides. It differs from POS annotation in the sense that while POS annotation contains only contextualized information, this process contains decontextualized information.

9.3 Some Early Works

Several research works have focused on the analysis of Bengali verbs in the last few years. To date, we have come across some morphological analyzers that are able to analyze Bengali verbs moderately. That means the requirement of a robust morphological analyzer for Bengali verbs is not yet over. The following list shows how different approaches are applied to accomplish the goal.

(a) 1996: Trie structure-based approach (Sengupta & Chaudhuri, 1996)
(b) 1997: Two-level morphologybased approach (Dash et al., 1997)
(c) 1999: Graphemebased approach (Sengupta, 1997, 1999)
(d) 2004: Feature unification-based approach (Dasgupta & Khan, 2004)
(e) 2005: Paradigm-based approach (Bhattacharya et al., 2005)
(f) 2006: PC-KIMMO-based approach (Islam & Khan, 2006)
(g) 2008: Rule-based approach (Sarkar & Bandyopadhyay, 2008)
(h) 2009: Statistics-based approach (Abu Zaher & Tyers, 2009; Banerjee et al., 2010).

Since the approaches are partly successful to serve purposes, we propose here a method that can hopefully generate better results. This method strips the suffix part from a conjugated Bengali verb to generate a verb root and a verb suffix database. Since this method is based on a large number of verbs collected from a Bengali corpus, it achieves a greater percentage of accuracy. This method is adopted with a belief that there is a scope to work in this area to understand the structure of Bengali verbs, develop a method that can analyze the structure of Bengali verbs, and separate root and suffix parts for developing a machine-readable lexical database for decomposing conjugated verbs. In essence, the development of a good method for verb analysis largely depends on information obtained from the analysis of inflected verbs (Minnen et al., 2001). This is addressed here with reference to Bengali inflected verbs.

9.4 Morpheme Structure of Bengali Verbs

Morphological analysis is an age-old method of structural analysis of words. It deals with an analysis of those words that are made with two or more morphemes. The Bengali inflected verbs are invariably made with two or more morphemes. Morphologically, Bengali verbs are divided into two parts: *dhātu* (root) and *bibhakti* (suffix). While the root part carries a basic sense of the action of a verb, the suffix part contains varieties of information relating to the aspect, person, number, tense, auxiliary, and particles (emphatic, negative, or both) of a verb. After combining root and suffix through concatenation, a conjugated Bengali verb is made in the following way (Fig. 9.1).

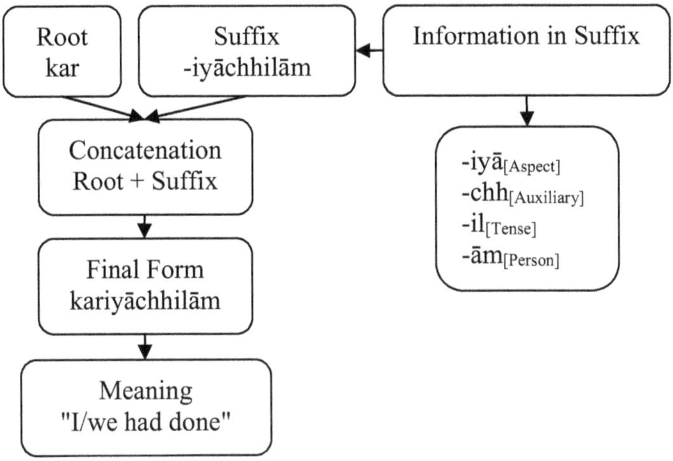

Fig. 9.1 Conjugated Bengali verb after rootsuffix combination

9.4.1 Root Part (dhātu)

Verb roots are analyzed based on their basic forms. They are divided into four subtypes (mentioned below). Moreover, based on their surface representation, Bengali verbs are divided into eight types (mentioned below), which helps in the decomposition of verbs. The conjugation patterns of Bengali verbs are also looked into to see how inflected forms are produced through the application of information of several types (i.e., *tense, aspect, moods, person, honorificity,* and *particles*). Since the categorization of Bengali verbs is controlled by the nature of rootsuffix conjugation, verbs are based on *gaṇa* (i.e., class) in our process of analysis and generation.

The root is the backbone of a verb. All markers of tense, aspect, mood, and person are tagged to it. Other verb-formative properties such as emphatic particles and negative particles are appended to a root after markers of tense, aspect, mood, person, and honorificity are tagged to root to generate a finite or non-infinite form. The term *root* is used in a specific sense here to refer to the units that are primarily used to form verbs only. Other types of the root (e.g., *pronominal root*) are ignored here because the present discussion is not intended to deal with ambiguity linked with the term (Banerjee et al., 2010).

The *dhātu* (root) of a verb denotes the type of action to be performed. Since it is not easy to identify a root in a verb, earlier scholars have suggested some rules for identifying the root of a verb. According to Jogeshchandra Ray Vidyanidhi (1912), after eliminating the final "-i" from a firstperson simple present tense form of a verb, the remaining part may be treated as *dhātu* (root) of a verb. On the other hand, according to Sunitikumar Chattopadhyay, "In modern Bengali, the present imperative for the 2nd person non-honorific form is the root of that verb" (Chattopadhyay, 1939: 122). In both cases, the resultant output is the same.

Table 9.1 Eight types of Bengali verbs that are regularly used in the language

No.	Verb type	Examples
1	Primary root (maulik dhātu)	kar, cal, mar, ýā, khā, dekh, śon, bal, par, rākh, tol, dhar, de, ne
2	Secondary root (sādhita dhātu)	ýāoyā, khāoyā, dekhā, karā, śonā, balā, deoyā, neoyā, tolā, parā
3	Gerundial root (nām dhātu)	ghumāno, dekhāno, śoyāno, śonāno, balāno, jānāno, upcāno, ugrāno, bāt̲lāno, dhamkāno
4	Finite verb (samāpikā kriyā)	kareche, balche, dharche, nemechila, dekhechila, paṛchila, balto, dekhten
5	Non-finite verb (asamāpikā kriyā)	kheye, kare, niye, giye, phele, pāliye, miśiye, mārte, śuniye, dekhte, balle, cāliye
6	Conjunct verb (nām kriyā)	upakār karā, uttar deoyā, hājir haoyā, mukhasta karā, praṇām karā, praśna karā, hāt tolā
7	Compound verb (ýaugik kriyā)	balte thāk, śunte pā, lege paṛ, uṭhe paṛ, śuye paṛ, jene rākh, kāmiye ne, bale ýā
8	Verbal compound (kriyā dvandva)	āsā-ýāoyā, dekhā-śonā, lekhā-paṛā, jānā-śonā, dharā-mārā

Bengali verb roots are largely derived from Sanskrit verb roots with a few offshoots gathered from dialects, neighboring, and foreign languages. The Sanskrit roots, after undergoing several morphophonemic changes at the *Prākṛt* and *Apabhraṃśa* stages, have taken modern shapes and are treated as Bengali verb roots. Besides, there are also a few verb roots that are derived from foreign languages like Arabic, Persian, and English. When combined, they count in the order of 1600 or more which are divided, based on the nature of roots, into the following four types:

(1) Primary verb roots (maulik dhātu): 800+
(2) Causative roots (praýojak/nijanta dhātu): 300+
(3) Denominative roots (nām dhātu): 300+
(4) Onomatopoeic roots (dhvanvātmak dhātu): 200+.

From the perspective of surface form, there are eight types of Bengali verbs, which are frequently used in modern Bengali texts (Sarkar & Basu, 1994: 199–213). They include the followings (Table 9.1).

9.4.2 Suffix Part (Bibhakti)

After the elimination of the root part from a conjugated verb, what remains is called *bibhakti* (suffix) or *kriyā bibhakti* (verb suffix). This part carries a large load of information of a conjugated verb: tense, aspect, and state of an action, persons involved in an action, the modality of an action, and information relating to an action and actor on the dimension of time. In a simple count, in standard Bengali, there are more than

160 verb suffixes, which are attached to a verb root to generate the final conjugated forms. However, it is not the case that all suffixes are tagged to all verb roots. There are restrictions at possible combinations between a root and a suffix. Due to this factor, we are extremely careful during the process of formation of a conjugated verb when we concatenate suffixes with roots to generate conjugated verbs (Dash et al., 1997).

9.5 Conjugation of Bengali Verbs

Bengali verbs are conjugated for tense, aspect, modality, person, and honorification. They do not inflect with gender and number of a subject or an object. Due to this phenomenon, final conjugated forms for masculine and feminine subjects as well as for singular and plural subjects are the same. The non-finite verbs are not conjugation sensitive. They do not change their forms based on properties that force finite forms to change their forms in conjugation. Taking this factor as a controlling element, we classify Bengali verbs into two broad types (Bhattacharya et al., 2005).

(a) Non-finite verbs (conjugation free)
(b) Finite verbs (conjugation controlled).

The non-finite verbs are further classified into four types based on their nature of use (a) conjunctives (*pūrbakālik asamāpikā*), (b) infinitives (*uddyeśak asamāpikā*), (c) participles (*bartamān asamāpikā*), and (d) conditionals (*bhūārtha/ ẏadyārtha asamāpikā*). The finite verbs, on the other hand, are adorned with suffixes for four tenses, three aspects, three moods, three persons, one honorification, one non-homorification along with three emphatic and three negative particles. All of these are tagged with verb roots to generate final conjugated forms. The verb-formative elements are listed below with their further subclassification:

(a) Tense: Present, past, future, and habitual past
(b) Aspect: Continuous, perfect, and perfect continuous
(c) Mood: Indicative, imperative, and subjunctive
(d) Person: First, second, and third
(e) Honorific: Non-honorific, neutral, and honorific
(f) Particle: Emphatic and negative.

Bengali verbs have another unique dimension in their conjugation relating to the variety based on the sobriety of use of a verb in written and spoken discourses. One is called the *sādhu* (chaste) version, and the other one is called the *chalit* (colloquial) version. Interestingly, the entire paradigm of the *sādhu* version is vigorously replicated in the *chalit* version, which doubled the list of conjugated forms of a verb. In application, the presence of two separate sets of conjugated forms of a verb becomes crucial in determining if a piece of text is written in a colloquial or chaste version. Taking these factors of conjugation in view, we make some observations about Bengali verb morphology in the following way. It helps in designing a method for analyzing Bengali verbs.

[1] There are two types of conjugation for Bengali verbs. One is for *sādhu* forms, and the other is for *chalit* forms.

[2] The conjugation pattern of *sādhu* verbs is systematic, regular, and ordered than that of *chalit* verbs.

[3] The vowel *ā* as the first character of a verb root changes into *e* when the verb is conjugated for first, second, and third person in present perfect and past perfect tense, e.g., *ās* "to come" changes into *esechhi, esechha, esechhen, ela; esechhilām, esechhile, esechhilen, and elen.* In the same way, it changes for the second person in the future imperative tense, e.g., *eso.*

[4] The roots which have vowels *i* and *u* as the second character of the string change into *e* and *o*, respectively, in some forms, e.g., *di: deoyā* "to give", *ni: neoyā* "to take," *dhu: dhoyā* "to wash", *śu: śoyā* "to lie."

[5] In case of the progressive and perfect tense, the auxiliary suffix *-chh* changes into *-chchh* if a verb root (to which it is to be tagged) ends with a vowel, e.g., *khāchchhi* (< √khā + chchh + i). This rule, however, presents a few exceptions for some roots. It remains unchanged even if the root ends in a vowel, e.g., *gāichhi* (< √gāi + chh + i), *nāichhi* (< √nāi + chh + i), and *chāichhi* (< √chāi + chh + i). This is, perhaps, becuase of the presence of the high front vowel [-i] immediately before the auxicliary form 'chh-', e.g., *khāchchhi* but *khāichhi, chāchchhi* but *chāichhi, gāchchhi* but *gāichhi*, etc.

[6] Root *ýā* has several allomorphic variations based on tense in both *sādhu* and *chalit* conjugation. In present tense, it is *ýā* (e.g., *ýāi* "I go"); in past tense, it is *ge* (e.g., *gelām* "I went"); in past perfect tense, it is *gi* (e.g., *giyechhi* "I have gone"); in habitual past, it is *ýe* (e.g., *ýetām* "I used to go"), and in future tense, it is *ýā* (e.g., *ýāba* "I shall go").

[7] There are incomplete and irregular verbs in Bengali: *āchh* and *baṭ*. These verbs are called incomplete in the sense that they do not have a full range of conjugation as noted for other verbs. These are called irregular in the sense that these forms undergo complete morphological change once the inflectional markers are attached (e.g., *āchhi: chhilām: thākba*). It is to be explored why these verbs are incomplete and irregular in Bengali while other verbs are regular, systematic, and complete.

[8] The causative forms (*nijanta dhātu*) of roots are typically formed by adding the suffix *-ā* with roots ending with consonants (*kar: karā, dekh: dekhā*) and *-oyā* with two-lettered roots ending with vowels (*ýā: ýāoyā, khā: khāoyā*).

[9] To form causative roots for roots having *i* or *u* as a first vowel, vowel *i* changes into *e* (e.g., *di: deoyā* "to give," *ni: neoya* "to take"), while vowel *u* changes into *o* (e.g., *dhu: dhoyā* "to wash," *śu: śoya* "to lie down," *ru: roya* "to plant").

[10] There is a set of negative verbs in Bengali (e.g., *nai, nao, nos, nan, nay*) which do not have a full conjugation paradigm like other verbs. They, however, perform a very strong role in the formation of negative sentences when other verbs are not present in a sentence (e.g., *se bhadra nay "he is not polite"*). The uniqueness of these forms is that they hardly change with tense, but change with person and honorification.

9.6 Categorization of Bengali Verb Roots

9.6.1 Verb Root Categorization

Considering the properties and features noted above (Sect. 9.4 and Sect. 9.5), the Bengali verb roots are divided into ten classes according to the manner of change in form and suffixes they accept during conjugation. Traditionally, Bengali verbs, after conjugation, are broadly classified into two types: *sādhu* verbs and *chalit* verbs. There is another issue with regard to the concatenation of verb suffixes with verb roots. It is noted that the addition of suffix with roots is controlled by the last character of a verb root. The last character is a vowel (or its allograph) (i.e., *a, ā, i, ī, u, ū, ṛ, e,* and *o*) or a consonant (hardly a cluster). Based on this factor, the use of the verb suffix with roots is often changed in Bengali. Keeping this in mind, Bengali verbs are divided into two subclasses:

(a) Verb roots ending in vowels, and
(b) Verb roots ending in consonants.

Keeping in view possible challenges involved in the processing of verbs, clarity in the analysis of verbs, and brevity in rule formation, we classify Bengali verb roots into the following ten classes (Table 9.2).

These classes are formed with close reference to structural similarity at the root level. That means, verb roots having the same type of spelling belong to the same category. They exhibit the same orthographic forms and the same types of conjugation patterns. For example, root √kar "to do," √cal "to move," and √bas "to sit" are put into one group because they follow the same kinds of conjugation patterns. Similarly, root √kāṭ "to cut," √sāj "to decorate," and √thāk "to stay" are put to another group

Table 9.2 Classification of Bengali verb roots into ten classes

No.	Class	Gana	Roots ending in vowel/consonant
1	Class 01	khā-ādi	(Class of vowel-ending *sādhu* roots)
2	Class 02	bal-ādi	(Class of consonant-ending *sādhu* roots)
3	Class 03	kar-ādi	(Class of consonant-ending roots)
4	Class 04	rākh-ādi	(Class of consonant-ending roots)
5	Class 05	likh-ādi	(Class of consonant-ending *chalit* roots)
6	Class 06	ha-ādi	(Class of vowel-ending *chalit* roots)
7	Class 07	cā-ādi	(Class of vowel-ending *chalit* roots)
8	Class 08	lāphā-ādi	(Class of vowel-ending *chalit* roots)
9	Class 09	pāoyā-ādi	(Class of vowel-ending *chalit* roots)
10	Class 10	āṭkā-ādi	(Class of vowel-ending *chalit* roots)

due to the same reasons. We have picked up the most frequently used verb roots as representative of the classes stated above.

9.6.2 Verb Suffix Categorization

In a simple count, there are more than 160 suffixes which can be added to a Bengali verb root. However, due to several linguistic (primarily, phonological, and morphological) reasons, all these suffixes are not permitted to be added to each verb root. Moreover, the number looks quite big due to the fact that it includes two sets of suffixes—one for resultant *sādhu* forms and the other for resultant *chalit* forms. Therefore, based on additive properties of suffixes with roots as well as taking into consideration the morphophonemic changes that take place during conjugation, verb suffixes are categorized into the following eight sets:

[1] Set 1: Suffixes for Root Class 1
[2] Set 2: Suffixes for Root Class 2
[3] Set 3: Suffixes for Root Class 3, Class 4 & Class 5
[4] Set 4: Suffixes for Root Class 7
[5] Set 5:Suffixes for Root Class 6
[6] Subset 5a:Suffixes for Root Class 8
[7] Subset 5b:Suffixes for Root Class 9
[8] Subset 5c:Suffixes for Root Class 10.

It is to be noted that these suffix sets share some structurally identical suffixes. For instance, the suffix *-len* is used with a root to generate a form that is either a simple past second person honorific form or a simple past third person honorific form (e.g., *āpni karlen* "you (hon.) did" vs. *tini karlen* "he (hon.) did"). Moreover, some suffix sets are subsets of other sets. For example, Set 5 has 3 subsets (5a, 5b & 5c). They differ in perfect tense conjugation only.

9.7 Issues in Lexical Decomposition

From a technical point of view, lexical decomposition is concerned with a study of the internal morphemic structure of a word. For the Bengali verbs, it looks at the structure, type, grammatical property, formation, meaning and functional roles of the morphs. All the aspects are empirically analyzed and interpreted with a minute study of the internal structure of Bengali verbs (Sarkar & Bandyopadhyay, 2008). Since Bengali is an inflectional language, it reduces lexical ambiguity by increasing compactness in lexical representation. Structurally, there are two primary types of finite verbs in Bengali. These are used quite frequently in the language.

Table 9.3 Structural composition of Bengali verbs

No.	Root	Suffix	Final form	Gloss
1	kar	-ø	kar	"to do"
2	kar	-i$_{[\text{Prsn}]}$	kari	"I do"
3	kar	-chh$_{[\text{Aux}]}$ + -i$_{[\text{Prsn}]}$	karchhi	"I am doing"
4	kar	-ite$_{[\text{Asp}]}$ + -chh$_{[\text{Aux}]}$ + -i$_{[\text{Prsn}]}$	karitechhi	"I am doing"
5	kar	-il$_{[\text{Tns}]}$ + -ām$_{[\text{Prsn}]}$	karilām	"I did"
6	kar	-chh$_{[\text{Aux}]}$ + -il$_{[\text{Tns}]}$ + -ām$_{[\text{Prsn}]}$	karchhilām	"I was doing"
7	kar	-iyā$_{[\text{Asp}]}$ + -chh$_{[\text{Aux}]}$ + -il$_{[\text{Tns}]}$ + -ām$_{[\text{Prsn}]}$	kariyāchhilām	"I had done"
8	kar	-ā$_{[\text{Cstv}]}$ + -no$_{[\text{Grnd}]}$	karāno	"make other do"
9	kar	-ā$_{[\text{Cstv}]}$ + -chchh$_{[\text{Aux}]}$ + -i$_{[\text{Prsn}]}$	karāchchhi	cause other do

(a) Verbs in root forms, and
(b) Verbs in inflected/conjugated forms.

The first group of verbs includes only the second person imperative forms, e.g., *kar* "you do," *bal* "you say," *śon* "you hear," *dekh* "you see," *ýā* "you go," *gun* "you count," *par* "you wear," *mar* "you die," and *sar* "you move." The second group of verbs, on the other hand, includes the following types:

(a) Finite forms, e.g., *karla* "he did," *karchhe* "he is doing"
(b) Non-finite forms, e.g., *kare* "doing," *karle* "doing"
(c) Infinitive forms, e.g., *karte* "to do"
(d) Causative forms, e.g., *karāte* "to make others do," *karālām* "made others do," and
(e) Gerundial forms, e.g., *karāno* "making others do," *karbār* "for doing," *karābār* "for making others doing."

The major morphological combinations that are used to produce conjugated Bengali verbs are structurally explained in the following manner (Table 9.3):

There are at least five different sets of information (i.e., *aspect, auxiliary, tense, person,* and *particles*) embedded within a verb suffix. However, since all information is not used always with each root, one or two sets of information are used based on the requirement. In some other cases, different sets are attached to roots. The linear sequential order of use of these suffixes with regard to verb root is more or less uniform. No suffix normally interchanges its position with others in respect to a verb root. Generally, root occupies the leftmost position followed by aspect, auxiliary, tense, person, and particle—all are taking place in sequential order as shown below.

- Root+ (1) + (2) + (3) + (4) + (5) = (6)
- kar + -iyā + -chh + -il + -ām + -i = kariyāchilāmi "I had done indeed".

One important point has to be noted here. In some cases, the emphatic particle (*-i* and *-o*) comes immediately after the aspect marker, when we put additional emphasis on verb root (e.g., *kariyāichhilām*). In a normal situation, the emphatic particle comes

Table 9.4 Morphological information found in a Bengali verb

No.	Root	Suffix	Function	Gloss
0	kar			"I had done indeed"
1		-iyā-	Aspect marker	
2		-chh-	Auxiliary marker	
3		-ila-	Tense marker	
4		-ām-	Person marker	
5		-i	Particle (Emphatic)	

as the last member at the end of the conjugated form of a verb (e.g., *kariyāchhilāmi*). When we decompose the final surface form of a verb and analyze formative components, we find the following set of morphological information in the following manner (Table 9.4).

When a particular suffix is dropped from its fixed position, its immediately following suffix occupies the vacated slot. Following this method, more than 160 conjugated verb forms (*simple, finite, non-finite, perfect, causative, and gerundial*) are possible to generate from a single verb root in Bengali (Dash, 2015: 120). Each suffix contributes to the linguistic identity of a verb. During the formation of an inflected Bengali verb, the suffixes are normally governed by the following two rules:

(i) **Rules of morphosyntax:** It restricts random conjoining of different morphemes with roots
(ii) **Rules of lexical generativity:** It controls morphophonemic (and morphographemic) restructuring of characters at the boundaries of conjoining morphemes.

The word formation rules that generate the final verb forms with constituent morphemes are mostly concatenative in nature. No morpheme is embedded within another morpheme during verb formation. However, due to the effect of the spelling rule, some verb forms are not the results of a simple concatenation of constituent morphemes. Spelling rules for words are quite complex in Bengali. They affect the rules that operate at morpheme boundaries. Therefore, a major problem of decomposing verbs in Bengali is the proper detection of morphemic boundaries, which are not as explicit as word boundaries. In certain contexts, the lexical projection of a verb is derived as a union of projections of constituent morphemes obtained through integrated morphosyntactic concatenation. Therefore, for extracting root and suffix parts from conjugated Bengali verbs, we need clear ideas about the verbs of the language. After structural analysis of verbs (conjugated and non-conjugated), we observe that there are two parts in a Bengali verb:

(a) Root part (verb root): It has independent use.
(b) Suffix part (verb suffix): It is attached to the root.

Table 9.5 Bengali verbal suffixes attached to the verb root

Finite verb form: baleichilām			
Root part:	√bal	Suffix Part:	-eichilām
		aspect	-e-
		particle	-i-
		auxiliary	-ch-
		tense	-il(a)
		person	-ām

From a deeper structural analysis of verb types, we find that Bengali verbs are formed as a result of the following processes:

(a) $[R_1]$: Single root without a suffix.
(b) $[R_1 + S_1]$: Single root with a single suffix.
(c) $[R_1 + R_2 = \mathrm{CR}_1]$: Two roots (as a compound root).
(d) $[\mathrm{CR}_1 + S_1]$: Compound root with a single suffix.

The final lexico-grammatical identity of a verb depends on the role it plays in a sentence. Therefore, by defining the syntactic and semantic role of a verb in a sentence, we identify if a verb is used as a finite verb or a non-finite one. On the contrary, identification of subclass of a verb in decontextualized existence (when it is not used in a sentence) is largely based on its surface structure. At this point, the identity of a verb depends on its suffix part that carries various types of grammatical information such as aspect, tense, person, number, and particle. For instance, *baleichilām,* in a decontextualized situation, is a finite verb because it has a root part, which is attached, in a fixed sequential order, with suffixes of aspect, particle, auxiliary, tense, and personall of them are arranged following the word formation rule applicable to Bengali (Table 9.5).

9.8 Method of Information Storage

We collect a large number of verbs from a Bengali corpus to compile a verb lexical database (VLD). This is the most useful resource at subsequent stages of verb decomposition. We structurally analyze more than two thousand Bengali verbs to identify and separate suffixes from roots. The following schema shows how we make preparation for verb decomposition (Fig. 9.2).

The primary stages that we apply at this level of the task are summarized in the following order:

[1] **Collection**: All kinds of Bengali verb (conjugated and non-conjugated) are collected from a Bengali text corpus.
[2] **Normalization**: Verbs are passed through this stage to find out if there is any error in spelling and if any non-verb is included in the list.

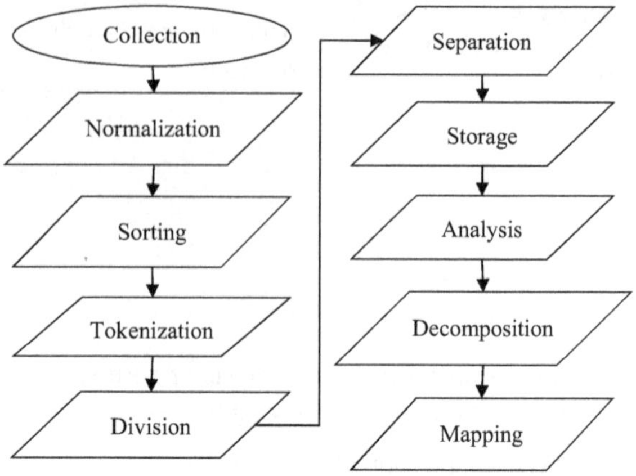

Fig. 9.2 Introductory preparation for verb decomposition

[3] **Sorting**: Verbs are sorted in alphabetical order. Attention is paid to see that all allomorphic variants are put under regular heads.

[4] **Tokenization**: Verbs are passed through tokenization to prepare a list of unique verbs with a single representation in the list.

[5] **Division**: Verbs are divided into non-conjugated and conjugated forms.

[6] **Separation**: Conjugated verbs are split into the root and suffix parts.

[7] **Storage**: Roots are stored in root lexicon (RL) and suffixes are stored in suffix lexicon (SL). Non-conjugated verbs are put in RL.

[8] **Analysis**: A large number of conjugated verbs are analyzed to find out grammatical rules underlying their surface forms.

[9] **Decomposition**: Large numbers of suffixes are decomposed to identify morphs, their morpheme class, and their role in verb formation. The morphs (*aspect, tense, person, honorific,* and *particle*) that combine with a root to generate final surface forms are identified.

[10] **Mapping**: Root–suffix mapping rules are framed to develop algorithms for automatic identification and analysis of Bengali verbs in texts.

The RL contains regular and irregular variants (allomorphs) of verb roots while the SL contains suffixes with possible allomorphic variations. To distinguish these from standard dictionaries, these are marked with separate indicators. During the initial training period, RL and SL are gradually augmented with new data and information. Also, grammatical mapping algorithms are modified to deal with new verbs, which are found in other texts but not available in the corpus. Dictionaries made with lists of roots and suffixes as well as mapping rules are indispensable for designing a tool for Bengali verb decomposition. The ways we analyze verbs and store information are not found in standard dictionaries available in the language. What makes it relevant in the present context is its elaborate analysis of the morphological structure of verbs, which is essential for designing a supervised or automated verb analyzer. As a result of this analysis, algorithms, with root and suffix lists and rules for grammatical mapping, are developed to decompose inflected verbs to produce outputs with all relevant morphological information.

The process of data storage is further substantiated with a standard general reference dictionary (GRD) that contains all kinds of verbs collected from the language. This dictionary is modeled after regular dictionaries so that regular lexicographic information of verbs (i.e., *root, etymology, meaning, usage, grammatical form*) is available in the GRD. In addition, possible variations in the spelling of some verbs are reproduced in the GRD so that a verb, due to spelling variation, is not left out or identified as a different one. Moreover, some English verbs that are used in Bengali are also included in this dictionary.

9.9 Decomposing Non-conjugated Verbs

Given a verb, our system considers it as a single lexical string. At this stage, the system does not know if the string is a conjugated verb or a non-conjugated one. Once the string is found, the system tries to find out an exact match of the string from the RL. If an exact match is found, the string is marked as a verb root, and information relating to the root is collected from GRD to be displayed to the users. In case a string is not found in RL, the system considers it as a conjugated verb and initiates the process applicable for conjugated verbs. Since non-conjugated verbs do not go through further processing, these are matched in RL and then analyzed based on information available in GRD. If the system fails at this point, it is assumed that either the verb root is not in RL or there is an error in the spelling of the root (Fig. 9.3).

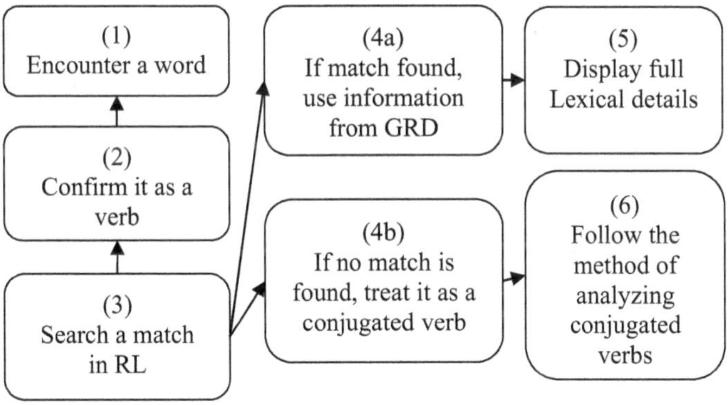

Fig. 9.3 Schema for processing non-conjugated verbs in Bengali

9.10 Decomposing Conjugated Verbs

Most of the conjugated verbs that are used in modern Bengali are in *chalit* form. They follow a more or less uniform pattern of conjugation. Due to this feature, the decomposition of conjugated verbs in Bengali is a systematic and regular process. The following diagram shows how conjugated Bengali verbs are decomposed using information from RL and SL (Fig. 9.4).

The method of decomposing conjugated Bengali verbs includes identification of conjugated verbs, separation of root and suffix parts, finding out valid root part in RL and suffix part in SL, identifying grammatical rules of root–suffix concatenation, and generation of results. For all the works, our system follows the above-mentioned steps in sequential order (Fig. 9.4). After the first step of searching out a conjugated verb is over, it breaks a verb into the root and suffix part by applying information obtained from RL and SL. It collects required morphological and grammatical information from GRD to present a total load of information on the display screen.

We apply a rule-based suffix stripping method to break conjugated Bengali verbs into the root and suffix parts. The input word is picked up from a sample set of verbs extracted from a corpus and stored in the VLD. The input string, after it is detected as a verb, is scanned through to search for a suffix. After detection, the suffix part is stripped from the input word, and the remaining part is treated as a root. The rootsuffix pair undergoes further checking based on word formation rules to find if

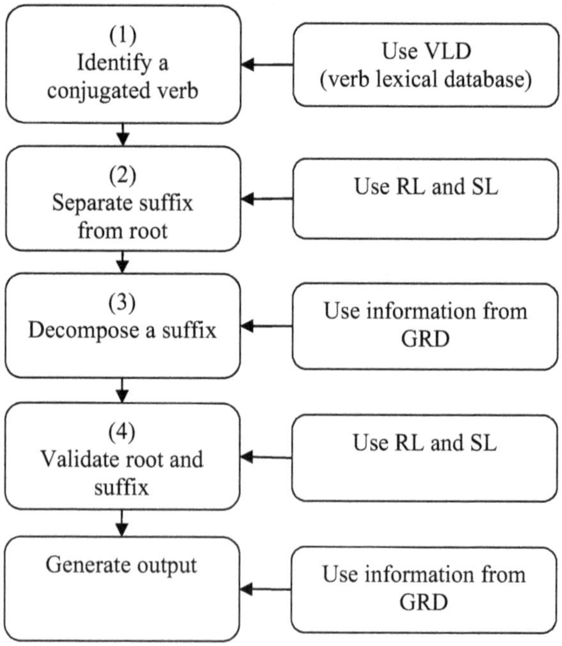

Fig. 9.4 Schema for decomposing conjugated Bengali verbs

a rootsuffix combination is a grammatically valid combination. When this checking result is positive, information stored in GRD is collected and presented for future use.

The most challenging part of the whole process is **suffix stripping**. It results in the separation of root and suffix parts from a conjugated verb form. For this, we apply a trial and error method based on heuristics. The success of this process is based on the robustness of the system. The system proceeds from left-to-right direction following the sequence of characters used to construct an inflected verb. With each character, it forms a subset and verifies the subset to see if it matches with any of the strings stored within RL. It goes on adding one more character (C) at each time ([C_{1+1+1+} … C_{n}]#) until it finds out a suitable match in RL, in the following manner:

First set	[C_1C_2 … C_n]#,
Second set	[$C_1C_2C_3$ … C_n]#,
Third set	[$C_1C_2C_3C_4$ … C_n]#,
Fourth set	[$C_1C_2C_3C_4C_5$ … C_n]#,
Fifth set	[$C_1C_2C_3C_4C_5C_6$ … C_n]#,
Sixth set	[$C_1C_2C_3C_4C_5C_6C_7$ … C_n]#,
Seventh set	[$C_1C_2C_3C_4C_5C_6C_7C_8$ … C_n]#, etc.

The subset formation and matching process follow the following algorithm:

Stage 1	Constitute a sub-string combining the first two characters.
Stage 2	Verify if the sub-string matches with a string stored in RL.
Stage 3	If a match is found, it considers it as root and other parts as a suffix.
Stage 4	If a no match is found, it adds one more character to the string.
Stage 5	It repeats the same process used in Stages 1 and 2.
Stage 6	It matches the suffix part with a suffix stored in SL.
Stage 7	If a match is found, it considers the word as a valid one.
Stage 8	It applies mapping rules for rootsuffix combination.
Stage 9	It matches the output string with the input string for validation.
Stage 10	It collects detailed linguistic information from GRD.
Stage 11	It produces the final result.
Stage 12	It encounters the next word string.

The system identifies a valid match with information collected from RL and SL. Once a root and suffix pair is matched with corresponding strings in RL and SL, it explores rules of the grammatical agreement between root and suffix to confirm validity. After validation, it treats the entire string as a valid verb and retrieves necessary information from GRD for presentation. After completion of the decomposition process, the final output looks like the following (Table 9.6).

Table 9.6 Lexical decomposition of a Bengali conjugated verb

Surface form of a verb	dekheochhilen
Lexical decomposition	dekh-e-o-chh-il-en
Root part	√ dekh
Suffix part	-eochhilen
Aspect	-e-
Particle (emphatic)	-o (emphatic)
Auxiliary	-ch-
Tense	-il- (past)
Person	-en (second/third)
Number	-Ø (Sing./Pl.)
Honorific	-en (second/third)
Part-of-speech	Finite Verb (FV)
Meaning	"you/he /they had also seen"

9.11 Data Creation and Storage

An exhaustive list of root and suffixes is needed for this kind of decomposition and analysis. The list should contain different forms of roots and suffixes as well as metadata related to roots and suffixes. For our purpose, we collect and analyze more than 2000 verbs made with different roots and suffixes. This has been our primary verb lexical database (VLD) which is gradually updated, normalized, and classified based on the patterns of use of suffixes with roots. To avoid data redundancy and to modify existing databases for future use, we divide the suffix database into two separate lists.

(a) **Primary suffix list**: For some linguistic reasons (i.e., *tense* and *person*), verb suffixes take different forms when they conjugate with roots. Keeping this factor in view, suffixes that conjugate with roots of Class 3 (Sect. 9.6.1) are put in the primary suffix list. The metadata that is linked with these suffixes is stored in a header file of this suffix list.

(b) **Secondary suffix list**: All other variant forms that a suffix can assume are stored in the secondary suffix list. Each of them has a pointer to relate with the corresponding suffix in the primary suffix list. When a match is found from the secondary suffix list, details of the suffix are extracted from the primary suffix list through a pointer.

The verb roots are stored in the **root lexicon**. Like suffixes, verb roots also take different forms (i.e., *allomorph*) when they conjugate with different suffixes. However, unlike suffixes, a few roots have varieties. For instance, root $\sqrt{gam}$ has four allomorphic variants: *ýā* (*ýāi* "I go," *ýāy* "she goes"), *gi* (*giyeche* "has gone"), *ge* (*geche* "has gone," *gela* "went"), and ýe (*ýeto* "used to go"). Therefore, it is necessary to keep allomorphs of the root in one list. To reduce searching time, roots are stored in alphabetical order in the list.

9.11.1 Suffix and Root Detection

When a verb is encountered as an input, it is scanned thoroughly to separate its suffix and root part. In Bengali, suffixes are added to roots. That is why the input word is scanned from the first to the last character. Each time a sub-string is matched with entries in the suffix lexicon. The sub-string, which is found as a match, is stored as a suffix. The remaining part is treated as a root and matched in RL. The following four possibilities are the outcomes of this operation,

(a) **Possibility 1**: Valid rootsuffix and valid root are found. In that case, the output is produced after the suffix–root mapping test.
(b) **Possibility 2**: Valid suffix is found but the valid root is not found. In that case, it is assumed that it might be an allomorphic variant of a root. If it is not true, then it may not be a verb.
(c) **Possibility 3**: Valid root is found but the valid suffix is not found. It may be considered as a second person present imperative form of a verb which is always in root form.
(d) **Possibility 4**: Neither the suffix nor the root is valid. In that case, it is considered that the input word is not a verb.

9.11.2 Suffix—Root Mapping

In order to discard some ill-formed (non-grammatical) verbs like **dekchhilām,* **khāchi,* and **karatechhilen*, a set of conjugation rules are implemented. For this, we identify the patterns in root–suffix conjugation and apply them in the process. Some Bengali suffixes undergo morphophonemic changes when they conjugate with the roots of a different class. For instance, *-chhi* remains unchanged when it conjugates with roots ending in a consonant (e.g., *par: parchhi, dhar: dharchhi, bas: baschhi, śun: śunchhi*). It changes into *-chchhi* when it conjugates with a root ending in the vowel *-ā* (*khā: khāchchhi, pā: pāchchhi*) (exception, *gāichhi*), *-i* (*di: dichchhi, ni: nichchhi*), and *-u* (*śu: śuchchhi, dhu: dhuchchhi*) (exception, *ruichhi*).

By using signal flags, we keep track of root classes and corresponding suffix classes. To achieve this, we mark each root class with a symbol (digit or letter) and keep a flag with the suffix list containing the same symbol. When a rootsuffix pair is detected, the symbol denoting a root class is matched with a flag of a suffix class. A match implies that a valid conjugation is possible. If it is not matched, we conclude that the conjugation is an instance of a non-grammatical pair. We also note (especially for *chalit* Bengali verbs) that a verb suffix has "one-to-many" mapping possibilities with multiple verb roots. This leads to the generation of a string of symbols instead of a single symbol for the flag stored in the suffix lexicon. Consequently, a string search operation decides whether a conjugation is possible (Fig. 9.5).

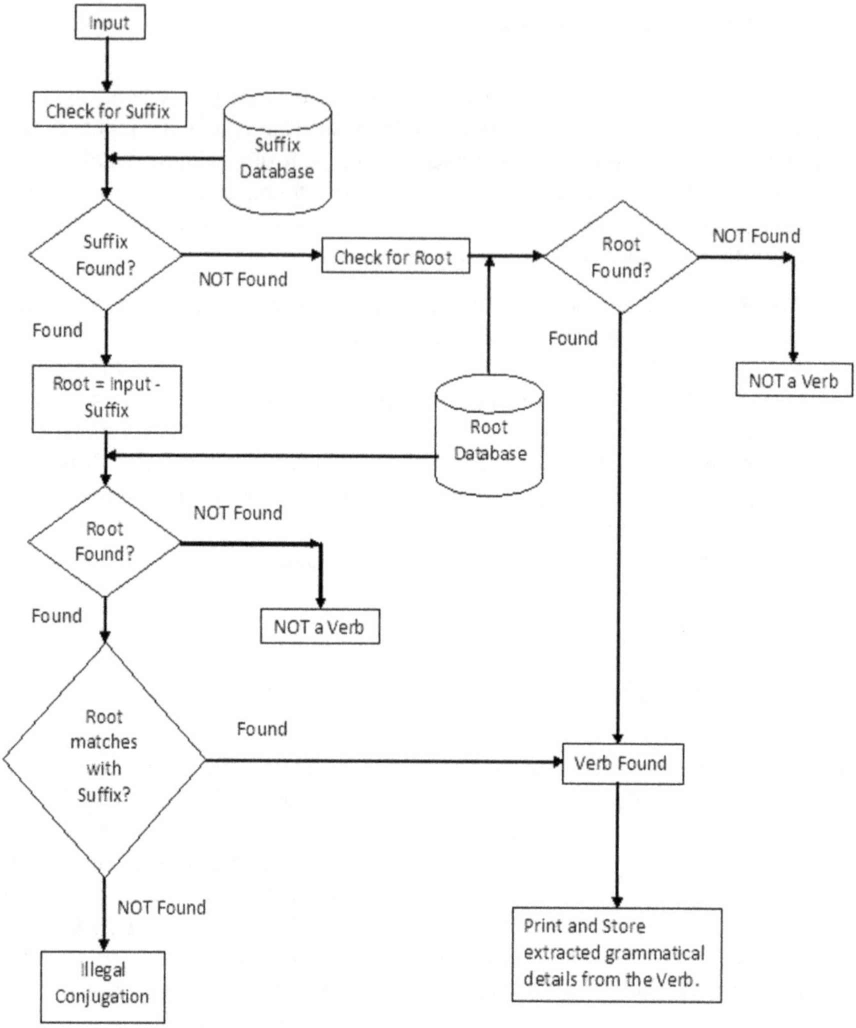

Fig. 9.5 Root–suffix mapping mechanism for Bengali verbs

9.12 Some Special Cases

The gap between what we expected and what we achieved is marred with a few shortfalls that are addressed here. We consider these instances as special cases that put challenges in the application of the process of verb decomposition in Bengali.

(a) There are two different types of negative verbs in Bengali. The first type is a kind of negative verb that is not made through conjugation. Forms like *nai* "I am not," *nao* "you are not," *nay* "he is not," *nei* "has not," and *nahe* "is not" belong to this group. They denote both action and negation together. These are usually indivisible.

(b) The other types of negative verbs (which are found in *chalit* (colloquial) Bengali) are formed by adding a negative particle with a verb. Particles like *nā, ni,* and *ne* are attached to finite verbs to produce the final form (e.g., *balinā* "I do not say," *balini* "I have not said," *baline* "I do not say"). Sometimes these particles are used as detached units also (e.g., *bali nā, bali ni,* and *bali ne*). Such inconsistency is a bottleneck in the process of decomposing Bengali verbs.

(c) Negation markers create more problems in the final identification of a verb. For instance, while *nā* is used for a verb of the simple present, *ni* is used for a verb of present perfect and past, and *ne* is used for a verb of simple present and present perfect. There is no negative marker for verbs of the past perfect tense. Therefore, to detect a verb as a negative verb, we have to identify the final negation mark of a verb. After removing the negation mark, we analyze a verb. This is a tedious error-prone task.

(d) In Bengali, there are two emphatic particles: *-i* and *-o*. These are attached to a conjugated verb. Since they are mutually exclusive, they never occur together in a single conjugated verb form. Usually, an emphatic particle is appended at the end of a conjugated verb (e.g., *balei* [bal-e-i] "says indeed," *baleo* [bal-c-o] "says also"). In simple cases, it is not difficult to identify and remove emphatic particles and analyze a verb in a normal way. Complexities arise when these particles are inserted in the middle of a conjugated verb (e.g., *baleichhiām* [bale-i-chhilām], *baleochhilām* [bale-o-chhilām]). In this case, it is difficult to decompose a conjugated verb because the suffix list fails to account for a different suffix string. A possible solution to this problem is the generation of a suffix list where suffixes are already attached to emphatic particles (e.g., *-eichhiām, -eochhilām*). This is, however, a challenging task for linguistic and technical reasons.

9.13 The Resultant Output

The approach discussed above is codified in Java. Root and suffix databases are stored in XML format. As a consequence, our present system is platform-independent. Although developed on the Linux platform, it produces satisfactory results when it runs on Windows 7 and Apple Mac. The input string is entered in Bengali orthography, and the analysis runs on that string. To input strings, we use a standard keyboard layout for Bengali which comes with the widely used Linux system. Windows and Macintosh also provide the Bengali inscription packages. The following diagram presents the results of a verb decomposition process in Bengali (Fig. 9.6).

1. Input word: balitechhila
   Meaning: She/He/They was/were saying.

Fig. 9.6 Morphological decomposition of an isolated Bengali verb

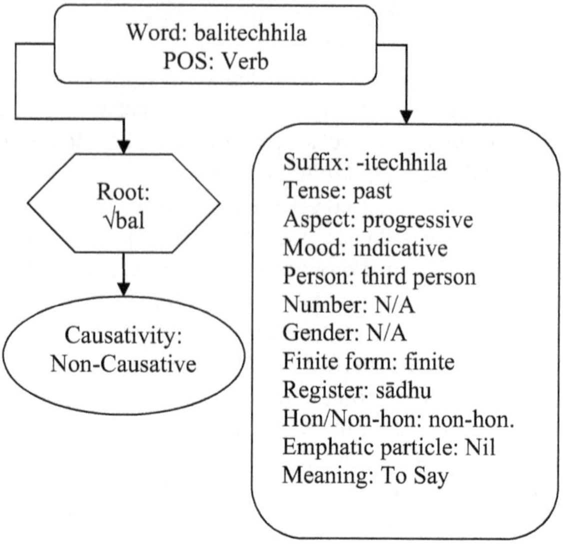

9.14 Performance of the System

After the initial run of the system on a large set of Bengali verbs, the outputs are put to verification and validation. Verification of the outputs shows that the system produces the following four types of results.

(a) Due to proper cutting and matching, some verbs are rightly decomposed.
(b) Due to multiple matches, some verbs are doubly decomposed.
(c) Due to false cutting and matching, some verbs are wrongly decomposed.
(d) Due to the non-availability of data, some verbs are not decomposed.

To make our system accurate and robust, we need to augment data in RL and SL. Also, we need to modify the linguistic rules that are used for generating grammatical mapping algorithms. Verification and validation of grammatical agreement largely depend on the information stored in the respective lexicons (RL and SL in VLD). Also, information about unacceptable subsets of root–suffix pairs is required to be incorporated. This enhances the processing capacity of a system to make it more robust, efficient, and accurate.

Decomposition of Bengali verbs is a daunting challenge—both linguistically and computationally. Building a comprehensive verb decomposer requires connections among lexicon, grammatical rules, and computation. Since the process discussed here is influenced by the strategy of lexicon access, we prefer a method for lexicon generation and storage in the system. The system needs to be improved regularly after considering the finer aspects of the morphemic structure of verbs. Moreover, different kinds of verbs are to be analyzed for augmentation of the existing lexical database and to enhance the grammatical mapping rules for designing a system as well as making it robust.

Given the complexity of Bengali verbs, it is a tough task to make an accurate decision always about their morphemic structure. Accuracy varies based on the load of information included in RL and SL. We have understood that it is easy to identify a word as a verb than to specify its embedded information (e.g., *aspect, tense, person, modality, honorification,* etc.). Therefore, occasional errors in decomposition of inflected Bengali verbs should not be taken as a major deficiency of a system. Errors will occur with certain types of ambiguous verb forms also. An interactive interface designed for checking decomposition results can make a system faster and reliable in processing as well as in generation of accurate outputs.

9.15 Conclusion

In this chapter, we present a method of decomposing Bengali verbs. While we try to reach this goal, we keep many options open for possible modifications of the present system. To achieve our goal, we develop two dictionaries (a) verb lexical database (VLD) and (b) general reference dictionary (GRD). Also, we develop two lexical lists (a) root lexicon (RL) and (b) suffix lexicon (SL). We use these resources in verb decomposition and utilize them as reference texts in other domains of descriptive, applied, and computational linguistics. Lexical lists are normalized to minimize the possibility of reference and duplication errors. The dictionaries and lexical databases are also utilized for decomposing verbs used in Bengali dialects.

It is a challenge to formulate and implement a set of rules that can clearly describe the patterns of Bengali for verb conjugation. It is equally a tricky game to design a set of mappings rules that determine possible combinations between a root and a suffix. In the present case, we use these rules to find a match between a root and a suffix. On the other hand, these rules can reversely be applied in the generation of Bengali verbs. We have tried to store data and information extracted from a verb in such a way that it can be used for many other works of text processing like part-of-speech annotation, lexical class determination, lemmatization, and word form generation. This approach is tested on nearly 5000 verbs with moderately good results. The ultimate goal is to make this system useful for decomposing all verbs available in Bengali in both context-free and contextualized situations. This is not a distant dream when the system is updated with new sets of data and information to decompose Bengali verbs in both situations.

References

Abu Zaher, M. F., & Tyers, F. M. (2009). Development of a morphological analyzer for Bengali. In *Proceedings of the 1st International Workshop on Open-Source Rule-Based Machine Translation* (pp. 43–50). Alacant, Spain, November 2009.

Banerjee, S., Das, D., & Bandyopadhyay, S. (2010). Classification of verbs: Towards developing a bengali verb subcategorization Lexicon. In *Proceedings of 5th Global WordNet Conference (GWC-2010)* (pp. 30–38). Mumbai: IIT-Bombay.

Bapat, M., Gune, H., & Bhattacharyya, P. (2010). A paradigm-based finite state morphological analyzer for Marathi. In *Proceedings of the 1st Workshop on South and Southeast Asian Natural Language Processing (WSSANLP), 23rd International Conference on Computational Linguistics (COLING)* (pp. 26–34). Beijing, August 2010.

Basu, R. (1962). *Chalantika: Adhunik Bengali Bhasar Abhidhan (Chalantika: A dictionary of modern Bengali language).* Kolkata: M.C. Sarkar.

Bharati, A., Chaitanya, V., & Sangal, R. (1995). *Natural language processing: A Paninian perspective.* New Delhi: Prentice-Hall of India.

Bhattacharya, S., Choudhury, M., Sarkar, S., & Basu, A. (2005). Inflectional morphology synthesis for Bengali noun, pronoun, and verb systems. In *Proceedings of the Conference on Computer Processing of Bengali (NCCPB 05)* (pp. 34–43). Dhaka, Bangladesh.

Chattopadhyay, S. K. (1939). *Bhasa Prakash Bangala Vyakaran (A grammar of the Bengali language).* University of Calcutta.

Chomsky, A. N. (1972). *Studies in generative grammar*. Mouton.

Dabre, R., Ambedkar, A., & Bhattacharyya, P. (2012). *Morphology Analyser for Affix Stacking Languages: A Case Study in Marathi, COLING 2012*, Mumbai, India, December 10–14, 2012 (poster paper)

Das, A., & Bandyopadhyay. S. (2010). Morphological stemming cluster identification for Bengali. In *Knowledge sharing Event-1: Task 3: Morphological analyzers and generators,* January 24–25, 2010, Mysore.

Dasgupta, S., & Khan, M. (2004). Morphological parsing of Bengali words using PC-KIMMO. In *Proceedings of the 7th International Conference on Computer and Information Technology (ICCIT2004)* (pp. 121-128). Dhaka, Bangladesh.

Dash, N. S. (2015). *A descriptive study of Bengali words.* Cambridge: Cambridge University Press.

Dash, N. S., Chaudhuri, B. B., & Kundu, P. K. (1997). Computer parsing of Bengali verbs. *Linguistics Today., 1*(1), 64–86.

Islam, M. Z., & Khan, M. (2006). Kimmo: A multilingual computational morphology framework for PC-KIMMO. In *Proceedings of the 9th International Conference on Computer and Information Technology, ICCIT 2006*, Dhaka, Bangladesh.

Minnen, G., Carroll, J., & Pearce, D. (2001). Applied morphological processing of English. *Natural Language Engineering, 7*, 207–223.

Ray Vidyanidhi, J. C. (1912). *Bengali Bhasha*: Pratham Khanda: Byakaran (Bengali language: 1st part: Grammar).

Sarkar, P., & Basu. G. (1994). *Bhasa Jijnasa (Language Inquiries).* Kolkata: Vidyasagar Pustak Mandir.

Sarkar, S., & Bandyopadhyay, S. (2008). Design of a rule-based stemmer for natural language text in Bengali. In *Proceedings of the IJCNLP-08: Workshop on NLP for Less Privileged Languages* (pp. 65–72). Hyderabad, India: Asian Federation of Natural Language Processing, January 2008.

Selkirk, E. O. (1983). *The syntax of words.* MIT Press.

Sen, S. (1993). *Bhasar Itivrittva (The history of language).* Ananda Publishers.

Sengupta, G. (1997). Three models of morphological processing. *South Asian Language Review., 7*(1), 1–26.

Sengupta, G. (1999). GS_Morph: A grapheme oriented structuralist morphological processor. In Presented at the *2nd International Conference on the South Asian Linguistics* (ICOSAL-II). Patiala, India: Punjabi University, January 9–11, 1999.

Sengupta, P., & Chaudhuri, B. B. (1996). Morphological processing of Indian languages for lexical interaction with the application to spelling error correction. *Sadhana, 21*(3), 363–380.

Web Links

http://wiki.apertium.org/wiki/Morphological_analysis
http://www.au-kbc.org/research_areas/nlp/projects/morph.html
http://www.cfilt.iitb.ac.in/~ankitb/ma/
https://blog.bitext.com/morphological-analyzer
https://langrid.org/playground/morphological-analyzer.html
https://ltrc.iiit.ac.in/showfile.php?filename=onlineServices/morph/morph_analyser.html
https://studfile.net/preview/2227003/
https://tdil-dc.in/index.php?option=com_vertical&parentid=60&lang=en
https://www.aclweb.org/anthology/L16-1409/
https://www.cs.bham.ac.uk/~pjh/sem1a5/pt2/pt2_intro_morphology.html
https://www.quora.com/In-simple-terms-what-is-a-morphological-analyzer-How-are-they-used-in-machine-translation
https://www.slideshare.net/akshatapandey/morphological-analysis-47051109

Chapter 10
Syntactic Annotation

Abstract We discuss in this chapter some of the basic challenges that are involved in analyzing sentences and designing a scheme for syntactic annotation. Here we define the basic concept of syntactic annotation with comments on its nature, method, and function in a language. Next, we focus on some goals and purposes behind developing a syntactic annotation tool for a language. There are some guidelines and instructions for developing a syntactic annotation tool for some advanced languages. We do not try to address these issues and strategies again in this chapter. Rather, we focus on the theoretical and practical importance of syntactic annotation in the process of extracting syntactic information from a sentence. During syntactic annotation, we supply a sentence of a natural language to a machine as an input and instruct the machine to identify phrases and mark their grammatical-cum-syntactic roles in the sentence. It implies that a machine has to learn how phrases are formed and organized so that it understands how a sentence is to be analyzed and interpreted from the perspective of syntactic function and semantic information of words and phrases. It also needs to learn how syntactic-cum-semantic roles of various syntactic units are functionally controlled based on their lexical associations and morphological functions in retrieving information embedded within a sentence. We address all these issues in this chapter and present some ideas and processes that are normally used in syntactic annotation. In course of formulating the basic ideas, we refer to the rules of context-free grammars and show how the outputs generated from syntactically annotated corpus can be used in a better description of a grammar of a language, teaching grammatical forms of a language with better information and analysis, understanding how human brain applies syntactic rules to form sentences, how syntactic rules can be designed to train a computer, and how applications relating to language can be developed with proper syntactic information of a language.

Keywords Syntax · Grammar · Skeleton parsing · Context-free grammar · Phrase structure grammar · POS annotation · Parser · Treebank

N. S. Dash, *Language Corpora Annotation and Processing*,
https://doi.org/10.1007/978-981-16-2960-0_10

10.1 Introduction

The term *syntactic annotation* is theoretically and practically related to the analysis of sentences used in a natural language according to the grammar of a language (Barnbrook, 1998: 170). Technically, it is referred to as **parsing**. It involves the practice of assigning phrasal marks to those syntactic structures that are used to form a sentence (McEnery & Wilson, 1996: 178). Normally, we carry out syntactic annotation after we identify and classify possible morphosyntactic categories of a language. These classified sets are accepted as syntactic tagsets which are later used in the process of annotation of sentences. In a simple sense, syntactic annotation (or parsing) is a process by which we identify phrases used in a sentence, classify them, mark out their types, assign a specific phrasal identity to them, see how they are syntactically linked, and explore how they generate different layers of information in a sentence (Greene & Rubin, 1971).

The methods and processes that are applied for syntactic annotation normally follow different grammar formalisms such as *phrase structure grammar* (Borsley, 1991; Sag & Wasow, 1999; van Valin, 2001), *context-free grammar* (Hopcroft and Ullman 1979, Sipser, 1997), *dependency grammar* (Mel'čuk 1987, Liu, 2009, Osborne, 2019), *extended affix grammar* (Koster 1991, Watt & Thomas, 1991), *tree adjoining grammar* (Joshi, 1985, Jurafsky and Martin 2000), and *lexical functional grammar* (Bresnan, 2001; Bresnan et al., 2015; Dalrymple, 2001). In most cases, we use the information and schematic frames proposed in these grammars to explain the hierarchical relationships of the morphosyntactic categories to understand their non-explicit syntactic relationships. It is, however, noted that a good syntactic annotation process may involve contextualized as well as decontextualized analysis of sentences using information collected from word-level processing (Souter and Atwell 1993).

Syntactic annotation is one of the most common and frequent yet highly complex forms of text annotation. It is used on a written corpus after the words of a corpus are passed through the stages of grammatical annotation. Before syntactic annotation, one has to do some standard syntactic analyses of sentences in texts according to the grammar of a particular language to identify phrases that are used as building blocks to construct sentences (Leech and Eyes 1993). This is needed because the most important goal behind syntactic annotation is to understand and explicate how constituents are arranged in particular syntactic orders to form valid sentences and what kinds of relational interface and dependency roles the constituents play in the realization of meanings of sentences (Briscoe & Carroll, 1993).

In the past, within the traditional frame of sentence analysis and interpretation, we used the syntactic analysis of sentences manually with rules and information available in grammar books. When we plan to do it automatically by a computer system, we realize the importance of grammatical rules that we form with information collected from various grammars and grammar formalisms. In both cases, existing rules of grammar of a language are simply indispensable. Whether we analyze a sentence manually, automatically, or by combining both the techniques, the outcome is an annotated version of sentences in which individual phrases are analyzed with a set of linguistic information to exhibit their syntactic properties and functions (Aarts et al., 2000).

In this chapter, we discuss some of the primary issues of syntactic annotation. In Sect. 10.2, we address ambiguities embedded in syntactic annotation; in Sect. 10.3, we refer to the transitional periods the syntactic annotation has passed through before it acquires the present sense; in Sect. 10.4, we mention the primary goals of syntactic annotation; in Sect. 10.5, we focus on challenges involved in syntactic annotation; in Sect. 10.6, we define the importance of syntactic annotation in language processing; in Sect. 10.7, we describe different methods of syntactic annotation; in Sect. 10.8, we focus on Treebank as an outcome of syntactic annotation; in Sect. 10.9, we highlight applications of syntactic annotation in various areas of applied linguistics and language processing; and in Sect. 10.10, we refer to the present state of syntactic annotation in some less-resourced languages.

10.2 Ambiguity of the Term

The term *syntactic annotation* is ambiguous. It refers to three significantly different ideas based on the domains of its application in traditional grammar, natural language processing, and cognitive linguistics. In traditional grammar, it refers to the act of identifying the subject(s) and predicates, phrases and clauses, main clauses, and subordinate clauses, and how these are interlinked to frame a sentence. It also involves the act of understanding single or multiple readings of a sentence that are embedded within a single surface construction (e.g., *Time flies like an arrow*).

(a) Reading 1: "Time" is a Noun Phrase (NP); "flies like an arrow" is a Verb Phrase (VP).
(b) Reading 2: "Time flies" is a Noun Phrase (NP); "like an arrow" is a Verb Phrase (VP).
(c) Reading 3: There is no Noun Phrase (NP); "Time flies like an arrow" is a Verb Phrase (VP).

In natural language processing and computational linguistics, it refers to the process of formal analysis of sentences by a computer automatically with the help of some predefined syntacticrules that are modeled as machine-readable algorithms. These algorithms are not only capable of interpreting the syntactic structures and recognizing constituent phrases, but also capable of defining the nature of syntactic dependencies of the constituents, resulting in the generation of parsed trees (known as Treebanks) (Kübler et al., 2008). The parsed trees exhibit syntactic relations of phrases, containing syntactic and semantic information, to each other in a hierarchical order (Fig. 10.1).

In cognitive linguistics, psycholinguistics, and neurolinguistics, syntactic annotation refers to the act of comprehension of a language text with all its syntactic properties and semantic nuances with an additional focus on extralinguistic information embedded in a sentence. In all three domains, *syntactic annotation* is used in

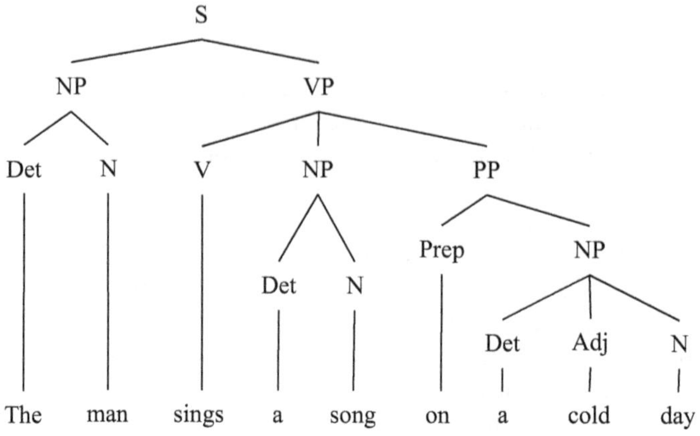

Fig. 10.1 Diagrammatic representational of syntactic annotation

an encoded sense to understand how language users analyze sentences in terms of grammatical constituents used in sentence formation, identify part-of-speech roles of words used in phrases, and reflect on syntactic relations of phrases by which they comprehend meaning(s) of a sentence.

All the different senses indicate one thing—that construction of a sentence in a natural language is a highly complex linguistic-cum-cognitive process which involves several rules, methods, strategies, constituents, and their relations that act as a thread to bind them into a coherent construction. Understanding a sentence is, therefore, not a trivial task. It is a challenge for human beings as well as for a computer; however, robust it maybe. On a positive side, syntactic annotation is a useful interpretation process that applies efficient strategies to understand how information and relation are generated, fabricated, embedded, processed, and maintained in meaningful sentence construction and comprehension.

The differences between grammatical annotation and syntactic annotation can be understood from their primary goals, application of processes, applicational scopes, and functional significance in analysis of texts (Leech, 1993). In case of grammatical annotation, which is also known as part-of-speech annotation and part-of-speech tagging, the tag list, which is used to assign grammatical marks to words, is designed to provide accurate part-of-speech information for each word used in a text. On the other hand, in case of syntactic annotation, the tag list is designed to identify and mark each phrase and extract exact grammatical information from phrases for identifying their syntactic roles in a sentence (Barnbrook, 1998: 127). Since syntactic annotation works at a higher level than grammatical annotation, it usually depends on the information available from the grammatical annotation. It is necessary to determine the grammatical roles of words before syntactic roles of phrases are identified and marked.

10.3 Transition of the Concept of *Syntactic Annotation*

Syntactic annotation has a history of its origin and changes over the centuries. Its synchronic identity is largely affected due to its diachronic transformation. In traditional grammar, the term is used to refer to the concept of breaking down a sentence into possible minimum elements in the form of words, and identification of part-of-speech of words according to their form, function, and relation with other words in building a sentence and expressing meanings. Based on this assumption, for centuries, we have treated syntactic annotation as an essential part of traditional grammar education. We have taught learners to understand how words are used in sentences; how we analyze morphological structures of words; how we understand lexico-grammatical roles of words; how we assign different parts-of-speech to words; how we specify different phrase categories and their properties; how we list complex syntactic relations of phrases with other constituents in a sentence, and how we can derive meanings of sentences through analysis of phrases and words.

There are some debates between the western and Indian grammarians with regard to looking at words in a sentence. Western grammarians are interested to look at words both at their context-free (i.e., *morphological identity*) and context-bound situations (i.e., *syntactic identity*). The Indian grammarians, on the other hand, are not interested to give much importance to words that are noted in a context-free situation. They are more interested to pay attention to words only when the words are used in a sentence. In traditional Indian grammar, it is argued that the identity and role of a word are best realized only when it is judged in the context of its use in a sentence. In Indian syntactic analysis, an investigator is interested to know the identity and role of a *pada* (i.e., *constituent*), not of a *śabda* (i.e., *word*).

A *śabda* (i.e., a word), in principle, can have multiple lexical-cum-semantic identities in the conceptual framework of the members of a language community. The members may like to visualize a word in different forms, representations, settings, meanings and purposes. But a syntactician—who is engaged in understanding the role of the constituents used in a sentence—is more focused on a predefined logical inquiry. He is more particular to know how these *padas* (i.e., *constituents*) behave within a sentence; how they build up latent syntactic relation with others; and how their individual identities contribute collectively in the generation and interpretation of meanings of a sentence. The process, which helps a grammarian to carry out all these tasks successfully and accurately, is *syntactic annotation*—a rational method suitable for analysis of sentences (Verma & Krishnaswamy, 1989: 330).

Syntactic annotation starts with the syntactic analysis of a sentence. At the very first stage, it involves the identification of the subject and predicate(s) of a sentence. In subsequent stages, it marks various objects used for a verb as well as specifies constituents that concord with other constituents in building unique grammatical relations. The entire process of analysis changes if an existing set of constituents are replaced by another set of constituents in the same syntactic frames. Therefore, a crucial part of understanding syntactic annotation is to identify the most important components of a sentence (i.e., *subject, predicate, main clause, subordinate clause,*

Table 10.1 Syntactic annotation of a sentence in traditional grammar

Sentence	The man killed the snake that entered the room
Subject	The man
Object	The snake
Predicate	Killed the snake that entered the room
Main clause	The man killed the snake
Subordinate clause	That entered the room
Matrix/Main verb	Killed
Lexical Verbs	Killed, entered

matrix verb, embedded clauses, etc.), which are arranged in specific syntactic orders in a sentence with single/several underlying meanings. For instance, we may refer to the following sets of data to understand how we are guided to look at a sentence in a traditional method of syntactic analysis (Table 10.1).

There are clear clues to attest to the fact that the traditional approach to the analysis of sentences (i.e., *syntactic annotation*) in a natural language is largely controlled by semantic information. Although informative and insightful, this strategy is less successful and less effective in modern contexts when the emphasis is given on the structural properties of sentences without much importance on the semantic information embedded in a sentence (Jurafsky and Martin 2000). In modern linguistics, *syntactic annotation* is looked at from a different angle and perspective to shade new insights into this linguistic phenomenon. It draws heavily from the **structure** of a sentence; not from its **content**. Within a technology fabricated framework, *syntactic annotation* is used in a generic sense to refer to a program-based computer-aided system of analysis of sentences of a text to retrieve machine-readable ingredients based on which a computer program can analyze and interpret other sentences of a language. Within this broader scheme, *syntactic annotation* is understood as a grammar-controlled and computer-operated process of sentence decomposition by which the complex structure of a sentence is broken into several formative constituent parts. These parts are further analyzed and interpreted to understand how these parts combine and how they generate valid and meaningful sentences. One of the most frequently used definitions of *syntactic annotation*, in a modern sense, is the following:

> "In parsing, the complex structures under consideration are natural language sentences and constituent parts are the building blocks in syntactic analysis, from clauses, and phrases down to words and morphemes." (Bunt et al., 2004: 1).

From the definition given above, we get an idea that in modern understanding, attention is not only on phrases but also on words and morphemes based on the form of a language. It is necessary to go to lexical, and even, to morphological level because much of syntactic information is encoded at these levels. Without proper consideration of such information, syntactic analysis of a sentence may not be complete and accurate. It is often noted that in the case of ambiguous sentences, where a multiplicity of meaning is hidden in the grammatical role of words, we require adequate information from the morphological level for multiple interpretations of a sentence. For instance, in a sentence like *Time flies like an arrow*, multiple readings are possible only when we consider morphological and grammatical ambiguities of words as the following sentences show.

10.1 Time$_{\backslash NN\backslash}$ flies$_{\backslash FV\backslash}$ like$_{\backslash ADV\backslash}$ an$_{\backslash DET\backslash}$ arrow$_{\backslash NN\backslash}$.
10.2 [Time$_{\backslash NN\backslash}$ flies$_{\backslash NN\backslash}$]$_{\backslash NN\backslash}$ like$_{\backslash FV\backslash}$ an$_{\backslash DET\backslash}$ arrow$_{\backslash NN\backslash}$.
10.3 ~~(You)~~$_{\backslash PN\backslash}$ time$_{\backslash FV\backslash}$ flies$_{\backslash NN\backslash}$ like$_{\backslash ADV\backslash}$ an$_{\backslash DET\backslash}$ arrow$_{\backslash NN\backslash}$.

In most of the cases, in both modern linguistics and language computation, the algorithms for syntactic annotation are designed after following various models of context-free grammars, such as *phrase structure grammar* (Chomsky, 1956, Pullum and Gazdar 1982, Shieber, 1985), *tree adjoining grammar* (Joshi et al. 1972a, 1972b), *lexical functional grammar* (Bresnan, 2001, Falk, 2001, Kroeger 2004), *relational grammar,* (Perlmutter, 1980, 1983) and others. These grammars try to provide a formal or structural representation of syntactic frames of a natural language. The basic advantages of these strategies are that they give us a better insight into the complex structure of sentences. They also provide us with a fair chance to analyze sentences in an organized manner with clear ideas about the structure, position, and role of phrases constituting sentences, as the following table (Table 10.2) shows.

The rules underlying the internal structure of phrases are primary frames based on which symbolic representation of sentences are constructed in the model of a tree diagram where branches originated from it replicate the phrases used in a sentence. Once this is understood based on a grammar of a language, syntactic annotation becomes an act of organized decomposition of sentences both by a human being and a machine (Fig. 10.2).

10.4 The boy played in the field.
10.5 [The boy]$_{\mathbf{NP}}$ [[played]$_{\mathbf{V}}$ [[in]$_{PP}$[the field]$_{\mathbf{NP}}$]$_{PP}$]$_{\mathbf{VP}}$.

Table 10.2 Rules used in context-free phrase structure grammar

(1)	S	→	NP + VP
(2)	NP	→	(Det) + (Adj) + N
(3)	VP	→	(Aux) + V + (NP) + (PP) + (NP)
(4)	PP	→	Prep NP
(5)	Det	→	a, an, the, that, some …
(6)	Adj	→	big, small, tall, high, good …
(7)	N	→	man, student, cow, time ….
(8)	Aux	→	will, can, may, shall …
(9)	Verb	→	eat, run, fall, call, give ….
(10)	Prep	→	in, at, by, for, with …

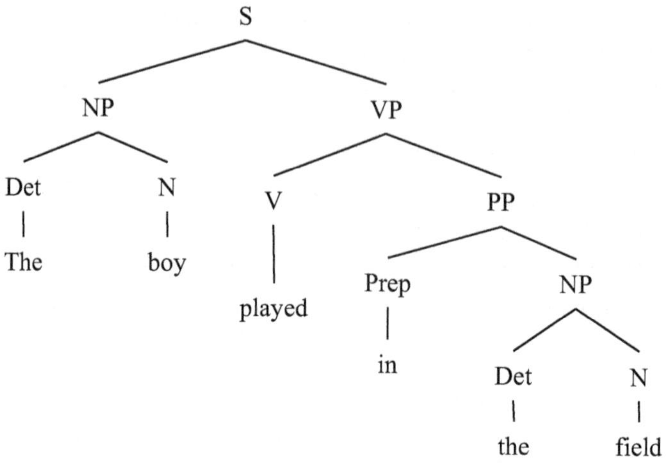

Fig. 10.2 Tree diagram of a simple declarative sentence

It is, however, to be noted that in syntactic annotation, knowledge accumulated from grammar formalisms is not much useful. Most of the grammars do not care to address all primary and advanced requirements for interpreting all kinds of sentences that occur in a text. Moreover, context-free grammar formalisms usually decline to preserve the occurrence of a form over an arbitrarily long lexical input. For instance, it is quite common in a natural language that a proper noun is declared much before it is further referenced in the subsequent parts of a text. In such a situation, context-free grammar may fail to refer to the noun, because it is mentioned long ago in the earlier part of a sentence.

On the contrary, more powerful grammar formalisms, which can handle this kind of constraint in a sentence, are not able to parse a sentence properly. More powerful grammar formalisms are more complex in nature and they usually put up many highly contextualized constraints that ask for additional contextual information from extralinguistic domains for generating accurate syntactic annotation. To avoid such complexities, it is rational to adopt a simple and common strategy of **simplified annotation** with a suitable model of context-free grammar. It can accommodate a superset of desired language constructions along with some invalid constructions (Aldebazal et al., 2009). While the valid constructions are approved with the application of accepted rules of the grammar of a language, invalid constructions are usually preserved for further analysis to understand how existing rules fail to accommodate these constructions and what kinds of modifications are needed to overcome the pitfalls in a syntactic annotation system. The second part is a tough challenge, which is taken up at later stages when all unwanted constructions are filtered out from outputs through contextualized analysis (Karlsson et al. 1995).

10.4 Goals of Syntactic Annotation

From a technical perspective, syntactic annotation is a practice through which we assign specific syntactic tags to varied syntactic structures that are used in a sentence in a piece of text. From a linguistic perspective, on the other hand, we view syntactic annotation as a process by which we understand how a sentence is formed, how phrases are used in a sentence, and how information embedded within a phrase is percolated into a sentence. Since this is a complex cognitive process, there is no simple way to understand this until we apply a cognition-based formal mechanism. This mechanism helps us, to a certain extent, to go into the underlying form and content of a sentence based on which it is possible to get ideas about the structure represented at the surface level of a sentence. The primary goals of syntactic annotation are, therefore, to perform all these tasks that are assigned to a human or an automated annotator (Fig. 10.3).

A syntactic annotation program performs all these tasks after it identifies morphosyntactic categories of constituents used in the formation of a sentence. And identification of these categories involves a tedious process of syntactic analysis—in both context-bound and context-free situations—after taking into consideration the lexicosemantic information acquired from analysis of words at the lexical level (Bunt & Tomita, 1996: 49). This implies that a successful process of syntactic annotation assimilates a large amount of information that is generated from lexicomorphic analysis of constituents.

Also, a successful syntactic annotation scheme applies different methods of grammar analysis to transfer all the morphosyntactic categories of words to the level of syntactic relationship. At this level, words are empowered to express their inherent grammatical relations with each other in a sentence based on the meaning that controls syntactic roles performed by the constituents. Since this is a process of mixing information at multiple layers of operation, a syntactic annotation system attests to the fact that insufficient information and improper data may lead to the generation of wrong results. Therefore, an algorithm, which is designed for syntactic annotation, needs to be enriched with adequate syntactic rules and patterns which are

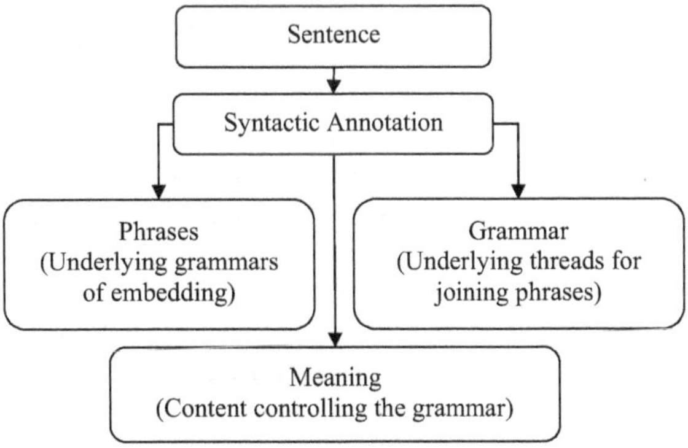

Fig. 10.3 Goal of syntactic annotation while analyzing a sentence

frequently used in a language. Whatever is the approach, technique, model, strategy, method, or scheme, the goals of syntactic annotation, in essence, are the followings:

[1] Identification of lexical units used in the construction of a sentence.
[2] Assignment of appropriate syntactic descriptions to each lexical unit.
[3] Chunking multiword units (e.g., *phrases*) and define their syntactic roles.
[4] Identification of word-group boundaries to be marked as phrases.
[5] Allocation of word groups to specific phrase components.
[6] Identification of specific syntactic roles of phrases.
[7] The naming of phrases based on their function in sentences.
[8] Identification of main syntactic constituents in a sentence.
[9] Identification of how constituents is syntactically linked.
[10] Identification of how constituents contributes to form a sentence.

The majority of syntactic annotation algorithms that are developed using rules of linguistic and grammatical formalisms (e.g., *Government and Binding Rules, Phrase Structure Rules,* and *Constituent Dependency Rules*) try to capture and express inherent syntactic roles and relations of constituents used to construct a sentence. This has been a common method in developing models for syntactic annotation. It is believed that the deployment of a syntactic annotation model based on specific grammar formalism is convenient and useful in encoding syntactic relations of constituents as well as achieving better results in analysis, interpretation, and comprehension of sentences (Brekke, 1991). However, the reality is that the application of grammatical formalisms has not produced any praiseworthy success which can be loudly canvassed and imitated. It eventually leads us to design methods based exclusively on human-crafted syntactic rules which are more computer-compatible and object-oriented. Since these rules are mostly man-made, they seek to encode inherent human understanding of a language to construct a creditable syntactic annotation mechanism for it. Also, information gathered from the analysis of a large set of examples produced in corpora by language users is used as a part of deep learning to train a computer so that it is able to analyze sentences with fewer ambiguities and errors (Johansson & Stenström, 1991).

10.5 Challenges Involved in Syntactic Annotation

Most of the challenges involved in syntactic annotation are linked with models and approaches applied. We try to bring different computational approaches together controlled by theoretical syntax, either in the form of a particular theory or as a general framework that draws on theoretical and descriptive analysis of sentences. We call it deep linguistic processing (DLP) as it tries to model the complexities of natural languages in rich linguistic representations. The DLP is concerned with the development of usable grammar formalisms that can annotate sentences successfully. However, the linguistic complexities and precisions in grammars, which we normally find in a natural language, require a more complex mechanism to interpret knowledge and information embedded in a sentence. The mechanism also requires necessary support to develop and maintain algorithms that are computationally robust and less expensive.

There is a good scope for designing a new syntactic annotation strategy with recent developments in computer hardware technology, advancements in syntactic annotation algorithms, and improvement in statistical learning models. These issues are incorporated in DLP as it tries to address the requirements of an ever-growing range of languages, domains, and applications. It, however, puts up several new challenges in the development of workable syntactic annotation algorithms. It requires a new method that includes a considerable amount of linguistic data and algorithms shared by existing syntactic annotation mechanisms. This new approach generates novel challenges in syntactic annotation and processing that are summarized below.

[1] **Grammar Engineering:** Workable framework for grammar evaluation; developing models for grammar engineering; cross-linguistic grammar comparison and generalization; and semantic representation of syntactic and lexical information.

[2] **Treebank Generation:** Frameworks for Treebanks; normalization and grammar extraction from Treebanks; interfaces between grammars and Treebanks; comparison among cross-lingual Treebanks.

[3] **System Development:** Computer-controlled linguistic works; grammar profiling; system architecture; system integration; text preprocessing; robustness enhancement.

[4] **Parser Development:** Algorithms for identification and interpretation of sentences; measurement of repeatability of grammatical rules; estimation of the correctness of annotated outputs.

[5] **Machine Learning:** Adaptation of effective syntactic annotation models in DLP; selection of annotated sentences based on ranks for application; deep lexical acquisition (DLA) from annotated sentences; induction of novel grammatical features and properties.

[6] **Applications:** Utilization of knowledge and information generated from the syntactic annotation in information extraction, deep learning, question answering, sentiment analysis, machine translation, dialogic-based query responses, and computer-assisted language learning.

10.6 What is a Syntactic Annotator (Parser)?

A syntactic annotator (or *parser*) is a machine-operated system or tool which is developed based on a set of predefined machine-readable syntactic rules of a language. It works like software that takes natural language sentences as input, analyzes sentences in a supervised or semi-supervised manner, and generates structures of sentences in the form of parsed trees, abstract syntactic trees, or hierarchical structures to present conceptually feasible structural representation of input sentences with attention on possible correct syntactic representation of the constituents. Since this is a complicated and lengthy process to be executed with a set of predefined algorithms, a syntactic annotator depends on preceding and following operations which are linked with an annotator for understanding the internal structure of sentences. Some of the operations include *lexical analysis, morphological processing, part-of-speech annotation, chunking, lexical collocation, local word grouping,* and *tokenization*. These operations are normally carried out in sequential order. They may be combined together in a single operational interface with a few sub-steps that operate in a synchronized fashion (Karlsson 1994).

In essence, a syntactic annotator is a primarily preprogrammed tool that works either automatically or semi-automatically on sentences. It is controlled by an "annotator generator" in both supervised and non-supervised options. The input to an annotator is provided in the form of a natural language sentence reframed into computer language since a computer is not able to comprehend a natural language sentence produced in known orthography. If an annotator is robust enough after rigorous training, sentences may be given in a natural language as less structured texts. The expectation is that the system will preprocess texts before texts are put to syntactic annotation. In most cases, the result is just an extraction of a text or components from it, rather than the formation of annotated trees of input sentences.

A syntactic annotator works in different manners and varied sequences. Given below is a list of interlinked tasks that a syntactic annotator carries out once a piece of text is supplied to an annotator as input. Each task is summarized in the following subsections.

[1] Detection of the terminal point of a sentence.
[2] Tokenization of words in a sentence.
[3] Identification of part-of-speech of words.
[4] Chunking larger lexical blocks (syntactic units).
[5] Finding out matrix verbs in a sentence.
[6] Identification of non-matrix clauses.
[7] Identification of phrases used in a sentence.

10.6.1 Detection of End of a Sentence

When a piece of text is given to a syntactic annotator in the form of a string variable input, the annotator divides the text into several valid sentences. It does this by using an algorithm which is developed with the information of a sentence terminator (i.e., *full stop, interrogative sign*, and *exclamatory sign*). If a text is written, for instance, in the Roman script, the annotator can identify the endpoint of a sentence based on the three indicators mentioned above. In case of a text produced in a non-Roman script, the system is trained to identify those sentence terminal markers which are used in that particular language. For Bengali, a typical terminal marker for a declarative sentence is *pūrṇachhed*. The system, for a Bengali text, therefore, has to learn that the terminal marker of a declarative sentence is a *pūrṇachhed* (not a *full stop*).

What we understand from this is that there are a good number of punctuation marks that work as sentence terminal markers based on practice and the norm of a language. Referring to the punctuation markers a syntactic annotator identifies the terminal point of a sentence. However, this method is not useful in those cases where the punctuation markers are used in the middle of a sentence. In that context, a syntactic annotator has to understand that a punctuation mark can appear at the middle of a sentence; and in that situation, the punctuation mark is not used as a sentence terminal marker but for some specific stylistic purposes.

10.6.2 Tokenization of Words in Sentences

Once sentences are separated and marked with a unique sentence identity code (SIC), a syntactic annotator invokes text processing techniques on a sentence to split it into "tokens" such as words, word groups, punctuations, and other units (Webster & Kit, 1992). The annotator must record the number of tokens and lexical identity of each token for further processing (Huang et al., 2007). The following scheme shows how tokenization works on a piece of text before the text is put to syntactic annotation (Table 10.3).

Table 10.3 Tokenization of words used in an English sentence

Sample Text (Times of India: 2 July 2018)		
The Center's decision to scrap the University Grants Commission (UGC) and bring in a new regulatory body in the higher education sector has not gone down well with academicians, who have questioned the move saying politicians should not be involved in academic matters		
Tokenization		
a (1)	academic (1)	academicians, (1)
and (1)	be (1)	bring in (1)
Body (1)	Center's (1)	Commission (1)
decision (1)	education (1)	gone down (1)
Grants (1)	has (1)	have (1)
higher (1)	in (2)	involved (1)
matters (1)	move (1)	new (1)
not (2)	politicians(1)	questioned (1)
regulatory (1)	saying (1)	scrap (1)
sector (1)	should (1)	The (4)
to (1)	(UGC) (1)	University (1)
well (1)	who (1)	with (1)

A sentence-splitting process is not adequate for syntactic annotation. An annotator has to use information from other text processing methods (e.g., *grammatical annotation, lexical collocation, local word grouping, and chunking*). For instance, information collected from grammatical annotation guides an annotator in the proper marking of words at the part-of-speech level before these words are put to tokenization and chunking (Huang et al., 2007).

10.6.3 Grammatical Annotation

Grammatical annotation is a method of tagging part-of-speech marks to words used in a sentence (Discussed in Chap. 3). The POS tagset that is used in this operation is developed with a list of coded abbreviations conforming to a particular tagging scheme designed elaborately taking into consideration the grammatical categories available in a language (Toutanova et al., 2003). Before obtaining an array of tokens from a sentence by tokenization, a syntactic annotator feeds the sentence to a grammatical annotator to tag words at the part-of-speech level. The grammatical annotator assigns part-of-speech to words based on grammatical-cum-syntactic-cum-semantic roles of words in a sentence. A grammatical annotator marks each word with its actual part-of-speech with a specific tag in the following manner (Brants, 2000).

10.6 She reads a book silently.
10.7 She\PN\ reads\FV\ a\DT\ book\NN\ silently\ADV\.

POS Tagset:	Noun	[NN]
	Verb	[FV]
	Adjective	[ADJ]
	Adverb	[ADV]
	Preposition	[PRP]
	Postposition	[PSP]
	Pronoun	[PN]
	Determiner	[DT]

At this stage, a grammatical annotator also takes into account those words that show a possibility of more than one syntactic or part-of-speech category. It, however, does not consider their possible different syntactic-cum-semantic identities and roles. Rather, it considers the exact syntactic-cum-semantic role the words play in the sentence. For instance, let us consider the English word *book* in the following sentences where the word is rightly tagged with its exact part-of-speech in the sentence.

10.8 You read a **book\NN**
10.9 You **book\FV** a taxi for this trip.

When a word is not used in a sentence, it can potentially have more than one part-of-speech value. But when it is used in a sentence, it is assigned to only one part-of-speech value which is syntactically exhibited in a sentence (Atwell et al. 2000). At this stage, a grammatical annotator guesses the part-of-speech of a word based on intrasentential and extra-sentential information and assigns a value. In the case of unknown words, it leaves them unmarked due to the paucity of adequate information. Alternatively, it may search through in-built dictionaries for necessary information for the identification of lexico-syntactic functions of unknown words in a sentence. After the grammatical annotation task is complete, a grammatically annotated sentence is returned to the syntactic annotator for further processing.

10.6.4 Chunking Larger Lexical Blocks

Chunking is the next step after grammatical annotation. After the completion of grammatical annotation, a syntactic annotator invokes a chunking algorithm to combine those words together which carry special syntactic-cum-semantic implications in a sentence. The combinations are marked as *chunks* so that these chunks correspond to phrases of different types, such as *noun phrase (NP), prepositionphrase (PP), determiner phrase (DP), verb phrase (VP)* (Hewlett & Cohen, 2011). However, it has to be kept in mind that a chunk is not always equal to a phrase. In many languages, a chunk may be made with several words which do not form a phrase but an idiom or a set expression. At the same time, it has to be understood that chunking is not equivalent to local word grouping. Local word grouping has a different characteristic and function in text analysis, processing, and cognition (Dash & Ramamoorthy, 2019: 85-86).

Chunking, at the operation level, is the immediately preceding stage of syntactic annotation. This does not imply that it is an indivisible part of the syntactic annotation. It can be useful in itself when we look for the units of meaning which, when combined, are larger forms than individual words but shorter than a sentence (Jurafsky and Martin 2000: 577–586). To perform chunking, a syntactic annotator requires a grammatically annotated sentence. The following example shows how a larger lexical unit is chunked in a hierarchical manner through an integrated process of assignment of phrasal identity tags to the chunks (Fig. 10.4).

10.10 [a young boy]$_{\mathbf{NP}}$ [walks]$_{\mathbf{VP}}$ [on [a slippery road]$_{\mathbf{NN}}$]$_{\mathbf{PP}}$.

10.6.5 Finding Matrix Verb in Sentence

The next step of syntactic annotation is the identification of a matrix verb and other verbs that are present in a sentence. A matrix verb plays the most pivotal role in a sentence. Since a syntactic annotator cannot find out verbs of its own from a sentence, it takes help from grammatically annotated texts and machine-readable dictionary

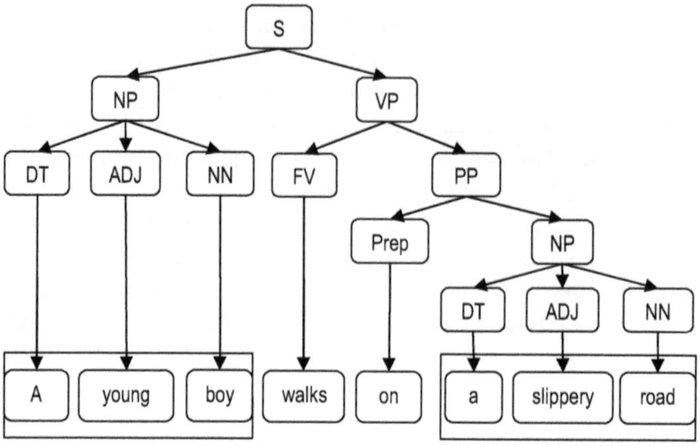

Fig. 10.4 Chunking on a simple declarative sentence

(MRD) to achieve its goal. It takes additional information from morphology and grammar when information taken from a grammatically annotated text and MRD is found inadequate (Staub et al., 2017). In grammar, a matrix verb is a "main verb" or "lexical verb" which controls syntactic structure and information of a sentence. Identification of matrix verb is necessary for a syntactic annotator for several reasons noted below.

(a) Matrix verb plays a pivotal role in a sentence. It is, therefore, necessary to identify and mark it at the first opportunity.
(b) Matrix verb is crucial in the identification of a matrix clause if a sentence contains several clauses.
(c) Matrix verb helps to recognize all other clauses and phrases that are used in a sentence.
(d) Matrix verb helps to recognize and locate all other verbs (i.e., *finite, non-finite, infinitive*) that are used in a sentence.
(e) Matrix verb helps to understand the dependency relations of subordinate clauses with the matrix clause.

At the time of identifying a matrix verb, a syntactic annotator has to keep in mind that a sentence may contain several clauses while a clause may contain, in certain situations, up to three or more (rarely observed) auxiliary verbs along with a matrix verb. At the time of annotation, it is the matrix verb that is the main concern of an annotator. The most useful way to find out a matrix verb in a sentence is to notice where a matrix verb appears in a sentence and how the meanings of the verbs are represented. In English, for instance, a matrix verb is usually tagged with inflection (e.g., *-s, -ed, -ing, -en*) as the following example shows.

10.11 She **is planning** to leave early from work as she has to go to the hospital to see her mother.

But the above argument has some limitations:

(a) Some verbs do not require suffix (e.g., *leave, go,* and *see* in the example above) as they can be used without suffix, and
(b) Some of the suffixes can also appear as affixes that are used with nouns for different linguistic functions.

Therefore, a syntactic annotator has to take the necessary precaution in the sense that affixes are not the only properties with reference to which it identifies a matrix verb in a sentence. A syntactic annotator has to consider auxiliary verbs (e.g., *be, am, is, are, was, were,* and *have*) as well as modal verbs (e.g., *can, may, might, will, would, shall, should,* and *ought*) because these verbs are also used as matrix verbs in a sentence when a matrix verb is absent.

10.6.6 Identifying Non-Matrix Clauses

When the syntactic annotation process is on, an annotator has to identify all the non-finite clauses used in a sentence. The non-finite clauses are to be treated as subordinate clauses of a matrix clause. There are language-specific rules and lexical indicators based on which an annotator identifies subordinate clauses (Dornescu et al., 2014). Once an annotator finds out the subordinate clauses, it becomes easier for an annotator to identify and mark how different clauses and phrases are related to each other in a sentence and how they are organized to form a grammatically valid sentence.

The non-finite clauses usually contain non-finite verbs. Moreover, these verbs are usually in their infinitive and participial (*past and present*) form and are not usually supported by an auxiliary verb. However, in some languages, there are examples where a subordinate clause may contain a finite verb (Joshi, 1985). Therefore, identifying the non-finite verbs alone cannot help an annotator to identify all the subordinate clauses used in a sentence. The annotator may need additional lexico-grammatical data and information from verbs and words of other parts-of-speech used in a sentence to mark out subordinate clauses.

10.6.7 Identification of Phrases

The next crucial step for a syntactic annotator is to identify the main phrase of a sentence and establish its transitivity. Since transitivity varies based on sub-categorization (i.e., *intransitive, transitive, ditransitive*) and thematic roles of a verb, an annotator has to understand the nature of transitivity of a verb so that it is able to identify the number of arguments a verb is able to carry within a phrase. It becomes crucial during the time of identifying phrases of a matrix clause as well as recognizing the subordinate clauses used in a sentence. The context-free phrase structure grammar formalisms, as well as language-specific grammar and syntactic rules, can help in this regard in the identification of phrases used in a language (Tateisi et al., 2005, Chen et al., 2020).

The resultant output of a syntactic annotation work is a combination of the results of several text processing tasks discussed above. It involves breaking sentences into clauses, clauses into phrases, and phrases into smaller building blocks (i.e., *multiword units*). All these stages are sequentially ordered and marked with specific notations used for syntactic annotation (Manning et al., 2014).

10.7 Types of Syntactic Annotation

Most of the syntactic annotation systems are designed with several complex logical networks of context-free grammars. Most of these systems usually have the same goal of identifying phrases, identifying the nature of dependencies, and marking specific syntactic roles of phrases (Leech & Eyes, 1993). The annotation systems are, however, not always similar in form, approach, operation, and representation (Kallmeyer, 2010). The primary differences among the systems are usually marked out by the following aspects.

(a) The number of types of constituents a system uses, and
(b) The methods a system uses to combine these constituents.

A syntactic annotation system usually makes distinctions between two types:

(a) Full syntactic annotation (FSA), and
(b) Partial syntactic annotation (PSA).

The full syntactic annotation (FSA) is known as **full parsing**, while partial syntactic annotation (PSA) is known as **skeleton parsing**. In case of FSA, an annotator provides a nearly detailed analysis of various phrase structures of a sentence as shown below (Fig. 10.5).

In case of PSA (i.e., *skeleton parsing*), an annotator presents less amount of syntactic information. It usually removes distinguished sets of constituent types and

Sample Sentence	Another new style feature is the wine-glass or flared heel, which was shown teamed up with pointed, squared, and chisel toes.
Full Syntactic Annotation	[S[Ncs another_DT new_JJ style_NN feature_NN Ncs] [Vzb is_BEZ Vzb] [Ns the_AT1 [NN/JJ& wine-glass_NN [JJ+ or_CC flared_JJ HH+]NN/JJ&] heel_NN ,_, [Fr[Nq which_WDT Nq] [Vzp was_BEDZ shown_VBN Vzp] [Tn[Vn teamed_VBN Vn] [R up_RP R] [P with_INW [NP[JJ/JJ/NN& pointed_JJ ,_, [JJ- squared_JJ JJ-] ,_, [NN+ and_CC chisel_NN NN+]JJ/JJ/NN&] toes_NNS Np]P]Tn]Fr]Ns] ._. S]

Fig. 10.5 Full syntactic annotation (*Lancaster–Leeds Treebank*)

Sample Sentence	For the members of this university this charter enshrines a victorious principle; and the fruits of that victory can immediately be seen in the international community of scholars that has graduated here today.
Partial Syntactic Annotation	[S& [P For_IF [N the_AT members_NN2 [P of_IO [N this_DD1 university_NNL1 N]P]N]P] [N this_DD1 charter_NN1 N] [V enshrines_VVZ [N a_AT1 victorious_JJ principle_NN1 N]V]S&] ;_; and_CC [S+[N the_AT fruits_NN2 [P of_IO [N that_DD1 victory_NN1 N]P]N] [V can_VM immediately_RR be_VB0 seen_VVN [P in_II [N the_AT international_JJ community_NNJ [P of_IO [N scholars_NN2 N]P] [Fr that_CST [V has_VHZ graduated_VVN here_RL today_RT V]Fr]N]P]V]S+] ._.

Fig. 10.6 Partial syntactic annotation (*Spoken English Corpus*)

ignores the internal structure of certain constituent types in a sentence (McEnery & Wilson, 1996: 45), as shown below (Fig. 10.6).

In both cases, annotation outputs are postedited by human analysts. This is necessary because automatic syntactic annotation has a low rate of accuracy. Therefore, it is important that annotated outputs are checked and certified by human experts. The main disadvantage of full syntactic annotation (FSA) is the irregularity in outputs by a system engaged in an annotation task. Although we give elaborate instructions to a system to overcome such limitations, ambiguities are simply inevitable. In most cases, ambiguities occur in those situations where the annotator generates multiple structures for a single phrase or clause (e.g., *John saw a man in the park with a binocular*).

As of now, some workable syntactic annotation systems are developed in some advanced languages (Bunt et al., , Kallmeyer 2010, Jelínek, 2016). Even in languages like Chinese and Japanese, we come across many efficient syntactic annotation systems developed in these languages (Kanayama et al. 2000, Xue et al. 2004, Hsieh et al., 2007). A similar claim is, however, not made for less-resourced languages used in South Asian and Central Asian languages. The development of a syntactic annotation system for the Indian languages has not been mush successful for many years. Decades ago, some efforts were made in this direction for developing a syntactic annotator for the Indian languages (Bharati et al., 1995). However, over the years, continuous efforts by a large number of scientists in this direction have produced some syntactic annotators that can moderately annotate sentences for many Indian languages (Begum et al. 2008, Palmer et al. 2009, Bharati et al., 2009, Vempaty et al. 2010, Antony et al. 2010, Antony et al. 2012, Makwana & Vegda, 2015). This, however, does not solve the problems of all the Indian languages. It will not be unfair if we argue that it is necessary to develop syntactic annotation systems for all the Indian languages. For achieving this goal, it is necessary to conduct an exhaustive analysis of the internal structure of sentences of the Indian languages. Adapting the methods and systems that are already designed for the advanced languages may serve only limited purposes as most of the Indian languages are typologically different from these languages.

10.8 Treebank

By applying a comprehensive syntactic annotation scheme, a system can assign phrase markers with labeled brackets to each phrase of a sentence following the schema of a context-free phrase structure grammar (PSG). The resultant output is a syntactically annotated sentence which we call a **treebank** (Taylor et al., 2003). It is called a *treebank* because syntactic and semantic information of a sentence, to a certain extent, is represented compositionally within a tree structure (Sampson, 2003). It presents a graphical layout which appears similar to a tree diagram used in phrase structure grammar (Fig. 10.7).

The true visual representation of a tree structure is, however, not available in the syntactic annotation of a sentence. Therefore, the same load of information is represented by using sets of labeled brackets. That generates even a more complex layout even for a simple sentence and becomes more challenging for a human user, if the user is not trained properly, to comprehend the annotation notation of the sentence. Thus, a sentence like *The young boy sat on a new chair* appears in a Treebank in a more complex form in the following manner (Fig. 10.8).

At the first level, the morphosyntactic information that is generated for each word—after it is used in a sentence—is attached to each word by an underscore (e.g., The_AT1). At the second level, each phrase is indicated by opening and closing square brackets annotated at the start and endpoint of a phrase with a notation of a phrase type (e.g., [NP The_AT1 young_AT2 boy_NP1 NP]). Finally, at the third level, the whole sentence is marked by square brackets both at the beginning and end of the sentence (e.g., [S … S]).

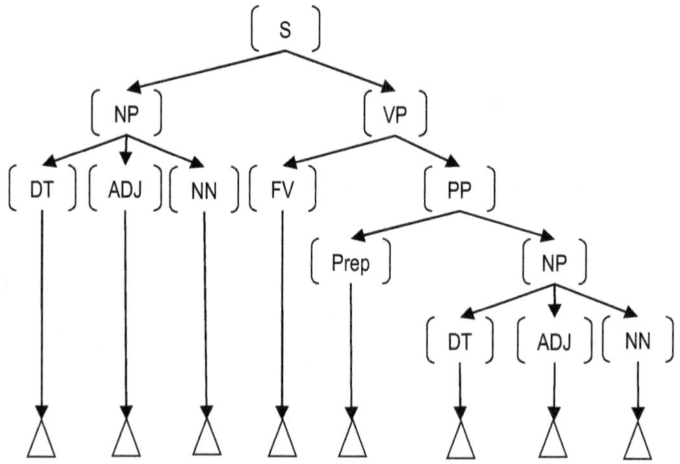

Fig. 10.7 Penn Treebank of the Stanford Parser (Sample Treebank)

```
Input Sentence: The young boy sat on a new chair.

Bracketing format:

[S [NP The_AT1 young_AT2 boy_NP1 NP] [VP sat_FV [PP on_II [NP a_AT1
new_AT2 chair_NN1 NP] PP] VP] S]

[S
        The_AT1 young_AT2 boy_NP1 NP]
                [VP sat_FV
                        [PP on_II
                        [NP a_AT1 new_AT2 chair_NN1 NP]
                        PP]
                VP]
S]
```

Fig. 10.8 Treebank in brackets following phrase structure grammar

Treebanks are very useful linguistic resources for various application purposes. They provide a good amount of hierarchical information of natural language texts at various levels of structure. At the word level, we see how words are combined to form phrases; at the phrase level, we see how phrases are formed, classified, and used in sentences; at the sentence level, we understand how phrases contribute to building structures and information in sentences; and at agreement level, we see how the constituents take part in the formation of function-argument structures. Due to such advantages, treebanks are referred to for developing models and methods for sentence decomposition, phrase analysis, grammar interpretation, sentence comprehension, machine translation, language description, and teaching. In the last three decades, treebanks are developed for many advanced languages (Nivre, 2008; Wallis, 2008). Efforts are also made for compiling representative treebanks for those languages that lack these (Han et al. 2014, Haug 2015, Mambrini, 2016). There are also initiatives for compiling treebanks for specific technological purposes. The *Penn Treebank* at the *University of Pennsylvania* is a fine example of a well-formed treebank. Other notable treebank projects are either completed or still in progress at various universities and research centres. We record below some references to a few well-known treebank projects.

(1) The *Penn Treebank of American English* contains 14 million annotated words. In it, 7 million words are grammatically annotated, 3 million words are syntactically annotated, 2 million words are annotated for predicate-argument structure, and 2 million spoken words are annotated for speech disfluencies (Marcus et al., 1993).
(2) The *Lancaster Parsed Corpus* contains a large number of sentences that are syntactically analyzed and annotated at phrase level with labeled bracketing. It follows the sentence analysis scheme outlined in the manual of syntactic annotation (Garside et al., 1987; Johansson et al., 1978).

(3) The *Tuebingen Treebank of Written German* is a syntactically annotated German newspaper corpus. It has a hundred thousand sentences from news reports from *Die Tageszeitung*. The annotation distinguishes four levels of information: lexical, phrasal, topological, and clausal. Besides, to encode grammatical functions, the annotated trees contain "edge labels" between "node labels" (Telljohann et al. 2012).

(4) The *Tuebingen Partially Parsed Corpus of Written German* is a large collection of sentences that are annotated at various levels. The sentences are annotated with clause structures, topological fields, and chunks. Also, they carry some low-level annotations (e.g., *parts-of-speech annotation and annotation for morphologically ambiguous classes*). Annotation is done automatically; it starts with paragraph braking, sentence marking, phrase marking, and ending with the segmentation of tokens (Müller, 2004).

(5) The *Arabic Treebank* (Part 3 v 1.0) contains 1 million words of Arabic texts which are annotated at the phrase level. Additional features include vocalization (including case endings), lemma IDs, and part-of-speech (POS) annotation for verbs and particles.

(6) The *Tubingen Treebanks of German* introduces an additional annotation layer of topological fields on the basic constituent structure of sentences (Hinrichs et al. 2000).

(7) The *Italian Syntactic–Semantic Treebank* uses two layers of annotation, the first one for constituent structure and the second one for dependency structure (Montemagni et al. 2003).

(8) The *Prague Dependency Treebank* carries surface-level dependency annotation as well as a layer of tecto-grammatical annotation involving case roles described as a semantically oriented deep syntactic analysis (Hajicova, 1998).

(9) The *Spanish Treebank* (Moreno et al. 2003), the *Penn Korean Treebank* (Han et al. 2002), the *Penn Chinese Treebank* (Xue et al. 2004), and the *Penn Arabic Treebank* (Maamouri & Bies, 2004) annotate constituent structures and grammatical functions of words together.

(10) The *ICEGB Corpus of British English* annotates constituent dependency and grammatical functions in the treebank (Nelson et al., 2002).

The treebanks for the Indian languages are still at their nascent stage. They are yet to come to a mature stage to be used in technology and linguistic works (Sharma et al., 2016). So far, the Indian Language Machine Translation (ILMT) project has produced some syntactically annotated sentences for a few Indian languages (Bhat et al., 2017a, 2017b). These are, however, too small to meet the requirement for language technology research and development works of the country. It is time to take up new projects to generate treebanks for the Indian languages to meet the current needs of industries and academia engaged in language technology resource and tool development and application activities.

The practice of building syntactically annotated treebanks reveals some truths before us. We understand that detail analytical descriptions of trees may become more theory-dependent with fewer potentials for applications. Many treebanks (e.g.,

Prague Dependency Treebank, *Italian Treebank*, *Turkish Treebank*, *Polish HPSG Treebank*, *Verbmobil HPSG Treebank*, and *Bulgarian HPSG Treebank*) now face this problem. It leads to a situation where the utilization of treebanks is a challenging task for human users. Human users cannot decipher information encoded in tagsets assigned to the constituents in a sentence. Only those machines which are adequately trained and programmed can understand such encodings and utilize them accordingly. It is, therefore, necessary to strike a balance so that the development of treebanks and linguistic theories are combined in a way to ensure uninterrupted information flow between the two ends.

10.9 Utility of Syntactic Annotated Texts

The recent advancements in computational linguistics, language processing, and language technology generate possibilities for applications of syntactically annotated texts. These are useful in understanding the form and construction of natural language sentences as well as applying information extracted from annotated texts in application-oriented tasks. We refer to some of the domains where syntactically annotated texts have good application possibilities (Bunt et al., 2004b: 3–5):

(a) **Information and Document Retrieval**: Recognition of syntactically annotated noun phrases and verb phrases in texts has much relevance in document identification and retrieval of linguistic information.
(b) **Question Answering**: Answering systems use information obtained from syntactically annotated texts to formulate answers. Many statistics-based systems also use web-data to find out answers to queries by applying matching algorithms on a syntactically annotated corpus.
(c) **Terminology Extraction**: Syntactically annotated parallel translation corpora are a good source for cross-lingual information retrieval as well as for the extraction of scientific and technical terms.
(d) **Lexicon Induction**: Lexical information of various types (e.g., *lexical collocations, lexical associations, lexical clustering, multiword units, compounds, and reduplications*) is retrieved from syntactically annotated corpora. Moreover, argument structures of sentences are determined by analyzing syntactically annotated texts.
(e) **Text Summarization**: Syntactically annotated sentences are used at the discourse level to produce shorter grammatical versions of sentences and compress several sentences into one.
(f) **Knowledge Extraction**: Systems depend on syntactically annotated texts in analysis of NPs, VPs, and PPs. Also, systems use syntactic annotation methodology for semantic analysis of texts.
(g) **Character Recognition**: Grammatically and syntactically annotated spoken sentences are used as inputs to recognize various characters and character combinations in texts.

(h) **Speech Recognition**: Syntactically annotated spoken texts are accessed to retrieve information to understand syntactic structures of spoken texts and to develop models for recognizing spoken texts.
(i) **Speech Understanding**: Syntactically annotated texts are analyzed to retrieve information for building interactive speech-based systems that can deal with disfluencies in speech.
(j) **Bilingual Text Alignment**: Syntactically annotated sentences are used in multilingual applications like text alignment at sentence and phrase level, cross-lingual information comparison, multilingual lexical mapping, and translation verification.
(k) **Machine Translation**: Almost all the models of machine translation (e.g., *grammar-based, rule-based, interlingua, transfer-based, example-based, statistics-based, and corpus-based*) utilize syntactically annotated corpora of a source language to generate equivalent syntactic outputs in the target languages.
(l) **Speech Translation**: Syntactically annotated corpora are also utilized to combine different approaches to speech recognition and speech translation into a frame that can translate source speech into target speech.

10.10 Conclusion

The present state of activities relating to the development of automatic systems for syntactic annotation in many languages is quite impressive. Some of the highly acclaimed syntactic annotators (e.g., *Helsinki Parser, Lancaster University Parser, Stanford Parser, Turin University Parser, and Penn Treebank Parser*) have achieved a high success although, at the initial stages, they recorded low accuracy (Greene & Rubin, 1971). Nearly after six decades, it is satisfying to know that much progress is made in this direction. It is encouraging to know that 100% accuracy is achieved in the grammatical annotation, (Jelínek, 2016) and this plays a major role in achieving a higher level of accuracy also in the syntactic annotation. The success achieved in syntactic annotation inspires us to hope that present advancement made in this domain will overcome all the difficulties involved in this work. In the next twenty years, we expect to have robust parsers for almost all major and minor languages of the world. More research toward this domain should be our present goal.

There are many difficulties and hurdles in the development of a robust syntactic annotator for a language. It is a time-consuming task. It may be achieved after many trials and failures. It is a collective task. It requires the involvement of computer experts and linguists with sound knowledge in grammar. It is a work that requires adequate technical knowledge for carrying out research on large amounts of language data through trials and experiments. The development of a syntactic annotator for resource-rich and resource-poor languages is a work that cannot be ignored just because it is a hard and daunting task. Once we realize the functional importance of a syntactic annotator in language description, application, cognition, and computation, we should dedicate ourselves to develop it for all languages even if it puts strong challenges before us.

References

Aarts, B., Wallis, S. A., & Nelson, G. (2000). Syntactic annotation in reverse: Exploring ICE-GB with fuzzy tree fragments and ICECUP. In: J. M. Kirk (Ed.) *Corpora galore: Analyses and techniques in describing english* (pp. 335-343). Rodopi.

Aldebazal, I., Aranzabe, M. J., Arriola, J. M., & Dias de Ilarraza, A. (2009). Syntactic annotation in the reference corpus for processing of basque: Theoretical and practical issues. *Corpus Linguistics and Linguistic Theory, 5*(2), 241–269.

Antony, P. J., Nandini, J. W., & Soman, K. P. (2012). Computational morphology and natural language parsing for Indian languages: A literature survey. *International Journal of Computer Science, Engineering and Technology, 3*(4), 136–146.

Antony, P. J., Nandini, J. W., & Soman, K. P. (2010). Penn Treebank-based syntactic parsers for South Dravidian languages using a machine learning approach. *International Journal on Computer Application, 7*(8), 14–21.

Atwell, E., Demetriou, G., Hughes, J., Schiffrin, A., Souter, C., & Wilcock, S. (2000). A comparative evaluation of modern English corpus grammatical annotation schemes. *International Computer Archive of Modern English Journal, 24*(1), 7–23.

Barnbrook, G. (1998). *Language and computers*. Edinburgh University Press.

Begum, R., Husain, S., Dhwaj, A., Sharma, D., Bai, L., & Sangal, R. (2008). A dependency annotation scheme for Indian languages. *Proceedings of the international joint conference on natural language processing (IJCNLP-2008)*. International Institute of Information Technology, January 2008, pp. 1–7.

Bharati, A., Chaitanya, V. and Sangal, R. (1995). *Natural language processing: A paninian perspective*. Prentice-Hall of India.

Bharati, A., Gupta, M., Yadav, V., Gali, K., & Sharma, D. M. (2009). Simple parser for Indian languages in a dependency framework. *Proceedings of the 3rd linguistic annotation workshop (LAWIII)* (pp. 162-165). SIGANN, 47th ACL—4th IJCNLP, Singapore (IJCNLP-2009).

Bhat, I.A., Bhat, R.A., Shrivastava, M., & Sharma, D. M. (2017). Joining hands: Exploiting monolingual treebanks for parsing of code-mixing data. *Proceedings of the 15th conference of the European chapter of the association for computational linguistics* (Vol. 2, pp. 324–330). April 3–7, 2017.

Bhat, R. A., Bhat, I. A., & Sharma, D. M. (2017). Improving transition-based dependency parsing of Hindi and Urdu by modeling syntactically relevant phenomena. *ACM transactions on Asian and Low-Resource Language Information Processing (TALLIP),* Article 17, 6(3), 1–35.

Borsley, R. (1991). *Syntactic theory: A unified approach*. Edward Arnold.

Brants, T. (2000). TnT—A statistical part-of-speech tagger. *Proceedings of the sixth applied natural language processing conference (ANLP-2000)* (pp. 37–42).

Brekke, M. (1991). Automatic syntactic annotation meets the wall. In S. Johansson & A.-B. Stenström (Eds.), *English computer corpora: Selected papers and research guides* (pp. 83–103). Mouton de Gruyter.

Bresnan, J. (2001). *Lexical-functional syntax*. Blackwell.

Bresnan, J., Asudeh, A., Toivonen, I., & Wechsler, S. (2015). *Lexical-functional syntax*. 2nd ed. Wiley Blackwell.

Briscoe, E., & Carroll, J. (1993). Generalized probabilistic LR syntactic annotation of natural language (corpora) with unification-based grammars. *Computational Linguistics., 19*, 25–60.

Bunt, H., & Tomita, M. (Eds.). (1996). *Recent advances in syntactic annotation technology*. Kluwer Academic Publishers.

Bunt, H., Carroll, J., & Satta, G. (2004a). Developments in syntactic annotation technology: from theory to application. In H. Bunt, J. Carroll, & G. Satta (Eds.), *New Developments in syntactic annotation Technology* (pp. 1–18). Kluwer Academic Publishers.

Bunt, H., Carroll, J., & Satta, G. (Eds.). (2004b). *New developments in syntactic annotation technology*. Kluwer Academic Publishers.

Chen, X., Alexopoulou, T., & Tsimpli, I. (2020). Automatic extraction of subordinate clauses and its application in second language acquisition research. *Behavior Research Methods*. https://doi.org/10.3758/s13428-020-01456-7

Chomsky, N. (1956). Three models for the description of language. *Information Theory, IEEE Transactions., 2*(3), 113–124.

Dalrymple, M. (2001). *Lexical-functional grammar*. No. 42 in *Syntax and semantics* series. Academic Press.

Dash, N. S., & Ramamoorthy, L. (2019). *Utility and application of language corpora*. Springer Nature.

Dornescu, I., Evans, R., & Orasan, C. (2014). Relative clause extraction for syntactic simplification. *Proceedings of the workshop on automatic text simplification: Methods and applications in multilingual society (ATS-MA 2014)* (pp. 1–10). Association for Computational Linguistics and Dublin City University.

Falk, Y. N. (2001). *Lexical-functional grammar: An introduction to parallel constraint-based syntax*. CSLI.

Garside, R., Leech, G., & Sampson, G. (Eds.). (1987). *The computational analysis of English: a Corpus-based approach*. Longman.

Greene, B., & Rubin, G. (1971). *Automatic grammatical tagging of English*. Technical Report. Department of Linguistics. Brown University.

Hajicova, E. (1998). Prague dependency treebank: From analytic to tectogrammatical annotation. *Proceedings of the first workshop on text, speech, and dialogue* (pp. 45–50).

Han, A. L. F., Wong, D. F., Chao, L. S., Lu, Y., He, L., & Tian, L. (2014). A universal phrase tagset for multilingual treebanks. Proceedings of the CCL and NLP-NABD 2014, LNAI 8801, pp. 247–258.

Han, C., Han, N., & Ko, S.(2002). Development and evaluation of a Korean treebank and its application to NLP. *Proceedings of the 3rd international conference on language resources and evaluation* (pp. 1635–1642).

Haug, D. (2015). Treebanks in historical linguistic research. In C. Viti (Ed.), *Perspectives on historical syntax* (pp. 188–202). John Benjamins.

Hewlett, D., & Cohen, P. (2011). Word segmentation as general chunking. *Proceedings of 15th conference on computational natural language learning* (pp. 39–47). 23–24 June 2011.

Hinrichs, E. W., Bartels, J., Kawata, Y., Kordoni, V., & Telljohann, H. (2000). The tubingen treebanks for spoken German, English and Japanese. In W. Wahlster (Ed.), *Verbmobil: Foundations of speech-to-speech translation* (pp. 552–576). Springer.

Hopcroft, J. E., & Ullman, J. D. (1979). *Introduction to automata theory: Languages, and computation*. Addison-Wesley.

Hsieh, Y.-M., Yang, D.-C., & Chen, K.-J. (2007). Improve parsing performance by self-learning. *Computational Linguistics, and Chinese Language Processing, 12*(2), 195–216.

Huang, C. R., Simon, P., Hsieh, S. K., & Prevot, L. (2007). Rethinking Chinese word segmentation: Tokenization, character classification, or wordbreak identification. *Proceedings of the ACL 2007 demo and poster sessions* (pp. 69–72). June 2007, Association for Computational Linguistics.

Jelínek, T. (2016). Partial accuracy rates and agreements of parsers: Two experiments with ensemble syntactic annotation of Czech. *ITAT 2016: Proceedings CEUR Workshop Proceedings, 1649*, 42–47.

Johansson, S., & Stenström, A.-B. (Eds.). (1991). *English computer corpora: Selected papers and research guides*. Mouton de Gruyter.

Johansson, S., Leech, G., & Goodluck, H. (1978). *Manual of information to accompany the Lancaster-Oslo/Bergen Corpus of British English*. University of Oslo, Norway.

Joshi, A. (1985). How much context-sensitivity is necessary for characterizing structural descriptions? In D. Dowty, L. Karttunen, & A. Zwicky (Eds.), *Natural language processing: Theoretical, computational, and psychological perspectives* (pp. 206–250). Cambridge University Press.

Joshi, A. K., Rao, K. S., & Yamada, H. M. (1972a). String Adjunct Grammars: I Local and distributed adjunction. *Information and Control, 21*(2), 93–116.

Joshi, A. K., Rao, K. S., & Yamada, H. M. (1972b). String adjunct grammars: II. Equational Representation, Null Symbols, and Linguistic Relevance. *Information and Control, 21*(3), 235–260.

Jurafsky, D., & Martin, J. H. (2000). *Speech and language processing.* Pearson Education Inc.

Kallmeyer, L. (2010). *Syntactic annotation beyond context-free grammars.* Springer.

Kanayama, H., Torisawa, K., Mitsuishi, Y. & Tsujii, J. (2000). A hybrid Japanese parser with hand-crafted grammar and statistics. *Proceedings of 18th international conference on computational linguistics (COLING 2000)* (Vo. 2, pp. 411–417). 31 July–4 August 2000, Universität des Saarlandes.

Karlsson, F. (1994). Robust syntactic annotation of unconstrained text. In N. Oostdijk & P. deHaan (Eds.), *Corpus-based research into language: In honour of Jan Aarts* (pp. 121–142). Rodopi.

Karlsson, F., Voutilainen, A., Heikkilä, J., & Anttila, A. (Eds.). (1995). *Constraint grammar: A language-independent system for syntactic annotation unrestricted text.* Mouton de Gruyter.

Koster, C. A. (1991). Affix grammars for natural languages. In: Attribute grammars, applications, and systems, *International summer school saga.* Springer.

Kroeger, P. R. (2004). *Analyzing syntax: A lexical-functional approach.* Cambridge University Press.

Kübler, S., McDonald, R., & Nivre, J. (2008). Dependency parsing. *Synthesis Lectures on Human Language Technologies., 2*(1), 1–127.

Leech, G., & Eyes, E. (1993). Syntactic annotation: Linguistic aspects of grammatical tagging and skeleton parsing. In E. Black, R. Garside, & G. Leech (Eds.), *Statistically-driven computer grammars of English* (pp. 36–61). Rodopi.

Leech, G. (1993). Corpus annotation schemes. *Literary and Linguistic Computing., 8*(4), 275–281.

Liu, H. (2009). *Dependency grammar: From theory to practice.* Science Press.

Maamouri, M., & Bies, A. (2004). Developing an Arabic treebank: Methods, guidelines, procedures, and tools. *Proceedings of the workshop on computational approaches to arabic script-based languages* (pp. 2–9).

Makwana, M. T., & Vegda, D. C. (2015). Survey: Natural language parsing for Indian languages. ArXiv. arXiv:1501.07005. pp. 1–9.

Mambrini, F. (2016). The ancient Greek dependency treebank: Linguistic annotation in a teaching environment. In G. Bodard & M. Romanello (Eds.), *Digital classics outside the echo-chamber: Teaching, knowledge exchange & public engagement* (pp. 83–99). Ubiquity Press.

Manning, C. D., Surdeanu, M., Bauer, J., Finkel, J., Bethard, S. J., & McClosky, D. (2014). The Stanford coreNLP natural language processing toolkit. In: *Association for computational linguistics (ACL) system demonstrations.* pp. 55–60.

Marcus, M. P., Santorini, B., & Marcinkiewicz, M. A. (1993). Building a large annotated corpus of English: The Penn Treebank. *Computational Linguistics., 19*(2), 313–330.

McEnery, T., & Wilson, A. (1996). *Corpus linguistics.* Edinburgh University Press.

Mel'čuk, I. A. (1987). Dependency syntax: Theory and practice. State University Press of New York.

Montemagni, S., Barsotti, F., Battista, M., Calzolari, N., Corazzari, O., Lenci, A., Zampolli, A., Fanciulli, F., Massetani, M., Raffaelli, R., Basili, R., Pazienza, M.T., Saracino, D., Zanzotto, F., Nana, N., Pianesi, F., & Delmonte, R. (2003). Building the Italian syntactic-semantic treebank. In: A. Abeille' (Ed.)*reebanks: Building and using parsed corpora* (pp. 189–210). Kluwer.

Moreno, A., Lopez, S., Sanchez, F., & Grishman, R. (2003). Developing a Spanish treebank. In: A. Abeille' (Ed.) *Treebanks: Building and using parsed corpora* (pp. 149–163). Kluwer.

Müller, F. H. (2004). *Stylebook for the Tübingen partially parsed corpus of written German (TüPP-D/Z).* University of Tübingen, 15 Jan 2004.

Nelson, G., Wallis, S., & Aarts, B. (2002). *Exploring natural language: Working with the British component of the international corpus of English.* John Benjamins.

Nivre, J. (2008). Treebanks. In: A. Lüdeling & M. Kytö (Ed.) *Corpus linguistics: An international handbook* (pp. 225–241). Mouton de Gruyter. Chapter 13.

Osborne, T. (2019). *A dependency grammar of English: An introduction and beyond.* John Benjamins.

Palmer, M., Bhatt, R., Narasimhan, B., Rambow, O., Sharma, D., & Xia, F. (2009). Hindi syntax: Annotating dependency, lexical predicate-argument structure, and phrase structure. Proceedings of the *7th international conference on natural language processing,* (ICON-2009) (pp. 14–17).
Perlmutter, D. M. (1980). Relational grammar. In: E. A. Moravcsik & J. R. Wirth (Eds.) *Syntax and semantics: Current approaches to syntax* (Vol. 13, pp. 195–229). Academic Press.
Perlmutter, D. M. (Ed.). (1983). *Studies in relational grammar 1.* Chicago University Press.
Pullum, G. K., & Gazdar, G. (1982). Natural languages and context-free languages. *Linguistics and Philosophy., 4*(4), 471–504.
Sag, I., & Wasow, T. (1999). *Syntactic theory: A formal introduction.* CSLI Publications.
Sampson, G. (2003). Reflections of a dendrographer. In A. Wilson, P. Rayson, & T. McEnery (Eds.), *Corpus linguistics by the Lune: A Festschrift for Geoffrey Leech* (pp. 157–184). Peter Lang.
Sharma, A., Gupta, S., Motlani, R., Bansal, P., Shrivastava, M., Mamidi, R., & Sharma, D. M. (2016). Shallow parsing pipeline—Hindi-English code-mixed social media text. *Proceedings of the 2016 conference of the North American chapter of the association for computational linguistics: Human language technologies* (pp. 1340–1345).
Shieber, S. (1985). Evidence against the context-freeness of natural language. *Linguistics and Philosophy., 8*(3), 333–343.
Sipser, M. (1997). *Introduction to the theory of computation.* PWS Publishing.
Souter, C., & Atwell, E. (Eds.). (1993). *Corpus-based computational linguistics.* Rodopi.
Staub, A., Dillon, B., & Clifton, C., Jr. (2017). The Matrix Verb as a source of comprehension difficulty in object relative sentences. *Journal of Cognitive Science, 41*(6), 1353–1376.
Tateisi, Y., Yakushiji, A., Ohta, T., & Tsujii, J. (2005). Syntax annotation for the Genia corpus. *Proceedings of the IJCNLP, Companion, 2005*, 222–227.
Taylor, A., Marcus, M., & Santorini, B. (2003). The Penn Treebank: An overview. In A. Abeillé (Ed.), *Treebanks: Building and using parsed corpora* (pp. 5–22). Springer.
Telljohann, H., Hinrichs, E. W., Kübler, S., Zinsmeister, H., & Beck, K. (2012). *Stylebook for the Tübingen treebank of written German (TüBa-D/Z).* University of Tübingen, January 2012.
Toutanova, K., Klein, D., Manning, C. D., & Singer, Y. (2003). Feature-rich part-of-speech tagging with a cyclic dependency network. *Proceedings of HLT-NAACL, 2003*, 252–259.
van Valin, R. (2001). *An introduction to syntax.* Cambridge University Press.
Vempaty, C., Naidu, V., Husain, S., Kiran, R., Bai, L., Sharma, D., & Sangal, R. (2010). Issues in analyzing Telugu sentences towards building a Telugu treebank. *Computational Linguistics and Intelligent Text Processing,* pp. 50–59.
Verma, S. K., & Krishnaswamy, N. (1989). *Modern linguistics: An introduction.* Oxford University Press.
Wallis, S. (2008). Searching treebanks and other structured corpora. In: A. Lüdeling & M. Kytö (Eds.) *Corpus linguistics: An international handbook* (pp. 738–758). Mouton de Gruyter. Chapter 34.
Watt, D. A., & Thomas, M. (1991). *Programming language syntax and semantics.* Prentice-Hall.
Webster, J. J., & Kit, C. (1992). Tokenization as the initial phase in NLP. *Proceedings of COLING-92,* Nantes, Aug 23–28, 1992. pp. 1106–1110.
Xue, N., Xia, F., Chiou, F. D., & Palmer, M. (2004). The Penn Chinese treebank: Phrase structure annotation of a large corpus. *Natural Language Engineering, 11*(1), 207–238.

Web Links

http://clu.uni.no/icame/manuals/LPC/LPC.PDF
http://nlp.stanford.edu:8080/corenlp/process
http://www.aclweb.org/anthology/P/P07/P07-2018.pdf
http://www.cis.upenn.edu/~Treebank/

http://www.cs.brandeis.edu/~clp/ctb/
http://www.ldc.upenn.edu/Catalog/
http://www.link.cs.cmu.edu/link/submit-sentence-4.html
http://www.sfs.uni-tuebingen.de/en_nf_asc_resources.shtml
http://www.sfs.uni-tuebingen.de/en_tuebadz.shtml
http://www.sfs.uni-tuebingen.de/en_tuepp.html
http://www.sfs.uni-tuebingen.de/en_tuepp.shtml
https://catalog.ldc.upenn.edu/LDC95T7
https://en.wikipedia.org/wiki/ANTLR
https://tdil-dc.in/index.php?option=com_download

Author Index

N. S. Dash, *Language Corpora Annotation and Processing*,
https://doi.org/10.1007/978-981-16-2960-0

Subject Index

N. S. Dash, *Language Corpora Annotation and Processing*,
https://doi.org/10.1007/978-981-16-2960-0

D

E

Q

Lightning Source UK Ltd.
Milton Keynes UK
UKHW020607110722
405674UK00001B/16

9 789811 629624